THE GREEK ECONOMY

Also by Nicholas G. Pirounakis

BASIC ECONOMICS FOR STUDENTS, MANAGERS AND POLITICIANS

FINANCIAL MANAGEMENT

HOUSING AND MORTGAGE CREDIT IN GREECE

The Greek Economy

Past, Present and Future

Nicholas G. Pirounakis
Consultant Economist
Economic Research and Analysis Ltd

First published in Great Britain 1997 by
MACMILLAN PRESS LTD
Houndmills, Basingstoke, Hampshire RG21 6XS and London
Companies and representatives throughout the world

A catalogue record for this book is available from the British Library.

ISBN 0–333–65422–6

First published in the United States of America 1997 by
ST. MARTIN'S PRESS, INC.,
Scholarly and Reference Division,
175 Fifth Avenue, New York, N.Y. 10010

ISBN 0–312–17517–5

Library of Congress Cataloging-in-Publication Data
Pirounakis, Nicholas G., 1955–
The Greek economy : past, present and future / Nicholas
G. Pirounakis.
p. cm.
Includes bibliographical references and index.
ISBN 0–312–17517–5 (cloth)
1. Greece—Economic conditions. 2. Greece—Economic policy.
3. Economic forecasting—Greece. I. Title.
HC295.P55 1997
330.9495—dc21 97–9653
CIP

---

10 9 8 7 6 5 4 3 2 1
06 05 04 03 02 01 00 99 98 97

Printed and bound in Great Britain by
Antony Rowe Ltd, Chippenham, Wiltshire

In memory of my father, George

To my mother, Anastasia

To Evlyn Macfarlane, who, at great personal cost and despite a great sense of humour, believed in me enough to teach me some measure of self-confidence.

To KaterinaTsitse, warm, fun-loving and tolerant companion.

To my colleagues, teachers and friends from my PhD days: David Donnison, Duncan Maclennan, John Parr, John Bannister, Michael Ball, Thereza Carvalho, and Sean Damer (whose vivid interest in Greece is well-known).

To my colleagues and friends in Athens: Panayotis Mandicas (whose thirst for tables of figures this book will probably satisfy), Basil Manessiotis, Chrysanthos Lazaridis (both of whom kindly had a look at some of the chapters), Odysseus Katsaitis, Albert Arouch.

To my Greek friends, Minnie Vassiliadou, Evi Kalessi, Anthony Spinakis, Dionysios Coulianthonis, Aleck Kotseroglou, Nick Panopoulos, Alexis Anagnostopoulos, Aleck Grech.

To my Scottish and English friends, Elisabeth Baird (who corrected the English of parts of the text), Claire Smith, Christine Lawrie, Frances Kinnear, Rachel Neville, and the wonderful Pettifer family: Robert, Mary, Rachel and Candice.

Finally, to the Greek weekly *Economicos Tachydromos*, for its incessant efforts to introduce sense, accountability and patriotism in the management of my country's affairs.

Contents

List of Tables x
List of Diagrams xii
Abbreviations xv
FactFile on Greece xvii

Introduction 1

I.1 What's special about the Greek economy? 1
I.2 A corkboard of questions 4

Chapter 1: An overview of the modern Greek economy 7

1.1 Current problems 7
1.2 The iron hand of history 10
1.3 A captive economy 14
1.4 A vicious circle 19
1.5 So, how do Greeks make a living? 24

Chapter 2: Economic performance since the civil war 34

2.1 Growth of Greece's official GDP 34
2.2 Comparative economic performance, 1966–90 37
2.3 The role of investment 42

Chapter 3: The public sector in Greek society 49

3.1 A self-serving state 49
3.2 'Democracy' and the non-rule of law 58
3.3 Caliban's palimpsests 61

Chapter 4: Public finances, taxes, and privatisation 70

4.1 Budget deficits and the public debt 70
4.2 Taxes and the informal economy 78
4.3 The failure to privatise 87

Chapter 5: Inflation, economic policy, and the drachma 94

5.1 The dynamic of Greek inflation 94
5.2 A Greek Phillips curve? 101
5.3 Would rapid depreciation help? 104

Appendix: Variables, data, explanations, and regression results 113

Chapter 6: Banking, insurance, and the Stock Exchange 121

6.1 An overview of the banking system 121
6.2 From regulation to deregulation 126
6.3 Banks and the state: Who finances whom? 131
6.4 Foreign banks in Greece 136
6.5 The insurance industry 140
6.6 The Athens Stock Exchange and unit trusts 145

Chapter 7: Social security – or the lack of it 151

7.1 Welfare in Greece 151
7.2 The Greek social security system 155
7.3 What needs to be done 164

Chapter 8: Aspects of the 'real' economy 170

8.1 Greek industry: from retreat to patchy recovery 170
8.2 Causes of uncompetitiveness 177
8.3 Transnationals lead 185
8.4 Foreign capital and attitudes to investment 190
8.5 Oligopolies and competition 197

Chapter 9: Housing miracle – planning blight 206

9.1 A nation of house-owners – not just owner-occupiers 206
9.2 Investment in housing 216
9.3 Housing credit 220
9.4 The future of Greek housing 223

Chapter 10: Tourism and environmental concerns 229

10.1 Myrina, Lemnos: a case study 229

10.2 Where Polyphemus treads 233
10.3 Prospects of Greek tourism 242

Chapter 11: Lessons and insights 250

11.1 How is Greece different? 250
11.2 Development and underdevelopment 256
11.3 'Keys' of economic and social recovery 264

Chapter 12: What future for Greece? 274

12.1 Rude awakening 274
12.2 Greece in the international arena 278
12.3 Two models of regional stability 281
12.4 Greece's responses to foreign challenges 284
12.5 Who will lead? 292

Bibliography and references 300

Index 315

List of Tables

Table 1.1	Greece: Population shares 1940–91, and GDP shares, 1951–91	16
Table 2.1	Seven political periods of Greek real GDP growth	35
Table 2.2	Rankings of OECD countries by period growth rates	38
Table 2.3	Deviations of OECD countries from expected trend of real GDP growth rates, 1966–90	43
Table 3.1	Educational profile of Greek public sector staff in 1991 vs respective population age-group	64
Table 4.1	Greek Maastricht-defined public debt, central government debt, and public-sector foreign debt	71
Table 4.2	Greece: Financing of net borrowing requirements (NBR) of broad public sector (including public-sector enterprises), 1978–95, and Bank of Greece credit to the Government	73
Table 4.3	An international comparison of taxation systems	80
Table 4.4	Structure of Ordinary Budget Revenue	82
Table 4.5	Greece, 1979–94: Evolution of personal taxation (1978 = 100)	84
Table 5.1	Greek inflation and the exchange parity of the drachma	106
Table 5.2	Real short-run interest rates, 1990–5: Greece vs five other countries	108
Table A5.3	Data for Chapter 5 regression models	116
Table A5.4	A Greek Phillips curve? Comparison of Greek inflation and unemployment rates from 1978 to 1996	120
Table 6.1	Assets and liabilities, typical of banking business, of banks in Greece, 1978–94	123
Table 6.2	The commercial banking sector of the European Union around 1990–91	125
Table 6.3	Greece, 1990–95: Financing of private sector by commercial banks, Greek and foreign	129
Table 6.4	Foreign banks in Greece	138
Table 6.5	Greek insurance industry: Basic data	142
Table 6.6	Athens Stock Exchange and unit trusts	146

Table 7.1	Aspects of welfare in the European Union, c. 1990	152
Table 7.2	Social insurance in the European Union, c. 1990	153
Table 7.3	Social insurance in Greece: Basic data	157
Table 7.4	Seven biggest Greek social security organisations: Financial trends, 1985–95, in current prices	159
Table 8.1	Basic data on Greek industrial companies, 1977–94 (millions of drs at 1986 prices)	172
Table 8.2	Profit- and loss-makers in Greek industry, 1988–94	174
Table 8.3	Greek external trade in industrial goods, 1973–95: Key ratios	176
Table 8.4	Greek industry: Changes in the labour force, 1961–92	178
Table 8.5	Greek manufacturing industry, 1974–95	180
Table 8.6	European Union: Infrastructrure data	184
Table 8.7	Greek and foreign industrial firms by sector, and comparison of profit per frim, 1992	187
Table 8.8	Biggest industrial, commercial, and construction firms in Greece, 1994	188
Table 8.9	Private long-term capital imported into Greece, 1960–95 ($US thousands)	192
Table 8.10	Direct Foreign Investment in EU-12 member-states, 1986–91	194
Table 8.11	Business units in Europe, 1992, and retail outlets per 1000 of population, 1990	199
Table 8.12	Greece: Market shares in selected sectors, 1993–94	200
Table 8.13	Market shares and import penetration in selected sectors of the Greek economy, 1992	203
Table 9.1	Basic data on the Greek housing system	207
Table 9.2	Environmental pollution in Athens and the rest of Greece (late 1970s–early 1990s)	211
Table 9.3	Housing ownership structure in Greece in 1981	212
Table 9.4	Housing ownership structure in Greece in 1991	213
Table 10.1	Greek tourist industry, 1993: Number of beds, skilled and unskilled staff	235
Table 10.2	Greece, 1980–95: Arrivals of tourists and receipts in FX and in drs	244

List of Diagrams

Diagram 1.1	The Greek economy: A dynamic overview	23
Diagram 1.2	Greece, 1958–95: Living beyond her means, thanks to a net inflow of invisible earnings (and foreign borrowing, which more than covers the difference)	25
Diagram 1.3	Greece, 1958–95: Tourism, shipping, expatriates' remittances, and European Community transfers as % of gross invisible earnings	27
Diagram 2.1	Annual growth rates of Greece's real GDP, 1966–90	40
Diagram 2.2	Annual growth rates of OECD's real GDP, 1966–90	40
Diagram 2.3	Relationship between slopes and vertical intercepts of lines depicting real GDP growth rate trend for each OECD country, 1966–90	41
Diagram 2.4	Actual and expected trends of Greece's real GDP growth rates, 1966–90	41
Diagram 2.5	Ranking of OECD countries by deviation of actual from expected trend of real GDP growth rates over the 1966–90 period	42
Diagram 2.6	Do changes in investment levels as % of GDP explain the deviations of OECD countries from expected real GDP growth rate trends?	44
Diagram 4.1	Greece, 1977–95: An unmistakable political business cycle emerges as of 1981, with peaks in public sector net borrowing requirement as % of GDP in every election year	72
Diagram 4.2	Greece 1957–95: Relationship between economic growth and government budget deficits	74
Diagram 5.1	Greece, 1958–95: Relationship between annual percentage change in real government budget deficit and inflation rate; no lag	96
Diagram 5.2	Greece, 1958–95: Relationship between annual percentage change in real money supply (MS3) and inflation rate; no lag	97

Diagram 5.3	Greece, 1958–95: Relationship between APC in real money supply and APC in total bank credit outstanding; no lag	98
Diagram 5.4	Greece, 1955–95: Relationship between inflation rate and real GDP APC; no lag	99
Diagram 5.5	Greece, 1955–95: Relationship between inflation rate and ratio of annual absolute change in money supply (MS3) to GDP (factor cost); one-year lag	100
Diagram 5.6	A Greek Phillips curve, 1979–96: Points after 1978 exhibit a negative relationship between unemployment and inflation rates	103
Diagram 5.7	Greece, 1963–95: Percentage deviations of imports (TM) price index from price index of primary & industrial production (PIP), and comparison to trend	107
Diagram 5.8	Nominal and real weighted exchange parities of the drachma, 1979–95	107
Diagram 5.9	Greece, 1950–95: When have savers with commercial banks received positive real pre-tax returns?	109
Diagram 6.1	Greece, 1964–95: All-bank financing to various sectors as percentage of total to private sector (outstanding claims at year-end)	130
Diagram 6.2	Greece, 1964–95: Bank financing of public-sector enterprises, social insurance organisations, and agencies purchasing agricultural products, as percentage of total bank financing (year-end balances)	132
Diagram 6.3	Foreign banks in Greece, 1976–94: Comparison of European to North American banks by advances to total assets	139
Diagram 7.1	Ageing populations and economic performance: OECD (except Turkey and Mexico)	163
Diagram 8.1	Greek manufacturing industry, 1974–95	173
Diagram 8.2	Evolution of Greek trade in industrial goods, 1973–95	175
Diagram 8.3	Work-hours lost due to strikes throughout the Greek economy in 1976–93, as percentage of period average (= 8.2 m. hrs)	182

Diagram 9.1 Comparative contribution of housing and industry to total gross fixed capital formation (GFCF) in the Greek economy, 1949–94 217

Diagram 9.2 Time series of housing investment in Greece, 1950–94 217

Diagram 9.3a Correlation between housing and industrial investment in Greece, 1949–94 218

Diagram 9.3b Correlation between housing and industrial investment in Greece, 1949–66 218

Diagram 9.3c Correlation between housing and industrial investment in Greece, 1967–94 219

Diagram 9.4 Comparison of outstanding bank loan advances to housing in Greece, to same for industry and tourism, 1975–94 219

Abbreviations

ΑΕΔΑΚ (Greek)	Mutual Fund Management plc
AITD	Area(s) of Integrated Tourist Development
APC	Annual Percentage Change
ASE	Athens Stock Exchange
ATE (Greek)	Agricultural Bank of Greece
ATM	Automatic Teller Machine(s)
BG	Bank of Greece
BEA (Greek)	Athens Chamber of Craft Industries
BSE	Bovine spongeiform encephalopathy
CAP	Common Agricultural Policy
CPG	Communist Party of Greece
CPI	Consumer Price Index
ΔΕΗ (Greek)	Public Power Corporation
ΔΕΚΟ (Greek)	Public-sector Enterprises and Organisations
DFI	Direct Foreign Investment
EBEA (Greek)	Athens Chamber of Commerce and Industry
ECU	European Currency Unit
EEC	European Economic Community
EFT-POS	Electronic Fund Transfer at Point Of Sale
EMU	Economic and Monetary Union
ΕΟΠ (Greek)	National Welfare Organisation
EOT (Greek)	Hellenic Tourism Organisation
ETB	English Tourist Board
ETBA (Greek)	Hellenic Industrial Development Bank
ETEBA (Greek)	Hellenic Investment Bank for Industrial Development
EU	European Union
FX	Foreign Exchange
GGBd	General Government Budget deficit
GDP	Gross Domestic Product
ICAP	a Greek consultancy firm specialising in the collection, processing and analysis of business data
IKA (Greek)	Social Security Foundation
IOBE (Greek)	Institute of Economic and Industrial Research
ΚΝΠΙΔ (Greek)	State-controlled entities of private-sector Law status
LCF	Loans and Consignments Fund (ΤΠΔ in Greek)
MD	Managing Director

MEDA	a EU programme involving assistance to Mediterranean countries
MEP	Member of European Parliament
MP	Member of Parliament
MS3	Money Supply 3
NAT (Greek)	Veteran Seamen's Fund
NATO	North Atlantic Treaty Organisation
ND	New Democracy (a Greek 'right-wing' political party)
NHBG	National Housing Bank of Greece
NMBG	National Mortgage Bank of Greece
NSSG	National Statistical Service of Greece
OAE (Greek)	Organisation for Restructuring Business Enterprises
OAEΔ (Greek)	Manpower Employment Agency
OC	Olympic Catering plc
OΓA (Greek)	Peasants' Assurance Organisation
OECD	Organisation for Economic Co-operation and Development
OEK (Greek)	Workers' Housing Organisation
ORBE	Organisation for Restructuring Business Enterprises
OTE (Greek)	Telecommunications Organisation of Greece
PASOK	Panhellenic Socialist Kinema [Movement]
PCD	Pharmaceuticals, cosmetics, detergents
PIB	Public Investment Budget
PLC	Public Limited Company
PM	Prime Minister
PPP	Purchasing Power Parity
PSNBR	Public-sector Net Borrowing Requirement
R&D	Research & Development
TEBE (Greek)	Professionals', Craftsmen's, Traders' Fund
TT (Greek)	Post Office Savings Bank
ΣΕΒ (Greek)	Confederation of Greek Industries
ΣΕΤΕ (Greek)	Union of Greek Tourist Enterprises
TAXIS	Tax Information System
ΤΣΜΕΔΕ (Greek)	Pension Fund of Public Works Contractors and Engineers
UBTO	Urban Bus Transport Organisation
UGB	Union of Greek Banks
VAT	Value Added Tax

FactFile on Greece

Area:	131 944 sq km (50 944 sq. miles).
Population in 1995:	About 11 m., including approx. 600 000 economic refugees from the Balkans, Poland and the ex-USSR. Number of tourists in 1995: 10.7 m.
Religion:	Christian Orthodox (97 per cent).
Capital:	Athens (with Piraeus, 30 per cent of population, officially, in 1991).
Main cities:	Thessalonica, Patra, Heracleion, Larissa, Volos, Cavala, Khania, Serres.
Political system:	Parliamentary republic since 1974. Military dictatorship in 1967–74.
Head of State:	President elected by Parliament, but real power rests with Prime Minister.
Currency:	Drachma (dr). In June 1996, £1 = 375 drs, $1 = 245 drs.

GDP per capita in 1991:	$US 7729 (at current prices using PPPs).
Size of informal economy:	Approx. 20 per cent of (recently adjusted) formal GDP.
Owner-occupation in 1991:	75.35 per cent (plus 4.25 per cent occupying gratis).
Structure of GDP in 1991:	16.4 per cent agriculture; 19.7 per cent manufacturing, mining, energy, and water; 7.1 per cent construction; 56.8 per cent services.
Main exports in 1991:	Textiles, olive oil, cereals, preserved fruit & vegetables, fresh fruit, aluminium-alumina, iron plates, other metals, cement, petroleum products.
Main minerals:	Bauxite, lignite, talc, copper, iron, silver, gold, bismuth, sulphur, marble; possibly oil and uranium.
Main industries:	Agriculture, tourism, construction, entertainment, shipping, food and drink, banking, petroleum products, textiles – clothing – white linen & footwear, retailing.

Public debt and budget deficit in 1995:	111.7 and 9.3 per cent of GDP (at market prices), respectively.
Foreign public debt per capita in 1994:	$US 2867, highest in the world.
Trade deficit in 1995:	16 per cent of (revised) GDP at market prices.
Inflation and unemployment in 1995:	8.1 and 10 per cent, respectively.

Important chronologies:

1821:	Greek revolution against Turkish rule.
1830:	Formal independence; European powers impose German king on new nation-state.
1843:	Revolt in Athens forces German king to agree to a Constitution.
1912–13:	More of Greece is liberated; Greece expands to nearly her present borders.
1922:	Following Greek–Turkish war of 1919–22, victorious Turks reconquer Asia Minor, throwing 1 m. Greeks out of their homelands.
1923:	Treaty of Lausanne affirms Greek control of the Aegean and Western Thrace, along with Greeks' rights in Turkish-held Constantinople and the islands of Imbros and Tenedos in the Northern Aegean.
1936–40:	Fascist dictatorship.
1940–49:	Second world war and civil war. The Left loses.
1947:	The Dodecanese (Rhodes, Cos and other near-by islands) becomes part of Greece, ceded by Italy.
1967–74:	Military dictatorship.
1974:	Turkish invasion of Cyprus. Restoration of parliamentary rule in Greece. Communist Party legalised.
1975:	Plebiscite abolishes foreign monarchy (70%–30%).
1981, Oct.:	Under Andreas Papandreou, 'socialist' PASOK party comes to power.
1989–90:	PASOK loses elections; 'Right-wing' ND party forms government.
1993, Oct.:	National election. PASOK returns to power.
1996, Jan.:	C. Semitis replaces ailing A. Papandreou as Prime Minister. Turkish aggression in the Aegean is elevated to territorial claims.
1996, Sept.:	National election. PASOK retains power. Prime Minister, C. Semitis.

Introduction

'Though this be madness, yet there is method in it.'
William Shakespeare. *Hamlet.*

I.1 WHAT'S SPECIAL ABOUT THE GREEK ECONOMY?

John Ioannou is one of Greece's best political cartoonists. Every Sunday the large-circulation daily *Eleutherotypia* ('Freedom of the Press') publishes a full-page illustrated political satire of Ioannou's weekly and witty comment on Greek current affairs. In one of his stories, published on 11 September 1994, Ioannou portrays Andreas Papandreou, then Greece's near-80-year-old socialist Prime Minister, on his flight to Thessalonica, capital of Macedonia. The city holds its 59th International Exhibition, and, according to tradition, the Prime Minister will deliver a speech on the state of the Greek economy. A journalist asks Papandreou for some preliminary remarks. Papandreou replies:

> These things are well-known . . . What our country produces is national issues . . . We sell them abroad, and in turn get Delors financial assistance packages. We distribute these among contractors, and they hand out wages for diggings here and there – the so-called 'great public works'. As soon as the Inland Revenue get a sniff of those incomes, they make a grab for a bit of the loot too . . . In short, this is our economy.

Funny – yet uncomfortably close to the mark. An educated Briton or American, who is looking for some mirth or a bit of the charmingly *outré* in economic and political affairs, does not have long to search: Greece offers ample scope for either. Books like this could even oblige him.[1] After all, another Greek statesman, C. Karamanlis, twice President of the Hellenic Republic, once said that modern Greece is an unbounded institution for the insane.

The danger, though, of this approach is to limit oneself to the satirical or the anecdotal – and fail to ask a number of questions about Greece that just might hold a wider significance. These are:

(a) Greece is neither an advanced economy, like Britain, nor a little-developed one, like Egypt. 'Middle', or perhaps 'stray', cases, are usually less well-studied, certainly less well-understood, than more typical ones, whilst they face special problems and challenges. One pertinent, albeit general, question, for example, might be whether such economies (Greece, Portugal, Ireland, the transitional economies of Eastern Europe) combine the best from both sides of the economic spectrum (as exemplified by, say, capital-rich Britain, and labour-rich Egypt), or, indeed, the worst.

(b) Greece is also a country which is underdeveloping in a literal sense. Around the 1960s she was closing the gap that separated her from advanced countries, while now the gap is widening. Her economic and social trends are worsening instead of improving. This is another area which has not attracted the attention it deserves in the literature – that is, the problems of an economy going down the drain (as opposed to simply going through recession), their causes, and what can be done about it. This is an obviously different perspective from one which assumes that the starting point is low and the way forward can be either up or blocked. It is also different from considering the challenge of country recovery after a war, like Japan,[2] or a revolution, like Eastern Europe. The possibility of 'backsliding' in the context of 'normal' circumstances, which Greece exemplifies, should therefore be of interest to relatively peaceful advanced countries like Britain or America.

(c) Greece has so many interlocked problems that overcoming them calls for very bold and imaginative engineering. Inventing the right blueprint, and, even more so, attempting to apply it, necessitates an appreciation of social and political, as well as economic, factors. For too long has this approach been neglected in mainstream economic analysis – Marxism being the main exception. Recently it has been rediscovered – partly through lack of satisfaction with conventional development theory,[3] partly through attempts to introduce capitalism in countries in the East, which were once supposed to be socialist. In a sense, Greece's problem has been of a more peculiar nature: although a long-standing member of NATO, the EEC, the OECD, the IMF, she has been a strongly statist country, Greek society fiercely resisting the spread of capitalist relations.

(d) Above all else, Greece shows how anti-social behaviour, from relatively major things like polluting the environment, building illicitly, taking bribes, and evading taxes, to relatively minor ones like jumping a queue, being impolite, shedding responsibility, or minimising work effort, is collectivised, legitimised, and institutionalised in the process

> of economic and cultural break-down. Greece, along with other Eastern European economies on their way to capitalism (if that), shows that even European societies at the end of the 20th century are not immune to lawlessness, black economy growth, degeneration of citizenship, and loss of cohesion any more than, for example, post-Roman Europe was. But whereas Eastern European societies have the excuse of having gone very recently through revolutionary upheaval, Greece's attempt at revolution of a very different kind failed in 1949. Hence, her present predicament is, at first reading, the result of more gradual, indeed systemic, factors.

Yet, in both cases – that of Eastern Europe, and of Greece – one finds that the common link is utopia betrayed. Many years after the events of the 1940s, modern Greece shows that failing utopia is not, sadly, without consequences for societies no less than for people. As a collective phantasm, it causes rot to spread over the body and soul of a nation for generations. Even a period of economic growth, like Greece had from the 1950s to the mid-1970s, may not be a safe antidote to broken dreams or pride.

Greece's predicament raises, therefore, two issues of direct concern to the rest of Europe: Can the countries of Eastern Europe ever hope to attain sustainable economic development towards a citizens' society, when they suffer from so much bitterness and disillusionment? Alternatively, can Western European societies go Greece's way? In particular, how long will it be before widespread and rising unemployment, poverty and exclusion, in the midst of a culture of selfishness and money worship, undermine social cohesion, and cultivate the kind of spiritlessness that in turn sustains and feeds on crime, neglect of citizenship, opportunism, economic malaise, and, finally, underdevelopment? It is hoped that a study of the Greek economy, in its historical context, may provide some clues, if not answers.

It is indeed ironic how, after many decades, or even centuries, of references to Greece's past as a source of ideals which the West rightly and ostensibly holds dear to heart (democracy, individualism, inquisitiveness), Greece is now an example of how things can go quite wrong. The 'wrongness' is mitigated, maybe substantially, certainly fortunately, by 20th century successes, such as the liberation of Greek territories from Turkish rule (1912–13), the resistance of the Greek people against Axis forces (1940–4),[4] and the country's enviable economic growth after the war. It is compensated by the presence of the Parthenon in Athens or of Delos in the Cyclades, the literary works of, among others, Cavafy, Kazantzakis, Seferis, Ritsos and Elytis,[5] the voice of

Maria Callas, the fiery passion of Melina Merkouri, the music of Vangelis and Theodorakis (to name but two of the best known Greek composers internationally), or larger-than-life images of ouzo-drinking against the backdrop of a sunset in the Aegean.

But most of those successes and images lie in the dust of the past, like a lot of other things Greek. The decadence, on the other hand, is here and now. Recently it has become only too real as a result of Turkish bullying, Greek weakness and ineptitude, and Western self-interest – to such an extent that Greece is rapidly becoming 'a land famous simply for being so often and so richly insulted'.[6] That is why a study of the Greek economy cannot be appropriately entertaining any more. What might have been comedy, up to ten years ago, is now evolving towards tragedy. But then, one might point out, Greeks should know about drama.

Such a state of affairs cannot be the result of 'pure' economic forces, even if such are supposed to exist – hence, the need to invoke history, with its myriad social and political ramifications, in order to interpret the problems of the Greek economy of to-day. 'Dry' magnitudes and indices, although necessary, are certainly not enough. The same can be said of quantitative techniques, like statistical regressions, which in what follows are used in order to assist the analysis rather than be a substitute for it.

There is, for example, a causal link between the 1979–80 oil-price shock and the observed deterioration in Greece's subsequent economic performance, which has kept going on until the present. But to attribute Greece's economic stagnation solely or mainly to that oil shock, is to ignore the way Greece recovered (although not spectacularly) after the 1973 oil shock and, more importantly, the way other countries eventually succeeded in overcoming the effects of both oil shocks. They succeeded of course for certain reasons. Why, then, didn't those reasons apply in Greece? What other factors played their part? Answering such questions will illuminate the workings of the Greek economy and society, provide a more thorough explanation of the determinants of Greece's economic performance, and perhaps enrich economic theory.

I.2 A CORKBOARD OF QUESTIONS

Besides the above-mentioned reasons for studying the Greek economy, one can pose a variety of more specific questions, which the book will try to answer. These are:

(1) Why did the Greek economy grow fast after 1950, and why did growth decelerate after 1973, and especially after 1979? Was it just the oil-price shocks or were there deeper reasons for both phenomena?
(2) What is the connection between history, politics, and economic performance in post-war Greece, down to the present? Is there, for example, a political business cycle in Greece?
(3) How do Greeks make a living? What are their main sources of income? Is it true that they consume more than they produce? How do they finance the difference? What is the role of Direct Foreign Investment, of invisible earnings, of foreign borrowing?
(4) What kind of economic policies did the Greek state pursue in the last 20 years or so? How has Greece's huge and growing public debt come to be? How does it affect the economy? How can Greece clean up the mess her governments have made of the public finances?
(5) Has a propped-up drachma in the last few years been good or bad for the economy?
(6) What are the causes of Greek inflation? How successful has the Bank of Greece been at fighting it? Can Greece hope to bring it down on a par with the European Union average?
(7) How have state policies, politics, and social practices affected Greece's micro-economy, particularly industry, tourism, and housing?
(8) What is the significance of a relatively low percentage of employees in the labour force in Greece? Of a very high percentage of state employees among all employees? Of a very wide distribution of dwelling wealth? Has Greek economic development suffered because of 'excessive' investment in dwellings or, on the contrary, been boosted by such investment? Has tourism been good or bad for Greece?
(9) What are the main characteristics of Greece's social welfare system, including, importantly, state policy on unemployment? Has it helped or hindered economic growth? What pressures does Greece's social security system presently face?
(10) Can Greece do better in the future? What is the role of the Turkish threat to her sovereignty and territorial integrity? How can a besieged, alienated country with a broken economy hope to move forward? What is required?

The last issue is probably the most important of all. In a book whose main thrust is descriptive rather than prescriptive, any solution proposed can only be tentative and in the nature of guidelines. But if, on the basis of the discussion that is going to follow, the conditions for the urgently needed radical reform of the Greek economy, polity, and society are better appreciated, the book will have made a useful impact. Frequently, having a clear understanding of the general goal is as important as attempting the precise steps to achieve it.

Notes

1. A reader seeking such should find Arouch's (1995a) collection of articles on Greek economic affairs a highly-satisfying source of entertainment.
2. Cf. Tsuru, 1993.
3. *The Economist*, 1996b.
4. Cf. the following extract from Dilys Powell's book *Remember Greece*, published in London in 1941 (p. 149): 'Few nations so far have come out of this war with reputations higher than those they took in. Greece at least has won honours which nothing, not the destruction of her cities nor the massacre of her people, can take from her as long as there are free men left living in the world.'
5. Seferis and Elytis were awarded Nobel prizes in 1963 and 1979, respectively, whilst Kazantzakis was not, in 1957, only because the Greek state and Church intervened against him for political and ideological reasons. Ritsos was awarded the Lenin prize by the Soviet Union in 1977.
6. The phrase was coined as a description of the fictitious kingdom of Sung, in Hugh Cook's book *The Wordsmiths and the Warguild* (Corgi, 1989).

1 An Overview of the Modern Greek Economy

'It is indeed desirable to be well descended, but the glory belongs to our ancestors.'

Plutarch. *On the Training of Children.*

1.1 CURRENT PROBLEMS

Although no economy is problem-free, some can boast of strengths that far outweigh their weaknesses. Not so to-day's Greece. True, by the mid-1970s the Greek people had managed to house themselves amply and satisfactorily (but at the cost of anarchic, thoughtless city-planning); almost all Greeks nowadays eat well (perhaps too well![1]), whilst many certainly spend more time enjoying themselves than working productively.[2] Above all, a Greek (or an Australian or a Spaniard) born in 1992 would expect to live longer (76.9 years) than a person from any other country but four: Japan (79.5), Iceland (78.2), Sweden (78.2), and Switzerland (78).[3]

The country's central bank, the Bank of Greece, has managed to supervise a well-developed banking system strictly, ethically, and with remarkable success, mitigating the inflationary effects of fiscal profligacy and preserving people's trust in the system. This the Bank of Greece has achieved even though many state-owned banks for political reasons got overburdened with bad debts at times, and some still are. The country's food-processing, food-serving, entertainment, supermarket, and fish-farming sectors are thriving. So are her shipping[4] (though not shipbuilding!) and petroleum products industries.[5] Her sprawling tourist industry, although short-sighted and opportunist, remains a big FX earner. But other than these achievements, some of which are of an ambivalent nature, the economy is fraught with problems. In combination, these pose a serious threat to Greece's chances of sustainable development, in both the short and the long term – unless, that is, Greek society is prepared to go through the dramatic changes that overcoming those problems requires. Ten of these are particularly acute. In short, Greece has:

(1) The biggest public sector, broadly defined and in percentage employment terms, among members of the OECD. (We will see why and how this is perhaps the root-problem of the modern Greek economy.)
(2) The biggest public-sector deficits (Maastricht-defined) as a proportion of GDP in the European Union (EU): 9.3 per cent in 1995, against 5 per cent for EU-15. (This partly explains the big public sector and partly is a result of it.)
(3) One of the three biggest public-sector debts as a proportion of GDP in the EU: 111.7 per cent in 1995 (only exceeded by Belgium's and Italy's), against 71.2 per cent for EU-15. In fact, in 1994 Greece had the highest per capita foreign public debt in the world.[6]
(4) Among OECD countries, one of the lowest rates of economic growth in 1981–93, 1.5 per cent (against 2.5 per cent for OECD), while from mid-1950s to mid-1970s Greece's was second only to Japan's.
(5) In the 1980s and 1990s the highest inflation rate in the EU, and the third highest in the OECD (only Turkey, Mexico and Iceland did worse in the 1980s, and only the first two in the early 1990s).
(6) Worst competitiveness record but Mexico's in the OECD, according to reports by the World Economic Forum (see Chapter 2).

In addition, Greece has:

(7) One of the least performance-oriented educational systems in the world (see Chapter 3).
(8) A bad welfare system, in quality as well as in quantity, combined with the harsh reality of an ageing and static population. (This suggests that, to a large extent, the big size of the public sector may have come about for reasons other than welfare – which is, in fact, the case. In a convoluted way, the abysmal level of state services also allows most Greeks to justify tax evasion.)
(9) One of the biggest informal economy sectors in the OECD, as a proportion of formal GDP, with the very probable exception of Turkey, Mexico and Italy (in that order). (The twin results of that are widespread corruption, and a highly regressive taxation system, which, in a country of smallholders, penalises property ownership, among other things.)
(10) The highest percentage of employers and self-employed people in the EU. (This helps sustain the black economy, reduces price-wage flexibility, and drives a wedge between house prices and wages.)

Some of these problem-features have been characteristic of the Greek economy and society almost since Greece became a nation-state, and even before – such as the dominant, pervasive central state, and the large number of smallholders. Others, like persistent inflation and abysmal competitiveness in the 1980s and 1990s, have resulted from the interplay of basic social and political characteristics with particular historical events and international economic developments. The outcome, which is the Greek economy and society of to-day, is not random, but, given the premises of each historical phase modern Greece has gone through, virtually inevitable.

This does not mean necessarily that the present mess Greece has made of herself can only get worse – if anything, history teaches that when bad situations become desperate enough, drastic solutions and appropriate leaders are usually found. Greece herself is no stranger to this pattern. In December 1893, a century ago, the Prime Minister of Greece, Ch. Tricoupis, is reputed to have addressed Parliament in these words: 'Gentlemen, unfortunately we have gone bankrupt!' He had won the elections of 1892 because of popular hopes that he would save Greece from economic bankruptcy, as he had already done once before in 1886.[7] The situation being worse this time, he didn't. Economic collapse happened in a context which is eerily reminiscent of the present. In 1897 Greece lost a war with Turkey, and was only saved – once again – by the intervention of the European Powers. Financial ruin, national humiliation, and deep disillusionment with the corrupt political parties of the day combined to bring about an army revolt in 1909. The revolution ushered in a period of modernisation and national expansion which had not been seen in modern Greece before. It also produced modern Greece's greatest statesman, Eleutherios Venizelos. In the Balkan wars of 1912–13 Greece more than doubled her size, liberating Greek territories and populations from Turkish rule, and defining most of her present borders (which in 1947 formally came to include the Dodecanese – that is, Rhodes, Cos, and other near islands – as defeated Italy was forced to surrender them to Greece).

Like then, Greece nowadays faces bankruptcy and economic collapse. Like then, she has annoyed her European economic partners with her continuous demands for special treatment and for funds, while she does not appear to be making any real effort to put her house in order. Like then, her relations with Turkey are very hostile, while Turkey, on the basis of her perceived military superiority, threatens Greece.[8] But more than then, the Western Powers, for their own geo-political[9] and economic[10] reasons, follow a policy of appeasement of Turkey. So the similarities between the two periods are many. Whether the cycle of economic collapse, national humiliation, and revival will repeat itself in some form or another this time, remains to be seen.

But how did post-war Greece come to this state of affairs? Why, in particular, is her economy in such a bad shape? After all, the Greek economy did grow remarkably fast from the late 1950s to the early 1970s. The answer has to do with the way her economy is structured, the way it operates, and the way the salient features of Greek society and of its political system have been transmitted to the present since Greece became a nation-state in 1830. Let's see the process and its outcome in more detail.

1.2 THE IRON HAND OF HISTORY

From the 15th to the beginning of the 19th century the Greeks were under the Turkish yoke (and many still were until 1920; some are even now). Yet, the social system in which they found themselves failed to develop any well-entrenched form of feudalism. It was not the first time such a failure took place. Certainly the period of Frankish rule over large parts of Greece from 1204 to the 15th century did not last long enough, neither was it cohesive enough, for feudalism to take lasting roots. In Byzantine times (4th century AD to 15th century) multitudes of smallholders in the countryside, west and east of the Aegean sea, were in constant strife with local magnates, who tried to subjugate them, but couldn't do so fully because the central state, in the city of Byzantium, also feared the rising power of such nobles. Inevitably, the two powerful groups antagonised one another to the detriment of the Empire. For example, 'the decrees of the "Macedonian" dynasty [10th-11th centuries] denounce again and again the implacable appropriation of peasant lands and subjection of the poor by the rural potentates of the time [ ]. The concentration of land in the hands of local oligarchies was fiercely resisted by the central imperial State, because it threatened to destroy its recruiting and tax-collecting reserves'.[11] Thus, the Byzantine Empire 'remained transfixed between slave and feudal modes of production [ ], in a social deadlock that could only eventually lead to its extinction'.[12]

The dominance of the central state continued after Byzantium fell to the Turks. The indigenous populations were made to pay taxes to the Sultan via his local representatives, who, significantly, were Turks and Moslem Albanians (even though, at a low level, Christian Greek notables did come to exercise some authority and power). As a result, the introduction of serf – despot relations in the countryside failed to generate the cultural, economic and political dynamics of western-type feudalism. Greeks, along with other Balkanians and ordinary Turks, missed the fruits of the Renaissance and the Enlightenment, since for about five hundred years they were subjected to the barbaric autocracy of the Sublime-Porte. The Ottoman central state, an Islamic, aggressive, and thoroughly uncivilised state at that,[13] was much stronger than in late Byzantine times, and, naturally, the fact that the rulers were both foreign and of a different religion did not help the moral legitimacy of either the political or the social order. The difficulty the peoples of the Balkans and of Asia Minor, Greeks included, have to this day in establishing true civil societies in their countries, is a result of the very long period of Turkish occupation, and, as regards the Turks themselves, of the despotic nature of that occupation.

So the Greek revolution of 1821 and the emergence of modern Greece as a nation-state in 1830 (with decisive help from Russia, France, and Britain) offered an opportunity to re-affirm the central state – smallholder symbiotic pattern of the Byzantine Empire, with nothing in-between the two groups. The crucial difference between this and Byzantine times was in the form the political system took – what N. Mouzelis has called 'early parliamentarism'.[14] Instead of an openly autocratic state, political parties and popular representation through elections to parliament were introduced very quickly to Greece. This was inevitable for three reasons:

(a) Because of the long centuries of Turkish occupation, there was no indigenous aristocracy, or any other kind of indigenous elite, or even recognised descendants of the last Greek King, to take over. (Constantine IA' Paleologos had died in 1453 defending the city of Byzantium from the Turks.) In fact, the new Greek state made a point of not recognising legally any claims to aristocratic lineage;
(b) the Greeks who had financed the liberation struggle and led it politically – although not militarily – were bourgeois Greeks (merchants, philologues, diplomats) of the diaspora; and
(c) most of Western Europe was firmly on the path to parliamentarism and constitutional monarchy anyway. Thus in 1843 a revolt in Athens forced the German king Otto, whom the European Powers had imposed on the new nation-state, to grant a Constitution.

The problem with a state mechanism imposed from above in this manner, against a social background of long-oppressed, at the same time distrustful and naive, peasants, especially when that state mechanism is combined with parliamentarism, is that it becomes a recipe for a statist-clientelist-populist, and inevitably corrupt, political system.[15] People, politicians and voters alike, learn to exchange favours for votes. More often than not, these favours involve the distribution by the state of perks, pensions, contracts, subsidies, or simply of jobs ('positions' is the usual Greek term) with the public sector, without regard to needs[16] or merit. It is a pattern which Greece began to experience very soon after she reformed into a modern nation-state on lands liberated from Ottoman rule and has gone on since.[17] This is demonstrated in the following excerpt from an article on Greek politics, written in 1896 but which could just as easily have been written in 1996:

> Not only does the life of the government depend on the MP, but also the honour, the fortune, the security, the daily bread or at least the fulfilment of some desire or other of most Greeks. 'Most' is not an exaggeration either, since not many are those Greeks blessed enough to have nothing to fear or hope for from an MP, no landplot capable of being squatted on or included in a city plan, no debt to or claim on the state, no pending trial, no position in the public sector in need of protection or one which they covet instead [the list goes on].[18]

How quickly parliamentarism was introduced to Greece is seen through a comparison with Britain. The franchise in Britain was extended very gradually, and at each stage it was linked to amount of property owned. For example, although the 1832 Reform Act 'enfranchised a quarter of a million new property-owning voters', the proportion of voters as a percentage of the population aged over 20 years was just 7.1 per cent. The 1867 Reform Act 'gave the suffrage in boroughs to all householders and to lodgers paying ten pounds a year or more, and added one million voters to the registers', but the proportion of voters in the population aged over 20 years increased to a mere 16.4 per cent.[19]

In contrast to what happened in Britain, all Greeks over 25 years of age who were 'owners or practising a craft in rural areas' were given the vote as early as 1844 – that is, 14 years after Greece formally re-established national boundaries. The franchise was extended in 1864 to all male Greek citizens over 21 years of age.[20]

Broadly over the same period, the lands which the departed Turks had left behind were nationalised, both after 1830 and after 1913 (when Macedonia and Epirus were liberated by Greece and added to her territory). These were subsequently distributed to peasants in the most long-drawn privatisation exercise history has known.[21] Even the extensive land-holdings, which some Greeks established in Thessaly, in central Greece, between 1881 and 1900,[22] were liquidated after 1909 through Venizelos' agrarian reform.

The significance for future economic developments of the above events is three-fold:

(a) A society of smallholders who, moreover, have an early opportunity to influence laws and policies, and a central state whose functionaries want, for their own reasons, to preserve and expand its big size and role, do not make for the best way to foster the capitalist – wage-earner relationship. The political game becomes centred around ways to reproduce and enhance the clientelist role of the state and the interests of smallholders rather than around the pangs of industrialisation or the distribution of its fruits. Thus, genuine capitalist economic development is retarded, replaced by a twisted form of state – smallholder capitalism.
(b) A consequence of this pattern is that Greek society has attached traditionally more importance to possession of property and position than to performance or actual merit. Other countries (for example, Ireland[23]) had had the same hurdle to overcome, but have made the transition more successfully than Greece has achieved so far.
(c) Even more importantly, the notions of citizenship, obligation, reward for effort, discipline, merit, and even politeness have either been conspicuously absent from most of post-war Greece, or discarded at first opportunity.

Come to think of it, citizenship and civil society cannot flourish in a country where the central state is accustomed to treating the people as subjects, and they, in turn, to viewing the state as a milk cow.[24] In the same vein, politeness or self-discipline require either a very close-knit folk community, or a long tradition of class or elite rule, which teaches people 'their place'. Modern Greece used to be made up of close-knit rural communities, but rapid urbanisation after 1960, a domineering state and modern tourism have destroyed most of them without offering any positive alternatives by way of social cohesion. On the other hand, Greece's small, indigenous national bourgeoisie, having gradually risen and influenced Greek politics from the 1860s to the 1930s, did not manage to achieve social and political hegemony either: It eventually dissolved as an authentic national and nationalist force, giving its place to social strata and political forces totally dependent on Britain first, the USA later, for their survival.

Its failure happened for two reasons. First, as a result of Greece losing Asia Minor to the Turks in the Greek-Turkish war of 1920–2, whereas a Greek victory then would have secured the national bourgeoisie's hegemony for decades to come;[25] second, because part of that bourgeoisie collaborated with the Germans during the Occupation, 1941–4; another part – to a certain extent overlapping with the first – became instrumental in British designs to reimpose a hated and foreign monarchy on Greek republicans after the Occupation. The immediate motive of both segments, as well as of Britain, was to resist communism. A third part joined the Left during the Resistance and the civil war that followed (1944–9), and were subsequently persecuted and dubbed traitors by the victors.

In short, the absence of a civil society from Greece, with its attendant moral qualities, and/or of a hegemonic, cohesive force ruling over it, makes it very difficult either to alter the traditional role of the state and of the political system, or to achieve the team work and work effort required for successful capitalist economic performance.

1.3 A CAPTIVE ECONOMY

In 1920 Greece tried to liberate the Greeks of Asia Minor from Turkish rule. She failed. In 1922 one million Greeks were thrown out of Asia Minor and sought refuge in mainland and island Greece. Almost overnight the population increased by 20 per cent – propertyless, desperate people, willing to work for any wage. Unsurprisingly, the 1920s coincide with the first wave of industrialisation in Greece.[26]

The second wave occurred between 1958 and 1973, under similar circumstances. The Second World War, and the civil war that followed, had destroyed much of the Greek countryside. In the 1950s the country was starkly, desperately poor. People flocked to cities, mostly Athens and Piraeus, or migrated. The main difference between the 1920s and the 1960s was in the degree of police repression, which was worse in the later period.

And yet . . . in both instances the remarkable thing is that Greek society very quickly managed to incorporate the propertyless and the desperate in its fabric without itself having to undergo dramatic changes. It retained its character as a statist smallholder society throughout the transition from rural to urban. Indeed, the most significant change was urbanisation, rather than in employee growth, the role of the state, or the distribution of property, whose wide spread was reproduced after the war – in an urban setting this time.

Thus Greece's urban population rose from 33 per cent of the total in 1940, to 38 per cent in 1951, and 43 per cent in 1961. Between 1961 and 1971 it registered the biggest rise in the 1940–91 period, going up to 53 per cent, gained five more basis points over the next decade, and has been virtually stable at 59 per cent since (Table 1.1).

Despite this massive increase in urban population, by 1986 employers and self-employed in Greece made up 35.3 per cent of the labour force – higher than any other EEC country.[27] The second country in the list, Portugal, was way below, with 26.2 per cent. In the UK, by comparison, employers and self-employed were 11.5 per cent of the labour force. Not only that: Greece had the largest percentage of family workers in the labour force, 15.4 per cent, again way above the second country, Spain, which had 6.8 per cent. That left Greece with the smallest percentage, by far, of employees in the labour force, 49.3 per cent, against 68.8 per cent for Portugal (which came second) and 88.5 per cent for the UK. More recent evidence suggests that the Greek pattern holds strong: in 1990 the percentage of self-employed in the service sector was 34.4 per cent, higher than in Italy, where it was 30.1 per cent, and far higher than the EEC average, which was 16.6 per cent.[28] In 1991 the proportion of employers, self-employed, and family workers in Greece's economically active population was 48 per cent.[29] Finally, in 1993 the proportion of non-employees[30] in civilian employment was 47 per cent in Greece, 29 per cent in Italy, 26 per cent in Portugal and Spain, and 24 per cent in Ireland (in Turkey, however, it was 60 per cent).[31]

In housing, an inter-temporal pattern of high rates of owner-occupation is further evidence of the ability of Greek society to reproduce its characteristic feature of a smallholders' society. In 1957 a survey of cities and towns of more than 5,000 inhabitants showed the percentage of owner-occupiers to be 65.1 per cent.[32] The national percentage must have been significantly higher since rural households overwhelmingly owned their homes. In 1993 the national percentage of owner-occupation in Greece was 77 per cent, against 81 per cent for Ireland, 78 per cent for Spain, and 67 per cent for the UK.[33] What's more, the comparative percentages hide an important qualitative distinction, namely, that most owner-occupying Greeks own their homes outright, while in other EU countries the percentage of owner-occupiers who are in the process of repaying a mortgage is higher (see Chapter 9).

Also, in 1991 the percentage of employees who got their pay packets

Table 1.1
Greece: Population shares, 1940–91, and GDP shares, 1951–91

POPULATION	1940	1951	1961	1971	1981	1991
Urban	32.8%	37.7%	43.3%	53.2%	58.1%	58.9%
Semi-urban	14.8%	14.8%	12.9%	11.6%	11.6%	12.9%
Rural	52.4%	47.5%	43.8%	35.1%	30.3%	28.2%
Total population	7 344 860	7 632 801	8 385 866	8 766 909	9 738 945	10 259 720
Increase (1951 = 100)		1.00	1.10	1.15	1.28	1.34
GDP		1951	1961	1971	1981	1991
Agriculture		30.7%	27.5%	18.2%	17.7%	16.4%
Manufacturing + MEW*		16.1%	18.7%	22.7%	23.0%	19.8%
Construction		4.0%	6.4%	9.1%	7.7%	7.1%
Services		49.2%	47.5%	50.0%	51.5%	56.7%
Total GDP**		80 511	143 772	278 551	416 515	504 744
Increase (1951 = 100)		1.00	1.79	3.46	5.17	6.27
Increase in GDP per capita		1.00	1.63	3.01	4.05	4.66

* MEW = mining, energy, water.
** At factor prices, million drs, 1970 = 0, Standard System of Accounts (that is, 'old' system of calculating GDP).

Source: National Statistical Service of Greece (NSSG).

directly or indirectly from the state was about 45 per cent of all employees (that is, wage-earners) in the economically active population[34] – far higher than any other OECD country. Considering that public-sector employees in Greece enjoy life tenure, whether officially or in practice,[35] that figure means that even a very large number of employees possess a kind of property – their right to an income for life, usually in return for nominal work. If we now add together the 1991 percentages for non-employees (48 per cent) and for public-sector employees (23 per cent) in Greece's economically active population, that leaves only about 29 per cent for private-sector, non-family employees. This may not be enough to give slack to the labour market, or room for price-wage flexibility to work – and we haven't even considered those with two jobs, one of which will in all likelihood be in the black economy.

Rapid urbanisation and repression were not the only after-effects of the 1944–9 civil war. The war itself can be viewed as the most recent, large-scale attempt by many Greeks to create what they saw as a genuine people's republic, and achieve true national sovereignty for their country. The Left, which lost the civil war, was an amalgam of authentic folk, national bourgeois, and proletarian elements. If popular feeling in Europe had been allowed free reign by the Great Powers of the time, then Greece would have surely turned socialist, whilst Poland, for example, capitalist. But the opposite happened. The tragedy for Greece was that Britain and the USA, in their desperate efforts to save Greece (and their interests) from communism, as they saw it, supported and relied on collaborators of the Germans during the Occupation, and on mostly royalist politicians and officers (who had supported the 1936 Metaxas dictatorship). When the smoke of the civil war had finally cleared, the Greek people found that, contrary to what had happened in the rest of Europe, the collaborators were government (or the true power behind government), whereas those who had fought the conquerors had been declared traitors – exiled, tortured, executed, denied jobs, or imprisoned. The reversal of moral values which this state of affairs brought about, and the bitter conclusion that self-sacrifice does not pay, reverberates through Greek society to this day. The direction of private investment to projects which promise a quick payback, rather than over the longer term, has been, in part, a result of this mentality.[36]

Of course the governments which were formed after the civil war were repressive and conservative. Miraculously, the political system was still based on parliamentarism, but within prescribed lines, as the Communist Party and communist activity had been outlawed. Within these confines the old pattern of clientelist politics was resumed. The central state, if anything, grew even more powerful and self-seeking. Under those circumstances, paying lip-service to the need for export-led growth[37] was outweighed by the fact of state bureaucratic interference in all walks of economic life. This was worse than if import substitution had been the express state policy. It happened not only because the repressive and inefficient[38] Greek state instinctively feared that it would be unable to retain as much control over the economy and society in the context of any other behaviour on its part; but, contrary, say, to the Taiwanese pattern of development, the clientelist parliamentarism of Greece, with its attendant corruption, inefficiency, and short-termism, lent strength to protection-seeking interests. In turn, protectionist demands played into the hands of state functionaries and politicians whose interests lay with a domineering public sector, and the pattern of post-war Greek development was set.

Initially, from 1958 to 1973, the Greek economy knew remarkably high growth rates – in fact, second highest in the OECD after Japan. Such growth rates are often observed when the starting point is very low, that is, when the country in question is very poor. Other factors also helped: Poverty made for low labour costs, which is usually good for investment. US aid gave the economy an initial but important multiplier impetus. Police repression made trade-unionist activity difficult, if not outright illegal. A dramatic migration of rural population to the cities, particularly Athens and Piraeus, took place. The exodus from the countryside was itself a result of the disruption in rural life which the civil war had brought about, of poverty, and of the fact that police repression was especially severe in rural areas. But urbanisation created a very strong demand for new housing, which in turn helped generate demand for a number of associated industries and professions. Housing investment also tends to have a high domestic value content, a factor which can help an economy struggling along a growth path.

Yet the miracle of the 1960s did not go on. Too many things about the Greek economy were wrong for such growth to be sustained. It is true that the beginnings of decline for the post-war Greek economy coincide with the two oil shocks, in 1973 and 1979. These hurt domestic production as well as Greece's export markets, while they fuelled inflation. But other countries recovered. Greece has not – precisely because its weaknesses and mistakes were already there, and even got worse as time went by. Greece has not even managed to make intelligent use, like, say, Portugal has, of its full membership of the EEC, which she has enjoyed since 1981 (see Chapter 8).

Primary among those weaknesses has been the way the Greek state has sustained, created, or expanded inefficiencies and an anti-meritocratic mentality throughout the economy – something which we have already pointed out and we'll return to time and again. Another weakness has been the short-termist mentality of most Greeks – born out of defeat as much as of the need to survive from one day to the next. In fact, the only investment which almost all Greeks would gladly contemplate is in family dwellings – not, strictly speaking, a directly productive investment, despite its substantial multiplier effects. A third weakness has been the resurgence of clientelist politics – with an added dose of virulent populism – after 1974, when parliamentarism was re-established after a seven-year period of military junta rule. This kind of politics has led relentlessly to the worst public finances Greece has seen since the end of the war.

The Greek economy has become a captive of its own political system – the state officials and politicians who do not want to relinquish control or opportunities for perks, power and office, the public-sector employees who do not want to lose their positions or be forced to do any real work,[39] and the general population, who keep participating in the game of exchanging votes for favours – such as getting away with unauthorised building. Very often, too, these favours are about positions with the public sector, either for the voters themselves or for their kin. Characteristically, whereas before 1974 the Greek secondary and higher education system suffered primarily from repression and shallow conservatism, after 1974 and the reintroduction of civilian rule its declining standards have been the result of it being viewed as, and having degenerated merely into, a vehicle for entry into the public sector – where merit is of no importance, but a paper token, like a certificate or degree, is.

1.4 A VICIOUS CIRCLE

No modern economy is immune to unemployment – sometimes for prolonged periods, or even in a major scale. In an advanced capitalist country like Britain, the unemployed are primarily taken care of by means of unemployment benefits or via re-training schemes. In Greece, unless they emigrate (which they did in the 1920s and 1960s), they are recruited by the public sector, or have been so until the present. That is partly the reason why the official unemployment rate in Greece in the 1980s, when the country was experiencing one of the lowest growth rates in the OECD, fluctuated between a low of 4.1 per cent (in 1981) and a high of 8.1 per cent (in 1984).[40] Otherwise, it would have been much higher.[41]

One might rush to say that the net result from the point of view of the Exchequer is the same – whether the unemployed are hired by the state, including state enterprises and organisations, or are given benefits. Unfortunately, it is not. First, the employed usually have more organised power, and greater ability to push through with their demands, than the unemployed. Second, their power and ability are enhanced when their employer is a monopoly or near-monopoly, as is certainly the case with government departments, and, more often than not, with public-sector enterprises and organisations. Third, when that is the case, the power and ability of public-sector employees can be further enhanced by the opportunity they have to politicise every issue and every grievance. This is so especially when no political party in Greece, to borrow a modern phrase, wishes to roll back the frontiers of the state, or change a political system that is based on the parties using the public sector – and public money – in order to win votes in exchange for favours.

In general, the economic effects of this situation are also three-fold. The direct cost to the Exchequer can easily go far beyond what would have been if the unemployed or the poor were simply being given benefits. The productivity losses from overstaffed departments, enterprises and organisations, from various mismatches, from the lack of meritocratic ethos, from employees who know that no matter how little or how ineffectively they work they will keep their positions, and from work-days lost in strikes aimed at preserving or enhancing those employees' privileges, drag down the productivity of the entire economy. Third, the bureaucratic quagmire, which such a public sector is, drowns the sector itself as much as the rest of the economy in red-tape, frequent policy changes, officialdom, and delays. The upshot is that domestic production and international competitiveness suffer.[42]

Around the Greek public sector, in particular, a sea of smallholders has facilitated the reproduction and growth of a well-entrenched and expansive black economy. Successive governments have not wished to eradicate it by bringing it under the taxman as in an essentially parliamentary political system such measures would carry a severe penalty in terms of votes, and even social unrest. Yet the public sector needs to be financed. The financing requirements, in fact, are the greater the more unproductive, bloated, and inefficient the public sector is.

To finance itself, and lacking sufficient tax revenue, the Greek state has been incurring rising deficits, particularly since 1981, mostly regardless of anti-cyclical considerations as such. The proceeds have been channelled into, by and large, consumption expenditures, including wages for work not really done, and for output not really produced. The public debt has been increasing. The need to service a large debt has begun, since the late 1980s, to exercise an autonomous influence on the borrowing requirements of the state, irrespective of any perceived need to finance other expenditures. Inflation has become endemic. At the same time, the poor welfare record of the state has become an excuse for further tax evasion, while its poor infrastructure record, particularly in the areas of telecommunications and transport, adversely affects international investment in Greece.

Stagnating material production and incomes generated in the public sector and the service, mostly black, economy have been sucking in imports at an alarming rate. The trade deficit has been expanding. The Greek state, therefore, has had to borrow foreign currency, in addition to its domestic borrowing, in order to cover current account deficits brought about by recurrent trade deficits. Up to 1993, if the domestic capital market could not or would not cover all of the state's domestic borrowing needs, the state would print money, or force state-controlled banks and pension-funds to lend it the necessary monies at terms dictated by the state itself. This particular intervention has helped undermine, among others, the social security system of Greece. As membership of the EU has become increasingly incompatible with such practices (particularly, since 1994, note-printing), the state has been borrowing from abroad more than it needs in order to cover the country's current account deficits alone. Consequently, in addition to the domestic public debt, whose servicing quite probably crowds out a sizable chunk of potential private investment, the external debt of the country has been rising too.

High borrowing needs and, in comparison to the EU average, high inflation rates have kept interest rates relatively high. At a period of capital movement liberalisation, high interest rates have helped the country avoid devaluation or even rapid depreciation of the currency (the drachma). Financial liberalisation and a resistant drachma have enabled, and relatively high interest rates have forced, domestic companies to seek finance in foreign currency (thus contributing to a net inflow of capital to offset the current account deficits). The interest rate factor has also motivated drachma holders to retain their holdings, and encouraged short-term, that is, speculative, capital imports from international financial investors (again helping to offset current account deficits).

In turn, the overvalued currency facilitates imports, while international competitiveness is reduced, and the trade deficit grows. This further discourages domestic material production. The latter was already suffering as a result of declining investment, poor infrastructure (including education), political activism, red tape, lack of meritocracy, and a work ethos which for too long has dissociated rights from obligations. Devaluing the drachma, on the other hand, an exercise which was most successfully carried out in 1953, is nearly sure to cause a strong upsurge in inflation for the following reasons: A good majority of Greeks now live in cities and towns rather than in the farm. They have higher incomes than in the 1950s. They have learnt to depend on imports for their standard of living.

Careful interest rate management is thus crucial in helping a Greek government steer the economy through the prongs of public debt reduction, on the one hand, and the threat of devaluation-related inflation, on the other. But to what end? The real challenge is for the country to utilise the time thus gained in order to effect the painful structural changes she needs in order to clean up her supply side. For political reasons this has not happened. Thus the Greek economy is well into a vicious circle of debt, deficit financing, inflation, low investment, trade deficits, and low growth (see Diagram 1.1).

By the end of 1995 a combination of frantic, albeit inefficient, tax collection, gradual reductions in interest rates (helped by still lower rates abroad), less fiscal expansion than usual, continuation of the hard drachma policy (begun after a 'mini' devaluation in 1985), more competition in various sectors, and hopes of an economic upturn by means of EU funding for a number of great public works (the so-called Second Delors package), had led to a couple of positive, yet precarious, changes. First, the rate of inflation, which was already dropping from a high of 22.8 per cent in 1990, but at a decreasing rate, dropped faster in 1995, coming down to 8.1 per cent, and to 7.5 per cent by the end of 1996 (despite an upsurge to 9.2 per cent in April 1996). Second, domestic interest rates dropped substantially, led by issues of government paper at lower and lower rates. Happily, because these rates were still internationally competitive in real terms, there was no flight of capital from Greece, or a rapid depreciation of the drachma. Of course the downward course of Greek interest rates can only last as long as interest rates elsewhere are sufficiently lower than Greece's to offset the risk the economy of the country poses to investors in drachmas – and as long as the inflation rate does not rebound. The latter condition appears, at this stage, far from secured. Worse, no political

Diagram 1.1:
The Greek economy: A dynamic overview

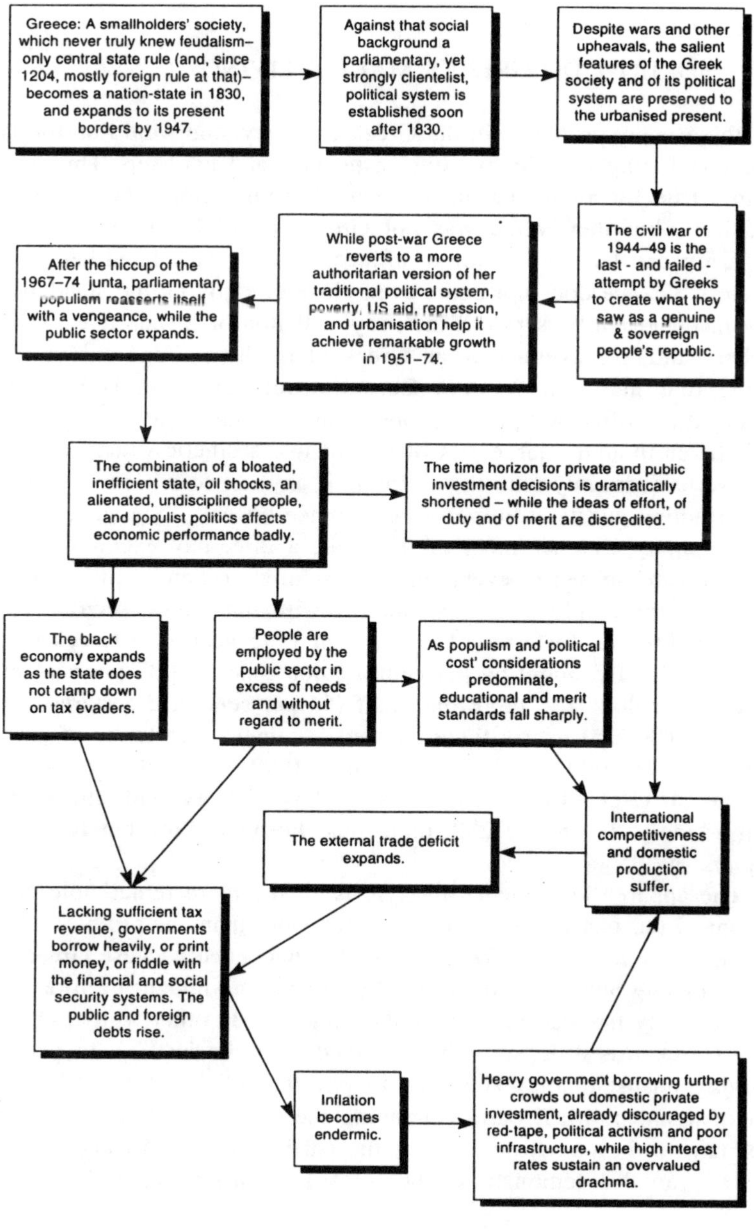

party seems willing to push for the dramatic clean-up act the country's economy and society need. Unsurprisingly, the people don't show much enthusiasm for the prospect either.

1.5 SO, HOW DO GREEKS MAKE A LIVING?

With so many problems in the Greek economy, one would be forgiven for concluding that Greeks live in poverty and hardship. This is certainly true for an increasing number of them, among the old in particular – but then when was not Greece poor? It's only in the last 20–25 years that the illusion of affluence has overwhelmed her. Nevertheless, Greece does not come even close to enjoying the standards of welfare and public services that, say, a Briton or Swede does. On the other hand, the average urban Greek of productive age enjoys a life style that many in Western Europe would envy: outright owner-occupation, often with extra property in the countryside; a vivid night life (even though a large part of it is of low aesthetic value); a visit to a taverna (certainly with the children, if any), or to a friend's place, or entertaining guests at home, once or twice a week; long summer holidays; sunny weather most of the year; a three-day excursion to the countryside on nearly every one of six long weekends; little pressure at work for employees, especially if with the public sector; family support for life. In terms of gadgets, in 1995 nearly all Greek households had a TV, about 64 per cent a colour one, and 33 per cent more than one colour TV; more than half (54 per cent) had a stereo, about half a VCR, and nearly three quarters a camera.[43] In terms of passenger cars per 1000 population Greece in 1990, with 169 cars, was last in the EU (Ireland had 228), but way above Turkey, with 29. (Perhaps surprisingly, Japan had 282, more than Portugal, 260, but fewer than Spain, 307.)[44]

The apparently affluent life style is all the more remarkable on account of the fact that Greece consumes more than she produces. Good for her, one might say! Yes, but this has happened because Greece has been raising debt, both domestically (with some bought by foreigners) and directly from abroad, at an alarming rate. In other words, much of the Greek life style, as it has evolved over the last 20–25 years, is simply unsustainable. The time to pay the bill has arrived, with all mainstream political parties dreading the day when they will have to explain to the Greek people that the party is well and truly over.

Diagram 1.2 demonstrates the point. From a ratio of trade deficit to

Diagram 1.2
Greece, 1958–95: Living beyond her means, thanks to a net inflow of invisible earnings (and foreign borrowing, which more than covers the difference)

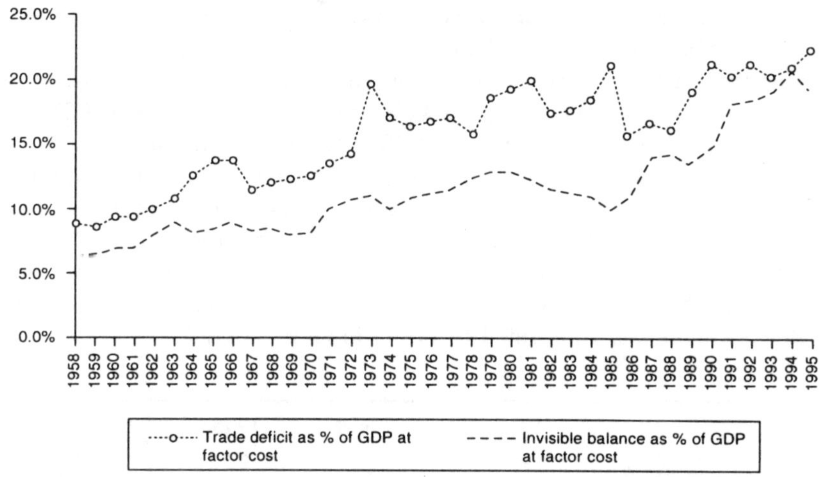

Source: NSSG (National Accounts), Bank of Greece Annual Reports.

GDP[45] equal to 9 per cent in 1958, the Greek economy went up to 22.3 per cent in 1995, higher than ever before. This ratio is more than simply a reference to the relative size of the trade deficit: it shows the extent to which Greece has been living beyond her means, that is, the excess of available consumption over production.[46]

The answer, therefore, to the question of how Greeks make a living involves three factors: first, national production, including, very importantly, a significant part which escapes the taxman; second, net invisible earnings to pay for the excess of imports over exports; third, net capital inflows, mostly representing foreign borrowing, in order to cover, or more than cover, any remaining difference. Let us look at them in greater detail.

The growing discrepancy between what Greece consumes and what she produces needs to be financed somehow. The main source of finance has been Greece's net invisible earnings, which from 1958 to 1995 have covered 71.5 per cent of the trade deficit, on average (see Diagram 1.2). Their importance has been growing, too: from 1986 to

1995, the proportion has averaged 83.2 per cent. The gap between net invisible earnings and the trade deficit is of course made good through net capital inflows, which have involved mainly foreign borrowing rather than direct foreign investment (DFI). Moreover, these inflows, as well as their foreign borrowing component, have typically been more than enough to finance the current account deficit.[47] The excess has helped governments finance large budget deficits, or, in recent years, to service the country's huge and growing public debt (see Chapter 4). As a result Greece's public foreign debt averaged 41.9 per cent of GDP in the 1986–95 period, rising from $US16 to $US34 billion.

Looking at invisible earnings in greater detail (Diagram 1.3), one discovers that as of 1986 the biggest items making them up have been tourist receipts and transfers from the European Communities[48] – the latter have actually been the single biggest category since 1989. On average, the contribution of the most important items to gross invisible earnings has conformed to the following pattern:[49]

	1958–95	1986–95	1995	1995 absolute values (in $US m.)
Tourism	22.3%	21.3%	19.9%	4135.8
Shipping	24.3%	12.5%	10.5%	2189.8
Expats' remittances	25.6%	14.7%	14.8%	3070.7
EC transfers	19.0%	22.8%	23.9%	4968.0

One sees that tourism and EC transfers together made up 44.1 per cent of gross invisible earnings in 1986–95. It hasn't always been like that: in the past the main sources of invisible earnings were expatriates' remittances (mainly from Germany, Australia, and the USA) and shipping (seamen's remittances). In 1959 and 1965, for instance, expatriates' remittances provided 38 per cent of gross invisible earnings, whilst shipping provided 36 per cent in 1974. The contribution of tourism, on the other hand, peaked in 1978 (30 per cent) and again in 1986 (28 per cent), dropped to 16.7 per cent in 1991 (lowest value in the 1969–95 period), and has been about 20 per cent since (although in absolute terms gross receipts from tourism have been growing – see Chapter 10). There can be no doubt, therefore, that when, or if, EC transfers to Greece stop, the country, already EU's biggest beneficiary in terms of net receipts,[50] will be hard-pressed to substitute other sources of invisible earnings for them.

Diagram 1.3
Greece, 1958–95: Tourism, shipping, expatriates' remittances, and European Community transfers as % of gross invisible earnings

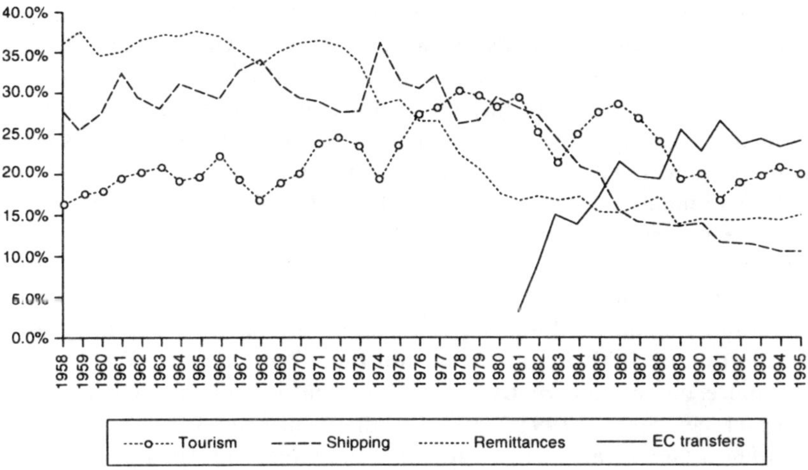

Source: Bank of Greece Annual Reports

Turning to Greece's national production (Table 1.1), one finds that from 1951 to 1991 GDP has increased in real terms much faster than population – which means that per capita income has risen (see Chapter 2). Expectedly, the share of agriculture has been declining since 1951. Industry (manufacturing, mining, energy and water provision) has lost share during the de-industrialising 1980s (see Chapter 8), while construction has stabilised around 7.5 per cent of GDP. This is not surprising considering how population growth, urbanisation, and economic growth have lost impetus since the mid-1970s (see Table 1.1 and Chapter 9). The peak of this activity apparently happened around 1971, facilitated by Greece's military government directing resources to the construction sector. Services are obviously on the increase, like in most countries. In 1991 they contributed 57 per cent of Greece's GDP, against 49 per cent in 1951. It is worth noting that in both the 1971–91 and in the 1981–91 periods, the bulk of the increase in the share of services has been at the expense of industry and construction (74 per cent), not agriculture (26 per cent) – in line with apparent international experience.[51] Conversely, in 1961–71, when industry and construction increased more rapidly than services, agriculture registered its biggest post-war share loss (9.3 basis points). The evidence suggests that it was easier for people to quit agriculture when they expected to work in industry or construction than when they expected to join the (relatively insecure?) service sector.

Linked to the question of how Greeks make a living is the issue of Greece's informal economy. Thanks to it many Greeks can afford a life style which they would not have been able to attain otherwise. Quantitative estimates of the informal economy are by definition quite difficult.[52] Regarding the Greek informal economy, these estimates have varied from about 28 per cent of formal GDP to 240 per cent! An added difficulty is that since 1988 the National Statistical Service of Greece has adopted a new method of calculating GDP,[53] which has resulted in an average increase in formal GDP by 22.3 per cent – presumably capturing in this way a significant part of the country's informal economy. Moreover, the size of the latter is not fixed as a proportion of GDP, but changes with time. For example, Turkey's informal economy apparently was 34 per cent of official GDP in 1992, and 41 per cent in 1994.[54] Equally, the Centre for Planning and Research, a Greek think tank, estimated the Greek informal economy as 27 per cent of official GDP in 1982, and as 31 per cent in 1988.[55] In 1990 Maria Negreponti-Delivani, a Greek economist, came up with a figure of 40 per cent,[56] her estimate echoed by the late A. Angelopoulos in 1994.[57] P. Pavlopoulos, an economist who pioneered research into the Greek informal economy in the 1980s, has concluded that in 1984 it must have been near 30 per cent, certainly no smaller than 25 and no larger than 35 per cent of formal GDP.[58] For that reason, the mentioned correction in Greece's national accounts must have substantially limited the size of her informal economy. Following, that is, the recent GDP review by the NSSG 'we can safely conclude that the most probable size of our country's informal economy is around 10 per cent plus or minus 2 basis points'.[59] On the other hand, if we accept Negreponti-Delivani's original estimate of 40 per cent (made in relation to the 'old' GDP), Greece's informal economy after the GDP review must be in the range of 20 per cent, provided of course that its size has not grown further since 1990.

Pavlopoulos, rightly, cautions against equating the percentage size of a country's informal economy with the percentage size of tax evasion (that is, unlawfully uncollected taxes as a proportion of tax revenue), which, he suggests, must be larger than 10 per cent.[60] But he dismisses exaggerated estimates (like Lecatsas' 240 per cent![61]) of the size of the informal economy since, among other reasons, in that case

Greece would in fact be so prosperous that her present economic mess would not be possible to explain.[62]

Why does Greece have such a large informal economy – at least by 'advanced' country standards? Negreponti-Delivani has identified a number of contributing factors.[63] First and foremost among these appears to be government consumption expenditures – the strongest positive influence on the country's informal economy. This makes intuitive sense: Greece's clientelist political system and corruption in the public sector combine in order to create incomes 'under the table'.[64] On the other hand, changes in the level of industrial investment seem to be negatively associated with informal economy growth. Again this makes intuitive sense, as the spread of industry tends to bring about greater organisation in social and economic life, which in turn tends to limit the scope of informal activities. (If this analysis is correct, the informal economy in 'advanced' countries should therefore be on the rise, along with their expanding service sectors.)

Useful as these statistical associations are, we shouldn't forget that even a small government, or a small public sector in general, can allow informal economy growth by default: all that it takes is inability and/or unwillingness on the part of the authorities to clamp down on tax evasion. To curry favour with the public, and avoid social unrest and, they say, capital flight, all Greek governments have therefore not taken radical measures to assess and tax people's true incomes. Only very recently, as a result of grave fiscal difficulties, are tentative and inefficient measures being taken to that direction.[65]

Notes

1. Certainly they spend a larger percentage of their total consumption on food than any other EU-12 member: 28.8 per cent against 14.9 for EU-12. *E Cathemerine*, 24.9.1995, p. 64, on the basis of EuroStat data for 1992. Happily, their diet is rapidly winning international renown as the world's healthiest: 'Amok with the Greek diet', *Ta Nea*, 7.12.1995, p. 43; 'The secret of longevity is Greek', *Ta Nea*, 13.12.1995, pp. 20–1.
2. According to research by IP ('Euro-Time Survey'), the Greeks sleep less, go to bed later, and rest longer than any other EU-12 member. 'How Europeans spend their time', *To Vema*, 8.11.1992, pp. E6–E9. On the other hand they do seem to have to work longer than, say, the Germans, the British, or the French, in order to buy the same goods: 'The cost of living has gone up', *E Cathemerine*, 18.4.1996, p. 7, on the basis of research by the Consumer Institute of Greece (INKA).

3. *UN Human Development Report 1995* (Oxford University Press: New York, 1995), p. 155.
4. At the beginning of 1995 the Greek-owned merchant fleet was the biggest in the EU, numbering 3142 ships of all types (14 per cent of world total), with a gross tonnage of nearly 72 million (9.2 per cent of world total); 69 per cent of the ships and 44 per cent of the gross tonnage came under the Greek flag (*E Cathemerine*, 10.2.1996 & 2.4.1996).
5. The petroleum products industry is dominated by the state-owned EKO, and the immensely successful, world-class enterprises of the Vardinoyannis and Latsis families, in the tradition of other Greek self-made tycoons like Onassis or Niarchos.
6. Yannaris, 1996.
7. Andronopoulos, 1993.
8. For example, on 22.9.1994 the Prime Minister of Turkey, Ms Tansu Ciller, threatened Greece with military attack if Greece extended her territorial waters from six to twelve miles – something which Greece was perfectly entitled to do after 16.11.1994, on the basis of the 1982 Convention on the Law of the Sea.
9. They see Turkey as a long-term counter-weight to Russia, as an attractor power to the Moslem populations of parts of southern ex-Soviet Union, and as a regional security force for Western oil ventures in the Caspian and the surrounding republics.
10. In order to justify the European Union policy of striving for a closer association between Turkey and the Union, Sir Leon Brittan said in November 1994 that in 1993 Turkey 'imported more Community goods than any other country' (Ploritis, 1994).
11. Anderson, 1978, p. 271.
12. Ibid., p. 270.
13. Anderson, 1979; Barber, 1988.
14. Mouzelis, 1986.
15. Mouzelis, 1978a, 1978b, 1986, 1988.
16. The practice continues unabated. In March 1996 the High Court in Athens decided for the reinstatement of 6000 part-time employees of PPC (Public Power Corporation, or ΔΕΗ), who had been fired in the end of 1993, after PASOK, the 'socialist' party, had come to power. PASOK's argument was that these people had been illegally placed with PPC by ND, the incumbent 'conservative' party, just before the October 1993 elections. Now PPC apparently, has to reinstate them at a time when, according to the PASOK Minister of Development, Ms Vasso Papandreou, PPC already has 7000 excess staff.
17. Tsoucalas, 1983, 1986.
18. Roidis, 1996, pp. 75–6.
19. Ryder & Silver, 1970, pp. 73–4.
20. *Eleutheroudakis*, 1929, vol. 5, p. 148.
21. Pirounakis, 1990. Even up to 1985 one could read in Greek newspapers items like these: '17,000 stremmas to landless peasants' or 'Awarded legal titles thirty years after' (*Ethnos*, 25.4.1985).
22. Anderson, 1979.
23. Lee, 1989.

24. The contrast with the ex-communist countries of Eastern Europe is unavoidable here. Fukuyama (1994), reviewing Gellner's (1994) book, notes that 'in reality socialist societies required excessively powerful states, which in turn destroyed all organic communal links and made their people individualistic, egoistical, and unable to co-operate among themselves'. One wonders, however, whether exactly the same statement could be accurately applied to, say, modern America, among others.
25. Exactly what the Turkish victory in the same war secured for Turkey's own governing, and strongly militarist, elite.
26. See El. Papayannakis, 'The different phases and the basic characteristics of Greek industrialisation', *Economicos Tachydromos*, 24.3.1983, pp. 70. In his view, the first wave actually occurred in 1870-90.
27. Eurostat, 1988.
28. *E Cathemerine*, 11.2.1994.
29. NSSG, 1991 Census.
30. Employers, self-employed, family workers.
31. Eurostat, 1995a.
32. Pirounakis, 1990, p. 322.
33. *Manager*, Nov. 1994, p. 52.
34. See Chapter 4 of this book.
35. This right has begun to be challenged since 1992 but only as a result of EU pressures and in a very hesitant manner. There have even been relapses: When PASOK came back to office in October 1993, it renationalised urban bus transport, which had been privatised only a few months before, and re-employed those bus company employees who had been made redundant. More poignantly, the same government in November 1994 passed a law granting life tenure to employees of the Greek Telecom (OTE), a fortnight before 25 per cent of the company was to be offered for sale. Inevitably, investors were not keen to buy, and selling any part of OTE was postponed until March 1996, under more favourable financial terms.
36. '. . . whereas public investments are rising substantially, private investments are lagging behind and continue being oriented largely towards non-productive purposes.' (*Bank of Greece Report for the year 1961*, p. 14.) '. . . a major portion of private investment activity was still [in 1963] concerned with projects of non-primary importance.' (*Bank of Greece Report for the year 1963*, p. 17.)
37. X. Zolotas, Governor of the Bank of Greece from the '50s to 1967 (when the colonels seized power in Greece) repeatedly exhorted various governments on the need to foster exports. His style is revealing of the small extent to which they listened to him: 'It is absolutely necessary to understand that the importance of developing exports of industrial products does not only lie in the necessity of maintaining balance of payments equilibrium. The need to turn towards the foreign markets is imperative mainly because rapid industrial development cannot be based on the limited capacity of the domestic market.' (*Bank of Greece Report for the year 1961*, p. 14.) Two years later Zolotas would write bitterly: '. . . the gap in the balance of trade which reflects the structural weaknesses of the Greek economy, continues to widen at a rapid rate, owing to the long-term trend

towards stagnation in the export trade.' (*Bank of Greece Report for the year 1963*, p. 17.)

38. '. . . government investment shows a tendency to stagnate. The causes can be traced to the lack of adequate and methodical planning, the failure to exercise a proper supervision during the implementation of projects and the insufficient utilisation of completed works.' (*Bank of Greece Report for the year 1963*, p. 16.)
39. J. Marinos, director of *Economicos Tachydromos*, Greek equivalent of *The Economist*, has repeatedly described the public sector employees of Greece as an occupation army (see, for example, Marinos, 1994b).
40. *Epiloghe*, 1994, p. 33.
41. By 1994 the percentage had risen to 10 per cent, as the need of Greece to converge with the other EU economies has limited – certainly not taken away – the ability of her governments to incur deficits in order to expand or preserve public-sector employment. The (official) rate has been about the same since, despite the influx of economic refugees into Greece.
42. See Chapter 2 for more on this.
43. 'A TV in every home', *Ta Nea*, 7.12.1995, p. 24, on the basis of research by Bari/Focus using an 11 000-strong sample. The research covered big cities throughout Greece, and rural areas in Crete and mainland Greece (that is, it left out the Aegean and the Ionian). For more important amenities, see Chapter 9.
44. OECD, 1994.
45. For consistency with historic data, the GDP used in most of the book is, unless otherwise stated, GDP at factor cost, calculated under the 'old' method employed by the National Statistical Service of Greece. In 1993 the NSSG began to employ a 'new' method, which it backdated to 1988 and has not, at the time of writing, applied to all subsequent years yet. The new method is more accurate than the old, having resulted in an appreciation of Greek GDP figures by 20–22 per cent. It thus captures a substantial part of Greece's informal economy.
46. Since $GDP = C + I + G + EX - IM$, adding back imports and subtracting what the country sells to foreigners gives total consumption by households, business firms, and the government. Therefore, the difference between total consumption and total production as a percentage of the latter is equal to the trade deficit as a percentage of GDP.
47. For example, in 1995 the net capital inflow to Greece was $US3161.8 m., against a current account deficit of $US2850.4 m. In 1994 the respective figures had been $US6903.5 m. and $US121.6 m., and in 1993 $US4400.0 m. and $US716.3 m. 26 per cent of the net capital inflow in 1995 was foreign borrowing by the public sector, the rest representing net capital inflow by the private sector. Even so, the largest part of the private sector inflow was debt, rather than DFI, real estate, or portfolio investment. Moreover, part of the latter was undoubtedly in Greek government securities. Thus the public-sector foreign debt must have been larger than officially registered for the year ($US34 b.), although in this way a part of it was denominated in drachmas rather than FX.
48. These began in 1981.
49. Source: Bank of Greece Annual Reports.

50. In 1994 Greece got 3812 m. ecus in net receipts from the EU, against Spain's 3006 m., Portugal's 1881 m. and Ireland's 1727 m. (*The Economist*, 1996d, p. 27.)
51. There are definitional and measurement problems here, as very often the growth in services in advanced countries is qualitatively different from that in less advanced. For example, contracting out services like programming, security or catering, which in the past might have happened in-house, statistically augments services and reduces industry, yet the economic importance of the latter has anything but diminished.
52. Connolly, 1985.
53. A presentation of the new system is in Botsari, 1994.
54. 'Turkish Finance and Industry: A Survey', *Financial Times*, 3.11.1993, p. i.
55. *E Cathemerine*, 13.12.1992, p. 44, and *Eleutherotypia*, 31.1.1993.
56. Negreponti-Delivani, 1990a, 1990b.
57. *Ta Nea*, 28.2.1994, p. 12.
58. Pavlopoulos, 1987.
59. Pavlopoulos, 1996, p. 152.
60. Pavlopoulos, 1996.
61. Lecatsas, 1995.
62. Pavlopoulos, 1996. See also Vamvoucas, 1990a.
63. Negreponti-Delivani, 1990a, 1990b.
64. See Nicolaou, 1995.
65. See Chapter 4; Karacottas, 1994; Manessiotis, 1995.

2 Economic Performance Since the Civil War

'Man can climb to the highest summits, but he cannot dwell there long.'

George Bernard Shaw. *Candida.*

2.1 GROWTH OF GREECE'S OFFICIAL GDP

At $US70.2 billion, Greece's official GDP in 1991, at current prices and current exchange rates, ranked ninth in the European Union (EU), above Portugal's ($US68.6 billion) and Ireland's ($US43.4 billion), and below Denmark's ($US130.3 billion).[1] In terms of GDP per capita, though, Greece, at $US6840 was last in the EU (Portugal: $US6991; Ireland: $US12 324).[2] The comparison with Portugal is all the more remarkable, since as recently as 1986 her GDP per capita, at $US2984, was quite below Greece's, which was $US3987. The change in respective rank reflects positively upon Portugal's efforts, but also the fact that after a period of high initial growth, as Greece was rebuilding herself after the wars of the 1940s,[3] the country's economic performance has deteriorated markedly since the mid-1970s. The pattern of Greek real GDP growth rates can make more sense if it is associated with appropriate periods of Greek post-war political history. Seven such periods have been identified, and are presented in Table 2.1. The decline has been greater than what would have been expected merely as a result of the two oil shocks (1973 and 1979–80), and of the drop in growth rates across the OECD (see next section). Indeed, if the problem had simply been finding ways to deal with these two factors, then applying appropriate economic policies might have sufficed. But the Greek economy has been doing consistently badly for 20 years now; her problems, therefore, must be caused by something deeper than possibly inappropriate economic policies.

George Alogoskoufis, a younger-generation economist, has attributed the bad performance of the Greek economy since the mid-1970s to 'the failure of our political system to substitute new institutions for

Table 2.1
Seven political periods of Greek real GDP growth (average rates of GDP growth in each period; GDP at factor cost and 1970 prices; NSSG Standard System of Accounts)

	Growth rate (%)
From 1951 to 1958 (Reconstruction, repression, yet parliamentary rule; period ends with the Left securing 24.4% of the vote in national elections)	6.3
From 1959 to 1966 (Political turmoil; struggle for democracy)	6.4
From 1967 to 1974 (Military dictatorship; ends with the Turkish invasion of Cyprus in July)	6.5
From 1975 to 1981 (Restoration of parliamentary order; rise of populism; expansion of public sector)	3.7
From 1982 to 1989 (First period of PASOK rule; rampant populism; further expansion of public sector; period ends with three general elections in less than a year)	2.2
From 1990 to 1995 (Both main parties under fiscal & EMU convergence constraints; political cost considerations still paramount)	1.0

those which contributed to the so-called economic 'miracle' of 1954–73'.[4] In that period, he writes, the following factors were strongly present, which were weakened thereafter:[5]

- A taxation system which favoured private investment (see Chapter 4).
- State-controlled industrial relations (this was, after all, the post-civil war period); post-1974 populism, on the other hand, freed trade-unionism from police control, but also devalued work effort and managerial prerogative.

- A stable currency (until the collapse of the Bretton Woods System in 1973).
- Fiscal discipline (see Chapter 4).
- Greater reliance on the price mechanism as a resource allocation device (whereas later, redistribution on the basis of political criteria came to dominate).
- A banking system forced to finance productive investments rather than 'lame ducks', as was increasingly the case after 1980.
- A more disciplined civil service.

In the same vein, Alogoskoufis feels that Greece's full membership of the EEC as of 1981 did not help matters because the transfer of substantial funds from the latter to the former veiled for a long time the bad shape of the Greek economy and the need for her thorough restructuring.

Although broadly correct, Alogoskoufis' analysis does not emphasise strongly enough the link between most of the factors he cites with underlying features of Greek society, while the lack of a stable currency after 1973 has not been confined to Greece, or been something that Greece could have avoided had she tried. It is precisely Greece's fundamental social features (see Chapter 1) which have created and reproduced time and again the statist-populist-clientelist orientation of her political system, whose roots go back to the 19th century. The confirmation of this trend after 1974, and especially since 1981, when PASOK, Greece's 'socialist' party came to power, has therefore been inevitable, accounting in turn for the reappearance of fiscal profligacy, indiscipline in the work place, and political favouritism. In this connection, as the historian Richard Clogg has wryly observed, 'what was different under PASOK was that whereas, in the past, [political] patronage had been mediated through the individual parliamentary deputy, now it was dispensed through the party'.[6]

For this reason the decline of growth rates after 1974 cannot be attributed solely to the lifting of repressive political measures or the re-introduction of syndicalism and parliamentarism. The decline would have probably happened anyway, and might even have been worse if military rule had continued, as repression alone cannot create an adaptable, dynamic economy, or guarantee sustainable development. For example, the military junta which ruled the country from 1967 to 1974, although it did adhere to fiscal discipline, did nothing, or very little, to introduce meritocracy in the broad public sector, streamline the social security system, modernise the financial system, clamp down on the informal economy, improve education and training, or, for that matter, strengthen the country's defence, or protect the picturesque physiognomy of Greek cities and villages. Often, it did the opposite. In this way, it wasted an opportunity to force through the radical changes that the Greek economy and society needed then, and still do.

On the other hand, given the nature of the Greek political system and social structure, once that system had been allowed free play, it was bound to lead to increasing inefficiency, incompetence, debts and decline. The pattern of real growth rates shows that much. Sadly, unless the root-causes of the Greek malaise are attacked, the chances are that the future will bring more decline, not less.

2.2 COMPARATIVE ECONOMIC PERFORMANCE, 1966–90

It was suggested in the previous section that the decline in Greek GDP growth rates since the mid-1970s has been worse than for the OECD as a whole. It is time we examined this claim in detail.

It is appropriate to compare Greece to the other member-states of the Organisation for Economic Co-operation and Development (OECD) because (a) member-countries are supposed to be advanced or 'qualifying' semi-advanced market economies, (b) 24 countries[7] are a wider sample than, say, the 12 members of the European Union (EU), and (c) the OECD has enough historical data on all 24 to make a comparison practicable.

Table 2.2 produces four rankings of the 24 OECD member-states: by real GDP[8] average annual growth rate for 1966–90, 1966–70, and 1986–90; and by the standard deviation of each country's annual rates for 1966–90 from their mean.[9]

As is well-known, growth rates dropped over the period. Greece in particular used to be a very good performer. She had the second highest growth rate in the 1966–70 period, bettered only by Japan, and the seventh highest in 1966–90. Yet Greece ended by being 21st (out of a total of 24 countries) in terms of her 1986–90 growth rate. This plunge is also depicted by Greece's variability of growth rates over the entire period, 1966–90: she had the third largest standard deviation, only exceeded by Iceland and Portugal.

So Greece has not done well. How badly though? It is not enough to point to the decrease in Greece's growth rates because (a) the OECD as a group suffered a drop also, and (b) in the long run, high growth rates are unsustainable. But then one cannot evaluate Greece's relative

Table 2.2
Rankings of OECD countries by period growth rates

	Mean growth rate of real GDP, 1966–1990 (%)		Standard deviation of growth rates, 1966–1990 (%)		Mean growth rate of real GDP, 1966–1970 (%)		Mean growth rate of real GDP, 1986–1990 (%)
Japan	5.73	Iceland	4.41	Japan	11.26	Turkey	5.94
Turkey	5.48	Portugal	3.52	Greece	7.24	Portugal	4.58
Ireland	4.44	Greece	3.41	Turkey	6.62	Japan	4.56
Portugal	4.28	Japan	3.39	Portugal	6.34	Spain	4.48
Canada	4.03	Luxembourg	3.13	Spain	6.24	Ireland	4.42
Iceland	3.98	Turkey	3.04	Italy	6.22	Luxembourg	4.34
Greece	3.96	New Zealand	2.92	Australia	5.70	Finland	3.46
Spain	3.84	Switzerland	2.65	Holland	5.50	OECD	3.32
Australia	3.79	Spain	2.60	France	5.38	Australia	3.22
Italy	3.67	Finland	2.55	Austria	5.30	Belgium	3.20
Finland	3.67	Italy	2.44	Germany	4.98	UK	3.20
Norway	3.64	USA	2.38	Belgium	4.86	EEC	3.16
Austria	3.41	Canada	2.33	Finland	4.80	Austria	3.10
OECD	3.39	Ireland	2.31	Canada	4.76	Germany	3.04
France	3.38	Belgium	2.20	Ireland	4.76	Italy	3.02
Luxembourg	3.20	Holland	2.14	OECD	4.64	Canada	2.98
Belgium	3.07	Germany	2.14	EEC	4.56	USA	2.98
EEC	3.01	Austria	2.12	Switzerland	4.24	France	2.92
Holland	3.01	Denmark	2.12	Sweden	4.12	Iceland	2.82
Germany	2.90	UK	2.10	Norway	3.78	Switzerland	2.78
USA	2.90	Australia	2.09	Denmark	3.74	Holland	2.66
Denmark	2.49	Norway	1.96	Luxembourg	3.72	Sweden	2.06
Sweden	2.45	France	1.82	New Zealand	3.40	Greece	1.66
UK	2.33	OECD	1.72	USA	3.08	Norway	1.58
Switzerland	2.20	EEC	1.72	UK	2.48	Denmark	1.52
New Zealand	2.16	Sweden	1.60	Iceland	2.40	New Zealand	0.36

Source: OECD Historical Statistics 1966–90.

performance without taking Greece's high starting point into account.

Let us look at Diagrams 2.1 and 2.2. Diagram 2.1 plots Greece's annual growth rates for 1966–90 against the years in the period. It also plots the trend of those growth rates. Diagram 2.2 does the same for the whole of the OECD.

A comparison of the two diagrams makes it obvious that Greece's decline has been steeper than for the OECD as a group – the trend line of Greece has a larger slope. On the other hand, the vertical intercept of the OECD trend line is lower than for Greece – a reflection of the fact that Greece started the period with higher growth rates than the average OECD country. The question is – is there a relationship between a country's 'starting point', as evidenced by the vertical intercept of her trend line, and the subsequent decline in her rate of growth, as evidenced by the slope of that line?

Diagram 2.3 shows the relationship between slopes and vertical intercepts for all OECD countries for the 1966–90 period, as well as the trend line which epitomises this relationship. One can tell that there is a significant association between the two variables. In fact, the equation of this line comes out as

$$\text{slope} = -\ 0.03904\ (\text{vertical intercept}) + 0.08272$$

while the co-efficient of determination (r^2), a statistical measure which shows the percentage of variations in the dependent variable explained by variations in the independent variable(s), is 76.5 per cent. This is fairly large, considering that r^2 can only take values between 0 and 1.

Now, if we take the above equation and solve it for the actual vertical intercepts of all 24 country trend lines, we will come up with the expected, as opposed to the actual, slopes of those lines – meaning, the slopes that would have prevailed if all countries had conformed fully to the kind of growth pattern dictated by their starting growth rates, and depicted by the equation. Further, if we take the difference between the expected slope and the actual slope, we will know by how much a country's actual trend of growth rates has deviated from her expected trend. Diagram 2.4 shows the two different trends – actual and expected – for Greece. In this case the line with the larger absolute slope – the actual trend – lies below Greece's expected trend, which tells us that Greece has deviated negatively from its expected pattern of growth rates.

The final step in our evaluation of Greek economic performance is to rank all 24 OECD countries by their deviations from their expected

Diagram 2.1
Annual growth rates of Greece's real GDP, 1966–90

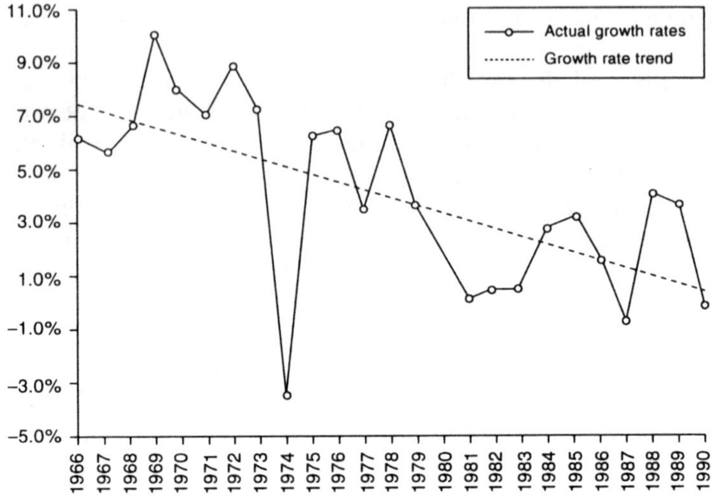

Source: OECD, Historical Statistics 1966–90 (GDP at market prices).

Diagram 2.2
Annual growth rates of OECD's real GDP, 1966–90

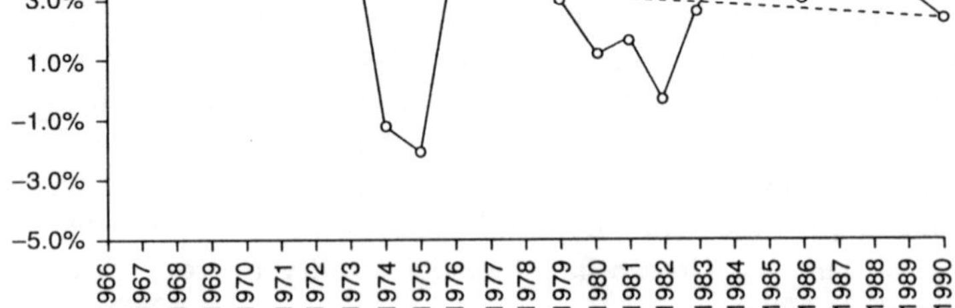

Source: OECD, Historical Statistics 1966–90 (GDP at market prices).

Diagram 2.3
Relationship between slopes and vertical intercepts of lines depicting real GDP growth rate trend for each OECD country, 1966–90

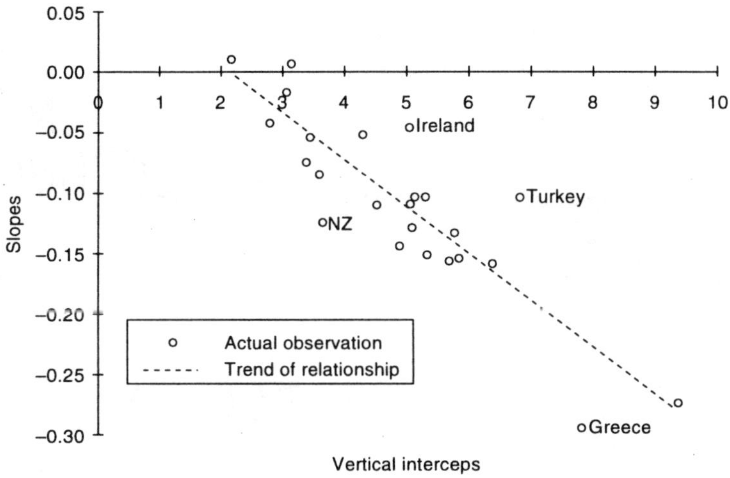

Diagram 2.4
Actual and expected trends of Greece's real GDP growth rates, 1966–90

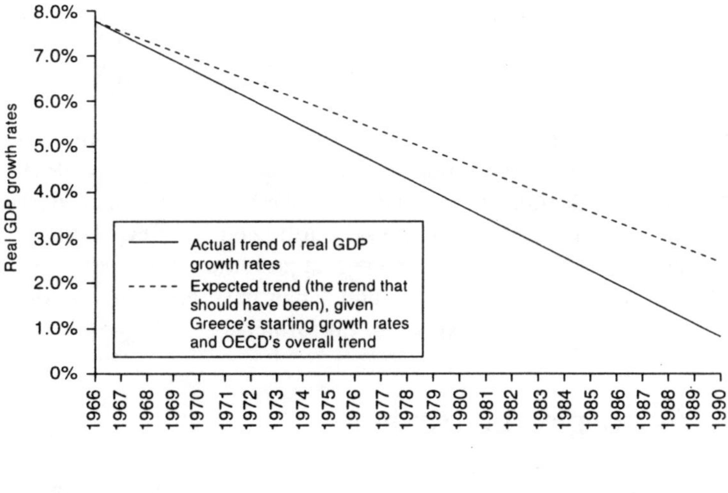

Diagram 2.5
Ranking of OECD countries by deviation of actual from expected trend of real GDP growth rates over the 1966–90 period

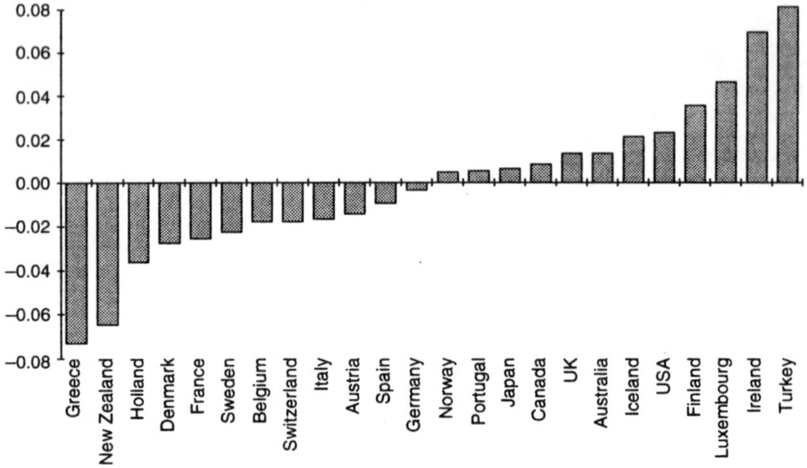

patterns of growth rates. The outcome is depicted in Table 2.3 and Diagram 2.5, where the countries with negative deviations are the worst performers (that is, their growth trends are worse than expected, or worse than what is dictated by the expected relationship between starting and subsequent growth rates for all 24 countries), and those with positive deviations are the best (that is, their growth trends are better than expected).

It is interesting to note from Table 2.3 and Diagram 2.5 that Greece has been the worst performer of the period. Her negative deviation (-0.0720) is 21.8 times the deviation of the best of the 'bad' performers, namely Germany). She is closely followed by New Zealand and Holland, whereas Turkey has been the best performer, followed by Ireland and Luxembourg. The USA, UK, and Japan have also been among the good, that is, better than expected, performers.

2.3 THE ROLE OF INVESTMENT

It is well-known that investment and growth are causally related. Investment powers economic growth, as it adds to a country's productive

Table 2.3
Deviations of OECD countries from expected trend of real GDP growth rates, 1966–90

	Vertical intercept of actual growth rate trend	Slope of actual growth rate trend	Expected slope* of growth rate trend	Deviation of actual from expected slope (that is, of actual from expected trend of real GDP growth rates)
Greece	7.7660	−0.2925	−0.2205	−0.0720
New Zealand	3.6160	−0.1225	−0.0584	−0.0640
Holland	4.8700	−0.1432	−0.1074	−0.0358
Denmark	3.5870	−0.0842	−0.0573	−0.0269
France	5.3550	−0.1519	−0.1263	−0.0256
Sweden	3.3810	−0.0718	−0.0493	−0.0225
Belgium	4.5200	−0.1114	−0.0937	−0.0176
Switzerland	2.7520	−0.0422	−0.0247	0.0174
Italy	5.7030	−0.1565	−0.1399	−0.0166
Austria	5.1070	−0.1307	−0.1167	−0.0140
Spain	5.8500	−0.1549	−0.1457	−0.0092
Germany	3.4510	−0.0553	−0.0520	−0.0033
Norway	5.0900	−0.1112	−0.1160	0.0048
Portugal	6.3720	−0.1606	−0.1660	0.0054
Japan	9.2850	−0.2733	−0.2798	0.0065
Canada	5.7690	−0.1339	−0.1425	0.0086
UK	2.1880	0.0108	−0.0027	0.0135
Australia	5.1500	−0.1048	−0.1183	0.0136
Iceland	5.3250	−0.1038	−0.1252	0.0214
USA	3.0980	−0.0152	−0.0382	0.0230
Finland	4.3400	−0.0517	−0.0867	0.0350
Luxembourg	3.1140	0.0069	−0.0389	0.0458
Ireland	5.0290	−0.0453	−0.1136	0.0683
Turkey	6.8370	−0.1044	−0.1842	0.0798

* Expected slope = −0.03904 (vertical intercept) + 0.08272.

capacity. The exact nature of the relationship is not straightforward, neither is investment the only factor affecting growth. One way to investigate that relationship in the context of the preceding discussion is by looking into the relationship over time (1966–90) between all 24 countries' deviations from their expected trends of GDP growth rates, and a proxy for the behaviour of investment over the period. An appropriate candidate is the ratio of average annual investment as a percentage of GDP during 1960–90 over average annual investment as a percentage of GDP during 1968–73, a period of remarkably high investment rates among OECD countries. Obviously, the higher a country's investment peak in the 1968–73 period, relative to her average for the entire period, 1960–90, the smaller the (inv. 60–90)/(inv. 68–73) ratio.

Diagram 2.6
Do changes in investment levels as % of GDP explain the deviations of OECD countries from expected real GDP growth rate trends?

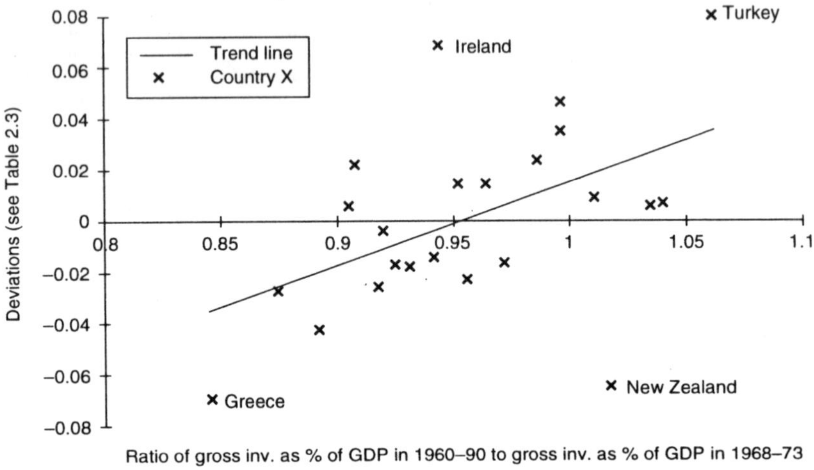

Consequently, a drop in levels of investment, as a proportion of GDP, between the beginning and the end of the period under consideration (that is, a relatively small (inv. 60–90)/(inv. 68–73) ratio) would go some way towards explaining a country's economic decline, as evidenced by a possibly negative deviation from her expected growth path. Our results showed this to be the case (Diagram 2.6).

Expectedly, the trend line in Diagram 2.6 is upward sloping; this means that the smaller the (inv. 60–90)/(inv. 68–73) ratio, the smaller the deviation. That is, those countries which suffered the biggest decline in investment as a percentage of GDP, relative to the percentage they were investing in 1968–73, also suffered the biggest (negative) deviations from their expected growth paths. What strikes one immediately is not so much the overall strength of the association (after all, the co-efficient of determination, r^2, is only 24.5 per cent); as the presence of four outliers, two above, two below the trend line. The two most obviously at discord with the general trend are Ireland (above the line) and New Zealand (below the line). Taking these explicitly into account,[10] increased r^2 to 68.2 per cent. Taking into account the other two also, which are Turkey (above the line) and Greece (below the line), further increased r^2 to 78.1 per cent. A number of observations are, therefore, in order.

First, the countries whose investment records deviate most from the norm (are further away from the X-axis in Diagram 2.6) are also the countries which are outliers when it comes to the relationship between starting rates of growth and their subsequent pattern (cf. Diagram 2.3).

Second, the outliers in Diagram 2.6 are also at the extremes of the ranking of all 24 OECD countries in terms of their deviations from their expected growth trends (cf. Diagram 2.5).

This implies that these countries are somehow special, relative to the rest of the OECD. Their investment patterns alone cannot explain their deviations from their expected growth trends, as well as those patterns can in regard to the rest of the OECD. Additional factors must have played a significant part.

On the other hand, Diagram 2.6 shows that Greece's large decline of investment as a percentage of GDP from its 1968–73 peak, relative to the entire 1960–90 period (84.6 per cent), is compatible with her poor growth performance. This is not New Zealand's case, for instance, where the country's large negative deviation from her expected growth path has taken place despite a relatively large (inv. 60–90)/(inv. 68–73) ratio (101.8 per cent).[11] Greece's investment record over the period has in fact been worse than those of the other 23 countries[12] – and so has her growth performance. Hence, Greece's decline must in the first place be sought in those factors which, directly or indirectly, have affected her investment behaviour pattern. Nevertheless, that pattern, as Diagram 2.6 makes clear, cannot have been the only cause of the bad performance of the Greek economy in recent years.

We have already suggested (Chapter 1) that additional possible causes involve the nature of Greece's public sector, her political system,[13] and her social structure. These have affected Greece's economic performance by first influencing her investment pattern, but also autonomously. For example, it is reasonable to expect that Greece's excessive public debt (itself a result of her inefficient and sprawling public sector, and her populist politics) would be crowding out private investment directly (say, through higher interest rates in order to service the debt); in addition, though, Greece's public sector, by employing nearly half of all of the country's employees without much regard to needs or merit (see Chapter 3), reduces price-wage flexibility, while it reproduces inefficiencies, corruption and red-tape throughout the economy (see Chapter 8). Inevitably, by 1990 returns to fixed capital in the Greek economy were the lowest in EU-12 in relation to what they had been in 1961–73: 52.3 per cent, against 124.9 per cent for Spain, 141.1 per cent for Ireland, 62.0 per cent for Portugal, and 92.5 per cent for

EU-12.[14] It goes without saying that Greece's diminishing returns to fixed capital in the last 20 years or so both reflect and cause relatively low investment levels. The Greek public sector has therefore been discouraging investment indirectly too, while, naturally, any inefficient use of existing resources does lead to less growth anyway.

It may, in fact, be that the negative impact of Greece's public sector on investment takes place more through indirect than direct means. A recent study by Basil Dalamangas,[15] another Greek economist, covering the 1958–94 period, has confirmed, on the one hand, that private investment in Greece is negatively affected by interest rate increases, and positively by GDP (as a proxy for aggregate demand), which is not surprising. On the other hand, though, interest rates turned out being less important, statistically speaking, than aggregate demand. Dalamangas concluded that

> the urgent emphasis given in recent years to the need to lower interest rates in order to raise investment does not seem warranted. It's quite possible that, despite a drastic reduction in interest rates, investment will not rise – or not rise commensurately –, as long as insufficient demand, low profit margins, the institutional framework governing the operation of markets, expectations . . ., social and political conditions, and so on, do not justify investment initiatives.

The combination of poor investment and the institutional factors mentioned have damaged Greece's economic performance in more than real GDP growth rate terms. First, Greece's international competitiveness has suffered. Repeatedly in recent years the World Economic Forum, a Switzerland-based institute, has placed Greece towards the bottom of the OECD league, lower even than Turkey.[16] Countries as diverse as Chile, Argentina, Brazil, Egypt, Korea, and Israel have also done better. From among OECD members only Mexico seems to have done worse than Greece in 1995 – but only just – while the WEF league was tailed by Poland, Hungary, Venezuela, and, at the very end, Russia.

Second, Greece's chances of being part of the Economic and Monetary Union (Emu) between EU members by 1999, or even later, have been reduced. True convergence, as two Greek economists, Alogoskoufis and Prodromidis, have recently pointed out,[17] requires more than meeting the formal criteria set forth in Maastricht. These are:[18]

(a) Annual change in consumer prices should be no more than 1.5 basis points above three lowest EU inflation rates. (Greece's inflation at the end of 1995 was down to 8.1 per cent.)

(b) General government budget deficit as percentage of GDP should not exceed 3 per cent. (Greece's figure was 9.3 per cent in 1995.)
(c) Yields of long-term government bonds should not exceed yields of the three lowest inflation countries by more than two basis points.
(d) General government debt as a proportion of GDP should not exceed 60 per cent. (Greece's was 111.7 per cent in 1995.)

To achieve these targets, and stick to them, Greece's GDP per capita, which is presently about half of its EU counterpart, must grow to being 80 per cent of the latter. This, Alogoskoufis and Prodromidis have calculated,[19] requires sustaining a real GDP growth rate of 12 per cent per annum from 1996 to 2000 (assuming a simultaneous real EU GDP growth rate of 2 per cent); should the growth rate of Greek GDP be 4.4 per cent, convergence of GDP levels between Greece and the rest of the EU will take place in 20 years. Obviously, if Greek GDP grows by only 2 per cent per annum, convergence will never happen, and if it grows by less than 2 per cent, there will be divergence instead. With a real GDP annual growth of only one per cent in 1990– 95 (according to Table 2.1), or 1.2 per cent, according to the Bank of Greece,[20] or even 2 per cent in 1995 alone,[21] Greece obviously needs to hurry up.

Finally, let us not forget that Greece's attempts at fiscal clean-up are taking place in a world of near-perfect capital mobility. This world Greece joined fully in June 1994, when she freed short-term capital movements (that is, she lifted exchange controls on such movements), with long-term ones having been freed the previous year. These developments hold a serious implication. Since, in such a world, 'there is little or no relation between the domestic investment in a country and the amount of savings generated in that country',[22] then, even if the Greek state's effort to service the public debt did not crowd out domestic investment, or even if the public debt problem were solved somehow, there is no guarantee that the Greeks would begin to invest domestically rather than abroad. To induce them to do so, the state would have to introduce and cultivate conditions securing high returns to capital domestically (a theme emphasised throughout the book). But this is asking the state to reform itself no less than Greek society.

Notes

1. OECD Economic Surveys: UK 1993–94 (OECD, 1994). At current prices and purchasing power parities, however, Greece's GDP, at $US79.4 billion, fell behind Portugal's ($US90.1 billion).

2. Ibid.
3. The late famous planner C.A. Doxiadis (1977) estimated in 1947 that Greece 'lost 23 per cent of her building wealth – a higher proportion than any other country' during the Second World War.
4. Alogoskoufis, 1995b, p. 72.
5. Alogoskoufis, 1995a, 1995b.
6. Clogg, 1992, p. 206.
7. The comparison has been based on data in OECD Historical Statistics from 1966 to 1990; Mexico joined the OECD after 1990.
8. At market prices.
9. A large standard deviation would indicate unstable growth.
10. The technique involves turning these countries into 'indicator' (or 'dummy') variables. These can only take 0s and 1s as values.
11. The corresponding figures for Ireland and Turkey are 94.4 and 106.3 per cent, whilst for the EEC and the OECD as a whole are 93.6 and 95.2 per cent, respectively.
12. The countries nearest to Greece, in that respect, are Holland and Denmark.
13. 'When an economy performs badly for twenty full years, that surely [ ] is a long-term structural problem related to the role of [political] institutions.' (Alogoskoufis, 1995b.)
14. The corresponding averages for 1986–90 (1961–73 = 100) were 47.5 per cent for Greece, 115 per cent for Spain, 121.1 per cent for Ireland, 56.7 for Portugal, and 89.1 per cent for EU–12. *Nautemporica*, 1991. Data are from *European Economy*, 4, April 1991.
15. Dalamangas, 1996.
16. Nicolopoulos, 1992; Butler, 1994; Mikhas, 1995.
17. Alogoskoufis & Prodromidis, 1995.
18. Barber & Marsh, 1994.
19. Alogoskoufis & Prodromidis, op. cit.
20. Bank of Greece Annual Report for 1995, p. 68. GDP at market prices, GDP-deflated.
21. Ibid.
22. Feldstein & Horioka, 1980, pp. 327–8.

3 The Public Sector in Greek Society

'. . . the 'Turkish' aspect of our polity [] humiliates the Greek as much as the Kemalist state[1] the Turkish citizen. The difference is that in Greece this tyrannical state is composed and sustained [] by us all [].'

Christos Yannaras, Greek theologian and philosopher.[2]

3.1 A SELF-SERVING STATE

It is nearly impossible to calculate the actual size of the public sector in Greece, whether in employment[3] or, more so, output or expenditure terms.[4] This should not be surprising. Accurate information presupposes transparency and good management. Both have been conspicuously absent from the Greek public sector. The reason, at least in part, is deliberate: more often than not, obscurity has allowed governments and individual politicians to employ people in the broad public sector, or divert funds to political friends or 'social' purposes, without due process of law, or accountability. The Greek public sector is a huge, sprawling and amorphous affair, intertwined with the rest of society through umpteen intricate interconnections, fed by expedience and convenience on the part of politicians, administrators, and 'subjects' alike. Many would add that the Greek public sector is ineffectual and incompetent. This criticism, however, might be misplaced: the Greek public sector has been relatively successful at discharging its raison d' etre, namely, to distribute jobs, grants, subsidies, and favours here and there, calculated to buy votes and/or secure apathy.[5] On top of that, public procurement practices[6] and the allocation of public works (see Chapter 8) often secure for politicians and public-sector officials lucrative pecuniary benefits in addition to political kudos, whilst lower-level functionaries have to make do with smaller bribes. With rare exceptions the sector has not been good at curbing economic and financial waste, creating conditions for successful economic performance, enhancing citizenship, carrying out public works that stand the test of time, protecting the environment, or offering high standards of education, health care, transport, communications, or even defence to the population, as these services have been at the bottom of its agenda, means rather than ends.

Like all free meals, the Greek state's social contract with the population could not last forever (see Chapter 4). But for EU fund transfers to Greece, which since 1981 have averaged 19 per cent of gross invisible earnings (and 24.1 per cent in 1991–5), Greece's current fiscal crisis would have broken out sooner. As things are, all Greek parties postpone, or do not press for, the deep structural changes that the country needs, each afraid to tell the Greek people the truth, namely, that the contract cannot stand any longer. They hope that, with a bit of luck, when the crisis comes another party will have to face it – and receive the blame.

But what was the contract about? Certainly there was never any explicit contract as such. One thing led to another, until enough people and groups had structured their interests and life-chances around favours from the state,[7] and then it was a case of a critical mass gathering momentum. Although the pattern goes back to the beginnings of modern Greece, in 1830 (see Chapter 1),[8] it was inevitably reaffirmed after the upheavals of the late 1930s and 1940s, combining the clientelist, paternalistic, parliamentary tradition of the Greek state with a stronger authoritarian twist than the country had known since before 1935. The more brutal and stupid aspect of that authoritarianism came to the fore with the military coup d' etat of 1967, only to retreat in shame and fear in 1974. Rather than utilise the opportunity to push ahead with long-due structural reform, the NATO-backed military regime used the housing and tourist sectors to curry favour with the public, and left it at that.[9] In its own ways it was as populist as the politicians it had replaced – or who were still to come.[10] When it collapsed, populism in parliamentary colours reasserted itself with a vengeance. In a social backlash against the colonels the twin notions of obligations to match rights, and of the rule of law, were widely considered fascist.[11] From there, it was a small step to combine the time-honoured practice of seeking favours from the state, funded of course by tax-payers' money or by government borrowing, with wanton irresponsibility and reckless individualism. Politicians, hungry after votes, and afraid of being labelled socially inconsiderate or even fascist, in turn tolerated and cultivated this behaviour on society's part. The 'contract' had been born: Greek society knew that it did not get high-quality services from its state, but at least it got favours, including opportunities for unauthorised building (see Chapter 9), unrepayable loans (see Chapters 6 and 9), and, very importantly, 'positions' (that is, jobs) in the public sector. In a poor country facing severe potential unemployment, who can tell whether that was wicked or silly of the Greek people? Another model of economic development, probably along Japanese lines,[12] might of course have helped contain unemployment without sacrificing long-term economic performance. But such a model was not implemented, probably because it would have required social cohesion, visionary leadership, good education, academic freedom, and, above all, advancement and reward on the basis of merit. These were not part of the baggage of the post-civil-war state – or of to-day's. So the public sector grew, and those who came to depend on it for their livelihood, whether as employees or politicians, would acquire more power, which they would wield only too readily in order to preserve or expand their share of the economic pie.[13]

Superficially this is the standard behaviour of bureaucracies everywhere, Niskanen-fashion.[14] The Greek peculiarity is that here the attempt to justify a bigger slice of the pie has only a little been based on setting organisational goals, whether in a narrow business sense, or for the common good;[15] neither has it been championed by 'managers'.[16] After all, why should the latter bother since (a) the top people, governors, general managers, or ministers, know that their time horizon extends only until the next election, if that long, and (b) the rest of the 'high officials', just like all public-sector employees, enjoy permanent tenure, statutory pay, and are not rewarded on the basis of merit? Their pay depends on years of service, familial characteristics (single, married, number of children), formal educational qualifications, and on rung in the hierarchy they occupy. Their advancement depends again on years of service and educational qualifications, but also on political party affiliation. The latter, more than anything else, determines whether someone will be employed in the public sector in the first place, whilst educational qualifications determine the initial level at which the applicant will be employed. Staff are typically promoted depending on which party comes to power, provided they have served the pre-ordained number of years for each post (and sometimes not even that). Since, on the other hand, staff cannot be demoted,[17] the end result is that the upper rungs of public-sector hierarchies get quite crowded, which reduces efficiency further. For example, in 1995, 60 per cent of the 15 160-strong staff of the National Bank, Greece's biggest, were in the upper rungs of the bank's hierarchy, and 32 per cent of the total in the high and highest rungs.[18]

Permanent tenure for civil servants was introduced in Greece in 1911, in response to the traditional practice of firing civil servants after a party had won the elections, so as to make room for new recruits, loyal to the victor. Except for the purge of known communists from the 1930s to the early 1970s, the ban on firing a civil servant has been adhered to until the present. It has been enshrined in the Greek Constitution, and tacitly extended to a large part of the broad public sector. Since, in these circumstances, in-coming governments cannot fire staff already employed in the public sector, they simply and conveniently have been appointing additional staff from among their supporters.

Inevitably the practice has added to the chaos in the Greek public sector. For instance, official research found in 1994 that[19]

(a) in a sum-total of 330 directorates distributed in 18 ministries there were
   - nine directorates with no departments
   - one directorate with one department
   - 79 directorates with two departments each, and

(b) in a sum-total of 1085 departments distributed in 18 ministries there were
   - 113 departments with one member of staff
   - 135 departments with two members of staff
   - 47 departments with no supervisor and no rank-and-file staff
   - 69 departments with a supervisor, but no rank-and-file staff
   - 124 departments with no supervisor, but with rank-and-file staff.

Thus the behaviour of organisational entities in the Greek public sector – itself a mixter-maxter of bureaucracies rather than a well-structured whole – is not simply a matter of budget-maximisation. That might explain things sufficiently if the sector operated along performance or goal-oriented lines. In turn this would presuppose, as well as encourage, a significant measure of autonomy and accountability on the part of the organisations concerned. If one is asked to fulfil a target or meet a performance criterion, one needs freedom from interference, whilst one also expects to give an account of oneself in the end. But the Greek situation is considerably more complex. The Greek public sector is first and foremost a tool used by governments, employees and governed alike in order to negotiate mutually advantageous deals, quite irrespective of specific organisational goals, economic efficiency, outputs and outcomes.[20] Even the physical work environment in large parts of the sector, for example the civil service, is neglected[21] as enhancing productivity has never been at the top of the agenda for either employees or their political masters. The sector is, in truth, 'a spineless servant of the political-electoral objectives of the party in power',[22] although whenever the issue of protecting their narrow interests has arisen, public-sector employees have not hesitated using their monopoly muscle ruthlessly and effectively (usually).

The Greek public sector's dichotomy between its actual and its formal role is reflected in, among others, the complete absence of job descriptions for employees, supervisors, or directors. Crucially, it is also reflected in the inability and/or unwillingness of the Greek state to formulate and implement a social policy for dealing with unemployment (benefits,[23] retraining, and the like), in counter-distinction to the adopted policy of trying to contain unemployment by expanding the public sector regardless of specific needs or merit. Inevitably the more the sector grows, the stronger the incentive for politicians not to let go of it becomes, and the greater the effective power of interest groups (like public sector employees) to press for benefits.

Thus the sector's ability to attract resources, expand, and resist privatisation (see Chapter 4) is mainly political rather than functional. Mysteriously, it sidesteps even the legal framework: although restrictions on hiring temporary staff in the public sector have often been announced, 'these never managed to avoid the creation of armies of temps demanding to be given permanent tenure [even though] appointment rules were becoming altogether more detailed and strict!'.[24] Even the European Commission urging the Greek government to reduce the size of the public sector has not proven persuasive, as the Maastricht definition of the sector does not include public-sector enterprises or state-controlled banks. In this the present Greek government (PASOK) saw an exploitable loophole. For instance, it passed a decree compelling the National Bank to take in government-appointed staff up to 8 per cent of the total.[25] Another source of pressure for hiring more staff in the public sector is existing employees. They systematically lobby for giving permanent posts to temps.[26] They have good reasons. The first is that this will obviously increase their collective power. The second reason relates to the nature of Greece's social security system (see Chapter 8): employees with public-sector banks and enterprises in particular have their own pension funds, which are usually better than IKA, Greece's main social security organisation for ordinary mortals. At the same time they are aware that unless new employees begin paying contributions to the funds, the relative, and already precarious, advantage of the latter cannot last.[27] The grip of existing employees over the public sector is in fact so strong that in a number of organisations (the Public Power Corporation, the National Bank, the Ionian Bank, and so on) they have managed to turn appointments into a family affair quite literally: employees' children have on occasion been given precedence over others.[28]

The parasitic–symbiotic relationship between Greek society and its public sector is now very difficult to break.[29] A successful attempt would require a restructuring of both poles in this relationship, which would need to go far beyond shedding even a few thousand public-sector employees or privatising a few 'lame duck' firms. The state-mediated handing out and receiving of favours and perks is so entrenched in Greece that, on occasion, it is done formally and officially, rather than in secret and in shame: the author of this book, for example, while waiting in the ante-room to the MD of a public-sector insurance company in 1993, glimpsed a big, hard-back dossier with the name 'favours' in Greek slang (that is, *rousfetia*) on it . . .

It is interesting that, as public sector employment has expanded, a parasitic–symbiotic relationship has been reproduced within the sector itself. Employees despise their organisations as by and large the latter offer them no chances to do anything useful or emotionally rewarding – but probably also because the vast majority of them have been hired not on merit but on the word of some, usually political, middleman. Unwillingness to work often matches the lack of work to do. In their ample spare time at 'work' many public-sector employees will rest, play,[30] or even pursue other lines of gainful employment, some of which constitute full second jobs. An example is a bank employee covertly selling insurance policies to customers. These activities must be protected, and then the 'favour' to negotiate with the state is about the 'right' to resist managerial authority or the 'intensification' of work. As a result 'work' in the public sector increasingly has come to mean formal presence in the premises rather than effort or results. Even that minimalist definition has been challenged, as apparently there have been cases of organisations instituting bonuses for 'presence' or 'timely arrival'[31] (rather than penalties for absenteeism or being repeatedly late). Through these practices public-sector employees attempt to 're-privatise' themselves,[32] that is, pursue their truer interests as best they see fit, once they have secured a life-long pay-packet, which has gradually regressed into little more than a generous unemployment benefit.

How successful has the post-war Greek state been at actually adhering to the peculiar 'contract' between itself and the people, which was mentioned above? Enough, probably, to keep the system going, but otherwise not much. It would have been surprising if it had been very successful, as such a state of affairs has an inherent tendency to affect adversely economic performance,[33] which, after all, is the ultimate source of wealth. For instance, the sector's frequent use as a convenient unemployment-curbing mechanism must be set against the following two facts: (a) That from 1955 to 1976 one million people, or 11.4 per cent of Greece's 1971 population, emigrated permanently from the country.[34] (b) Despite the massive exodus, Greece's unemployment rate from 1960 to 1973 was 4.6 per cent, against 2.3 for EU-15 and 3.2 for OECD.[35]

On the other hand in 1974–9 Greece's unemployment rate was 1.9 per cent, in 1980–9 6.6 per cent, and in 1990–3 8.3 per cent, when the respective figures for EU-15 were 4.6, 9.2, and 9.4 per cent.[36] Over the same periods, Greece's economic performance deteriorated, both in absolute terms and in comparison to that of EU-15. Greece's annual real GDP growth rates were[37]

3.7 per cent in 1974–9,
1.8 per cent in 1980–9, and
0.9 per cent in 1990–3;

while the corresponding EU–15 rates were

2.5 per cent in 1974–9,
2.2 per cent in 1980–9, and
1.2 per cent in 1990–3.

Given these figures, Greece's slightly better unemployment record can be explained by (a) massive subsidies to peasants,[38] which managed to keep most of them on their farms (after all, the European Common Agricultural Policy has played this role for decades), (b) the high frequency of smallholder, often informal, economic activity, in the farm or out of it (see Chapter 2), and (c) the increasing role of the public sector as a haven for the potentially unemployed. Even though individually any one of these factors might have sufficed for an explanation, it is certainly the case that from 1970 to 1995 the number of regular civil servants with the ministries (excluding policemen and firemen, and also temporary staff) went up from 99.5 thousand[39] to 233.1 thousand[40] (or to an average of 226.2 thousand for the period 1991–5); in other words, the number has been rising at a rate of nearly 3.5 per cent per year, at a time when the Greek population has been increasing at about 0.7 per cent per year.

Consequent upon these trends, Greece's public administration (including policemen and firemen) accounted for 7.2 per cent of total employment in 1993, against 7.9 per cent for EU-12, but also for 13.5 per cent of all employees (that is, wage-earners), against 9.5 per cent for EU-12: a higher percentage than any EU member.[41] Taking into account a broader view of the Greek public sector (adding part-time employees with ministries, public enterprises, social security organisations, local authorities) would give anything from 570 000[42] to 650 000,[43] or even 750 000,[44] employees circa 1991, whilst a still broader view (adding military officers, priests, doctors with the National Health Service, and 'problem' companies under state-control as well as companies controlled by state-owned banks) apparently would raise the figure to more than 900 000.[45] If approximately true, the latter figure would suggest that in 1991 about 45 per cent of all wage-earners, or 23 per cent of the economically active population, got their pay packets from the state, or state-controlled entities. Since Greek employees (that is, wage-earners) are no more than half of the economically active population, it therefore seems appropriate to characterise Greece as a statist smallholder capitalist society.

Of course the influence of the Greek public sector extends far beyond the number of people it actually employs. For example, the state has traditionally controlled agricultural co-operatives,[46] something important in a country where in 1991 17.3 per cent of the economically active population were still engaged in agriculture. In 1994 state-owned banks accounted for around three-quarters of deposits (and bank bonds), as well as of outstanding loans (the corresponding figure in 1978 was around 87 per cent) (see Table 6.2). A state-owned company (Ethnike) was among the first three in life as well as car insurance in 1994. The state has a complete or near monopoly in air, rail, and collective urban transport, electricity production, the fertiliser industry, water and gas supply, telecoms, higher education, and hospital care. It owns most of the country's shipyards (all of them 'lame ducks'), dominates the petroleum industry, has a substantial presence in the chemicals sector, and 'looks after' dozens of 'problem' companies, many private, some state-owned, others anything in between.[47] It even 'owns' the country's local authorities, which in Greece have very limited taxation powers of their own.

Greek local authorities are funded mostly by means of central state grants, plus the proceeds of certain duties and levies, some of which the central state collects for them. For example, in 1994 they got 2.6 per cent of the Government Ordinary Budget revenue, which, together with duty and levy income, covered 77.5 per cent of the local authorities' current account revenue. Greek local authorities have traditionally had little else to do other than collecting garbage, issuing birth and death certificates, authorising the operation of shops, restaurants and clubs, street-sweeping, and, in cases of semi-urban and rural municipalities, supplying water and sewers. Significantly, in the 1980s they also became responsible for aspects of town-planning. Their finances, however, are poor: bad management, overambition on the part of the bigger municipalities (like Athens and Piraeus), and growing needs in their functional areas (to meet which many authorities, insufficiently funded by the central state, have had to borrow), have brought many of them close to bankruptcy.[48] Some, utilising certain entrepreneurial powers recently given them, have been known to reproduce the clientelist politics for which the central state has become infamous – and, when in financial difficulties, to ask the government to bail them out.

In response, the central state has on occasion assumed the debts of local authorities to the Loans & Consignments Fund, the state-owned credit institution which they usually borrow from. This is in line with state practice elsewhere in the economy (see Chapter 6), but is clearly not conducive to ethical, let alone efficient, management on the part of either central or local government.

In 1994 the PASOK government hastily introduced a so-called 'local authority level of the second degree' (Laws 2218/94 & 2240/94), that is, an attempt at decentralisation involving direct elections of county, or prefecture, councils (again, with very limited taxation powers of their own). Their purpose, extent of authority, and duties are still unclear.[49] Although a fine idea in principle, in Greece's little developed civil society autonomy at county level will probably fare no better, if not worse, than at townhall level, while adding another layer of red tape to the state apparatus. Townhall autonomy is already known to have frequently reproduced the inefficiency and corruption characteristic of the central state in general, with the added twist of providing an institutionalised venue in which to disregard central government decisions no less than national laws and regulations or public interest, if that suits infuential locals. These can range from gambling casinos (like the one recently opened in Loutraki, near Corinth[50]) to businessmen who operate noisy pubs or discos late into the night, shopkeepers who fear competition from a new supermarket, property-owners who build outside a town plan, or a municipality itself which borrows from a bank and does not repay. On occasion such disregard may express genuine environmental or life-style concerns on the part of local communities resisting what they see as the unfair or inconsiderate acts, or failures to act, of a distant and condescending central state (see below). More often than not, however, it runs in the opposite direction (as to why this is so, see Chapter 10), being in the service of narrow individual, or even group, interests, and damn the environmental or life-style consequences. This makes it doubly dangerous.

Things being so, the fact that county and local authorities have limited taxation powers of their own may be a blessing in disguise, as many of them would almost certainly come to abuse the power. The way forward probably involves the central state continuing to collect most of society's taxes, then allocating some to local authorities, but under more effective institutional checks and balances, and guarantees of citizen control at local, county, and central level. Since, presently, many Greeks evade taxation anyway, one might therefore say that in Greece representation without taxation is the norm rather than the exception. Now, isn't that something the Americans never thought of?

3.2 'DEMOCRACY' AND THE NON-RULE OF LAW

One of the experiences the writer of this book has had with the Greek public sector shows how this paternalistic state demotes its own (and, if it gets the chance, other countries') citizens to the level of subjects. In August 1986 Olympic Airways, Greece's national air-carrier which Onassis had founded and a 'right-wing' government nationalised in 1974, raised its prices, an act obviously within any firm's rights. But OA went further than that, compelling even those who had bought return tickets prior to the price increase, and had already completed the first leg of their journeys, to pay the difference in order to fly them back, a blatant breach of contract.

In January 1996 a citizen regained possession of his property, which for 20 years had been leased to the Ministry of Public Order and used as a police station. He was immediately informed by the Water Supply Company that he had to pay 2 108 000 drs (£5636) for water bills going back to 1994. They told him that they would never cut off the supply of water to a government agency, even though the latter was not paying the bills, and, moreover, they were now holding him responsible since 'he is the person whom they know to be the landlord'.[51]

In 1984 a tax assessor, on the basis of inappropriate comparative data, asked for a bribe – nothing unusual, here – in order to lower the taxable value of a tax-payer's property under transfer. The citizen involved said yes, then had the official framed. A court, subsequently, confirmed the attempt at bribery, and condemned the official. Still, out of solidarity with their colleague, the tax office concerned absolutely refused to lower the taxable value of the property, and even raised it, even though the tax-payer produced official comparative data invalidating the tax office's excessive claims. The hapless citizen eventually had to sue the Inland Renenue over the matter, incurring additional expenses, and bitterly decided never again to try and expose corruption in the system.[52]

In 1986 the Parliament voted a law (1599/86) obliging all public sector agencies and organisations to supply all and any administrative documents and data (except for those concerning defence, police work, and individual privacy) to citizens wishing to have them, no questions asked. Nine years later the Ministry of the Presidency felt obliged to remind the civil service, which it supervises, that they do have to apply the law . . .[53]

If these four instances, among many, are about the tyrannical aspect of the Greek public sector, they are matched by umpteen others, which are about its lax, permissive, indulgent aspect. Like Janus, the two-faced Roman god, the Greek state combines both visages in sharp relief. Its second aspect, no less irresponsible, disheartening, and oppressive than the first, allows governments to fulfil a very large part of their implicit 'contract' with Greek society by tolerating and turning a blind eye to individuals' activities aimed at short-term gain, irrespective of social or long-term consequences. From this point of view Greece is a liberals' paradise – or hell, considering the fruits of all this permissiveness. Notwithstanding cries to the contrary, extreme indulgence of this kind is of course deeply and inherently undemocratic, as it invalidates the rule of law, whilst the resultant atmosphere of lawlessness, arbitrariness, and corruption suppresses merit and damages economic performance at least as much as overt tyranny might. Greece's lower than expected economic growth over the last 20 years (see Chapter 2) must in part be attributed precisely to this pattern. The following are only a few examples of the state of the non-rule of law, characteristic of modern Greece:[54]

(1) A police officer was removed from his post in 1991 for stopping locals from building illegally.[55]
(2) In 1984 a woman from a Greek village, heeding a new law from the Ministry of Planning, went to the nearest Planning Office in order to pay a fine and buy a permit for her unauthorised building.

The officials came and saw it, only to tell her they could not give her a permit after all, neither would they allow her to finish the construction. When she pointed out that all dwellings near by were also unauthorised, they replied, 'true, but they did not come to us admitting their breach of the law, like you have'![56]

(3) In 1985 university students imprisoned their professor in his office for failing them, and released him only after the dean had promised to pass them.[57]

(4) On 17 November 1995 about 500 people in their 'teens and twenties occupied the Technical University of Athens. It was far from the first time, as it has become something of a routine for an obscure assortment of students, pseudo-anarchists, and layabouts to occupy this particular building on the anniversary of the students' genuine uprising against a fascist dictatorship in 1973. Not for the first time, either, they set fire to furniture and dissertations, destroyed labs and priceless paintings, looted and soiled the place thoroughly. They also burned Greek flags. Actually 1995 was the first time, since the practice began, that the police got permission from the University Senate to enter the premises and make arrests, as the concept of academic asylum in post-1974 Greece apparently covers anything from arson to rape and murder, as long as they take place within the ivory towers of higher learning.[58] Expectedly, those arrested got off very lightly.

(5) But government and police inactivity are not confined to watching calmly while academic institutions burn. In March 1995 farmers blocked the national highway joining Athens to Thessalonica for more than a week until a frightened, yet 'democratic', government promised them more subsidies. In November 1995 the inmates of Korydallos prison, in Piraeus, revolted, burned part of the building, killed or wounded one another, and repeatedly attempted escape, while government officials spent a week in polite negotiations until the situation petered out.[59] In June 1996 people living near places in Attica, where the government was contemplating establishing garbage dumps for Athens, protested by blocking public roads, burning cars, spoiling with garbage water mains supplying Athens, and brandishing firearms, whilst the authorities watched from a distance, and garbage accumulated uncollected throughout the nation's capital.[60] Generally, the tiniest group of protesters is allowed as a matter of course to block traffic for hours in downtown Athens, as stopping them is widely considered 'undemocratic'.

(6) Not paying taxes, loans received, or contributions due has become

a national sport in Greece, whilst government ministers and governors of state-controlled organisations and banks have often encouraged the practice by cancelling outstanding debts or not taking requisite measures to collect them.[61]

(7) In 1991 it was found that 40 employees of the Greek Telecoms Organisation (OTE) had been appointed on the basis of forged documents. The President of OTE admitted this, but added that the law does not make it possible for him to fire the forgers. Once again, it became apparent that breaking the law pays in Greece.[62]

(8) In March 1991 an MP and the local mayor broke down the door to the police station in the village of Sarti and freed people arrested for building illegally. In the same vein, the Ministry of Agriculture sued one of its employees because he had the 'audacity' to tear down an illegally raised wall in a piece of woodland.[63]

Corruption, of course, is rampant in this atmosphere. Research by Professor Coutsoukis disclosed that one in two civil servants is in a position to describe cases of bribe-taking in his or her department (while an equal percentage consider their work conditions wretched).[64] Nevertheless, Greece is not the world corruption champion. In a 40-country list comprised as a result of research by the University of Gottingen and published in *Der Spiegel*, on the frequency of 'corruption' in allocating big business contracts, Greece appeared as the 11th most corrupt country, the first three places going to China, Pakistan, and Venezuela. Least corrupt in the list were Singapore, Denmark, and New Zealand, whilst Germany and Britain ended 28th and 29th, respectively. Italy, incidentally, was the only EU country to beat Greece, occupying 8th place in the list, whereas Turkey appeared less corrupt – just – than Greece, coming up 12th.[65]

That Greece is not the most corrupt country in the world is small consolation though, and a pathetic thought. Societies, like people, must aim high; and Greece, with a state which on the one hand belittles its own citizens, and on the other denies them the safety of the rule of law and pride in equity, has a long way to go towards true democracy.

3.3 CALIBAN'S PALIMPSESTS

Since the Greek public sector has been hiring people without regard to merit or actual need, but, ostensibly at least, on the basis of formal educational qualifications, a parasitic relationship has developed between the state and the educational system, with crucial repercussions for the country's economic performance. The process works like this: people know that in order to find jobs in the public sector and secure themselves for life they need a formal qualification. The higher the latter is, the better of course, as this will determine their initial pay. The content of the qualification, the actual knowledge or skill involved, does not matter at all. A certificate, diploma or degree, typically referred to in Greece as a 'paper', is the all-important formal prerequisite (whilst political affiliation supplies the informal selection criterion). This being so, the whole idea of education, at whatever level, is not to receive training but a 'paper', which will allow one to proceed to the next level, and, if one is lucky, all the way to a recognised university degree. To get the latter one must attend a Greek public-sector university, or go abroad, as private universities on Greek soil are constitutionally banned. The only relatively hard obstacle throughout this process is the university entrance examinations, something of a national agony day every year. Still, students are not asked to demonstrate critical thinking. This, secondary, or any other, education in Greece has never attempted to cultivate (except for two or three private schools, but even they are not what they used to be). Rather, students have to be good at memorising excerpts or solutions to problems. Once in the university students know that they will get their degree no matter what. Among others, they have the right to take an unlimited number of resits on any number of courses – a Greek world exclusive, conducive to a continuous deterioration of the ratio of 'active' to registered students: 51 per cent in 1994, against 76 per cent 10 years earlier.[66] In 1992 the government of New Democracy ('right-wing') tried to restrict this right by making participation in 3rd and 4th year exams conditional upon passing all 1st and 2nd year courses, but in 1994 a PASOK government ('socialist') reverted to the old system. Other rights, informal but popular, are no less in effect, like the 'right' to at least a passing grade on account of 'democracy', or the 'right' to cheat.[67] Any notion of reward for merit or effort goes out the window, just as in the broad public sector. Over time educational standards have suffered to the point where now

> the system of higher education has almost totally [] deviated from the central aims and mission that by definition is supposed to serve. [] It is even wrong to think that the higher education system does its formal job, only inefficiently. Truth to tell, it serves a different goal, and rather effectively at that [].[68]

The different goal, of course, is the provision of merely formal, certainly mediocre, qualifications to those seeking employment in the public sector, which in turn is content with mediocre employees.[69] Table 3.1 provides data on people with higher education qualifications employed in the public sector as a percentage of the respective population age group (20–64) in 1991. The figure is about 34 per cent, but without taking into account graduates employed by state-controlled 'problem' companies and other entities. Altogether the 'true' figure should approach 45 per cent of the total, which is a little below Tsoucalas' (1986) estimate for 1980. In fact, taking graduates who are not in the labour force (for example, housewives or people doing their national service) out of the age group, the State's proportion of graduate employment must be more than 50 per cent, and much higher still – perhaps more than 75 per cent – if one limits oneself to graduates who work as employees rather than employers or self-employed professionals.[70]

The downgrading of true skills and knowledge, and conversely, the apotheosis of formality, have in fact reached such an extent that recently (April 1995) the Parliament voted a decree granting court clerks, who have only finished secondary education, university graduate status.[71] On current trends the time is probably not far when the Greek state will pass a law awarding every Greek a diploma! Inevitably Greek university degrees have increasingly come to be considered not much better than high-school certificates: job adverts have begun to appear in the Greek press requiring applicants for jobs in the delicatessen, fruit, and fish sections of big supermarkets to be university graduates![72] This is certainly an affront to quite a few bright young Greeks who go on to pursue postgraduate education in good universities abroad, some very successfully. It is only fair to say that such students shine despite the Greek higher education system rather than because of it. In the meantime most Greek university students, graduates and the State zealously guard the latter's monopoly of higher education[73] because (a) the simultaneous operation of private-sector universities would probably hasten the qualitative and financial[74] collapse of public-sector ones, and (b) many feel that competition among graduates for places in the public sector would intensify. The second argument really suggests a gut reaction rather than balanced judgement, since already in 1992 more Greek students, as a proportion of the total EU population of university students, studied outside their own country than students from any other EU country: 9.7 per cent, against a EU average of 1.3 per cent.[75] Moreover, Greece is now spending nearly U$250 m. per year on students studying abroad (not just in the EU), a large part of which could

Table 3.1
Educational profile of Greek public sector staff in 1991 vs respective population age-group

	Public administration staff**	Staff of state-controlled entities of public-sector Law status (NΠΔΔ)	Local authorities staff	Staff of state-controlled entities of private-sector Law status (KNΠIA)#	Total staff with respective educational qualification
Total staff:	116 799	116 439	45 094	217 358	495 690
Finished:					
University education	25.6%	12.6%	5.0%	12.9%	74 967
College or polytechnic education	10.0%	15.3%	3.4%	6.9%	45 964
Secondary education (6 or 3 forms)*	46.6%	45.5%	45.4%	46.9%	229 865
Primary education	17.8%	26.6%	46.2%	33.3%	144 894
Percentage totals	100.0%	100.0%	100.0%	100.0%	495 690
	Strength of age-group 20–64 with respective educational qualification in 1991 ##	Those with respective educational qualification as % of age group 20–64 in 1991 ##	Managers of member-firms of Athens Chamber of Small-scale Manufacturing Firms (BEA) in 1994 §		Public sector staff as % of age-group 20–64 with same educational qualification §§
University education	557 830	9.1%	12.0%		34.1%
College or polytechnic education	178 199	2.9%	7.0%		25.8%
Secondary education (6 or 3 forms)*	2 225 277	36.4%	56.0%		10.3%
Primary education	2 447 939	40.0%	25.0%		5.9%
Totals	5 409 245	88.4%	100.0%		11.3%

* Including those who were university, college, or polytechnic students in 1991.
** Excluding teachers (approx. 115 000), all of whom are higher-education graduates, police & fire dept staff (about 52 000), armed forces salaried staff (about 40 000), priest (about 11 000).
# But not staff of a, rather large, subset of state-controlled, private-sector 'problem' companies or of 'problem' companies fully dependent on state-controlled banks, as well as staff of agricultural co-operatives (who are ultimately paid by the Agricultural Bank), altogether nearly 200 000 people.
Total strength of age group, 6 114 076, but 11.5 per cent of that were people who had not finished primary school.
§ Sample of 4000 member-firms. *Eleutherotypia*, 7.5.1995, p. 73.
§§ Taking teachers into account. If teachers are not included, then the proportion of public-sector staff with university qualifications was 13.4 per cent.

Sources: Bulletin of statistical data on public-sector staff, census of 31.12.1991, Ministry of the Presidency, Athens, 1994; NSSG, 1991 Population Census.

be spent domestically if private universities were allowed; but the structure of interests around the State's monopoly in higher education wishes to ignore this. The struggle to preserve that monopoly has led, among others, to the ludicrous situation whereby if a person has finished a private college in Greece, and then gone on to earn a MSc or PhD degree from any renowned foreign university, to all intents and purposes the Greek public sector will consider that person a high-school graduate only, 'on account of the first degree having been obtained from a non-recognised institution'.[76]

Higher education is not the only educational level that has deteriorated in Greece. According to research by the NSSG,[77] in 1991 more than 4.5 m. Greeks (that is, 45 per cent of the total) were functionally illiterate:

> . . . they cannot read newspapers, use a telephone directory, fill in an application form or cheque, make sense of departures-and-arrivals boards, perform simple calculations, give correct change, or interpret percentages on receipts.

In an era where economic success lies in the production and marketing of information, of high-technology goods and of technology-intensive services, and all production requires improved 'soft' skills (from team work and information handling to customer care and total quality), functional illiteracy of this kind implies that the pool out of which competent staff are selected in Greece is that much smaller. This is especially sad for the country which first proclaimed the value of education and knowledge, and disastrous for a country that is seriously lacking in 'raw' economic resources, like land, labour and capital.[78]

The deterioration of overall educational standards has been assisted by another trend, which began in 1976 and was given impetus in 1982–3. Formal modern Greek, a well-structured form of the language which served as a link to ancient Greek, was abolished from official or school usage, along with a significant part of the spelling (for instance, accents),[79] and the teaching of ancient Greek. This sad development,[80] itself related to transforming the entire educational system merely into a certificate production line for the utilitarian purpose of enabling access to the public sector,[81] has had far-reaching as well as catastrophic consequences. High school or university students, and graduates of recent years, nowadays have a far poorer vocabulary than their predecessors; and the link of the country's population, particularly her youth, to ancient, Byzantine, and modern Greece's cultural heritage has been severed, perhaps irrevocably.

Before 1976 the educational system may not have encouraged free thinking, but at least, however inadequately, attempted to cultivate Greece's link to her past. After 1976 the system has drowned on a surfeit of 'freedom', and been blinded by utilitarianism. Vulgarity and intellectual poverty reign, vengefully erasing from the collective psyche ideals that once inspired modern as well as ancient Greeks.[82] A fast-spreading identity crisis has developed among the younger generation, which, together with the country's demographic and economic stagnation, is inexorably condemning the Greek nation to oblivion.[83]

If this analysis is correct, then 'rolling back the frontiers of the state' in Greece might do the nation a greater service than merely enhancing economic performance. Since the process would revolutionise Greek society, the hope is that in this way radical improvements would be introduced in all sectors of the nation's life, including education and culture. It would of course be deeply wrong, as well as naive, to expect that Greece's renaissance would happen merely as a result of a crush privatisation programme. Something else is also needed, desperately: political and spiritual leadership. Who will provide it, remains to be seen.

Notes

1. Mustafa Kemal Ataturk (b. 1880, Thessalonica): Founder of the modern Turkish state, inspirer of its secular orientation, and its first President (1920). A political and military genius, he – with decisive help from France, Italy and the Soviet Union – led Turkey to victory over the Greeks in the 1919–22 war, reconquering Asia Minor. The state he founded, however, has been deeply and inherently authoritarian, and under the strict control of the military.
2. Yannaras,1995a.
3. Lacopoulos,1994; Calliri, 1995b.
4. The author's rough estimate is that the public sector contributes more than 50 per cent of Greece's true GDP, formal (revised calculation) and informal.
5. See Arouch,1994.
6. Panayotarea,1995.
7. Petras,1984; Tsoucalas, 1983; 1986.
8. Tsoucalas, 1983; Calliri, 1993.
9. In the writer's view, this would have happened sooner or later even if civilian rule had not been broken. Still, the military regime never ran deficits in the Ordinary Government Budget, the way subsequent civilian governments, especially PASOK, did. The overall deficits it did ran originated with the Public Investment Budget alone.

10. One of its first acts was to cancel all outstanding liabilities of peasants to the state-owned Agricultural Bank, the country's only institution specialising in farm credit.
11. Marinos, 1987; 1995.
12. See P. Mourdoukoutas', 1994 fictitious account of such a possibility.
13. Marinos, 1988; 1994b.
14. William Niskanen (1971) described bureaucracies as self-serving, budget-maximising agencies.
15. For example, public-sector enterprise in Greece have never operated on the basis of business plans; only in 1995 the government began to contemplate passing a law making such plans obligatory for them, and introducing other elements of modernisation. See 'New-type administration for ΔΕΚΟ [public-sector enterprises and organisations]', *E Cathemerine*, 15 April, p. 22.
16. The very term 'managers' may be inappropriate: it is normally associated with a certain degree of autonomy, competence, and professionalism. In a public sector like Greece's it's better to speak of 'high officials'.
17. In cases of severe misconduct, they can be thrown out, though.
18. Mirkos, 1996.
19. Calliri, 1994b, on the basis of research conducted by the National School of Public Administration on behalf of the Ministry of the Presidency, which supervises the civil service.
20. The two should be distinguished from one another (Jones, 1985): Outputs refer to what is visibly produced, like so many hospitals or schools; outcomes refer to ultimate influence on social conditions.
21. Calliri, 1996, p. 23.
22. Spanou, 1994.
23. See Table 7.1.
24. Spanou, 1994.
25. Mirkos, 1996.
26. See, for instance, 'ΔΕΚΟ [Public-sector enterprises & organisations] want to hire 10 000 employees', *E Cathemerine*, 22.3.1995, and 'ΔΕΚΟ: 10 500 appointments', *E Cathemerine*, 18.1.1996.
27. Copsine, 1996c.
28. *Ta Nea*, 15.9.1994, p. 17.
29. George Papandreou, father of Andreas and himself Prime Minister of Greece in the 1960s is reported to have once said that it would be folly to try and set right, or even touch, anything in the Greek public sector, as this might cause it to collapse in its entirety.
30. Sometimes this is the sensible thing to do. In the following example it is also a reflection of the easy-going, bon-viveur life in the Aegean. On a day in the mid-1980s head-office inspectors from the National Bank of Greece arrived in the small island of Enousses, between the Greek island of Chios and the Asia Minor coast, in order to check on the bank's tiny branch there. Finding the branch closed, they sought the manager and his assistant; upon which they were shown a dot in the horizon, which turned out to be a fishing boat with the missing staff. It was fun, cute, and no harm done, since in that tiny island relations between bank staff and the locals were highly informal.

31. Tsoucalas, 1986, pp. 143–4.
32. Ibid., p. 144.
33. Magheiros, 1993.
34. Emigration data from *Epiloghe*, 1984, p. 65.
35. OECD, 1995, p. 45.
36. Ibid., p. 45.
37. Ibid., p. 50.
38. Originating with the CAP, but also coming from the Greek government budget and the Agricultural Bank of Greece, itself an instrument in the state's agrarian policy.
39. Gritzalis, 1992.
40. *Greek Government Budget for 1996*, p. 43.
41. *EuroStat Labour Force Survey 1993*, Lux. 1995
42. *E Cathemerine*, 5.4.1992.
43. Calliri, 1994a, 1995a.
44. *Kerdos*, 24.9.1991.
45. Vamvoucas, 1992a.
46. It has achieved this by monitoring the flow of farmers' subsidies through the co-operatives, by managing the peasants' indebtedness to the state-owned Agricultural Bank of Greece, and by having – usually – pro-government officials elected (or, in the past, appointed) at the head of the Pan-hellenic Confederation of Unions of Agricultural Co-operatives. (See also Papageorgiou, 1995.) Following the new GATT and CAP restructuring, however, it is doubtful whether the state can look forward to an acquiescent countryside any longer. But then, no political party told Greek farmers in the 1980s or later that EU subsidies were meant to help them modernise their farming rather than merely augment their income (Papatheodorou, 1995).
47. For more on the size and role of the state in the Greek economy, and of public-sector enterprises in particular, see Pirounakis, 1995b, and Drosos et. al., 1996.
48. Nicolacopoulos, 1995; Galati, 1996b.
49. An attempt at interpretation is in Sakellaropoulos, 1996.
50. *Eleutherotypia*, 11.8.1996, p. 50.
51. *Economicos Tachydromos*, 14.3.1996, p. 152.
52. *Economicos Tachydromos*, 11.8.1988, pp. 75–6.
53. Lacopoulos, 1995.
54. See also Chapter 8; Sterghiou, 1994; Khaicalis, 1994.
55. See note 19 in Chapter 9.
56. Marinos, 1991.
57. Marinos, 1995.
58. Pirounakis, 1996a.
59. Some time before that incident, the 'Mafia' (inmates, prison personnel and 'powers that be' from the outside) which actually runs Greece's prison system had succeeded in forcing Mr Kouvelakis, Minister of Justice, to resign his post, following pressures by Mr Livanis, A. Papandreou's aide, not to try and change things in the system. Mr Papandreou, who was then Prime Minister, asked Mr Kouvelakis to remain without, however, promising to back him up. Apparently Mr Kouvelakis replied by saying that he had

given Mr Papandreou and PASOK his life, but his honour was his to keep. (Source: confidential.)

60. 'The dump and the protests', *E Cathemerine*, 8.6.1996, p. 3.
61. Sterghiou, 1994.
62. Marinos, 1991.
63. Ibid.
64. 'Corruption in the civil service', *Ethnos*, 16.5.1995, p. 19.
65. *E Cathemerine*, 11.7.1995.
66. *E Cathemerine*, 21.10.1994.
67. Marinos, 1995.
68. Sophoulis, 1996.
69. Frankos, 1995.
70. Tsoucalas, 1986, p. 128.
71. Diamantopoulos, 1995.
72. Continent advert, *Ta Nea*, 16.1.1994. AB Vassilopoulos advert, *Ta Nea*, 5.10.1994, p. 57.
73. Although people from both big parties, particularly New Democracy, have increasingly begun to talk about the need for private-sector universities. The idea is also part of the proposals for Greek higher education reform suggested in a recent OECD study (Kharalampopoulou, 1995).
74. Karaiskaki, 1995.
75. *E Cathemerine*, 30.10.1994.
76. Formal wording in answers to relevant petitions.
77. *E Cathemerine*, 20.11.1994. See also Yannaras, 1995b; Arouch, 1995b; *E Cathemerine* 8.9.95, p. 6
78. At the root of the problem lies the tendency of the educational system to reward memorisation rather than critical thinking. Evidence from other educational systems suggests that Greeks can do quite well in the right circumstances. For example, research by the Inner London Educational Authority found that Greek pupils had achieved above-average performance scores in 1987. In particular, they had done better than the 'English, Scots, Welsh', 'Turkish', or 'other white', and worse than the 'other European' or 'Indian', ethnic groups. 'Home life is key to top marks at school', *The Guardian*, 9.3.1990, p. 10.
79. An English speaker may appreciate what happened by means of the following example: It was like ruling that henceforth the name 'Paul' will be written as 'Pol', or that it is alright to write 'I says' in newspapers, reports, documents, science journals and books.
80. On arguments for it see Rallis, 1996. George Rallis, Education Minister in 1976, was the man who initiated the reform.
81. Other victims of the post-1974 educational reforms have been the grade system and discipline. Of course, before 1974 discipline was not much different from repression, but apparently society decided later to throw away the baby along with the bath water.
82. Yannaras, 1996, quite rightly, considers Rallis' and subsequent educational reforms a catastrophe for Greece comparable to the Asia Minor disaster of 1922 (see Chapter 1).
83. Cf. Sterghiou, 1995c.

4 Public Finances, Taxes, and Privatisation

'If we fail to achieve fiscal health and discipline, to-day's implicit bankruptcy of our country will become patently real.'
Alexander Papadopoulos, Greek Finance Minister, 13 March 1995.

4.1 BUDGET DEFICITS AND THE PUBLIC DEBT

Not for the first time in her modern history (see Chapter 1), Greece is having grave difficulties with her public finances. A series of Government Ordinary Budget[1] deficits run in the 1980s in order to curry favour with the electorate, plus pervasive tax evasion, have placed Greek governments in the 1990s in a vicious circle of running deficits (that is, borrowing) in order to service what is, apparently, EU's third largest public debt. In the same vein, all Greek governments' singular failure to privatise almost anything adds to the budgetary difficulties, themselves a result, in part, of Greece's populist version of democracy.

All available data point to 1981 as the year of the onset of fiscal profligacy and indiscipline in post-war Greece. In that year:

- Central government debt went up by 42 per cent as a percentage of GDP at factor cost, from 31.1 per cent in 1980 to 44.3 per cent in 1981, a higher rise than ever before (see Table 4.1).
- A discernible political business cycle appeared in Greece, as with hindsight is now known (Diagram 4.1).
- Public-sector net borrowing requirement (PSNBR) rose by 73 per cent as a percentage of GDP at factor cost, from 9.4 per cent in 1980 to 16.3 per cent in 1981 (Table 4.2).
- The Government General Budget Deficit (GGBd) as a percentage of GDP at factor cost went up from 5.1 per cent in 1980 to 10.5 per cent in 1981 (that is, it more than doubled), whereas from 1957 to 1980 the annual increase of this figure had averaged 3.9 per cent, with a standard deviation of 0.99 per cent (Table 5.3 in Appendix to Chapter 5).

Table 4.1

Greek Maastricht-defined public debt, central government debt, and public-sector foreign debt

	Maastricht-defined public-sector debt as % of new GDP # at market prices (target = 60)	Central government (CG) debt (bil. drs)	Of which: foreign (%)	CG debt as % of old GDP at factor cost	CG debt as % of old GDP at market prices	CG debt as % of new GDP at market prices	Factors contributing to rise in CG debt (bil. drs): Primary surplus (−) or deficit (+)	Interest payments (not including interest payments to service armed forces debt)	Other ##	Public-sector foreign debt #@ ($US m.)	Public-sector foreign debt as of old GDP at factor cost	Debt service ratio (int.+cap. repayment as % of FX receipts from exports and invisibles)
1977*		216	23.02	25.5			NA	14	NA			
1978*		341	17.79	33.6			NA	20	NA			
1979*		395	19.88	31.7			NA	32	NA			
1980*		474	23.43	31.1	27.7		48	43	−12			
1981*		822	19.28	44.3			179	63	106			
1981**		672	24.26	36.2	32.8		179	62				
1982		929	25.30	40.6	36.1		154	68	35			
1983		1 269	30.50	46.9	41.2		177	104	59	10 562	34.3	13.0
1984		1 883	33.14	56.8	49.5		149	164	301	12 318	41.8	15.7
1985		2 673	38.46	64.6	57.9		300	240	250	15 530	51.9	19.3
1986		3 230	39.85	66.3	58.6		169	295	93	18 032	51.8	19.7
1987		4 046	36.36	73.9	64.5		176	408	232	18 562	45.9	23.8
1988		5 383	31.19	81.3	71.1	59.2	390	549	398	17 753	38.0	22.4
1989		6 699	27.93	85.5	76.1	61.9	812	630	−126	18 830	39.0	20.3
1990		9 383	22.16	101.8	88.9	72.3	523	1 163	998	22 030	37.9	20.1
1991		12 335	22.42	111.4	95.7	77.8	191	1 432	1 329	23 914	39.4	24.2
1992	89.4	15 557	21.46	124.1	104.9	85.3	−259	1 405	2 076	23 599	35.9	32.0
1993	111.8	23 431	19.13	163.2	139.8	113.7	−9	2 122	5 761	26 564	42.4	23.8
1994	110.4	28 093	22.18	175.8	149.0	121.1	−453	3 063	2 053	33 091	50.2	22.1
1995	111.7	31 928	20.74	181.6	154.3	123.8	−661	3 085	1 411	34 174	45.0	26.3

* Apparently including substantial long-term loans in FX arranged through the Bank of Greece on behalf of the Government (source: Gov't Budget Statement for Financial Year 1982, March 1982, p. 110).

** Apparently not including such loans (part of 'other assets' in Bank of Greece balance sheets). Hereafter data are from GBS for Financial Years 1986 (p. 72), 1995 (p. 119), and 1996 (p. 122).

\# 'New' GDP refers to the new method of calculating GDP, which the NSSG adopted in 1993, and backdated to 1988. The new 'GDP' is about 22% larger than the 'old' one, and nearer Greece's true GDP.

\#\# State guarantees called in, assumption of the debt of various entities (like banks or social insurance organisations), and so on. See Doukas, 1993.

\#@ This is larger than central government foreign debt alone, as it includes the foreign debt of, for example, public-sector enterprises. (Source: Bank of Greece Annual Reports.)

Sources: (a) For 1995 CG debt, E Cathemerine, 23.4.1996. As of 1994 central gov't debt includes armed forces debt. (b) For Maastricht-defined public-sector debt. Bank of Greece Annual Report for 1995, p. 176. (c) Last three columns: Bank of Greece Annual Reports. (d) Other columns: See above.

Diagram 4.1
Greece, 1977–95: An unmistakable political business cycle emerges as of 1981, with peaks in public sector net borrowing requirements as % of GDP in every election year

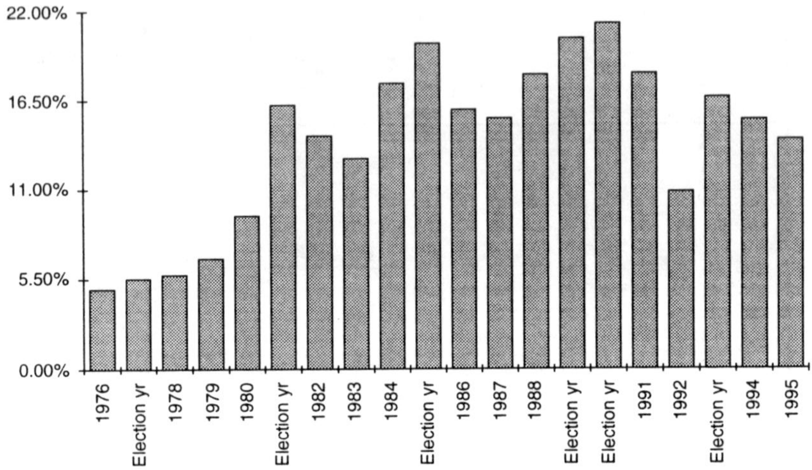

Source: Table 4.2

- Between 1980 and 1981 the GGBd increased by 105 per cent in 1978 prices (while in the period 1976–5 to 1980–79 it had been going up at an average of 1.7 per cent per year) (Table 5.3 in Appendix to Chapter 5). As a result, in 1981
- Government General Budget deficits deviated sharply upwards from their previous long-term trend (Diagram 4.2).

A relevant development in 1981 was the coming to power of a supposedly socialist party (PASOK) for the first time in Greek history.[2] This happened in October. PASOK alone could not of course have been responsible for the fiscal deterioration that marked the year (although it was only too happy to continue the trend), but the populist terms under which the election campaign was fought dragged the incumbent 'right-wing' New Democracy (ND) party along for more than a year before the elections took place. Already a series of ND governments since the end of 1974 had failed to keep the GGBd as a percentage of GDP at its pre-1975 level, but to a large extent this was both inevitable and understandable: in the aftermath of the Turkish invasion of

Table 4.2

Greece: Financing of net borrowing requirements (NBR) of broad public sector (including public-sector enterprises), 1978–95, and Bank of Greece credit to the Government (in m. drs)

Year	Public sector NBR	PSNBR as % of GDP at factor cost	Foreign borrowing to finance PSNBR	Foreign borrowing as % of PSNBR	Domestic borrowing: treasury bills to banks	Domestic borrowing: treasury bills to private sector	Domestic borrowing from Bank of Greece	Domestic borrowing from banks et al.	Total domestic borrowing	Foreign plus Bank of Greece borrowing as % of PSNBR	Treasury bills as % of PSNBR	Increase in Bank of Greece loans & advances to Government	Increase in Bank of Greece holdings of treasury bills & gov. bonds
1976	35 491	4.9										13 223	1 618
1977	46 586	5.5										18 799	150
1978	58 453	5.7	9 716	16.6	41 017		−53	7 773	48 737	16.5	70.2	44 375	−2 004
1979	83 745	6.7	3 919	4.7	31 968		37 397	10 461	79 826	49.3	38.2	31 223	−91
1980	143 346	9.4	34 842	24.3	44 095		37 671	26 738	108 504	50.6	30.8	48 853	−572
1981	302 337	16.3	42 887	14.2	44 744		164 066	50 640	259 450	68.5	14.8	154 393	−117
1982	328 524	14.4	59 198	18.0	56 361	−761	148 297	65 429	269 326	63.2	16.9	266 544	55
1983	350 632	13.0	121 543	34.7	180 217	−1 340	−15 719	65 931	229 089	30.2	51.0	54 728	1 787
1984	585 274	17.6	169 065	28.9	194 144	−219	95 079	127 205	416 209	45.1	33.1	348 586	−1 372
1985	828 387	20.0	270 330	32.6	335 362	8 852	116 278	97 565	558 057	46.7	41.6	626 869	3 505
1986	776 150	15.9	220 584	28.4	223 637	21 030	72 523	238 376	555 566	37.8	31.5	236 575	6 959
1987	843 853	15.4	74 899	8.9	304 895	169 553	56 029	238 477	768 954	15.5	56.2	254 046	53 673
1988	1 201 020	18.1	42 534	3.5	567 983	374 389	−17 205	233 319	1 158 486	2.1	78.4	383 218	72 330
1989	1 594 704	20.3	208 991	13.1	673 054	301 417	159 804	251 438	1 385 713	23.1	61.1	430 810	64 858
1990	1 957 480	21.2	236 641	12.1	315 962	844 133	292 737	268 007	1 720 839	27.0	59.3	379 526	−13 272
1991	2 015 944	18.2	251 323	12.5	34 935	1 370 681	101 119	257 886	1 764 621	17.5	69.7	828 300	−27 600
1992	1 362 885	10.9	152 057	11.2	−242 438	970 029	212 530	270 707	1 210 828	26.8	53.4	1 169 400	27 458
1993	2 408 114	16.8	764 550	31.7	394 521	1 031 501	−20 265	237 807	1 643 564	30.9	59.2	1 528 880	148 177
1994	2 450 610	15.3	289 939	11.8	450 192	1 621 596	14 807	74 076	2 160 671	12.4	84.5	−135 381	−28 129
1995	2 475 819	13.9	491 018	19.8	338 126	2 088 000	−437 901	−3 424	1 984 801	2.1	98.0	−288 421	−5 624
Mean				18.2						31.4	52.7		

Source: Bank of Greece Annual Reports.

Note: The increase in Bank of Greece credits to the Government (taken from the category 'loans & advances to Government' from the Bank of Greece balance sheet) includes, among others, the 'current receipts & payments account', the 'oil products account', and from 1985 to 1992, the 'FX valuation differences account'. Prior to 1985 the latter account is subsumed under 'other assets' in the BG balance sheet, whilst as of 1993 the balance of this account is part of 'loans & advances to Government', under the heading 'FX-denominated long-term loans & securities'. The increase in BG credits to the Government does not include 'treasury bills & government bonds', whose increase is shown separately in the next column. Finally before 1982 substantial FX loans to the Government were subsumed under 'other assets' rather than 'loans & advances to Government'. Any such are therefore not included here.

Diagram 4.2
Greece, 1957–95: Relationship between economic growth and government budget deficits

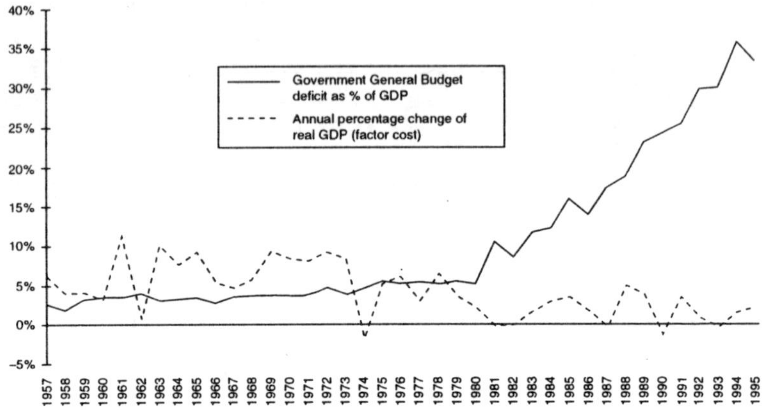

Source: Table 5.4 in Appendix to Chapter 5

Cyprus, in July 1974, Greece felt a strong need to increase her defence spending.[3] Thus in 1975 the GGBd as a percentage of GDP exceeded the 5 per cent mark, for the first time since 1957, never to drop below it again (Table 5.3 in Appendix to Chapter 5).

In 1978, however, the rate of growth of defence spending was exceeded by that of other budget categories, notably education and social services (even though 20.3 per cent of the government budget for 1978 was still earmarked for defence, the largest single category).[4] By 1981 increases in defence spending were definitely not among the most important:

> In contrast to revenue, Ordinary Budget expenditure exceeded estimates by . . . 14.2 per cent . . . This increase stemmed from all categories of expenditure, particularly from increased outlays for grants, public debt servicing, tax refunds and rebates on export financing costs, and other consumer outlays.[5]

That is why 1981, when PASOK's ascendancy ushered in a period of rampant populism, can be said to mark the country's firm orientation towards economic decline, even though the onset of that decline can be traced back to 1973 (first oil price shock), and particularly 1979–80 (second oil price shock). This is apparent in Diagram 4.2, which relates Greek economic growth to GGBd as a percentage of GDP from 1957 to 1995: low rates of economic growth since 1981 are associated with rapid rises in GGBd/GDP. In other words, at a time when Greece needed to effect a restructuring of her economy in response to international cost pressures (not only from the price of energy, but also from the prices of imports), PASOK chose to do nothing in that direction; instead, it tried to make the Greek people 'feel good' by spending more (and borrowing for the purpose), with disastrous results. To a lesser extent, however, a precedent had already been set by a series of ND governments even before 1981, and strongly so in that year. New Democracy (a 'right-wing' party, mind you) in fact initiated the wave of nationalisations[6] which PASOK was to take up later. PASOK's expansionist economic policy (with a brief interlude in 1986 – see Diagram 4.2) came to be taken so much for granted by its voters that in the infamous 1989 election (involving an orgy of handouts) they came up with the slogan, 'Tsovola, dos'ta ola' (that is, 'Tsovola, give it all'), the person named being PASOK's minister of public finance at the time.

Of course all Greek governments since at least 1957 had run budget deficits (see Table 5.4 in Appendix to Chapter 5). The difference is that up to 1978 these arose only as a result of deficits in the Public Investment Budget; the Ordinary Budget, on the other hand, was either in obvious surplus or in near-zero, positive balance. From 1957 to 1978 the net result of the Ordinary Budget was on average 4.8 per cent (a surplus) of Ordinary Budget expenditure, with a standard deviation of 3.8 per cent. From 1981 to 1995 the respective figures were 30.3 per cent (a deficit) and 11.3 per cent. The only years when the Ordinary Budget was not in obvious surplus but in near-zero, positive balance were 1965, 1974, 1975, 1977, and 1978. After the last year, however, the Ordinary Budget itself began to be in deficit, contributing to, and then dominating, the rise in General Budget deficits. The reason was not defence spending. From 1974 to 1977, as was mentioned, there were very substantial increases in defence spending, yet the Ordinary Budget was either in balance or in surplus. The reason, as of 1979, for Ordinary Budget deficits was increases in spending for other purposes, which after 1980 came to dominate. Inevitably, expanding deficits in the General Budget since 1980, and particularly since 1981, have been associated with a rising central government debt ever since (Table 4.1).[7]

The cause of those increases in spending must be sought in the populist politics, which, although never quite forgotten in post-war Greece, came to the fore rapidly after 1974, and have completely overwhelmed the nation's life since 1981. The fact that Greece's government budget is planned on an incremental, rather than zero, basis, has not helped matters either. But then, an incremental-basis budget is too convenient for politicians, public-sector employees and the voters to let go. The late Ath. Canellopoulos, Finance Minister in 1979–80 under a ND government, did attempt to introduce zero-based budgeting during his short spell in office,[8] but his successor at the Ministry, Mr Evert (of the ND party), reverted to the old system in no time. Presently, there is again talk of moving on to zero-based budgeting, and resistance is already bulding up to the idea.[9]

It is interesting to dwell a little on the specific factors contributing to the increase in central government debt, since, after a point, the budget deficits became an effect of the need to service the debt rather than the cause of the latter's growth. This became apparent for the first time in 1984, then in 1986, and decisively so as of 1990, when interest payments to service the debt exceeded the primary budget deficit (Table 4.1, boxed columns). In fact, since 1992, when the Government General Budget began to register a primary surplus, the main positive influence on the still growing debt has been interest payments. The other positive influence on debt growth, since again 1984 and in particular since 1990, has come from outside the budget. It has involved a miscellany of factors such as state guarantees called in, or assumption by the government of the debt of various banks, public enterprises, social insurance organisations, and so on.[10] In essence, these are instances of the profligacy and financial irresponsibility which have characterised most of the Greek public sector since the early 1980s.[11]

By 1995 the Greek public-sector debt, according to the definition of the public sector adopted in Maastricht (that is, central government, local authorities, social security organisations, other state-controlled entities of public-sector Law status – but not public-sector enterprises) was 111.7 per cent of Greece's 'new' GDP at market prices. This placed Greece in third place from top in the EU, with Belgium (133.7 per cent) and Italy (125.1 per cent) occupying first and second place. (Some have argued that Greece's debt as a percentage of GDP is actually higher if the debt of public-sector enterprises is included, or even highest in the EU if the calculation is done on a gross basis.[12]) Greece's high percentage certainly makes it very difficult for her governments to bring the public-sector debt down to 60 per cent of GDP, which is one of the criteria for European economic and monetary union by 1999, set down in Maastricht (see Chapter 2). It also presents the gravest threat to the country's stability and well-being, right after the Turkish threat to her territorial integrity. True, in 1946 the American and British public debt/GDP ratios were 120 and 260 per cent, respectively (just after a period of heavy defence spending).[13] Greece's debt, however, rose to its present heights as a result of budget deficits which since the early 1980s have had very little to do with defence (although, with hindsight, it would have been a welcome thing if the reason had been defence rather than electioneering). Moreover, the consequences of the fiscal profligacy of the 1980s have yet to unfold fully, as various 'problem' enterprises and banks under state control may force the government to assume their debts also, something already done before (see Chapter 6), while miscellaneous state guarantees keep being called in. Should the government, in addition, fail to bring inflation down, or at least keep it in check, getting out of the vicious circle of having to borrow in order to service the debt will prove next to impossible – at a time when the need to finance a huge defence programme has become essential to Greece's survival. But even if relations with Turkey were, or become, friendly, the size of Greece's public debt is cause for very serious worry on account of the following facts:

- Even though fiscal measures were being taken to keep the debt under control, by the mid-1990s it was still showing a mildly increasing trend (Table 4.1).
- By 1995, 21 per cent of central government debt was owed to foreigners, whilst the total public-sector foreign debt was 45 per cent of 'old' GDP at factor cost (or about 31 per cent of 'new' GDP at market prices) (Table 4.1).
- Greek real interest rates, on account of well-justified government and Bank of Greece fears that there would, or will, be a capital flight if Greek state securities are not internationally competitive, have been quite higher than Greece's real GDP growth rates. This, without being the primary factor behind Greece's poor growth performance, does affect the latter negatively anyway. In the meantime, Greece-based companies have been utilising the opportunity to borrow in FX – but the 'hard' drachma which makes this sensible (itself a result of Greece's high interest rates) also sucks in imports at an alarming rate (see Chapter 5).

These three facts make Greece's debt, although equal to America's and much smaller than Britain's in 1946, a much more difficult affair to handle. Handle it, though, Greece must – and do so by means of cutting expenditure, privatising state controlled assets and damping down on tax evasion, rather than by defaulting on her debt payments or allowing galloping inflation; the alternative (until, that is, the cleansing power of an all too likely crisis has had time to shape subsequent developments) is economic ruin in the worst possible international circumstances for Greece since the end of the German occupation (see Chapter 12).

By 1996 government efforts to reduce the debt still centred around lowering the cost of its servicing. The attempt hinged crucially on success in the fight to curb inflation, as, in an era of capital mobility, offering government securities to the public at low or negative real rates was correctly foreseen to be a sure way to speed up government bankruptcy (see Chapter 5). On the other hand, the failure to cut down government primary expenditure, tap informal economy incomes, privatise 'problem' companies under state control, or effect structural changes in the economy and society, was blatantly obvious, and no less inexcusable than before. Sadly the pattern was repeated in the 1997 Ordinary Budget (prepared in November 1996), which once again centred around the government's feeble attempt to improve the state's finances by raising planned tax revenue (by 8.5 per cent in real terms) rather than reducing expenditure (which was forecast to go down by 1.6 per cent in real terms), whilst drastic measures to curb tax evasion were still not implemented (see next section). Significantly, there was no planned revenue from privatisations, which were only given cursory mention in the Budget. In addition, some of the rise in planned tax revenue was forecast to result from the introduction of new property taxes, on the precarious assumption that possession of property and income-generating ability correlate strongly with one another – which is simply not the case in Greece (cf. Chapter 9).

4.2 TAXES AND THE INFORMAL ECONOMY

One of the main 'proximate' reasons behind Greece's big government budget deficits since the early 1980s has been tax evasion, something of a national sport. Having emphasised the political causes of the deficits, however, it is doubtful whether, *ceteris paribus*, a larger annual tax revenue would have constrained ND in 1980–1 or PASOK thereafter from spending more than they collected in taxes. Greece's two main parties would have done so anyway, still incurring deficits as a result. To believe differently is to miss the point of the political dynamic of fiscal expansionism: it's not about running a deficit in order to meet urgent needs (like defence, for example), but about winning elections. A balanced budget, at whatever level, although not neutral in terms of its effects on GDP, is not as conducive to the 'feel good' factor affecting the electorate as spending more on them (the more, the better) than they give away in taxes.

On the other hand, it may well be true that if governments clamped down thoroughly on tax evasion as a matter of course, they would probably also show greater fiscal restraint, thus ensuring lower rates of public debt growth. That is, the mentality of the political system, and the institutions making it up, would be different across the board. Italy, for example, which, like Greece, has a very high public debt/GDP ratio, also has a very extensive informal economy. The two are often related: since the informal economy is precisely about incomes that do not become known and are therefore not tax-assessed, a large informal economy means a relatively 'low' official GDP at the same time that the government of the country gets a smaller amount of tax revenue than is theoretically possible to collect. There is some doubt, however, as to how close the connection between clamping down on tax evasion and avoiding running big budget deficits really is. In the USA, for example, a very strict and efficient taxation system has often not stopped governments from spending far more than they collected in taxes, although defence spending has accounted for a large part of the discrepancy. Still, as President Clinton found to his dismay in 1995–6, a hostile Congress can bring the federal civil service near bankruptcy by not allowing the Administration to borrow more.

Probably because tax evasion is so extensive in Greece, the country's taxation system is highly regressive, and getting more so with time. For example, in 1980 income taxation revenue plus social security contributions (a more meaningful measure of the regressiveness of a taxation system than direct taxes, as these often include taxes on property and on bank deposits[14]) made up 52.3 per cent of Greece's total tax revenue (which placed Greece in the third lowest place in the OECD, after Portugal and Ireland). By 1992 the corresponding figure had gone down to 48.9 per cent, lowest in the OECD (Table 4.3).

Not counting social security contributions also throws up the regressiveness in Greece's taxation system: in 1992 indirect taxes were about twice the size of direct ones as a proportion of GDP (Table 4.3), a higher ratio than any other OECD country. Greek data confirm the predominance of indirect taxes in the country's taxation system: in 1979–95, direct taxes made up only 30 per cent of the government's

Table 4.3
An international comparison of taxation systems

	Revenue from taxation and social security contributions as % of GDP		Direct taxes, incl. taxes on property, as % of GDP		Indirect taxes as % of GDP		Personal & corporate income taxes plus social security contributions as % of all tax revenue	
	1980	1992	1980	1992	1980	1992	1980	1992
France	41.3	43.6	9.1	9.8	12.7	11.7	60.8	61.9
Greece	29.7	40.5	7.0	9.2	12.1	18.7	52.3	48.9
Ireland	33.2	36.6	14.1	15.8	14.8	14.7	50.8	54.1
Italy	29.4	42.4	9.5	17.6	8.0	11.4	69.1	70.4
Portugal	28.4	33.0	6.1	10.3	12.9	14.2	49.2	54.2
Spain	24.3	35.8	7.4	12.5	5.0	10.2	74.6	66.8
Turkey	17.8	23.1	10.4	8.0	4.6	6.9	65.8	52.9
UK	34.8	35.2	17.7	15.5	10.3	12.1	54.8	53.9
Japan	25.3	29.4	13.8	15.6	4.2	4.1	75.2	75.2
USA	29.3	29.4	16.7	15.5	4.9	5.0	73.6	71.4
EU	36.6	41.4	14.3	15.9	11.3	13.1	62.7	62.5
OECD	34.7	38.8	15.4	16.3	10.6	11.8	63.6	62.0

Source: Revenue Statistics of OECD Member Countries, OECD, Paris, 1994.

Ordinary Budget tax revenue on average, against 70 per cent for indirect taxes (Table 4.4). Even more aptly, the proportion of direct personal taxes in direct tax revenue has dropped, from 58 per cent of direct tax revenue in 1979–90 to 42 per cent in 1991–5, while over the respective periods the proportion of taxes on wealth has gone up from 5.6 to 19.8 per cent (Table 4.4).

On the other hand, Greece's total tax burden (all taxes plus social security contributions) as a proportion of GDP was, at 40.5 per cent, on a par with the EU average in 1992 (41.4 per cent), only a little higher than the OECD average (38.8 per cent). It appears that the tax-evading Greeks are simultaneously taxed as much as the rest of the EU, only less fairly.[15] But this is misleading since, precisely because so many Greeks evade their income taxes, and, in addition, Greece's true GDP is higher than the official estimate,[16] the true income tax burden on the Greek people is less, probably much less, than the above figures suggest.

If that is the case, then, as is sometimes argued, the income tax burden must fall more heavily on those who cannot hide their incomes, like employees, than on the rest, like self-employed professionals, companies, or shopkeepers. Certainly peasants in Greece by law used to pay no tax on their farm incomes, although since 1995 they do so a little.[17] The funny thing is that, again leaving aside social security contributions, the real average personal tax in Greece has been coming down since 1979, from 18 277 drs in that year to 7416 drs in 1994, at 1978 prices (Table 4.5). So has the average tax rate on personal declared income, from about ten per cent in 1979–80 to about five per cent in 1993–4 (Table 4.5).[18] Although this reflects, in part, the regressiveness of the Greek taxation system (that is, the decreasing reliance on direct taxes, a large part of which is personal income taxes), it also proves that the real personal income tax burden has become less for all, including those who cannot hide their incomes as easily as the rest. In fact these may have benefited most. On the other hand, the very regressiveness of the system means that the true tax burden (not just personal income tax) falls more heavily on those with lower incomes anyway, whether they declare those incomes to the Inland Revenue or not.

Dropping levels of real average personal income tax appear all the more curious in light of the following three trends:

First, the real average taxable income as a proportion of the real 'maximum marginal rate' income has been rising since 1979, by 1994 the former being about 34 per cent of the latter (Table 4.5). This means

Table 4.4
Structure of Ordinary Budget Revenue

	Ordinary Budget total revenue (m. drs)	Of which: Non-tax revenue (%)	Of which: Privatisation revenue (m. drs)	Direct taxes* as % of Ordinary Budget tax revenue	Direct personal taxes as % of direct tax revenue	Direct corporate taxes as % of direct tax revenue	Wealth taxes ** as % of direct taxes	VAT as % of indirect taxes	Capital transfer tax as % of indirect taxes
1979	312 360	8.1		28.1	53.2	13.6	7.3		4.7
1980	358 216	9.2		32.1	55.3	13.7	6.4		4.1
1981	422 542	7.9		31.8	54.5	14.2	6.2		3.3
1982	589 148	6.7		31.8	54.0	14.6	5.4		2.5
1983	733 397	7.4		29.6	59.0	9.3	5.8		2.3
1984	929 262	8.7		29.9	61.1	11.1	5.3		2.1
1985	1 110 819	7.7		29.50	64.70	12.20	4.70		2.40
1986	1 457 901	6.8		28.50	58.20	15.60	4.80		2.60
1987	1 723 934	7.4		27.60	59.60	22.40	4.90	43.10	2.30
1988	1 929 027	7.4		29.10	62.70	14.10	5.20	47.30	3.00
1989	2 126 331	7.2		29.40	59.90	21.10	5.30	51.30	3.80
1990	2 878 161	6.2		30.50	54.10	17.60	5.50	51.20	4.10
1991	3 661 457	7.1		30.10	51.00	18.80	16.60	50.10	2.70
1992	4 587 924	10.3	138 156	29.00	42.30	19.90	20.30	49.20	2.70
1993	4 970 981	8.5	26 402	29.90	38.90	21.10	23.40	48.40	2.60
1994	5 861 791	10.6	10 000	33.90	37.80	20.60	21.80	49.60	2.70
1995	6 730 000	11.1	21 000	35.70	39.80	22.00	17.10	50.20	2.70

* As of 1991 including tax on interest on the public's bank deposits, initially at 10 per cent, and from 1.9.1992 at 15 per cent. Direct taxes also include social security contributions by civil servants.
** On bequests, gifts, and property transfers from parents to children.

Source: Bank of Greece Annual Reports.

that the threshold after which the maximum tax rate applies has been brought down.

Second, due to measures aimed at increasing income tax revenue (like assessing a taxpayer's 'true' income on the basis of life-style or property-ownership criteria, and, as regards small companies and sole traders, on the basis of quite arbitrary 'objective' income criteria,[19] applied for the first time in 1995), total personal taxable income has as of 1989 been larger than total personal declared income (Table 4.5). This, considering the progressive structure of Greece's personal income taxation system, should mean, *ceteris paribus*, more tax as a proportion of income – not less, as has actually happened.

Third, personal income tax avoidance (the ratio of tax credits and exemptions to declared income) has become less over time, from 41.5 per cent in 1979 to 8.1 per cent in 1994 (Table 4.5).

At closer inspection, though, there is no oddity here. The government, once in 1989 and again in 1993, simply reduced the personal income tax rate scale sufficiently to offset, and even reverse, the effects of the above three trends. Thus, in 1989 the maximum tax rate was made 50 per cent, down from 63 per cent in 1988, and was again lowered in 1993, to 40 per cent (Table 4.5). In 1994 the three lowest tax rates (0, 5, and 15 per cent) applied to 61 per cent of declared income, and 85 per cent of the taxpayers.

The reversal was in fact more than enough to counter the effects on real average personal income of fiscal drag, although, in line with the regressiveness of the entire tax system, fiscal drag due to the sum-total of direct and indirect taxes appears to have reduced real incomes, particularly low ones.[20] Indeed, taking a broad view of the tax system, the above-mentioned three trends (the decrease in tax avoidance, the arbitrary increase of taxable personal income by the Inland Revenue, the rising ratio of average taxable to maximum-rate income) are consistent with efforts to tax the people more than before.

So, probably in response to protests that those who do pay taxes pay 'too much', a series of governments have alleviated the personal tax burden, which is the immediately obvious one to the taxpayer, and directed their attention to other kinds of taxes, both direct (like taxing interest on bank deposits and property transfers) and indirect – thus re-burdening the citizens but, like we said, in a more unfair way than otherwise. The other solution, namely clamping down on tax evasion, still appears too difficult and/or too sensitive to apply.

Yet it can be done – provided there is the political will.[21] Even now the government is trying to set up a computerised taxation system,

Table 4.5

Greece, 1979–94: Evolution of personal taxation (1978 = 100)

Year	Number of taxpayers	Maximum tax rate %	Applied on taxable incomes over drs	Which in real terms meant drs	When real average taxable income was drs	Real aver. tax. income/ real max. rate income %	Total declared income (m. drs, cur. prices)	Total taxable income (m. drs, cur. prices)
1979	1 437 955	60.0	3 000 000	2 403 846	129 829	5.40	367 389.7	232 986.8
1980	1 547 262	60.0	3 000 000	1 904 791	124 709	6.55	458 671.6	303 902.6
1981	1 631 199	60.0	3 000 000	1 554 931	110 289	7.09	559 382.9	347 097.0
1982	1 723 461	60.0	3 580 000	1 533 514	111 471	7.27	711 172.2	448 494.6
1983	1 805 778	60.0	4 456 000	1 584 028	115 649	7.30	911 405.3	587 471.7
1984	1 881 398	60.0	5 332 000	1 599 519	111 619	6.98	1 079 705.6	700 037.5
1985	1 989 433	63.0	4 880 000	1 171 141	116 227	9.92	1 353 448.1	963 491.0
1986	2 102 428	63.0	4 880 000	1 001 831	124 492	12.43	1 785 242.3	1 274 932.2
1987	2 176 204	63.0	4 673 000	829 158	117 632	14.19	2 054 427.4	1 442 731.5
1988	2 324 268	63.0	4 673 000	727 331	111 720	15.36	2 398 188.4	1 668 325.3
1989	2 405 769	50.0	4 700 000	637 224	166 244	26.09	2 946 831.2	2 949 886.6
1990	2 521 529	50.0	5 362 000	592 002	161 089	27.21	3 675 239.7	3 679 022.1
1991	2 655 446	50.0	6 109 000	571 590	164 053	28.70	4 594 478.5	4 655 951.3
1992	2 904 160	50.0	7 500 000	613 408	160 571	26.18	5 627 573.3	5 701 620.7
1993	3 096 390	40.0	7 000 000	510 717	158 944	31.12	6 473 248.8	6 745 544.5
1994	3 218 723	40.0	7 000 000	460 521	158 163	34.34	7 435 624.9	7 738 152.1

	Tax credits & exemptions (m. drs)	Extent of tax avoidance (= tax cr. & ex./decl. income) (%)	Total tax (m. drs)	Average tax in drs	Real average tax in drs	Average tax rate on declared income	Average tax rate on taxable income	Taxable income as % of declared income
1979	152 346.1	41.5	32 799.1	22 810	18 277	8.9	14.1	63.4
1980	171 100.0	37.3	47 751.4	30 862	19 595	10.4	15.7	66.3
1981	217,669.6	38.9	51 292.7	31 445	16 298	9.2	14.8	62.0
1982	268 111.3	37.7	70 899.5	41 138	17 622	10.0	15.8	63.1
1983	337 221.3	37.0	92 850.2	51 418	18 278	10.2	15.8	64.5
1984	409 917.1	38.0	107 675.4	57 232	17 169	10.0	15.4	64.8
1985	418 204.9	30.9	155 760.1	78 294	18 790	11.5	16.2	71.2
1986	535 305.1	30.0	184 638.3	87 821	18 029	10.3	14.5	71.4
1987	639 438.5	31.1	229 526.8	105 471	18 714	11.2	15.9	70.2
1988	760 642.1	31.7	262 788.8	113 063	17 598	11.0	15.8	69.6
1989	439 120.6	14.9	251 866.0	104 693	14 194	8.5	8.5	100.1
1990	560 589.6	15.3	314 875.3	124 875	13 787	8.6	8.6	100.1
1991	701 847.8	15.3	419 824.7	158 100	14 793	9.1	9.0	101.3
1992	850 147.3	15.1	508 136.4	174 968	14 310	9.0	8.9	101.3
1993	519 151.7	8.0	273 382.7	88 291	6 442	4.2	4.1	104.2
1994	604 075.6	8.1	362 836.1	112 727	7 416	4.9	4.7	104.1

Source: *Statistics of the Declared Income of Physical Persons and Its Taxation*, NSSG, Athens (financial years 1979 to 1994).

called TAXIS (Tax Information System),[22] which purportedly will allow Inland Revenue offices to cross-check company invoices and taxpayers' profiles, on the basis of the Tax Register Number each taxpayer has. On its own TAXIS is not likely to defeat tax evasion, so the government, sooner or later, will have to abolish the confidentiality of bank accounts, reintroduce, only genuinely this time, the 'whence' clause, whereby tax authorities can ask taxpayers to justify their ownership of various assets, and, third, start and finish the country's long-overdue Land and Property Register. It is highly unlikely, at this stage, that the government will have to resort to collecting taxes at gunpoint, the way it has happened, for instance, in Peru![23]

In the past fears of capital flight stopped Greek governments from breaching the confidentiality of bank accounts. Today, however, banks in almost all advanced countries refuse to accept suitcases of bank notes for fear of encouraging money-laundering. Money transfers from one country to another have to take place electronically, mediated by banks. So a Greek government truly bent on tapping undeclared incomes could simply extend TAXIS to include reporting by Greece-based banks of fund transfers overseas or into Greece, at the same time obliging banks (as is the case already) not to effect the transfer unless they jot down the sender's or recipient's Tax Register Number. Also, since most Greeks love investing in property, a full-fledged Land and Property Register would allow the Inland Revenue to have real-time knowledge of the most important elements of most people's wealth, variations in which taxpayers would then be called upon to justify. In this way, a substantial net against tax evasion would be put in place, which would be quite difficult to fool. But of course, the very reason why Greece has still not had a Land and Property Register put in place, is precisely because that would threaten the myriad interests that over the decades have been structured around tax evasion.[24]

The latter is not of course confined to personal income tax. VAT is another area where it is rampant,[25] even though VAT revenue seems to have stabilised at 50 per cent of indirect taxes (Table 4.4). Even this may be a success, when, for example, by 1996 the UK's famously efficient taxation system was finding it increasingly difficult to tap VAT-involving transactions, experiencing a significant fall in VAT revenues as a result.[26] Which of course goes to show that being an advanced country is not a safeguard against informal economy growth and the spread of tax evasion.[27]

Until Greece does put TAXIS in place, and the results are as hoped, couldn't government needs to borrow more in order to service the country's huge and growing public debt be mitigated by means of a crash privatisation programme? Quite probably yes; in practice things are not that simple, as 'rolling back the frontiers of the state' in Greece represents a far more radical breach with the past, and the way Greek society is structured and operates, than, for instance, it was ever the case in the UK. True, the Germans privatised almost everything in East Germany after unification,[28] and, say, the Hungarians or the Czechs have not been far behind.[29] The difference is that in Greece, privatisation is likely to bring about social upheaval, whilst Eastern European countries embarked on their privatisation programmes after they had experienced a revolution.

4.3 THE FAILURE TO PRIVATISE

The Greek state's income from privatisations was 3 per cent of Ordinary Budget total revenue in 1992, 0.5 per cent in 1993, 0.2 per cent in 1994, and 0.3 per cent in 1995 (Table 4.4). The only lasting, big-scale privatisation that ever took place in Greece involved the Hercules Cement plc in 1992, which the state-owned National Bank of Greece sold to an Italian firm, and even that sale was shrouded in still festering accusations of scandal, on the basis of which a terrorist group assassinated the bank's governor, Michael Vranopoulos, in November 1993.

There have been reversals too: after a brief spell in the private sector, the Athens & Piraeus Urban Bus Transport Organisation (UBTO), Olympic Catering and Eleusis Shipyards were brought back in the state fold, the first two just after PASOK's electoral victory in October 1993, the third in 1995.

The UBTO case is particularly interesting.[30] Its original predecessor was nationalised in 1971 by the 'right-wing' military junta which governed Greece from 1967 to mid-1974. After various transformations in the intervening years, while it remained state-controlled and accumulated deficits, its descendant was privatised in August 1992 by an ND government. There was no blanket sale to a single capitalist; the government, fed up with continuous deficits, decided to assume any existing debts of the company, compensate staff made redundant, and sell the buses to eight co-operative enterprises made up of old drivers and new ones wishing to join the scheme. The planning and monitoring of bus routes was still done by a board under the Ministry of Transport. During its short life the system worked more effectively than the old one, yet in December 1993 urban bus transport in Athens & Piraeus was renationalised by PASOK, which now had to compensate the previous owners. The UBTO is currently doing worse than when it was in private hands, while the Greek state still has to meet compensation claims in the order of at least 10 billion drs (about £27 m.) by members of the co-operatives, some of whom have sued the government at the European Court.

In 1991 49 per cent of the loss-making firm Olympic Catering, affiliate of Olympic Airways (another 'problem' company owned by the Greek state), was sold to Rosehill plc. The latter also bought the right to buy another 17 per cent of OC by 31.12.1995, and the last 34 per cent by 30.6.1996. Apparently the sale took place without due process of Greek law, but the party responsible was clearly the Greek state, not the buyer. At any rate, the new owner turned OC around, which began to register profits again. But after its electoral victory in October 1993 PASOK arbitrarily appointed a new Board of Directors in OC, which in turn refused to honour Rosehill's 17 per cent right, on the grounds that the initial sale had been illegal.[31] Subsequently the foreign investor sued OC at an international court, demanding 12 billion drs (£32 m.) by way of compensation.[32]

The Eleusis Shipyards, near Piraeus, were privatised in 1992. In August 1995 the owner withdrew, and the state took over the company again. The owner accused the Greek state of having deceived him in the first place: the financial situation of the Shipyards had proven to be worse than what the state-controlled creditor banks, who were also shareholders of the company, had guaranteed it was; the same shareholder-banks had signed contracts with the Greek Navy, which were not advantageous to the company; and there had been continuous government pressures not to make staff redundant.[33]

Eleusis Shipyards was not the only Greek shipbuilding firm which the state failed to privatise. On a day in October 1995 a group of Korean investors, visiting the grounds of Greek Shipyards plc (also known as Scaramanga Shipyards), in Piraeus, in order to assess the wisdom of buying the bankrupt firm from the Greek state, were shouted out by the workers there. No wonder: rather than face an unknown future in the private sector, involving, no doubt, a lot of hard work for those who would not be laid off, the workers preferred to keep receiving their pay packets from the state in return for no real work, since the Scaramanga Shipyards are heavily overstaffed anyway.

The episode occurred while the European Commission had been applying increasing pressure on the Greek government to stop subsidising the Shipyards. Finally, in September 1995, the government was forced to act.[34] It proposed to the European Commission, and the latter accepted, a plan whereby 51 per cent of the firm would go to ETBA (a state-owned development bank, itself on the verge of bankruptcy), and 49 per cent to the workforce. There would be some lay-offs, under generous compensation terms, while others would be reinstated elsewhere in the broad public sector. The remaining workers would pay for the shares through portions of their wages. In return, the European Commission would allow a huge debt write-off,[35] underwritten ultimately by the Greek tax-payer.

It is unclear, at this stage, where those wages will come from, since the firm is deeply in the red. Also unclear is the extent to which any loan financing will or will not be another form of subsidy, or, more to the point, will or will not be considered so by the European Commission.[36] The example has a double significance: it shows how thoughtlessly the Greek state lost one more chance to clean up one of its ailing companies at minimal cost to itself, with the added benefit of some foreign investment; and it shows the complete inability, as well as unwillingness, of the Greek state and society to come up with a welfare system that keeps unemployment benefits clearly apart from the running of business firms.

In many other cases Greek taxpayers foot the bill for government timidity as regards privatisation. For example, by July 1996 Piraiké-Patraiké, once Greece's biggest textile company, had reached 13 years under government control, had absorbed more than 200 billion drs (£533 m.) in government subsidies and had gone through four failed attempts to sell it off to the private sector, with the government contemplating ways to transfer some of its 1000 remaining employees elsewhere in the public sector and pension others off.[37] The debts of another 'lame duck' under government control, Athenian Papermaking, were on the rise also, amounting to 34 billion drs (£91 m.) by the same month, whilst the debts of Greece's biggest 'problem' firm, Larko, which employed 2500 staff, stood at 55 billion drs (£147 m.), yet the government had no plans to privatise it.[38]

The failure to privatise to any significant extent goes far beyond utility or strategic activities, like urban bus transport, water supply, school building, power generation and distribution, air transport, or telecoms. On social or defence grounds companies involved in some of those activities should perhaps continue under state control, on two conditions: they should never have or hire redundant staff; and they should not have a statutory monopoly of their respective sectors.[39] But the failure also extends to (a) other organisations or enterprises in the broad public sector, including affiliates or 'dependants' of state-controlled banks; (b) once private, 'problem' companies which in the 1980s were taken over by the Greek state for the specific purpose of helping them recover, and then selling them back to the private sector. All of them together – utilities, 'other', and 'lame ducks' – were found in 1991 to amount to 698 entities, 252 of which the state was planning in October of that year either to sell as the first wave of an ambitious privatisation programme, or else wind up.[40] One year later only 27 had been sold, and 60 were in the process of being wound up (Laws 1386/83, 1892/90, 2000/91).[41]

The instrument which the state used in order to deal with private-sector 'lame duck' firms was the Organisation for Restructuring Business Enterprises (ORBE, or, in Greek, OAE), founded in 1983 (Law 1386/83). Until 1990 the ORBE had absorbed 271 billion drs (£723 m.) in subsidies of various kinds,[42] only then deciding (that is, the government deciding) to start reprivatising the companies in its portfolio. By mid-1995, out of 74 'problem' companies which the ORBE had taken in, 27 had been sold, as said, 40 were being wound up, and 7 were operating on 'competitive' terms.[43]

Why the delays and the reversals? In addition to general opposition to privatisation, shared by the majority of Greek society and its political representatives, three reasons, really:[44] (a) There is the ever-present danger that a government attempting to privatise state-controlled assets will be accused by the Opposition, the press, or trade-unionists of selling 'national property' cheaply; (b) the legal framework governing ORBE privatisations in particular is highly vague and self-contradictory;[45] (c) more broadly, the management of state-controlled entities, in alliance with staff, typically undermine privatisation attempts, even if those managers have been put in the helm specifically in order to oversee them.[46] It is, after all, in their, as well as the staff's, interests to do so, especially since the Greek social security system, or the country's re-training schemes, are not equipped to assist the unemployed effectively or for long (see Chapter 7). It goes without saying that PASOK, in particular, is even less enthusiastic about privatising anything than the 'right-wing' ND was in 1990–3, so resisting privatisations at company level does receive political backing from higher up too.

It is hard to see how widespread and effective privatisation can take place in Greece, barring really radical developments. The failure to push it through makes management of the country's public debt that much more difficult, whilst any privatisations that have taken place at all (like selling to the general public 8 per cent of the Greek Telecoms Organisation in March 1996) have been aimed at securing extra revenue for the state budget rather than enhancing the operation of markets, promoting productive efficiency, increasing consumer welfare, or protecting investors.[47] Such concerns appear to be small print for the state no less than for the employees and government-appointed managers who want to keep their public-sector jobs and perquisites.[48]

Notes

1. The Greek Government Budget is composed of two parts: the Ordinary or Regular Budget, which finances functional spending by government ministries and the servicing of the public debt, and the Public Investment Budget, which finances infrastructure projects and other gross fixed capital formation by the government. The two components together make up the Government General Budget.
2. Andreas Papandreou, PASOK's founder and leader, achieved this mainly because he managed to present himself to the electorate as a radical yet feasible and realistic alternative to the Left no less than to the traditional Right. See 'Leader who "hijacked" the Left', *E Cathemerine*, 11.6.1996, p. 24.
3. This was underlined in a series of Bank of Greece Annual Reports: for 1974 (p. 101), for 1975 (p. 91), for 1976 (p. 85), for 1977 (p. 81), for 1978 (p. 110). Sadly, in later years defence spending and preparations, despite the purchase of some aircraft in the 1980s (an act of dubious value as regards both the kind of aircraft bought and the wisdom of neglecting other defence equipment), did not attract the attention they deserved.
4. *Bank of Greece Annual Report for 1978*, p. 100.
5. *Bank of Greece Annual Report for 1981*, p. 94.
6. From 1974 to 1981 ND decisively 'rolled forward the frontiers of the state' by nationalising a number of big private companies, including Commercial Bank, Ionian Bank, Olympic Airways, and Eleusis Shipyards.
7. Cf. Drettakis, 1996.
8. What his efforts threw up was truly amazing: for example, an amount of money earmarked annually for guarding Mount Parnes, to the NW of Athens, from Davelis, a 19th century country robber and kidnapper who used to haunt the area. Who actually pocketed the money, after so many decades, was unclear.
9. See Nicolaou, 1996.
10. For a more detailed account, see Dukas, 1993.
11. See Sterghiou, 1995a.
12. See Vamvoucas, 1994b, 1994c; Kephalas, 1994b; *European Economy* (a European Commission publication), 58, 1994. For example, Vamvoucas, 1994c estimated Greece's public debt in 1994 at 128.6 per cent of 'new' GDP at market prices, rather than 110.4 per cent, after he had included public-sector enterprises; while the European Commission estimated it in

1994 at 154 per cent on a gross basis, which made it the EU's biggest. (Belgium: 142.6 per cent; Italy: 123.3 per cent; EU-12: 69.8 per cent).
13. 'The vicious circle of the public debt', *E Cathemerine*, 16.4.1995, p. 59; reprint of a 1995 *Economist* article.
14. There are countries, too, Denmark being an example, where social security contributions are part of direct taxation, unlike elsewhere.
15. Cf. Claudianos, 1990.
16. See Chapter 2; also, Tett, 1996; Norman, 1996.
17. See Law 2238/94 and *E Cathemerine*, 1994b.
18. In 1995 the average tax rate on taxable income became 5 per cent, while the number of taxpayers increased to 3 840 071, total declared income to 9 748 059.2 m. drs, total taxable income to 9 956 119.4 m. drs (or 102.1 per cent of declared income), total tax to 501 068.3 m. drs, and tax credits and exemptions to 723 614.0 m. drs (or 7.4 per cent of declared income). *E Cathemerine*, 5.3.1996.
19. Cf. Karacottas, 1995.
20. See Vamvoucas 1990b, 1991b, 1994a.
21. See Manessiotis, 1995; Claudianos, 1995; Karacottas, 1994; Marinos, 1994a; reprint of the Casanegra report in *Economicos Tachydromos*, 1995.
22. E Cathemerine, 1.12.1994, p. 23.
23. Bowen, 1991.
24. Cf. Apostolou, 1995; Khaicalis & Collias, 1995; Pirounakis, 1993a.
25. 'More than one trillion drs [£2.7bn], the annual VAT evasion', *E Cathemerine*, 14 June, p. 17.
26. Kelly & Tett, 1996. According to Treasury sources in April of that year 'VAT revenue – at about £43bn – is likely to be £6bn lower than the projections made 18 months ago, and £1bn lower than the Treasury's forecast last November'.
27. In 1995 the informal economy in Germany and Belgium probably amounted to 10 and 20 per cent of formal GDP, respectively (Norman, 1996).
28. Cf. Gaunt, 1991.
29. Cf. Dempsey, 1990; Taylor, 1991.
30. Drosos et al., 1996.
31. Kephalas, 1994a.
32. Delithanassi 1995.
33. Hassiotis, 1995.
34. *E Cathemerine*, 12.9.1995, p. 18.
35. *E Cathemerine*, 22.9.1995, p. 19.
36. *Express*, 16.11.1995.
37. *E Cathemerine*, 17.7.1996, p. 17.
38. Ibid.
39. For a fuller discussion of the pros and cons of privatisation, see Pirounakis, 1995a.
40. Chrysolora, 1991.
41. Tringa, 1994a, p. 23.
42. Ibid.
43. ORBE data as of 20.6.1995. Mimeo.
44. Cf. Kephalas, 1991.
45. Interview by Christos Pikis, MD of ORBE, to Sterghiou, 1995b. Additional

problems keep coming up: for instance, in January 1996 the Commercial Bank of Greece sued ORBE, claiming 8.5 bn drs (£23 m.) in overdue loan repayments, whilst it requested a temporary halt to any change in the legal status of all companies in ORBE's portfolio (*E Cathemerine*, 17.1.1996).

46. Drosos et al., 1996, p. 76.
47. Papathanasiou, J., 1995.
48. Many of those perks are ludicrous, like the 'presence' bonus (see Chapter 3), or the 'productivity' bonus. Not for the first time, the latter was all the rage in 1995–96. Employees with public-sector enterprises, in particular, also receive large discounts when buying from their employers, chief examples being the Public Power Corporation, the Telecomms Organisation of Greece, and Olympic Airways. Overall, dozens of different bonuses (not necessarily the same from one public-sector entity to the next) constitute, in many cases, a second wage or salary, or more. Byzantine in its complexity and obscurity, the structure of bonuses in the Greek public sector makes achieving genuine performance-related pay extremely difficult, even supposing that interested parties might really wish to try it. The system also encourages the casuistic determination of public-sector pay, while it is a source of serious fiscal and cost pressures, as a bonus given employees of one public-sector entity is quickly claimed by other employees, whether in the same entity or elsewhere. Unbelievably, there is even (in the Public Power Corporation – ΔΕΗ) a 'bonus for those who receive no other bonus'! (*E Cathemerine*, 15.6.1996, p. 16.)

5 Inflation, Economic Policy, and the Drachma

'... the core of inflation was influenced only very slowly by the current contractionary monetary and fiscal policy.'

Bank of Greece Annual Report for 1995, p. 24

5.1 THE DYNAMIC OF GREEK INFLATION

Greek inflation is something of a mystery. The bane, as well as the prime concern, of all governments since 1973, it has fluctuated between 31 and 8 per cent, or around a 1973–95 average of 17.5 per cent, with a standard deviation of 5.8 per cent. The mystery, or perhaps miracle, is that during that period it has not become galloping inflation, but then it has also resisted dropping to one-digit levels. Only recently has the Greek inflation rate actually fallen below 10 per cent (8.1 in December 1995 and 7.5 per cent in December 1996, with a rebound to 9.2 per cent in April 1996); whether the rate will continue moving downwards remains to be seen, but it will be far from easy. Within the extreme values of the 1973–95 period, Greek inflation has shown sharp fluctuations: easy to shoot up, easy to come down.

A reasonably steady price level is pivotal to Greece's effort to reduce its public sector's deficits and debt, converge with the rest of the EU, and be part of European Emu. A much reduced inflation rate, say, near 5 or even 3 per cent, should help Greek economic growth quite irrespective of the three targets mentioned; achieving these into the bargain, should offer a real boost to the Greek economy, although the latter's long-term growth prospects depend on much more than securing low inflation. Should Greece fail to 'tame the inflation monster' (in the words of Stephanos Manos, Greek economic minister in 1992–3), her governments will have to service the country's huge and growing public debt under no better terms, and probably much worse, than they have done in the last four years (1992–5), as interest rates on government paper will have to rise in line with the rise in prices. The alternative will be for the Greek state to embrace bankruptcy, as, in an era of free capital movements, depositors and portfolio investors will seek to place their funds elsewhere. Of course a very substantial as well as sudden devaluation of the drachma, combined with the reintroduction of foreign exchange and banking system controls, might leave domestic savers with no option but to buy government paper. The price the economy will pay, though, will be terrible: A lower international credit rating, rapid inflation anyway (on account of higher import prices and pessimistic expectations), exclusion from the process of European integration, and a hard blow to an already battered real economy, to mention but the gravest of the implications. Either way Greece's public debt burden will strangle her, at a time when she desperately needs resources in order to tackle her social security problem, finance capital formation, and counter the Turkish threat.

The fiscal aspect of post-1980 Greek macroeconomic policy has shown a (precarious) anti-inflationary bias only since 1991. Before, primary deficits were incurred as a matter of course in order to help win elections and tackle unemployment. The last ill has been dealt with by fiscal and other means, often irrespective of possible inflationary consequences. One of those means, perhaps the most important, has involved hiring potentially or actually unemployed people in the broad public sector (see Chapter 3). Another factor that, until the early 1990s, helped keep the problem of unemployment at bay, has been the limitless support Greece's young people receive from their parents, and still another the pervasiveness of the informal economy. At best (that is, before 1981), Greek fiscal policy has been mildly expansionary, and at worst (after 1980) strongly so, and for the wrong reasons (see Chapter 4). Lacking a deliberately counter-cyclical dimension, its determinants have come from elsewhere:

- before 1981, government budget deficits were meant, almost entirely, to finance desirable infrastructure and utilities projects
- after 1980, deficits were incurred in order to finance an unsustainable social policy and to curry favour with groups of voters, and
- after 1988, in particular, deficits were run of necessity in order to service Greece's increasingly unmanageable public debt.

Monetary policy, on the other hand, carried out by the Bank of Greece, has often been applied counter-cyclically, which to all intents and purposes has meant a fight to curb inflation. It could be argued that there is a functional discontinuity between fiscal and monetary policy in Greece, the first bearing no relationship to annual inflation rates (Diagram 5.1),

Diagram 5.1
Greece, 1958–95: Relationship between annual percentage change in real government budget deficit and inflation rate; no lag

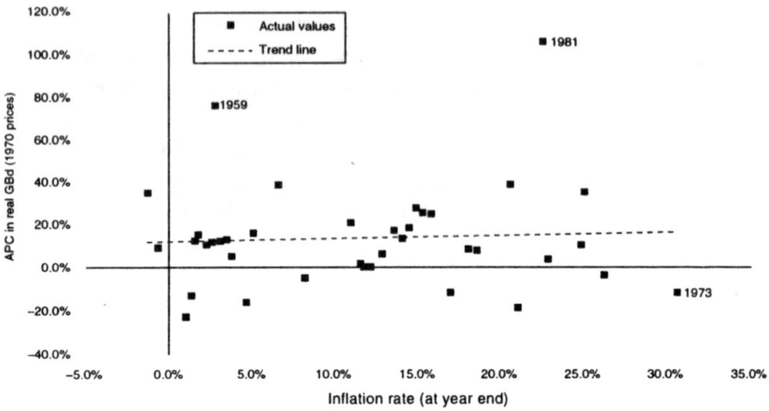

the second attempting, within the confines of government pressures, to remedy the inflationary effects of profligate fiscal decisions and supply-side policy mistakes (Diagram 5.2).[1] Thus, monetary, along with exchange rate, policy have been the only aspects of true macroeconomic policy in Greece, at least until 1990.

This is where any discontinuity stops, though: for from the point of view of the monetary, and ultimately the inflationary, consequences of each policy, the two have overlapped to a substantial extent. The reason is that government budget deficits have in part, yet systematically, been financed either by the Bank of Greece directly (for example, through the printing of new notes) or by government borrowing from abroad in foreign currency – or both. According to data in Table 4.2 the contribution of foreign borrowing in financing the broad public sector's net borrowing requirements (PSNBR) from 1978 to 1995 has on average been 18.2 per cent, and that of foreign borrowing plus government borrowing from the Bank of Greece 31.4 per cent.[2]

Financing government budget deficits by raising foreign debt may well rise in the future – unless Greece manages to clean up her public finances – in order to compensate for the fact that, since 1 January 1994, the Bank of Greece is not allowed to finance the government budget deficit through monetary means. An attempt to reduce the frequency of resorting to printing new money in order to finance PSNBR had supposedly been made in 1983,[3] in the form of raising the contribution

Diagram 5.2
Greece, 1958–95: Relationship between annual percentage change in real money supply (MS3) and inflation rate; no lag

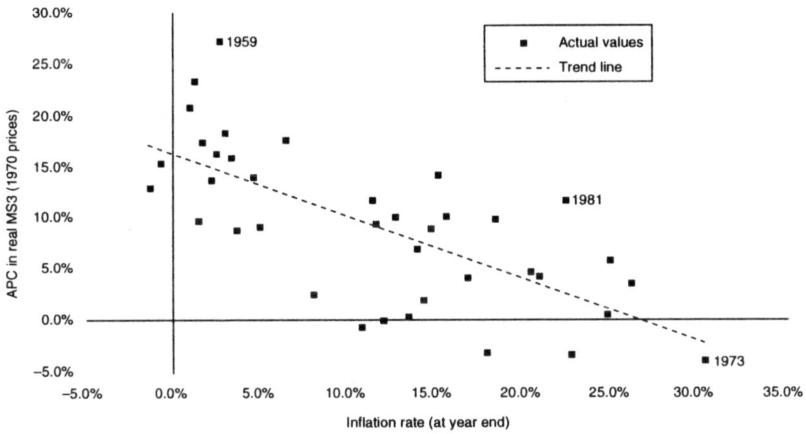

of treasury bills in financing PSNBR from 17 per cent in 1982 to 51 per cent in 1983 (Table 4.2); however, as Table 4.2 shows, the effort was not consistent, while in 1977 the percentage had been higher still. More to the point, financing a PSNBR through treasury bills does not necessarily leave the money supply unchanged; a lot depends on whether the Bank of Greece herself acquires treasury bills through printing new money or from banks; certainly, the Bank's holdings of treasury bills increased throughout the period (Table 4.2).

In fact, the remarkable thing in the recent history of the Bank of Greece is that, given the frequent occasions when it has had to act as the government's banker, she has consistently attempted, through her control of Greece's banking system (Diagram 5.3), to counter the inflationay repercussions of the ways part of the government budget deficit has been financed, or of 'too careless' credit expansion by banks. In this, the Bank of Greece has been reasonably successful (Diagram 5.2), all things considered. Indeed, if the Bank had been less dedicated or effective in her anti-inflationary stance,[4] Greek inflation would have probably gone much higher than its 1973–95 average of 17.5 per cent.

Overall, the main causes of Greek inflation have been a combination

Diagram 5.3
Greece, 1958–95: Relationship between money supply (MS3) increases and total credit expansion by the banking system; no lag

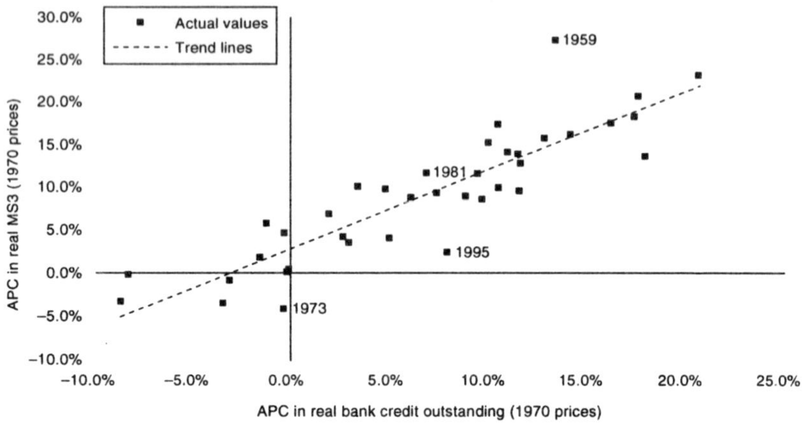

of faltering real economic growth and 'excessive' money supply increases, with a couple of oil price shocks added in for good measure. An x-y chart between Greek inflation rates from 1954 to 1995 and real GDP annual percentage changes delivers an expected negative relationship (Diagram 5.4). On the other hand, a corresponding x-y chart between inflation rates and the previous year ratio of the broad money supply (MS3) to GDP exhibits a positive relationship (Diagram 5.5). The two associations together mean roughly that, with lower growth, given increases in the money supply as a proportion of GDP have tended to raise prices. In fact, since the ratio MS3/GDP has tended to rise over time along with GDP (on account of Greece's low starting point after the war combined with her characteristic as a predominantly agrarian country at the time), it is a good idea to separate the effect on inflation of a rising MS3/GDP ratio as such from the effect on inflation of deviations of MS3/GDP from its long-run growth path. We will see that those deviations become more important as we shorten the time period examined whilst coming nearer the present. The reason is that, when we do that, the influence on inflation of the long-run trend in MS3/GDP is pushed to the background, and the medium-term deviations from the trend come to the fore. A number of statistical

Diagram 5.4
Greece, 1955–95: Relationship between inflation rate and real GDP APC; no lag

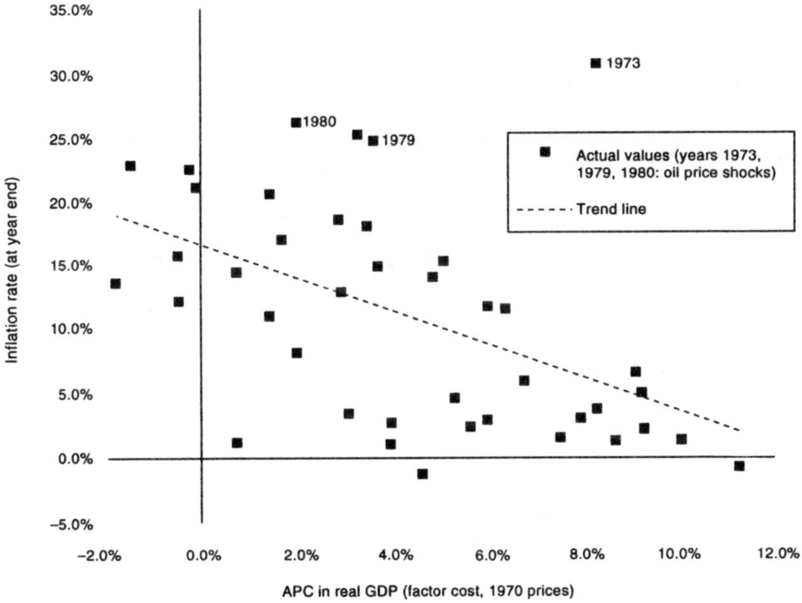

regressions, each for a different time period and each yielding a reasonably good fit, confirm this.[5]

Greece will find it very difficult, however, to achieve, let alone sustain, inflation rates lower than 10 or 8 per cent – the 'core' of inflation in Bank of Greece parlance. For that she first needs to achieve and sustain higher real growth rates than in the 1980s and 1990s, whilst keeping a tight rein on money supply increases. In turn, faster growth presupposes removing all the structural, political, and even social impediments to good economic performance. For example, protectionist distortions of competition in many sectors of the economy will have to go; so must legal obstacles to achieving economies of scale (see Chapter 8), public sector red tape and inefficiency, and so on (see Chapters 3 and 8). The very size of the public sector will have to be reduced as the budget deficits its upkeep involves have been a prime factor behind

Diagram 5.5
Greece, 1955–95: Relationship between inflation rate and ratio of annual change in money supply (MS3) to GDP (factor cost); one-year lag

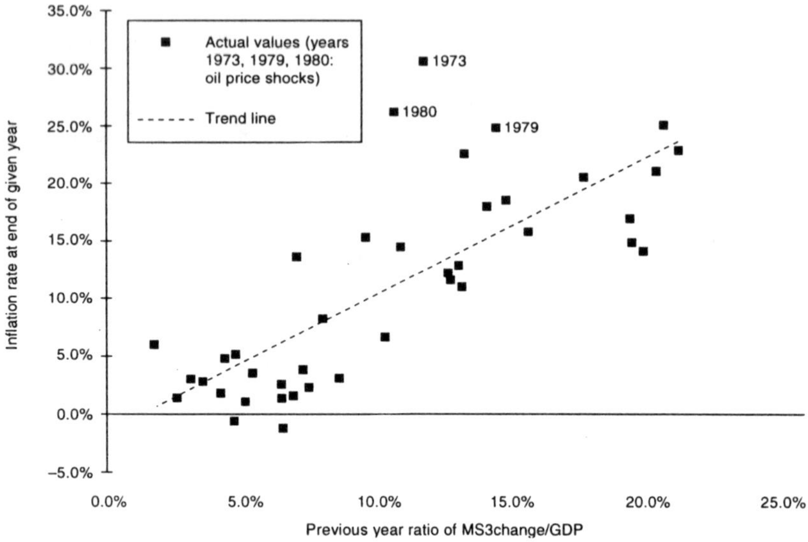

Greece's poor economic performance in the last 20 years or so – as well as a source of inflationary pressures.

There is serious doubt, too, as to whether fiscal policy in the difficult 1990s has assisted the fight against inflation as much as it could, or as much as monetary policy has. Almost all expenditure items are considered 'inelastic' (that is, resistant to cuts). The term as used by politicians means that the items concerned can only get bigger, not smaller, a convenient assumption considering that the state is still planning its annual budget on an incremental, rather than zero, basis. Moreover, in real price terms the government Ordinary Budget for 1996 involved a slower increase in revenue, and a faster increase in expenditure, than the 1995 Budget had achieved. This was forecast to lead to a smaller percentage rise in primary surplus for 1996/95 than in 1995/94.[6]

Expectedly, many of the sector's monopolies – quite a few in their own right – are notoriously inefficient:[7] whether, on account of that, they sell to consumers at higher prices than what is technically possible, or at government-subsidised prices, their contribution to the anti-inflation cause leaves a lot to be desired. So unless the Greek real economy is put on a healthier course, any gains in the fight against inflation will be necessarily precarious, open to reversal at the merest external shock.

Not that such a shock is really required in order for inflation to flare up. As long as the fight against inflation does not extend to restructuring the public sector and, in general, the supply side of the economy, Greece's high real interest rates will, ceteris paribus, keep propping up the drachma – causing both the trade deficit to expand, and FX to flow into the country, which of course augments the money supply. That is why monetary policy alone, even if it becomes more systematically contractionary than it has been so far (which would mostly happen if it were helped by a harshly contractionary fiscal policy), cannot defeat inflation. Although necessary, it is simply not enough.[8]

5.2 A GREEK PHILLIPS CURVE?

A negative statistical relationship between inflation and unemployment, called the Phillips curve, is supposed to exist in the short-to medium run, higher inflation rates being associated with lower unemployment rates, and vice versa. Apparently such a relationship has been confirmed, among others, for the UK from 1861 to 1913,[9] and from 1955 to 1966,[10] as well as for the USA from 1954 to 1969.[11]

The trouble with the Phillips curve is that it tends to change position in response to supply-side shocks.[12] In the meantime, that is, as long as an established supply-side pattern or situtation holds, variations in the money supply cause variations in aggregate demand, in turn causing variations in both the inflation and the unemployment rates, but to opposite directions. This stands to reason: a demand-side boost to the economy will reduce unemployment, but, given the relatively fixed supply-side conditions, will also raise prices. It might be that the extra workers employed will add to output, which should help absorb the pressure on prices, but the latter effect is unlikely for the following reasons.

(a) This idea ignores the reason why those workers were or became unemployed in the first place. Usually this happened because the particular labour-capital-technology mix of the economy (or of specific sectors in it) was not sustainable. For example, product X could be produced more cheaply elsewhere, using either cheaper labour or more advanced technology. If the result is also a higher-quality product, then the pressure on the country, sector, or firm with the wrong 'mix' increases. Under these conditions, a demand side boost to the economy may postpone, rather than induce, any necessary adjustment in wages or in production technology, whilst allowing many firms to keep producing costlier or inferior products than can be had from elsewhere. In such circumstances, any extra output that the extra workers will produce will not be able to absorb fully the pressure on prices resulting from the initial boost in aggregate demand, whilst the gains in employment will be small, anyway.[13]

(b) In addition to that, still assuming relatively fixed supply-side conditions, any extra workers employed will probably have to be linearly combined with larger quantities of other inputs (for instance, energy). But stronger demand for the latter will raise their prices.

(c) Again assuming given supply-side conditions, any movement towards full employment will eventually reach a total output and a productivity ceiling. Then any money supply increases become purely inflationary.

(d) Finally, the form of the increase in aggregate demand is very important in establishing whether the increase will lead to more output capable of absorbing the pressure on prices. If the increase takes the form of more money (representing a net increase in the money supply) for government ministries, agencies, and enterprises, it is then quite likely that rises in the number of workers employed by those entities will far exceed rises, if any, in their real output. Of course this will happen if the corresponding capital to labour ratios drop, but often it will happen even if they rise, should X-inefficiency[14] be present. The situation will only get worse if neither more workers nor more capital are really required, considering the scale or nature of operations of each of those entities. The reason behind these dismal possibilities regarding the public sector is mostly political, involving, that is, a country's political system: in the Greek case there is certainly ample evidence (see Chapter 3) to support this view. Whatever the reason, the result, for a time, will be a Phillips curve: there is pressure on prices since the extra spending does not call forth a commensurate increase in real output, even though employment has gone up. The situation will become even more counter-productive if part of the extra spending, financed through monetary means, takes the form

Diagram 5.6
A Greek Phillips curve, 1979–96: Points after 1978 exhibit a negative relationship between unemployment and inflation rates

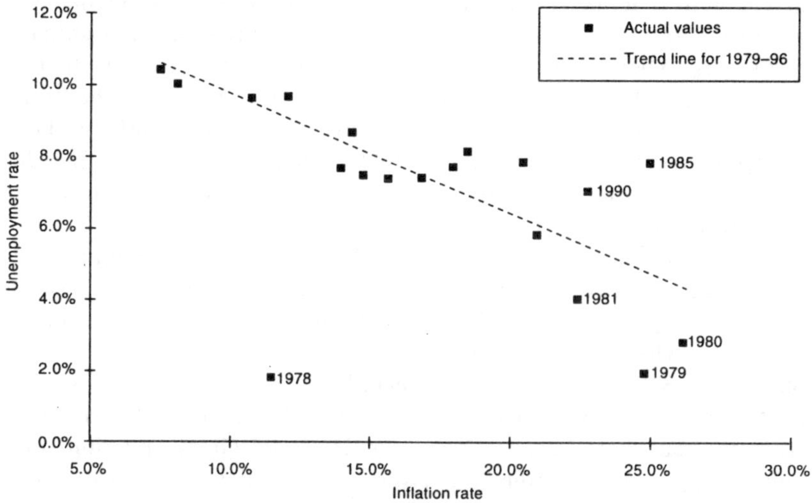

Data from Table A5.4 in Appendix to Chapter 5

of transfer payments. To some extent it will be like giving each citizen a gift of cash straight from the printing press.

In short, demand-side boosts will help an economy in the long run only in combination with positive supply-side policies. Since the latter are often painful to apply in the short to medium run, a number of governments in the past, and certainly a series of Greek governments down to the present, have avoided taking steps to restructure the real economy until, perhaps, the onset of crisis.

A Greek Phillips curve has certainly existed in the 1980s and early to middle 1990s, and even seems to have shifted as of 1979; the last inflation rate vs unemployment rate combination before that year (on the basis of available data[15]) lies far back from the curve, as Diagram 5.6 demonstrates. This should not be surprising: in 1979 and 1980 Greece suffered her second oil price shock, which pushed the economy to a completely new phase in relation to the past. Moreover, Greek governments responded to the shock and its aftermath not through supply-side means, but almost exclusively through borrowing more and spending more. They would recklessly employ people in the broad public sector without regard to needs or consequences (see Chapter 3). As long as this kept on, high inflation rates came to be associated with low unemployment rates. When the 1990s arrived, Greece found herself burdened with a huge and growing public debt. The situation made it necessary for Greek governments in the 1990s to reduce the profligacy of the past. They have even managed to start incurring primary budget surpluses (see Chapter 3), and have stopped hiring people in the broad public sector at past rates – but still have done nearly nothing about effecting structural changes in the real economy. As a result, the decrease in the inflation rate since 1990 has been associated with higher unemployment rates – typical Phillips curve result.

Notably, on the basis of the unemployment trend in Diagram 5.6, Greece can achieve a 5 or 3 per cent inflation rate at the cost of an 11.5 or 12.1 per cent unemployment rate, respectively. Not bad, on the face of it, when her 1995 inflation rate vs unemployment rate combination was 8.1 vs 10.0 per cent. Since, however, the range 10 to 3 per cent appears to represent the 'core' of Greek inflation (as evidenced from the fact that since 1972 only in 1995 did Greek inflation drop below 10 per cent), further reductions in the inflation rate will probably have to be associated with substantially larger rises in unemployment, at a time when there are already about 400 to 600 thousand economic refugees in Greece from the Balkans and the ex-USSR. On the other hand, if Greece fails to 'tame the inflation monster', her already weak real economy will suffer, whilst interest rates on government paper will have to rise in order to service the public debt. This will damage the real economy further. Yet it is not now possible to repeat the 1980s policy, when many of the potentially or actually unemployed were hired in the public sector (a practice which contributed crucially to the present size of the public debt). That is why, in such an eventuality, the country is set to face a stagflation problem of fearful and unprecedented proportions – certainly worse than anything in her post-war economic history.

5.3 WOULD RAPID DEPRECIATION HELP?

In the battle against inflation a relatively strong drachma policy is all-important. If Greece had failed to adhere to this policy, pursued since the 15 per cent devaluation of October 1985, then Greece's average inflation rate from 1991 to 1995 would have probably been about

8 basis points higher than what it was, or about 63 per cent more. This, however, is a conservative estimate, as the calculations have not taken into account the inevitable chain reactions from higher inflation to lower growth and more pessimistic expectations.

The above conclusion has been reached on the basis of a comparison of two inflation rates, from 1963 to 1995: the actual, and a derived one, incorporating the effect of the long-run trend in the price index of imports. The comparison has involved the following steps (see Table 5.1):

(a) Taking the deviations of the wholesale price index of imports from the corresponding wholesale price index of primary and industrial production. The two indices together, it must be noted, make up the wholesale price index of final products for domestic consumption, which in turn is very closely associated with the CPI-based general price level.
(b) Estimating the long-run trend of those deviations in the form of a straight line (see Diagram 5.7).
(c) Finding out the inflation rate corresponding to each of the expected deviations, given the true inflation rate corresponding to each of the actual deviations.

Mind you, a 'strong' drachma pattern emerges, since 1987 at least (as there are no available data before that), only in terms of its real weighted (against basket of appropriate currencies) exchange parity, that is, after inflation differentials between Greece and her main trading partners have been taken into account[16] (see Diagram 5.8). Otherwise, if one looks only at the nominal weighted exchange parity of the drachma, one finds that the currency has been losing value continuously since 1979 at least (Diagram 5.8).

Since the Greek economy has been performing consistently badly since 1973, experiencing low growth, high inflation and current account deficits, the main thing that has been sustaining the drachma's positive real exchange parities is Greece's internationally competitive real short-term interest rates (Table 5.2). These have resulted from governments' need to attract enough savings in order to run big budget deficits, which, particularly since 1988, are dominated by the need to service the public debt. In these circumstances, the overvalued drachma will last only as long as the relatively high Greek interest rates do (unless the real economy improves enough to justify the current parities).

A few Greek economists – certainly not the Bank of Greece herself

Table 5.1
Greek inflation and the exchange parity of the drachma

	Price index of primary & industrial production (PIP)	Price index of imports (IM)	Price index of final products for domestic consumption	Actual % deviation of IM index from PIP index	Trend % deviation of IM index from PIP index	Actual inflation rate %	Expected inflation rate on the basis of trend %
1963	20.8	18.1	20.1	−12.98	−19.76	1.3	2.0
1964	21.4	18.7	20.6	−12.62	−18.50	1.5	2.2
1965	21.9	18.3	21	−16.44	−17.24	5.0	5.2
1966	22.7	18.3	21.7	−19.38	−15.98	4.6	3.7
1967	23	18.1	21.8	−21.30	−14.72	−1.3	−0.9
1968	23.1	17.9	21.9	−22.51	−13.46	2.5	1.5
1969	23.9	18.6	22.7	−22.18	−12.20	2.2	1.2
1970	24.7	20.2	23.6	−18.22	−10.94	3.7	2.2
1971	25.2	22.3	24.4	−11.51	−9.69	3.0	2.5
1972	26.4	24.9	25.8	−5.68	−8.43	6.5	9.6
1973	31.9	30.6	31.4	−4.08	−7.17	30.6	53.8
1974	42.2	40	41.7	−5.21	−5.91	13.5	15.3
1975	45.7	44.6	45.4	−2.41	−4.65	15.2	29.4
1976	51.6	51.3	51.6	−0.58	−3.39	11.7	68.2
1977	58.3	57.5	58.1	−1.37	−2.13	12.8	19.9
1978	64.4	65	64.6	0.93	−0.87	11.5	−10.8
1979	77.6	77.9	77.7	0.39	0.39	24.8	24.7
1980	100	100	100	0.00	1.64	26.2	
1981	124.4	131	126.1	5.31	2.90	22.5	12.3
1982	146.7	150.9	147.8	2.86	4.16	21.0	30.5
1983	175	183.2	177.1	4.69	5.42	20.5	23.7
1984	208	227.2	212.9	9.23	6.68	18.5	13.4
1985	248	280.2	256.1	12.98	7.94	25.0	15.3
1986	292.8	348.8	303.2	19.13	9.20	16.9	8.1
1987	319.6	391.6	333	22.53	10.46	15.7	7.3
1988	352.1	427.9	366.3	21.53	11.71	14.0	7.6
1989	397.6	481.3	413.7	21.05	12.97	14.8	9.1
1990	474.3	541.7	486.9	14.21	14.23	22.8	22.8
1991	563.2	620.6	573.9	10.19	15.49	18.0	27.4
1992	631.2	699	643.8	10.74	16.75	14.4	22.5
1993	706.9	784	721.3	10.91	18.01	12.1	20.0
1994	767	856.2	783.7	11.63	19.27	10.9	18.1
1995	824.7	915.92	841.75	11.06	20.53	8.1	15.0

Source of indices data: National Statistical Service of Greece. Base year = 1980.

Diagram 5.7
Greece, 1963–95: Percentage deviations of imports (IM) price index from price index of primary & industrial production (PIP), and comparison to trend

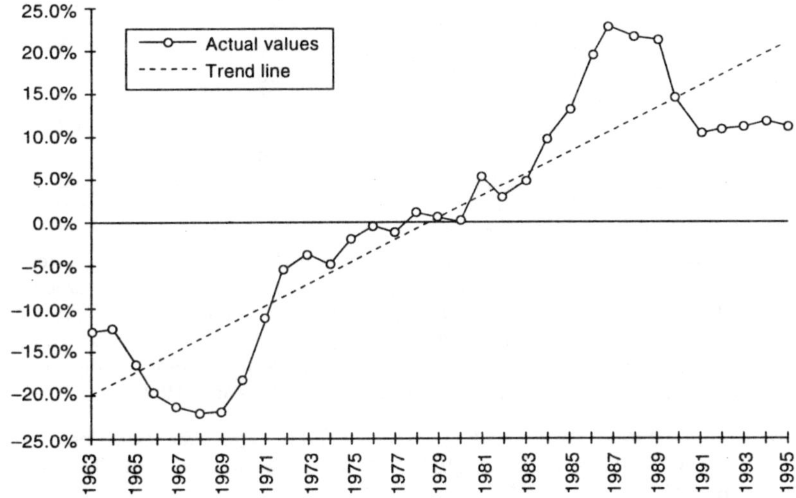

Diagram 5.8
Nominal and real (that is, adjusted for inflation differentials) weighted (against basket of appropriate currencies) exchange parities of the drachma, as estimated by the Bank of Greece, 1979–95; percentage changes over previous year.

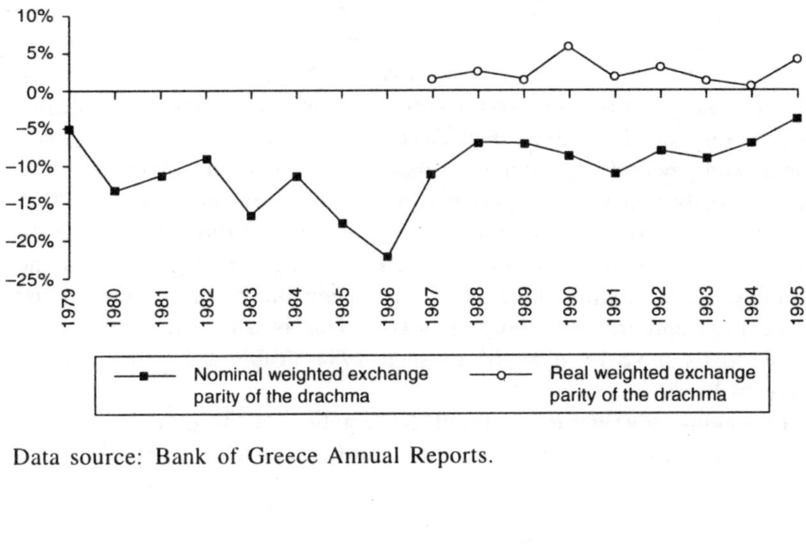

Data source: Bank of Greece Annual Reports.

Table 5.2
Real short-run interest rates, 1990–95: Greece vs five other countries

	1990 %	1991 %	1992 %	1993 %	1994 %	1995 %
USA	3.8	2.1	1.1	1.0	2.7	3.4
Germany	5.1	5.2	4.9	4.0	3.1	2.3
France	6.9	6.1	7.9	6.1	4.6	4.3
UK	7.8	4.7	5.1	2.5	3.7	4.4
Switzerland	3.0	2.5	5.0	2.6	2.8	1.5
5-country average	5.3	4.1	4.8	3.2	3.4	3.2
Greece	2.6	4.2	6.6	5.9	12.1	6.9

Note: To interpret Greek interest rates, one must take into account that Greece abolished foreign exchange controls in regard to short-term capital movements in May 1994, an act which forced the Greek government to raise interest rates substantially in order to stave off a run on the drachma. Controls governing long-term capital movements had been lifted since March 1993, having been preceded by sporadic deregulatory measures since the early 1990s.

Sources: For 1995 & 1994, *Bank of Greece Annual Report for 1995*, pp. 216 & 223. For 1993 down to 1990, *OECD Historical Statistics*, 1960–93, 1995 edition, p. 107.

– feel that the 'strong' drachma policy is wrong,[17] as it encourages imports, discourages exports, and, through the high interest rates it necessitates (though saying this is a bit like putting the cart before the horse), makes servicing the public debt that much more difficult. This view, however, ignores two important aspects of the problem:

(a) A rapid depreciation, let alone devaluation, of the drachma will cause, in all likelihood, a dramatic and probably persistent rise in the inflation rate. The government, no less than banks, will have no choice but to raise interest rates (on government securities and on bank deposits, respectively), first, because of competition for funds between them, and, second, in order to compensate savers-cum-investors, who have already had bitter experience of negative real interest rates: that was the case from 1973 to 1986, and again in 1990 (Diagram 5.9). Not to do so, will cause an unprecedented flight of capital from the country, since capital movements have been increasingly deregulated since 1991 and are now completely free. That is why real interest rates on deposits have been positive since 1991 (Table 5.2): they simply have to be.

Following devaluation or rapid depreciation of the currency (which in the short- to medium-term can mainly happen as a result of an

Diagram 5.9
Greece, 1950–95: When have savers with commercial banks received positive real pre-tax returns?

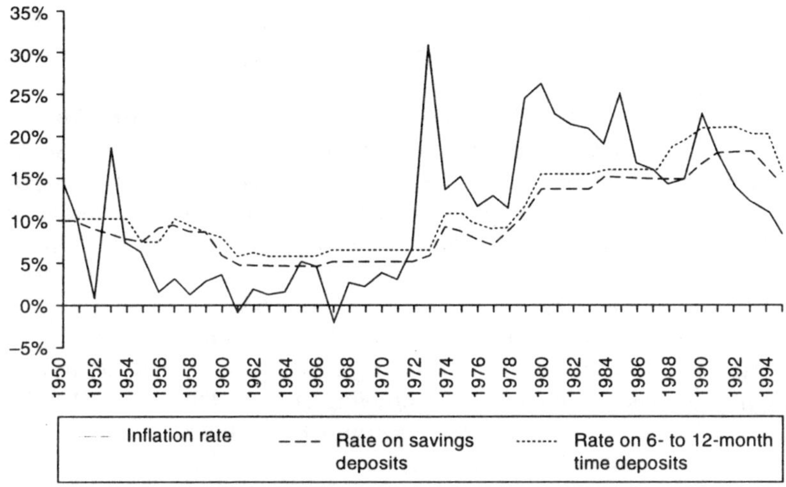

Source: Bank of Greece Annual Report and Monthly Statistical Bulletin, various year

excessive reduction in real interest rates), only a reintroduction of banking system and foreign exchange controls might stave capital flight off,[18] but to do so would be very unwise (see Section 5.1, above). If, on the other hand, the government does raise interest rates following, say, a devaluation, then, again because of the present free regime governing capital movements, this will cause the drachma to re-appreciate fast. Under a deregulated regime, the only reason that the drachma will not appreciate back to its pre-devaluation level when the government raises interest rates again, will be that in the meantime these 'games' and the upsurge in inflation that will certainly take place because of them, will have unbalanced the economy further. Despite inflation, servicing the public debt in those conditions will hardly become cheaper than to-day.

(b) As regards Greece's external trade, there is, in general, something suspect about attempts to enhance a country's international competitiveness through devaluations and such. It is an easy, and therefore temporary, solution, which substitutes tricks for efforts to tackle fundamental problems of the real economy. It may, as such, become counter-productive, lulling entrepreneurs, workers and politicians in a false sense of success. Moreover, in Greece's case rapid depreciation or devaluation would be disastrous for the many firms – let alone the state itself! (see Chapter 3) – who have borrowed in foreign currency over the last few years. It would also discourage imports of machinery and equipment, which have been rising lately (see Chapter 8).

True, on 9 April 1953 Greece's Minister of Co-ordination, S. Markezinis, devalued the drachma substantially, with positive consequences for the economy. But 1997 is not 1953. At that time the majority of Greece's population were peasants, and subsistence peasants at that, incomes were very low, and households' dependence on imports was minimal. To-day the largest part of the population lives in cities and towns, incomes are much higher (about 56 per cent of Austria's, in purchasing power parity units,[19] and without considering the large informal economy), and people have become accustomed to buying imported goods and travelling or studying abroad. These factors mean that a devaluation or rapid depreciation of the drachma will have a large and immediate inflationary impact.

Of course a 'hard' drachma policy that ignores the fundamentals of the real economy (like a widening trade gap) cannot be sustained in the long run, since the markets usually do pay attention to underlying trends, even if a government won't. Apart from being the inevitable consequence of Greece's high interest rates, a 'hard' drachma makes sense as a deliberate policy goal only to the extent it buys the country time in which to effect changes in her real economy. Greece certainly has had ample time to do that since 1988, when her first post-war fiscal crisis came to the fore – and stayed. But that time has been wasted because no Greek government has dared take and enforce the structural and institutional measures which the country's economy needs. For this reason the positive implications of the 'hard' drachma policy (positive by default rather than design) will become increasingly pointless, even though the country cannot afford to relax the policy (see also Section 11.3).

Notes

1. For co-efficients of determination and explanations, see Appendix to Chapter 5.
2. In Greece monetary financing of the government budget deficit has taken

place through the following four asset accounts of the Bank of Greece: (a) the current receipts and payments account, (b) the oil products account, (c) foreign exchange valuation differences, and (d) treasury bills and government bonds. Note that increases in the last account contribute to monetary financing of the deficit only if the Bank of Greece has bought the securities involved from the government directly, as opposed to obtaining them from banks. In addition, annual changes in the aforementioned accounts do not add up to the part of the public sector's net borrowing requirement financed by the Bank of Greece (see Table 4.2), first, because the public sector is a broader entity than the government, and, second, because there are accounting entries and transfers that obfuscate the relationship between the two sets of data. At any rate, as of 1 January 1994 any Bank of Greece-originated monetary financing of the government budget deficit has stopped, on account of it being illegal in the context of Greece's commitment to the European Union.

3. The assertion is contained in the Government Budget Statement for Financial Year 1986 (Athens, Nov. 1985), p. 73: 'Let us not forget that since 1983 financing the Ordinary Budget deficit is done through issuing treasury bills, something which, to the extent that it absorbs surplus liquidity, constitutes a healthy means of borrowing for the State, as in this way resort to printing new money, with consequent inflationary results, is avoided.'
4. See almost all Bank of Greece Annual Reports (BGAR) since 1973. For example, 'as in the previous year, the main aim of economic policy in 1980 was to reduce the rate of inflation', from BGAR for 1980, p. 17. 'The monetary programme for 1987 is consistent with and supports the objectives of the Government's economic stabilisation policy. In particular, . . . a reduction of inflation to 10 per cent by the end of 1987 . . . To achieve the final policy goals, the programme calls for a further significant decline in the growth rate of broad money (MS3), . . . and in total domestic credit expansion', from BGAR for 1986, p. 28. 'In 1990, as in previous years, monetary policy had to bear the main burden of containing inflation, supporting the balance of payments and imposing economic discipline', BGAR for 1990, p. 27. In June 1996 the Bank of Greece intervened once more in the banking system, trying to contain liquidity in the economy in the hope of controlling inflation. See 'New measures on liquidity', *E Cathemerine*, 13.6.1996, p. 17; Kephalas, 1996.
5. See regression results in Appendix to Chapter 5.
6. Pirounakis, 1995c.
7. Papasoteriou, 1991.
8. Cf. Aperghis & Carfakis, 1995.
9. Phillips, 1958. Notice that in its original formulation the Phillips curve associated unemployment rates to wage, rather than price, inflation.
10. Sloman, 1991, p. 522.
11. Baumol & Blinder, 1991, p. 328.
12. See Baumol & Blinder, 1991; Sloman, 1991; and Ormerod, 1994.
13. This situation can lead to a vicious circle where the initial causes of unemployment are not tackled, and a government is called upon to keep pumping money in the economy; unemployment is reduced, or kept at

bay, but only temporarily, while inflation rises. Eventually, unless the supply side recovers, stagflation is bound to appear, causing the Phillips curve to breakdown.

14. Term coined by the American economist H. Leibenstein in 1966, to describe a situation where production takes place at higher than the technically minimum cost, given the level of output.
15. See also Dalamangas, 1995, p. 4.
16. A nominal depreciation of a currency, say, 5 per cent, holding inflation differentials constant, means that a foreigner can now buy a representative basket of the country's goods and services paying 5 per cent less of his own currency. If, however, inflation in the given country has exceeded inflation abroad by more than 5 per cent, then that basket is now actually more expensive to foreigners than before, despite the currency depreciation.
17. Vardas, 1994a, 1994b; Paleologos, 1995. Cf. Hope, 1994.
18. The chances of such controls being successful are slim, as they have never fully stopped Greeks from building their foreign bank accounts. An interesting precedent occurred in 1982, first year of Greece's government by PASOK, which was also the first 'socialist' party in Greece's history to become government. Greek companies and individuals, obviously fearing PASOK's initial socialist promises increased their deposits with foreign banks outside Greece by 170.9% in relation to 1981. By the end of 1982 these deposits totalled \$5.12 bn, whilst by the end of 1992 they had reached \$10.9 bn (*E Cathemerine*, 16.3.1994.)
19. *E Cathemerine*, 4.5.1996, p. 32, on the basis of Eurostat data from 1995.

Appendix to Chapter 5: Variables, Data, Explanations, and Regression Results

A DETERMINANTS OF THE INFLATION RATE

An attempt was made to identify variables which influence the Greek inflation rate over different time periods, and to measure the linear strength of the emerging statistical relationships.

1955–95 period

Two primary candidates were fluctuations in real GDP (1970 = 100), and some appropriate measure of the money supply. The original idea behind the interest in these variables was that inflation is caused by 'excessive' money supply rises – which are not, that is, absorbed by commensurate rises in real output. Thus, when real GDP grows, reasonable increases in the money supply will not be inflationary, whilst they may in fact help the growth of real output. When real GDP drops, and at the same time the supply side of the economy suffers from rigidities, bottlenecks, or – worse! – cost shocks, further increases in the money supply will cause inflation.

There are thus two different factors at work here. One, the secular tendency of the money supply to move with output over the long term; another, the possibly inflationary impact of money supply rises that are not justified by the long-run trend, and therefore deviate from it.

To capture the influence on Greek inflation of these two factors in the 1955–95 period, it was thought, first, that the ratio of money supply annual changes (in absolute, not percentage, terms) to GDP would provide a basis on which to estimate the long-run trend in the money supply, in relation of course to GDP. By 'money supply' was meant broad money, MS3, which in Greece includes currency in circulation, private-sector sight deposits, time and savings deposits, repurchase agreements (repos) in the private sector, and bank bonds outstanding. Once the long-run trend in 'MS3change/GDP' was estimated, the next step was to calculate deviations (dev.) from the trend (actual 'MS3change/GDP' values – trend values). It was found that regression of the inflation rate on the two independent variables together – named for convenience 'Trend ΔM/GDP' and 'Dev. ΔM/GDP' – yielded a co-efficient of determination equal to 59.4 per cent (unadjusted), or 57.3 per cent (adjusted). It is worth noting that the two variables were associated with the inflation rate on a one-year lag, that is, the 1954 deviation, for example, was made to correspond to the 1955 inflation rate. This, because it was thought that it takes some time for 'excessive' money supply variations to affect the price level – an intuition which was borne by the analysis during the exploratory phase.

Three years, however, 'spoiled' the fit considerably: 1973, 1979, and 1980. Unsurprisingly, these were the years of oil price shocks, not just for Greece, but for every country in the First World. Taking their influence into account (by introducing an 'oil-price shock' dummy variable), improved the 'goodness' of the regression to 81.4 per cent (79.9 per cent adjusted).

Finally, it was found that also taking into account the deviations of annual percentage changes of real GDP from their trend values ('Dev. GDP%') yielded an r^2 equal to 84.2 per cent (82.5 per cent adjusted). Overall the regression confirmed the expected positive relationship between inflation and (a) MS growth as a percentage of GDP, and (b) deviations from trend MS growth as a percentage of GDP. It showed too a negative relationship between inflation and deviations of real output growth from its trend path – that is, inflation will tend to occur if real output does not grow fast enough to absorb fully the increases in the money supply that accompany the growth in output anyway.

Other Periods

As we move nearer the present, an interesting development occurs: the influence of the long-run (secular) trend in 'MS3change/GDP' on inflation seems to wane, whilst the deviations of actual 'MS3change/GDP' values from the trend values become increasingly more important. This is logical, since in the medium run the differences between consecutive real GDP levels tend not to be very great. This allows any 'excessive' deviations of the money supply from what is required in order to sustain long-term GDP growth to exercise a less adulterated influence on inflation than otherwise. Of course, at the same time, the shorter the time period becomes, the more other factors, of a short-term or specific nature, are likely to affect the inflation rate.

Thus, inflation rates from 1975 to 1995 were regressed on 'oil-price shocks', deviations of actual from trend 'MS3change/GDP' values, and 'Dev. GDP%'. The resultant linear fit was less good than the previous one, yielding an r^2 equal to 69.7 per cent (64.3 per cent adjusted).

Finally, inflation rates from 1985 to 1995 were regressed on 'Dev. ΔM/GDP' alone. The fit gave an r^2 equal to 57.2 per cent (52.4 per cent adjusted).

Below are the formal results of the above three regressions, including F- and t-ratios, confidence intervals and prob values. Finally, Table A5.3 includes data on almost all the variables used in the regressions, or referred to in the chapter, whilst Table A5.4 gives inflation and unemployment rates, on the basis of which Diagram 5.6 (in the Chapter) has been constructed.

B REGRESSION RESULTS

(a) Period 1955–95:
Dependent variable is: Inflation rate, 1955–95
No Selector
R squared = 84.2%   R squared (adjusted) = 82.5%
s = 0.0365 with 41 − 5 = 36 degrees of freedom

Source	Sum of squares	df	Mean squares	F-ratio
Regression	0.255483	4	0.063871	48.0
Residual	0.047863	36	0.001330	

Variable	Coefficient	s.e. of Coeff.	t-ratio	prob
Constant	−0.035255	0.0157	−2.24	0.0312
Trend M/GDP	1.26685	0.1414	8.96	≤0.0001
Oil shocks	0.159740	0.0220	7.25	≤0.0001
Dev. M/GDP	0.907799	0.1757	5.17	≤0.0001
Dev. GDP%	−0.529571	0.2094	−2.53	0.0160

0.025 confidence interval for 36 degrees of freedom:

(b) Period 1975–95:
Dependent variable is: Inflation rate, 1975–95
No Selector
R squared = 69.7% R squared (adjusted) = 64.4%
s = 0.0312 with 21 − 4 = 17 degrees of freedom

Source	Sum of squares	df	Mean square	F-ratio
Regression	0.038137	3	0.012712	13.1
Residual	0.016545	17	0.000973	

Variable	Coefficient	s.e. of Coeff.	t-ratio	prob
Constant	0.152198	0.0074	20.5	≤0.0001
Oil shocks	0.092631	0.0233	3.98	0.0010
Dev. M/GDP	0.595432	0.1642	3.63	0.0021
Dev. GDP%	−0.926108	0.3628	−2.55	0.0206

0.025 confidence interval for 17 degrees of freedom:

(c) Period 1985–95:
Dependent variable is: Inflation rate, 1985–95
No Selector
R squared = 57.2% R squared (adjusted) = 52.4%
s = 0.0340 with 11 − 2 = 9 degrees of freedom

Source	Sum of squares	df	Mean square	F-ratio
Regression	0.013876	1	0.013876	12.0
Residual	0.010402	9	0.001156	

Variable	Coefficient	s.e. of Coeff.	t-ratio	prob
Constant	0.154596	0.0103	15.0	≤0.0001
Dev. M/GDP	0.685812	0.1979	3.46	0.0071

0.025 confidence interval for 9 degrees of freedom: 2.26

Table A5.3
Data for Chapter 5 regression models

Year	Inflation rate	GDP Deflator (1970=100)	MS3 (outstanding balance at end of year) (m. drs)	MS3 (outstanding balance at 1970 prices) (m. drs)	MS3 (absolute change from previous year) (m. drs)	APC in real MS3	Gross Domestic Product* (GDP) (m. drs)	Real GDP at 1970 prices	APC of GDP at 1970 prices	Trend of ΔGDP% from 1955 to 1995	Deviation of ΔGDP% from trend
1953	18.9%	53.49	4 944.7	9 243.7			48 834.0	91 291.0			
1954	7.3%	59.64	5 948.0	9 972.8	1 003.3	7.89%	56 137.0	94 123.0	3.1%		
1955	5.9%	64.17	7 640.7	11 907.0	1 692.7	19.39%	64 512.0	100 533.0	6.81%	7.77%	–0.0096
1956	1.3%	68.36	9 968.8	14 582.0	2 328.1	22.47%	74 706.0	109 277.0	8.70%	7.59%	0.0110
1957	2.9%	68.70	14 062.1	20 467.9	4 093.3	40.36%	79 598.0	115 858.0	6.02%	7.42%	–0.0140
1958	1.0%	68.85	17 013.9	24 710.4	2 951.8	20.73%	82 955.0	120 481.0	3.99%	7.25%	–0.0326
1959	2.7%	68.99	21 694.5	31 446.6	4 680.6	27.26%	86 448.0	125.308.0	4.01%	7.08%	–0.0307
1960	3.4%	71.56	26 059.0	36 414.1	4 364.5	15.80%	92 460.0	129 201.0	3.11%	6.91%	–0.0380
1961	–0.7%	72.57	30 456.0	41 966.3	4 397.0	15.25%	104 339.0	143 772.0	11.28%	6.74%	0.0454
1962	1.7%	76.34	37 600.0	49.256.4	7 144.0	17.37%	110 390.0	144 612.0	0.58%	6.56%	–0.0598
1963	1.3%	75.64	45 913.0	60 696.8	8 313.0	23.23%	120 402.0	159 171.0	10.07%	6.39%	0.0368
1964	1.5%	78.57	52 271.0	66 526.8	6 358.0	9.61%	134 496.0	171 177.0	7.54%	6.22%	0.0132
1965	5.0%	81.25	58 904.0	72 500.0	6 633.0	8.98%	151 939.0	187 009.0	9.25%	6.05%	0.0320
1966	4.6%	84.44	69 739.0	82 591.0	10 835.0	13.92%	166 354.0	197 011.0	5.35%	5.88%	–0.0053
1967	–1.3%	87.37	81 415.0	93 180.0	11 676.0	12.82%	180 144.0	206 176.0	4.65%	5.70%	–0.0105
1968	2.5%	88.46	95 817.0	108.316.7	14 402.0	16.24%	192 750.0	217 895.0	5.68%	5.53%	0.0015
1969	2.2%	90.62	111 495.0	123 038.5	15 678.0	13.59%	215 853.0	238 201.0	9.32%	5.36%	0.0396
1970	3.7%	100.00	133 657.0	133 657.0	22 162.0	8.63%	258 000.0	258 000.0	8.31%	5.19%	0.0312
1971	3.0%	103.18	163 187.0	158.150.4	29 530.0	18.33%	287 422.0	278 551.0	7.97%	5.02%	0.0295
1972	6.5%	108.55	201 871.0	185 962.5	38 684.0	17.59%	329 977.0	303 973.0	9.13%	4.85%	0.0428
1973	30.6%	130.05	231 969.0	178 368.4	30 098.0	–4.08%	428 216.0	329 269.0	8.32%	4.67%	0.0365
1974	13.5%	156.92	280 392.0	178 686.6	48 423.0	0.18%	507 328.0	323 307.0	–1.81%	4.50%	–0.0631
1975	15.2%	174.55	355 933.0	203 913.8	75 541.0	14.12%	593 181.0	339 833.0	5.11%	4.33%	0.0078

1976	11.7%	202.20	450 792.0	222 941.1	94 859.0	9.33%	728 735.0	360 399.0	6.05%	4.16%	0.0189
1977	12.8%	227.65	558 208.0	245 205.5	107 416.0	9.99%	844 628.0	371 022.0	2.95%	3.99%	–0.0104
1978	11.5%	257.52	704 926.0	273 733.1	146 718.0	11.63%	1 016 709.0	394 803.0	6.41%	3.81%	0.0260
1979	24.8%	304.39	837 069.0	274 998.1	132 143.0	0.46%	1 245 187.0	409 075.0	3.61%	3.64%	–0.0003
1980	26.2%	364.96	1 039 018.0	284 697.5	201 949.0	3.53%	1 523 724.0	417 510.0	2.06%	3.47%	–0.0141
1981	22.5%	445.78	1 417 117.0	317 895.3	378 099.0	11.66%	1 856 745.0	416 515.0	–0.24%	3.30%	–0.0354
1982	21.0%	549.85	1 821 407.0	331 254.0	404 290.0	4.20%	2 288 314.0	416 169.0	–0.08%	3.13%	–0.0321
1983	20.5%	640.72	2 221 528.0	346 722.1	400 121.0	4.67%	2 706 100.0	422 351.0	1.49%	2.96%	–0.0147
1984	18.5%	763.24	2 905 670.0	380 702.4	684 142.0	9.80%	3 317 770.0	434 696.0	2.92%	2.78%	0.0014
1985	25.0%	920.49	3 707 253.0	402 748.3	801 583.0	5.79%	4 136 852.0	449 419.0	3.39%	2.61%	0.0078
1986	16.9%	1 065.74	4 466 804.0	419 125.5	759 551.0	4.07%	4 872 730.0	457 214.0	1.73%	2.44%	–0.0071
1987	15.7%	1 203.98	5 555 463.0	461 423.3	1 088 659.0	10.09%	5 478 103.0	454 998.0	–0.48%	2.27%	–0.0275
1988	14.0%	1 387.50	6 842 503.0	493 154.0	1 287 040.0	6.88%	6 620 725.0	477 170.0	4.87%	2.10%	0.0278
1989	14.8%	1 583.65	8 500 859.0	536 790.6	1 658 356.0	8.85%	7 838 252.0	494 950.0	3.73%	1.92%	0.0180
1990	22.8%	1 890.54	9 799 308.0	518 333.2	1 298 449.0	–3.44%	9 218 908.0	487 633.0	–1.48%	1.75%	–0.0323
1991	18.0%	2 193.49	11 001 948.0	501 572.0	1 202 640.0	–3.23%	11 071 526.0	504 744.0	3.51%	1.58%	0.0193
1992	14.4%	2 463.43	12 588 514.0	511 015.7	1 586 566.0	1.88%	12 531 000.0	508 681.0	0.78%	1.41%	–0.0063
1993	12.1%	2 836.30	14 474 814.0	510 340.8	1 886 300.0	–0.13%	14 359 099.0	506 261.0	–0.48%	1.24%	–0.0171
1994	10.9%	3 111.96	15 755 474.0	506 287.9	1 280 660.0	–0.79%	15 979 071.0	513 473.0	1.42%	1.07%	0.0036
1995	8.1%	3 356.04	17 401 786.0	518 521.8	1 646 312.0	2.42%	17 816 664.0	523 742.0	2.00%	0.89%	0.0111

* GDP at factor cost, Standard System of Accounts (NSSG).

Table A5.3
Data for Chapter 5 regression models (*continued*)

Year	Government General Budget* deficit (GGBD) (m. drs)	Real GGBD (m. drs)	APC of real GGBD	GGBD as% of GDP	Effects of oil price shocks	Annual change in MS3 as % of GDP	Trend of MS3 change as % of GDP (1955–95) (lag variable)	Deviation of ΔM/GDP from trend (lag variable)	Total bank credit (TBC) to the economy (m. drs)	Real TBC (1970=100) (m. drs)	APC of real TBC
1953					0				8 215	15 358	
1954					0	1.79%			10 511	17 623	14.75%
1955					0	2.62%	3.51%	–0.0172	11 576	18 040	2.37%
1956					0	3.12%	3.85%	–0.0123	14 635	21 407	18.67%
1957	–2 013	–2 930.0		–2.53%	0	5.14%	4.19%	–0.0108	18 631	27 118	26.68%
1958	–1 554	–2 257.0	–22.97%	–1.87%	0	3.56%	4.54%	0.0060	21 964	31 899	17.63%
1959	–2 741	–3 973.1	76.04%	–3.17%	0	5.41%	4.88%	–0.0132	24 963	36 184	13.43%
1960	–3 205	–4 478.6	12.72%	–3.47%	0	4.72%	5.23%	0.0019	29 234	40 851	12.90%
1961	–3 548	–4 888.9	9.16%	–3.40%	0	4.21%	5.57%	–0.0085	32 635	44 969	10.08%
1962	–4 296	–5 627.8	15.11%	–3.89%	0	6.47%	5.91%	–0.0170	37 947	49 711	10.55%
1963	–3 695	–4 884.8	–13.20%	–3.07%	0	6.90%	6.26%	0.0021	45 400	60 018	20.73%
1964	–4 304	–5 477.8	12.14%	–3.20%	0	4.73%	6.60%	0.0030	52 632	66 986	11.61%
1965	–5 156	–6 346.1	15.85%	–3.39%	0	4.37%	6.95%	–0.0222	59 264	72 944	8.89%
1966	–4 480	–5 305.6	–16.40%	–2.69%	0	6.51%	7.29%	–0.0292	68 717	81 381	11.57%
1967	–6 251	–7 154.3	34.84%	–3.47%	0	6.48%	7.63%	–0.0112	79 434	90 913	11.71%
1968	–7 057	–7 977.6	11.51%	–3.66%	0	7.47%	7.98%	–0.0150	91 823	103 801	14.18%
1969	–7 972	–8 797.4	10.28%	–3.69%	0	7.26%	8.32%	–0.0085	111 004	122 496	18.01%
1970	–9 236	–9 236.0	4.99%	–3.58%	0	8.59%	8.66%	–0.0140	134 390	134 390	9.71%
1971	–10 691	–10 361.0	12.18%	–3.72%	0	10.27%	9.01%	–0.0042	162 817	157 791	17.41%
1972	–15 590	–14 361.4	38.61%	–4.72%	0	11.72%	9.35%	0.0092	199 149	183 455	16.26%
1973	–16 466	–12 661.2	–11.84%	–3.85%	1	7.03%	9.70%	0.0203	237 725	182 794	–0.36%
1974	–23 286	–14 839.6	17.20%	–4.59%	0	9.54%	10.04%	–0.0301	286 285	182 442	–0.19%
1975	–32 486	–18 611.2	25.42%	–5.48%	0	12.73%	10.38%	–0.0084	353 631	202 595	11.05%
1976	–37 626	–18 608.1	–0.02%	–5.16%	0	13.02%	10.73%	0.0201	439 967	217 588	7.40%
1977	–44 963	–19 751.0	6.14%	–5.32%	0	12.72%	11.07%	0.0195	547 689	240 585	10.57%

1978	−51 623	−20 046.0	1.49%	−5.08%	0	14.43%	11.42%	0.0130	678 432	263 445	9.50%
1979	−67 341	−22 123.2	10.36%	−5.41%	1	10.61%	11.76%	0.0267	800 802	263 083	−0.14%
1980	−77 694	−21 288.6	−3.77%	−5.10%	1	13.25%	12.10%	−0.0149	988 259	270 789	2.93%
1981	−195 150	−43 777.1	105.64%	−10.51%	0	20.36%	12.45%	0.0081	1 290 415	289 473	6.90%
1982	−194 998	−35 463.7	−18.99%	−8.52%	0	17.67%	12.79%	0.0757	1 633 606	297 099	2.63%
1983	−315 460	−49 235.0	38.83%	−11.66%	0	14.79%	13.13%	0.0453	1 897 093	296 086	−0.34%
1984	−405 035	−53 067.9	7.78%	−12.21%	0	20.62%	13.48%	0.0131	2 368 630	310 339	4.81%
1985	−660 655	−71 772.2	35.25%	−15.97%	0	19.38%	13.82%	0.0680	2 820 414	306 404	−1.27%
1986	−675 233	−63 357.9	−11.72%	−13.86%	0	15.59%	14.17%	0.0521	3 429 302	321 775	5.02%
1987	−953 504	−79 195.7	25.00%	−17.41%	0	19.87%	14.51%	0.0108	4 006 148	332 741	3.41%
1988	−1 247 116	−89 882.4	13.49%	−18.84%	0	19.44%	14.85%	0.0502	4 707 061	339 248	1.96%
1989	−1 815 025	−114 610.6	27.51%	−23.16%	0	21.16%	15.20%	0.0424	5 698 742	359 850	6.07%
1990	−2 244 387	−118 716.6	3.58%	−24.35%	0	14.08%	15.54%	0.0562	6 564 084	347 206	−3.51%
1991	−2 824 913	−128 786.0	8.48%	−25.52%	0	10.86%	15.89%	−0.0180	6 951 409	316 910	−8.73%
1992	−3 753 519	−152 369.6	18.31%	−29.95%	0	12.66%	16.23%	−0.0537	7 681 018	311 802	−1.61%
1993	−4 322 877	−152 412.4	0.03%	−30.11%	0	13.14%	16.57%	−0.0391	8 107 072	285 832	−8.33%
1994	−5 723 524	−183 920.3	20.67%	−35.82%	0	8.01%	16.92%	−0.0378	8 615 116	276 839	−3.15%
1995	−5 861 768	−174 663.4	−5.03%	−32.90%	0	9.24%	17.26%	−0.0925	10 026 183	298 751	7.91%
							17.60%	−0.0836			

* The Government General Budget is composed of the Regular and the Public Invesment Budgets. It does not include the important (deficit) category 'management of agricultural products and government supplies'.

Source: Bank of Greece 1980, pp. 83–7, Bank of Greece Annual Reports from 1979 to 1995, Bank of Greece Monthly Statistical Bulletin, and, for GDP, National Accounts as supplied by the NSSG.

Table A5.4
A Greek Phillips curve?
Comparison of Greek inflation and unemployment rates from 1978 to 1996

	Inflation rate	Unemployment rate	Trend * unemployment rate
1978	11.5%	1.8%	
1979	24.8%	1.9%	4.8%
1980	26.2%	2.8%	4.3%
1981	22.5%	4.0%	5.6%
1982	21.0%	5.8%	6.1%
1983	20.5%	7.9%	6.3%
1984	18.5%	8.1%	6.9%
1985	25.0%	7.8%	4.7%
1986	16.9%	7.4%	7.5%
1987	15.7%	7.4%	7.9%
1988	14.0%	7.7%	8.4%
1989	14.8%	7.5%	8.2%
1990	22.8%	7.0%	5.5%
1991	18.0%	7.7%	7.1%
1992	14.4%	8.7%	8.3%
1993	12.1%	9.7%	9.1%
1994	10.8%	9.6%	9.5%
1995	8.1%	10.0%	10.4%
1996	7.5%	10.4%	10.6%
If	5.0%	then	11.5%
If	3.0%	then	12.1%

* Trend equation for 1979–96: Unempl. rate = 0.13141 – 0.335645 * infl. rate.

Source: On inflation (year-end values), Bank of Greece Annual Reports; on unemployment, *Epiloghe*, 1996, p. 24. On 1996 unemployment rate, *Eleutherotypia*, 6.4.1997, p. 93. Original data from NSSG.

6 Banking, Insurance, and the Stock Exchange

'In pursuing a tight credit policy in 1979, the monetary authorities took special care not to create any problems for the financing of particularly desirable activities [].'

Bank of Greece Annual Report for 1979, p. 60.

6.1 AN OVERVIEW OF THE BANKING SYSTEM

The importance of banks in Greece cannot be overstated. All the bigger banks, and some of the smaller ones, are owned by the State. The latter traditionally, and, some might say, unscrupulously, has used the banking system, ostensibly in order to streamline the Greek post-war development effort, but ultimately in order to support 'problem' companies and inefficient public-sector enterprises (even beyond the point where some of the banks became 'problem' cases themselves), in order to finance a government's political friends of the day, in order to exercise social policy via bank money, and in order to dispose easily and conveniently of treasury bills meant to finance the public-sector debt. That is a pity since the virtual absence of other sources of external business finance until 1987 had assigned to banks the responsibility of seeing that the Greek people's savings were invested wisely. Indeed, were it not for the Bank of Greece, the country's central bank, which by and large has done a good job supervising the banking system, the irresponsibility of Greek governments, especially after 1980, would have led many state-controlled banks to direr straits, and much sooner, that has actually been the case. Having said that, it is also true that on many occasions Greek banks have been bulwarks against the rough seas of a frail economy. For instance, Greece's four biggest commercial banks (one of them private) helped the government defend the drachma during the May–June 1994 currency crisis.

The Greek banking system is dominated by state-owned banks. On the deposit side, the biggest in 1994 were the National (Ethniké), which is by far the biggest (with 29 per cent of deposits), the Agricultural

(Agrotiké), the Mortgage (Ktematiké; biggest real estate bank), ETBA (biggest investment bank; it's financed through bonds though, not deposits), and the Commercial (Emporiké). On the loan side, the biggest were the National (with 17 per cent of outstanding loans), the Agricultural, the Commercial, the Post Office Savings Bank (TT), and the Mortgage. Only two of these – the National and the Commercial – were true commercial banks in 1994. For example, the Agricultural Bank of Greece, or ATE, was a specialised credit institution until July 1991, when it became a plc as an ostensible first step towards independence from the state. The practical significance of the transformation was realised three years later, when ATE was put on a par with the other commercial banks in that it was obliged to redeposit a certain percentage of its deposits with the Bank of Greece for liquidity control purposes. Banks which, at the time of writing, were still free of this obligation were the other remaining specialised credit institutions: the real estate banks, the investment banks, the TT, and the Loans & Consignments Fund (LCF) – all state-owned, but for a small real estate bank (Aspis Bank, affiliate of an insurance company).

The importance of the National Bank in the Greek banking system extends beyond the percentages of deposits and loan business it accounts for directly, as it has significant shareholdings in other banks. For instance, in 1994 it had 56.81 per cent of the investment bank ETEBA, 44.62 per cent of the Mortgage Bank, and 86.74 per cent of the Housing Bank. The Commercial Bank also had such interests: 62.59 per cent of the Ionian Bank (fourth biggest commercial bank in Greece), 66.83 per cent of the small Attica Bank, and 86.90 per cent of the very small Investment Bank. Many of the bigger Greek banks have additional interests in non-banks, ranging from agricultural co-operatives to construction, leasing, hotel, insurance, investment, credit card, and research and consultancy companies, as well as unit trusts.

The private-sector banks are topped by the Alpha Credit Bank (which is actually the third biggest commercial bank in the country, and the sixth biggest overall), and the ErgoBank. By 1994 there were seven public-sector and eight private-sector commercial banks, and 24 foreign banks in Greece.

Table 6.1 presents a break-down of deposit and bond liabilities, as well as of loan assets, in the Greek banking system by type of bank. The state-controlled banks altogether account for the largest percentage of either. In 1994 they had 76.6 per cent of deposit and bond liabilities (against 86.9 per cent in 1978), and 73.9 per cent of loan assets (against 88.3 per cent in 1978). Greece's banking system is clearly

Table 6.1
Assets and liabilities, typical of banking business, of banks in Greece, 1978–94

Shares of deposits and bank-issued bonds by type of bank* in Greece, 1978–94

	1978 (%)	1982 (%)	1986 (%)	1990 (%)	1994 (%)
Public–sector commercial (7 banks)	59.0	57.2	59.1	55.4	45.3
Private–sector commercial (8 banks)	5.1	5.5	6.8	9.0	13.4
Agricultural Bank	6.0	8.1	9.9	11.0	11.5
Post Office Savings Bank	13.2	10.9	9.5	8.5	7.9
Real estate banks*	3.8	4.4	6.0	7.1	7.3
Investment banks***	4.9	3.6	2.6	1.9	4.7
Total of Greek banks	92.0	89.7	93.8	92.8	90.0
Foreign banks (24 banks)	8.0	10.3	6.2	7.2	10.0

Shares of loan advances and credit discounts by type of bank* in Greece, 1978–94

	1978 (%)	1982 (%)	1986 (%)	1990 (%)	1994 (%)
Public–sector commercial (7 banks)	44.6	39.9	39.3	36.0	32.2
Agricultural Bank	20.4	20.3	20.3	22.9	20.6
Private–sector commercial (8 banks)	3.7	3.5	5.0	7.3	12.6
Real estate banks	8.7	8.3	8.5	10.2	9.5
Investment banks	6.3	5.5	5.5	7.1	8.9
Post Office Savings Bank	8.3	11.7	13.7	10.6	2.8
Total of Greek banks	91.9	89.2	92.3	94.3	86.5
Foreign banks (24 banks)	8.1	10.8	7.7	5.7	13.5

* The Loans & Consignments Fund is not included.
** Mortgage Bank, Housing Bank, and, since 1993, Aspis Bank (privately owned).
*** ETBA, ETEBA, Investment Bank.

Sources: *Epiloghe*; ICAP; the Post Office Savings Bank. The number of banks cited is at end of 1994.

oligopolistic. In 1989 the top four banks had 64 per cent of the bank market (Table 6.2). Only Ireland and Holland showed a higher concentration ratio that year. Still, considering that all four Greek banks were state-owned (as well as three out of the top four commercial banks), Greece's must have been the least competitive market.

It could also be argued that Greece's apparent top place in the EU in terms of number of inhabitants per bank branch (Table 6.2) is a reflection of her oligopolistic banking system; namely, that Greece's banks do not make an as great an effort as those of other countries to get near the customer and expand their deposit base. There is an element of truth in that, but one must take into account the nature of the country also. With a total area three times that of Holland, with some of the poorest regions in the EU (Epirus, Thrace, the Aegean), and with nearly a third of her population living in Greater Athens and Piraeus, Greece tends to render the building of very extensive deposit collection networks both unnecessary and loss-inducing. In many cases (for instance, many islands) the only reason to open a bank branch has been in order to assist the overall development of the place – not to make a profit. The only banks inclined to think in those terms, as well as capable of shouldering the relevant costs, have been the big state-owned banks, particularly the National and the Agricultural. Needless to say, as soon as they open a branch in some unprofitable, backward place, other banks find it even harder to open there too, and compete for the tiny pool of local savings. This is one area where the oligopolistic element of the Greek banking system comes to the fore, but obviously with socially beneficial results.[1]

In other respects, though, the oligopolistic structure of the system does not always work in the best interest of the customer. Table 6.2 shows that in 1993 Greece topped the EU league of rate spreads (the difference between bank lending and borrowing nominal rates). By contrast Britain, Luxembourg, and Spain, who have very competitive banking systems[2], appear to have enjoyed the lowest spreads.

Table 6.2 shows another interesting relationship. In 1992 Greek banks required more employees than banks in any other EU country in order to obtain and sustain a given ECU amount of total assets (column g). Greece's position was not accidental. In part it reflected the lower development level of the country in comparison to most other EU countries. Portugal, for example, the other least-developed EU member, was second in the EU after Greece in this respect. In part, however, Greece's low asset/employee ratio resulted from the bigger Greek banks being state-owned; from the state systematically trying to contain unemployment

Table 6.2
The commercial banking sector of the European Union around 1990–1

Country	Banks	Bank employees	Percentage of bank employees to service sector employees	Total assets (ECUs b.)	Advances (ECUs b.)	Total assets per bank employee (ECUs m.)	Advances to total assets (%)	Inhabitants per branch	Rate spreads (basis points) in 1993	Deposit market share of top 4 banks* (%)	Deposit market share of foreign banks (%)
(a)	(b)	(c)	(d)	(e)	(f)	(g)	(h)	(i)	(j)	(k)	(l)
Gt Britain	511	397 400	2.8	1 750.8	1 245.9	4.41	71.2		2.24 (6)	27	60
France	419	200 400	2.4	1 119.6	413.6	5.59	36.9	1 200		42	16
Italy	319	327 192		822.8	359.7	2.51	43.7	2 000	7.73 (4)	25	3
Germany	334	221 700	2.6	760.5	527.6	3.43	69.4	1 500	6.74 (2)	15	4
Holland	109	115 563	2.2	448.2	308.4	3.88	68.8	1 700	6.55 (1)	69	10
Spain	159	152 025	2.5	381.5	174.4	2.51	45.7		2.13 (1)	21	11
Luxembourg	213	17 592	9.4	357.9	88.3	20.34	24.7	1 750	2.58 (5)	24	91
Belgium	93	49 574	2.9	325.4	169.3	6.56	52.0	850	5 (1)	42	46
Denmark	119	47 560	2.9	123.6	63.3	2.60	51.2	1 050	3.9 (3)	47	1
Portugal	35	60 722		96.1	37.0	1.58	38.5	5 000	5.4 (4)	57	3
Ireland	43	20 731	3.0	55.5	27.3	2.68	49.2	7 000		74	11
Greece	40	40 188	2.8	47.6	12.6	1.18	26.5	7 700	9 (3)	64	7
Total	2394	1 650 647		6 289.5	3 427.4	3.81	54.5				

Sources: Columns (b), (c), (e) to (h): *E Cathemerine*, 30.8.1994, on the basis of European Union Banking Federation data for 1992.
Column (d): *Express*, 16.1.1994, on the basis of EuroStat data for 1991.
Column (i): *Ta Nea*, 2.3.1992, p. 18, on the basis of Bank Employees Union of Greece data for 1991.
Column (j): *Galiatsos*, 1994, p. 14. Legend: (1) = Nov.; (2) = Oct.; (3) = June; (4) = July; (5) = March; (6) = August.
Columns (k), (l): *Express*, 10.1.1991, p. 8, on the basis of European Commission data for 1989.

* There are some question marks on the criteria used. For instance, it appears that total deposits for Greece include those with the Post Office Savings Bank. Yet the latter, although big enough, has not been included among the top four banks, probably because it is not a commercial bank; but then the Agricultural Bank and the Mortgage Bank apparently have been included, along with the truly commercial banks National (the biggest) and Commercial.

through hiring people rather than giving them unemployment benefits and retraining them; and from the state extending the same policy to the banks it has traditionally controlled.

6.2 FROM REGULATION TO DEREGULATION

The deregulation of the Greek banking system, grudgingly begun in the late 1980s, was nearly completed in 1994. In that year the government took three very important steps:

(a) It freed short-term capital movements in addition to long-term, which had already been substantially freed in 1993.
(b) It removed the obligation of banks to buy government IOUs.
(c) It also removed their obligation to finance public-sector enterprises and social security organisations (ΔΕΚΟ).

Prior to 1994 the system was heavily regulated, although a number of controls had been gradually removed from the late 1980s to the early 1990s. Until the end of 1988 the core of the control mechanism was the so-called 'engage–disengage' (or 'e–d') system governing the allocation of loanable funds in the context of broader monetary policy targets, but even after 1988 specific controls remained. The 'e–d' system consisted in compelling banks to redeposit ('engage') at the Bank of Greece different amounts of their deposits in direct proportion to their advances to designated sectors, and in allowing them to receive back ('disengage') other amounts, again in proportion to other types of lending. In this way unfavoured sectors would be penalised, and favoured ones rewarded. The 'e–d' system, however, had an additional function, ostensibly at least: in conjunction with lending and borrowing rates determined by the Bank of Greece, it was supposed to equalise effective returns on lending business between different banks.

It turned out that the system did not manage to achieve either goal fully. The reason was that it ignored the level of risk associated with different sectors of the economy.[3] Banks, on the other hand, had to take this into account in determining the structure of their loan portfolios, at least in so far as they could. Different sectors would obviously mean different degrees of risk to different banks. Some banks, therefore, would be willing at any one time to have larger amounts of their funds 'engaged' at the Bank of Greece than what was dictated by nominal 'engagement' and interest rate profiles, in order to extend loans to less risky sectors. Moreover, for the Bank of Greece to have achieved true return parity between banks through the 'e–d' mechanism, she would have needed far more accurate information on loan demand than it was possible to have.[4]

In the context of the mechanism just described, but also in addition to it, specific statutes were indicative of the priorities adopted by a series of Greek governments. Thus:

(a) In 1981 commercial banks' compulsory investments in treasury bills (government IOUs) were raised from 36 to 37 per cent of their drachma and FX deposits. In August 1984 that was raised to 38 per cent, in 1989 to 39 per cent, and in 1990 to 40 per cent, also allowing investment in bonds issued by public-sector enterprises. In 1991 that was reduced to 35 and then to 30 per cent; in 1992 it was reduced to 20 per cent and then to 15 per cent. In 1994 the obligation was removed.
(b) In 1981 commercial banks were required to finance public-sector enterprises, to the tune of 2.5 per cent of their drachma and FX deposits as of December of that year. In 1984 that was raised to 3.5 per cent, and in 1987 to 10.5 per cent, also allowing financing of public-sector social security organisations out of the deposits earmarked so. In 1990, however, that was reduced to 9.5 and then to 9 per cent. In 1994 the obligation was removed.
(c) In 1981 the obligation of Greek banks to set aside 15 per cent of their deposits for medium and long term loans meant to finance 'productive' investments was extended to foreign banks. In 1986 that was raised to 16, 17, 18.5, and finally 19.5 per cent, the difference from 15 per cent meant to finance public-sector enterprises and social security organisations. In July 1987 the obligation was removed.
(d) In 1981 banks' compulsory 'engagement' of 7 per cent of their deposits for loans to small-scale manufacturing firms was raised to 10 per cent. In 1992 that was reduced to 8, 7, 6.5, and 5 per cent, and the obligation was finally removed in July 1993.

Until 23 November 1987 the Bank of Greece determined the interest rates and other terms on time deposits and savings deposits with a notice period. Until the first week of June 1989 it also determined the rates on current accounts and ordinary savings accounts. Until 8 March 1993 it did require banks to preserve a minimum rate on savings deposits, though. Full deregulation of time deposits happened only on

5 August 1994, when the 7-day limit on such deposits was removed. Broadly over the same period lending rates were deregulated also.

Nowadays the Bank of Greece exercises control over the banking system through reserve requirements and its own discount rate, whilst open market operations had still not been introduced by the middle of 1996. In the first half of that year reserve requirements involved 11 per cent of commercial bank deposits,[5] of which 50 per cent would be carried at zero interest, and the rest at 12.5 per cent. The latter rate was much lower than the banks' lending rates, but only a little lower than the rate on government paper. Any remaining controls stem from the legal framework[6] (mainly Law 2076/92, Law 2114/93, BGGA[7] 2246/93, Law 2324/95) governing banking business: freedom of establishment, home country control, a deposit guarantee scheme, capital adequacy, solvency rating. In turn this legal framework is for the most part[8] in accordance with EU directives (89/646/EC, 92/121/EC, 91/308/EC, 93/6/EC, 94/19/EC, and others). An interesting recent development has been preparation by the Union of Greek Banks of a long-due Code of Banking Practice.[9]

By the end of 1995 the results of deregulation had begun to unfold. For example, over the 1990–5 period the rate of increase in commercial bank financing of 'consumer credit' surpassed that of any other category, with 'commerce', 'housing' and 'other' also going strong. In contrast, more traditional sectors, like 'manufacturing' and 'tourism' were increasing more slowly, and losing share as a result (Table 6.3). Manufacturing, however, had been losing ground even before the onset of deregulation (Diagram 6.1), as it was facing problems of its own (see Chapter 8). Taking, therefore, a more long-term view, and looking into financing of the private sector by all banks (not just commercial ones), it becomes apparent that the main losers because of deregulation have been agriculture and small-scale manufacturing, whilst the main beneficiaries have been commerce and consumer credit (Diagram 6.1 and Table 6.3). Housing, despite its mildly increasing trend since 1977, is nothing to be excited about either (Diagram 6.1). Consumer credit, in particular, became the object of concern on the part of the Bank of Greece in June 1996, which tightened the prevailing rules a bit, but that intervention had nothing to do with pre-deregulation practices of trying to direct bank funds to 'desirable' sectors. The intervention was aimed, rather, at protecting banks from over-exposure and also at controlling inflation, both perfectly legitimate central bank goals even (especially!) in the context of a deregulated banking system.[10]

Since 1989 there has certainly been greater competition and product

Table 6.3
Greece, 1990–5: Financing of private sector by commercial banks, Greek and foreign

Year	Total financing (yr–end balance; bn drs)	Of which: in FX (%)	Financing of manufacturing (%)	Financing of commerce (%)	Financing of housing* (%)	Financing of tourism (%)	Financing of cosumer credit (%)	Financing of other sectors (%)
				Percentage increase in sectoral financing, 1990=100				
1990	2 146.7	6.8	100	100	100	100	100	100
1991	2 443.0	10.9	106	125	136	125	114	128
1992	2 868.0	13.5	114	163	180	137	149	174
1993	3 362.8	16.2	123	205	236	145	198	232
1994	3 957.9	20.5	138	241	314	155	350	281
1995	5 149.9	26.1	166	308	463	216	626	389
					Percentage sectoral shares			
1990	100		59.1	22.6	1.6	4.3	3.0	9.4
1991	100		54.9	24.9	2.0	4.7	3.0	10.5
1992	100		50.3	27.6	2.2	4.4	3.3	12.2
1993	100		46.3	29.6	2.5	4.0	3.8	13.9
1994	100		44.1	29.6	2.8	3.6	5.7	14.3
1995	100		40.9	29.1	3.2	3.9	7.8	15.2

* Most housing finance in Greece takes place through specialised banks and credit institutions (see Chapter 6). Commercial banks are relative newcomers.

Source: *Bank of Greece Economic Bulletin*, 7, March 1996, p. 75.

Diagram 6.1
Greece, 1964–95: All-bank financing to various sectors as percentage of total to private sector (outstanding claims at year-end)

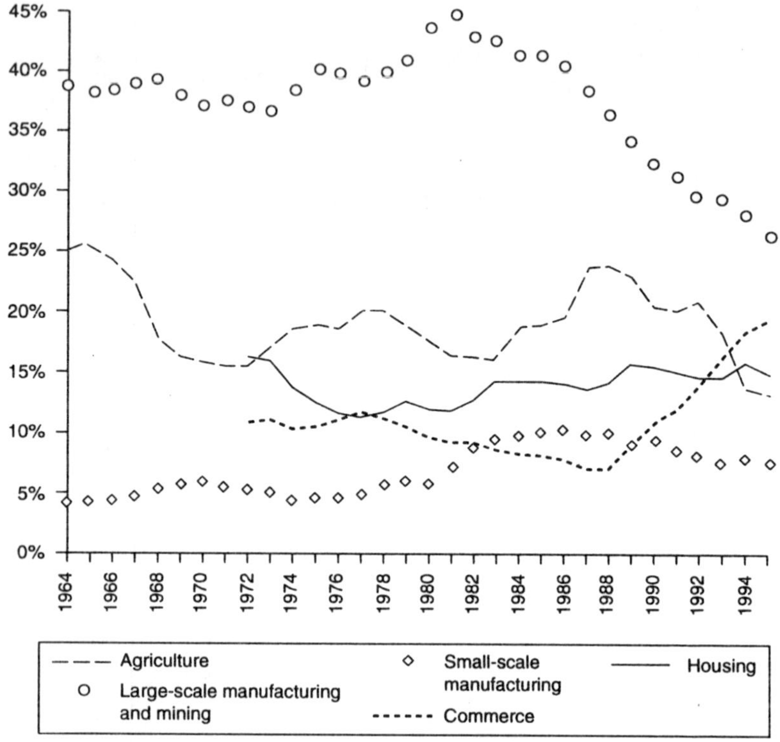

Source: Bank of Greece Annual Reports.

variation, and more pressure to expand in other financial fields. In terms of efficiency, cost-cutting, and productivity the Greek banking system has still some way to go.[11] For example, in 1993 the number of ATMs per one million inhabitants was 70 in Greece, whilst in 1990 it was:

199 in Western Europe;
304 in the UK;
308 in Spain;
357 in Switzerland;

421 in Norway;
581 in Finland, and
800 in Japan.[12]

Most directors as well as most employees of state-owned banks have traditionally viewed modernisation and competition more as threats to entrenched interests (like a salary structure that is based primarily on seniority and family status) than as opportunities for improving performance.[13] What's more, they oppose others, like private and in particular foreign banks,[14] who are not afraid to modernise, or link rewards to merit. There has also been talk of privatising a number of state-owned banks (Attica, Central Greece, Ionian, Crete),[15] but the Greek State shows a singular reluctance to privatise truly anything (see Chapter 4). For example, in 1996 the PASOK government 'privatised' the Bank of Attica by letting ΤΣΜΕΔΕ (a state-controlled pension fund) and the LCF (a credit institution directly controlled by the Ministry of Public Finance) have 49.5 per cent of it! So far the only thorough bank privatisations have been those of Piraeus Bank in December 1991 (bought by a group of Greek investors), and of the Bank of Athens, a small traders' bank, in January 1993 (bought by the Korean Hanwha Group[16]).

6.3 BANKS AND THE STATE: WHO FINANCES WHOM?

From the preceding section it is apparent that the heavy regulation of the Greek banking system prior to 1994 had very little to do with genuine prudence or performance considerations, a little more to do with supporting 'productive' investments, and a lot to do with financing the state. In addition to having to buy government paper, another activity became very important in the 1980s: financing state enterprises and social security organisations (ΔΕΚΟ), as well as government agencies purchasing agricultural products. Compelling banks to finance these entities began gaining momentum in 1980, when the 'pro-free-market' New Democracy (ND) party was in power. In October 1981 'socialist' PASOK succeeded it, and was only too happy to continue the pattern until 1989. At that point Greece entered a period of political turmoil which lasted well into 1990. It involved three general elections in about 12 months (two in 1989, one in 1990), ND's return to office, and lending to the aforementioned entities shooting up to a record-high of 30.4 per cent of total bank lending (Diagram 6.2).

Buying government paper and financing ΔΕΚΟ was not the worst

Diagram 6.2
Greece, 1964–95: Bank financing of public sector enterprises, social insurance organisations, and agencies purchasing agricultural products, as percentage of total bank financing (year-end balances)

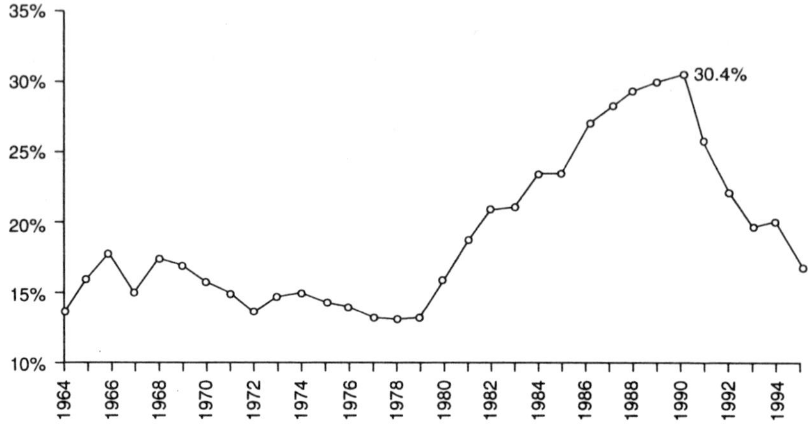

Source: Bank of Greece Annual Reports.

thing the banks were obliged to do. Especially after 1990, buying Greek treasury bills was a profitable as well as low-risk investment. In that year Greece's public sector debt problem was recognised as crucial, forcing governments to offer high-rate paper in order to acquire the funds with which to service the debt. More serious, therefore, for the banking system have been two other state practices: repeatedly forcing banks to extend loans to 'problem' and/or politically sensitive companies or sectors; and playing social policy with bank money. The two practices have overlapped often. For example, a series of governments from the 1970s to the early 1990s tolerated many borrowers not repaying their housing loans, particularly those who had been nominated by the Workers' Housing Organisation, and had subsequently been financed by the Mortgage Bank. Over the same period the importance of housing credit grew, not only because traditional sources of housing finance waned (see Chapter 9), but also for political reasons. The Mortgage Bank was the main policy instrument in the field, to such an extent that in 1989 its 'deposits and bonds were not enough to allow the Mortgage Bank to finance its particularly high credit expansion, so it had to borrow from the interbank market and overdraw its current account with the Bank of Greece'.[17]

By 1993 this kind of social housing policy had resulted in 13.4 per cent of the Bank's outstanding claims from housing loans being overdue (in addition to 24 per cent of its outstanding claims from hotel and construction loans, or 16.3 per cent altogether). In order to alleviate the Mortgage Banks' plight, in 1993 and 1994 the State took over those housing loans (rather than force repossession of the overdue debtors' homes), and gave the Mortgage Bank 46 billion drs (£123 m.) worth of government bonds instead.

At this point it is important to explain that the financial statements of Greek banks have hardly ever reflected their true profit-and-loss situations – or, for that matter, the consequences of actions and activities they have had to pursue as a result of government-inspired laws and regulations, or political pressure. One reason is that under Greek bank accounting law banks were obliged until 1992 to count as income all interest due, irrespective of whether it was actually collected, and without having to state the overdue amount. Another, that the management of state-owned banks were happy with this arrangement. Write-offs of non-performing loans were effected with the greatest possible reluctance (under Law 396/68). The situation changed in 1992 (Law 2076/92), when banks were obliged to count as interest income only interest from loan repayment instalments which have not been due longer than a year. Even that may be too convenient an arrangement: first, because a lot of uncollected interest still counts as income in this way; second, because it falls short of proper disclosure requirements as, of all Greek banks, only the Mortgage Bank actually breaks down its published outstanding claims into loans due and overdue. Since the accounting system does not require banks to disclose this kind of information, most choose not to. The only concession they make to the public in this connection involves publishing provisions for bad debts in accordance with the dated stipulations of Law 396/68.

Besides the Mortgage Bank, other state-owned banks have also had to extend loans in unwise ways, the state in effect making free with depositors' money – and ultimately having to shoulder the clean-up costs. Prominent among those banks have been the National, the Agricultural, the Commercial, and ETBA. For example, in 1993 and 1994 the Commercial received 19.5 and 16.8 billion drs, respectively, in government bonds, in exchange for overdue state-guaranteed loans, whose guarantees had been called in. In 1994 the Agricultural was saved from bankruptcy through the infusion of 620 billion drs (£1653 m.) in state funds. The liabilities involved had resulted from older contracts between the bank and the State, and from the bank supporting agricultural co-operatives on state orders.[18] The worst case, however, may have been ETBA, Greece's biggest investment bank. In the beginning of 1995 the relevant dilemma for the state apparently was either to close the bank down, at the cost of 1013 billion drs (£2701 m.) as well as of a lower international credit rating for Greece, or to spend 403 billion drs in an effort to make ETBA recover.[19] The second alternative was eventually chosen, at a projected nominal cost of 492 billion drs in the form of government bonds given to the bank from 1995 to 1999, in exchange for loan write-offs and other losses.[20] Still, the Greek State found it impossible to accept the necessary redundancies: since, on account of promises given the European Commission, it could not employ those people in central government, neither did it have a proper welfare policy, it decided to second them to various local authorities instead.[21]

By the middle of 1995 the National's overdue loans to about 12 000 firms were more than 200 billion drs (£533 m.),[22] or 27.5 per cent of her 1994 outstanding loans to non-banks. This may well force the Greek State to bail the National Bank out in the near future, typically by assuming most of that debt in exchange for government bonds (increasing, in effect, the public debt substantially). A remotely similar arrangement between the government and the National Bank reached in 1991 does not count as state assistance on account of the odd terms contained therein: At that time the government bought 102 bn drs (£272 m.) worth of National Bank convertible bonds, part of a 119 bn drs, 4 per cent issue. But the government did not actually pay in cash: it bought the National Bank bonds by giving the bank a government promissory certificate, which the bank had no right to sell; in turn, the government certificate was backed by 12 per cent government bonds worth 102 bn drs, which the National Bank bought for cash! The only nominal benefit from this deal to the bank was the interest rate spread,[23] while the various disadvantages of the scheme outweighed even that.[24]

How did a situation like that, involving banks and the State in an ever-widening cycle of debt-creation and debt-assumption, come to be? In many ways its development was inevitable since the State practically owns the banking system, and both the State and the state-owned banks have become accustomed to using political and social, rather than financial or performance, criteria in evaluating credit requests or business proposals. Government measures taken from 1982 to 1986 (period of strictest controls) exemplify precisely this mentality:

(a) Early in 1982 (under a PASOK government) 'a temporary credit relief programme was initiated to cope with the serious liquidity problems of ailing enterprises. Under this programme, commercial banks were required to set aside an amount equal to one per cent of their drachma deposits for the financing of enterprises characterised as problematic'.[25] That requirement was revoked on 31 December 1985.

(b) In 1983 debt payments by farmers and livestock breeders, who had suffered losses from forest fires in 1982, by earthquake victims in various regions, and by hotel and other tourist enterprises, were suspended. Also, repayment of loans to livestock breeders was rescheduled.[26]

(c) In January 1984 'debts falling due on 30.11.1983 on account of loans extended by commercial banks to hotels and other tourist catering firms and travel agencies for working capital during the period 1982–3 were rescheduled'.[27]

(d) In March 1984 'commercial banks were authorised to reschedule, at their discretion, the overdue debts of manufacturing and mining companies. However, the banks must first have established the viability of these companies through feasibility studies'.[28] To those who are not familiar with the way the Greek State operates the emphasis of the previous phrases on discretion and viability may seem like steps to less control than before, and towards the introduction of sound banking criteria in credit assessment. On the contrary, since most big banks were state-owned anyway, such 'freedom' to banks was often a way to overcome older and more stringent rules governing the extension of credit. A minister would simply pick up a telephone and tell a bank governor to finance firm X, and/or a bank governor would do the same to one or other of the bank directors.

(e) Not all measures aimed at helping 'problem' enterprises have involved central bank (that is, government) decrees as such. Some of the measures have taken other forms, and some again have resulted in losses for banks anyway, probably because the Greek State has hardly ever thought of banks as business firms. An example is Development Law 1892/90. An article in the law made compensation agreements between an enterprise in the red and a proportion of its creditors compulsory for all of them. Such a company, therefore, would come to a deal with 'cowboy', possibly bankrupt, companies, whereby the latter would appear as creditors of the 'problem' company. A general creditors' meeting would be called, which would result in an 'arrangement' between the indebted company and those present – an arrangement binding on

> all creditors. Eventually various banks and social security organisations – true creditors of the 'problem' company – would be informed that their claims had been substantially – and legally! – reduced.[29]

Against this background, it is not surprising that the government was taken aback in 1995, when for the second time in Greek banking history state-owned banks appeared unwilling to play the part of relief agencies.[30] On this occasion the issue of contention was extending loans to earthquake victims on the basis of government guidelines. The Minister of Planning went so far as to accuse banks of 'undermining the government's efforts for quick rehabilitation of the earthquake victims'.[31] Without doubt instances of bank rebellion will multiply in the future, as the new deregulated environment increases competitive pressures on all banks. The State will have to face up to the problem of putting in place and streamlining a genuine, multi-faceted social policy, with a transparent cost structure and transparent sources of funding. Laudable as the alleviation of hardship is, profit-making and profit-dependent banks are not the best instruments to use in order to achieve it.[32]

6.4 FOREIGN BANKS IN GREECE

As of 1994 there were 24 foreign banks with branch status in Greece, themselves having about 106 sub-branches and employing nearly 3600 staff. They accounted for 10 per cent of banking system liabilities to the public, and 13.5 per cent of outstanding advances (Table 6.2). Within foreign banks, Citibank and NatWest accounted for 26.5 per cent and 11 per cent of deposits, whilst Barclays and ABN-AmRo accounted for 14 per cent and 12 per cent of outstanding advances, respectively.[33]

Foreign banks in Greece arrived in three waves. The first wave took place from 1964 to 1972 (except for American Express which, nominally at least, has been in Greece since 1921); the second from 1974 (year of parliamentary restoration) to 1981; the third began in 1989, when Bayerische Vereinsbank became a full-fledged branch, and still goes on. Not all foreign banks who have come have stayed: for example, Continental lasted from 1972 to 1985, the First National of Chicago from 1971 to 1987, and the Bank of Scotland ran out fast in 1993, after three years of unfortunate experience with Dorian, a small private Greek bank. The Royal Bank of Scotland, on the other hand, has been doing well with its wholly-owned subsidiary in Piraeus, specialising in shipping, whilst Midland has developed a positive reputation in the field of investment banking, and NatWest has won renown for customer-friendliness.

Typically the arrival of foreign banks in a country has been linked to DFI flows to that country.[34] This correlation will probably lose much of its force as the on-going liberalisation of capital movements is completed at the international, and particularly the EU, level. Nevertheless, the correlation was initially based on the idea that foreign banks will arrive at a country in order to support manufacturing or trading companies of a multinational character from the banks' own countries, which have come to the given country first, having undertaken DFI there. Such support continues and affirms an already developed relationship between a bank and its client. It will be interesting to investigate whether the Greek experience confirms this pattern or not.

Taking into account that foreign banks in Greece do not publish income statements, and very little by way of balance sheets, there is not much relevant information around to use. Still, one can correlate the national origin of most of DFI into Greece over one or more time periods, and the following three variables:

(a) the nationality of most banks arriving at Greece over the same period(s);
(b) the ratio of advances to total assets for all foreign banks (a higher ratio in the earlier years, before the present trend towards portfolio investment and free capital movements, would be consistent with the support hypothesis), and
(c) the ratio of advances to total assets for foreign banks from the dominant national group compared to the same ratio for banks from other groups (if most DFI in a given period has been American, one would expect American banks to show a higher ratio of advances to total assets than, say, European banks).

Table 8.9 shows time series of long-term private capital imported into Greece for business purposes. The first series (column b) is capital imported under Law 2687/53, Greece's main law in support of DFI. Then there is other business capital (column e). After 1967 the latter flows become much larger than flows under Law 2687/53; but they do include financing for working capital purposes in addition to possible DFI. Table 6.4 shows Greece's foreign banks by year of establishment. It appears that up to 1974 only North American banks were in Greece, the last having arrived in 1972. But then, from 1960 to 1972 the following amounts of business capital were imported:

Table 6.4
Foreign banks in Greece

	Country of origin	Year of establishment	Staff in 1994
American Express	USA	1921	341
Citibank	USA	1964	650
Chase Manhattan	USA	1968	76
Bank of America	USA	1968	47
Bank of Nova Scotia	Canada	1969	119
First National Bank of Chicago*	USA	1971	
Continental Illinois**	USA	1972	
Royal Bank of Scotland §	UK	1974	65
NatWest	UK	1974	182
ANZ Grindlays Bank	UK, originally	1974	86
ABN – AmRo	Holland	1974	193
Barclays	UK	1978	296
Bank Saderat Iran	Iran	1978	13
Societe Generale	France	1979	130
Arab Bank	Of Arab interests	1979	63
Banque de Paris et Pays Bas	France	1980	58
Midland	UK	1981	197
Credit Commercial de France	France	1981	69
Banque Nationale de Paris (BNP)	France	1982	117
Credit Lyonnais §§	France	1982	108
Citibank Shipping	USA	1989	NA
Bayerische Vereinsbank	Germany	1989	56
Interbank #	France/Greece	1990	435
Bank of Cyprus	Cyprus	1991	140
European Popular Bank	Cyprus	1992	90
Istituto Bancario San Paolo di Torino	Italy	1994	15
			3 546

* Left Greece in 1987.
** Left Greece in 1985.
§ Formerly Williams & Glyn's Bank; acquired by the RBS in 1983.
§§ Formerly Banque FrancoHellenique, founded in 1982 by Credit Lyonnais and the Greek investment bank ETEBA. Credit Lyonnais became majority shareholder in 1993, and renamed the bank in 1994.
# Founded by Greek insurer Interamerican and Banque Worms; bought fully by French insurer UAP, owner of Banque Worms, early in 1996; then acquired by John Latsis' Euromerchant Bank.

From the Americas, $207 186 thousand under Law 2687/53 and $321 669 thousand as other capital; $528 855 thousand altogether.

From Europe, $64 625 thousand under Law 2687/53, and $375 921 thousand as other capital; $440 546 thousand altogether.

Diagram 6.3
Foreign banks in Greece, 1976–94: Comparison of European to North American banks by advances to total assets

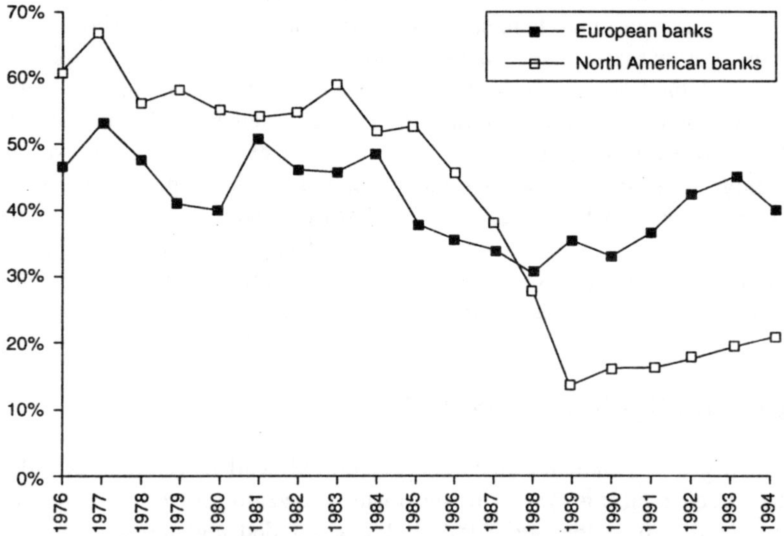

Source: Processing of *Epiloghe* and ICAP data, and banks' December accounting statements. Total assets exclude memorandum accounts.

Thus over the stated period 221 per cent more funds for DFI came to Greece, essentially from the USA and Canada, than what came in from Europe; 20 per cent more, if 'other' capital is also taken into account. This is certainly consistent with the exclusive presence of North American banks in Greece in the same period, as well as with the support hypothesis.

Diagram 6.3 takes care of the other two suggested correlations: it appears that, at least around 1976, foreign banks, both American and European, had a larger percentage of their assets in the form of loans and acceptances than what they had in later years; more importantly, the percentage was higher for North American than for European banks, and remained so until 1989. In other words, North American banks appear to have played a supportive role more systematically than European banks – in line with larger amounts of business capital coming into Greece from North America than from Europe (Table 8.9). The latter trend was reversed in 1992 (three years after the advances to total assets ratio of European banks topped that of North American banks), probably on account of developments in the process of integration between Greece and EU, but this does not mean that North American banks will have less reason to stay in Greece in the future. For all international banks, reasons for staying and/or arriving in a country nowadays have – within limits – increasingly more to do with personal banking services, assisting fund transfers, commission earning, deposit collection, lending other banks, and portfolio investment than with traditional lending.[35] In Greece, for example, the largest percentage of foreign bank customers come from the upper middle class (52.3 per cent), whereas 25.4 per cent of the customers of public-sector banks, and 36 per cent of the customers of Greek private banks, come from that class[36] (although in absolute terms more upper middle class people bank with Greek than foreign banks).

6.5 THE INSURANCE INDUSTRY

The insurance industry in Greece is not as well developed as either the Greek banking system or the insurance sectors of other EU countries; still, since the late 1980s it has expanded and modernised rapidly – some might say too rapidly for its own sake. At the same time the insurance industry is becoming an important pillar of the financial system. For instance, the outstanding investments of insurance companies in treasury bills, from 50 bn drs (£133 m.) in 1988, or 44 per cent of their total investments, reached 254 bn drs (£677 m.) in 1993, or 57 per cent of their total investments.[37] Those 254 bn drs represented about 25 per cent of treasury bill sales to non-banks by the government, or 15 per cent of total domestic borrowing by the government, in that year.

At the beginning of 1995 there were about 1.5 m. insurance contracts outstanding in Greece. These were held by approximately 1.2 m. insured parties. The number amounted to 12 per cent of the population, which industry practitioners feel it can go up to 20 per cent.[38] Certainly the sector appears to have a lot of growth potential, considering that in 1991 direct life premium income per capita in Greece was the lowest in the EU, and very much so in regard to direct non-life premium income (Table 6.5). In 1993 the sector accounted for 2.3 per cent of Greece's GDP, while in Italy, Spain, and Portugal the corresponding figures were 3.2, 4.3, and 4.4 per cent, respectively, and in Great Britain 12.3 per cent.[39] In the meantime, after dramatic growth in 1988–91, there are clouds on the horizon, both in the life and in the non-life branches of the industry.

A large part of the problem has to do with the many 'cowboy' firms which make up the sector. Industry sources say that the current number of firms is too large, and that the Greek market really has room for only 15 to 20 properly managed firms. They point to the declining number of firms to confirm this (Table 6.5). 'Cowboy' firms, however, are primarily a problem of poor supervision on the part of the authorities. The sector is supervised by the Ministry of Trade (presently part of the super-Ministry of Development); there are complaints, from within as well as from outside the Ministry, that it doesn't have the staff, and to a large extent the staff don't have either the training or the incentives, in order to do a proper supervising job.[40]

'Cowboy' firms have been particularly active in the car insurance business. They attract customers by charging premia that are too low; when they run into trouble, the so-called Assistance Fund foots the bill – and through that, the member-companies. (This is a Fund set up by all insurance companies doing car business, whose purpose is to indemnify victims of unknown or uninsured drivers, as well as rightful claimants for damages when the insurer has gone bankrupt or whose license has been revoked.[41]) Thus, at the end of 1995, the Assistance Fund had a deficit equal to 11.4 bn drs (£30.4 m.), or 10 per cent of the industry's car insurance premium income for 1995,[42] which the industry was called upon to make good. The Fund finances are not strained only because of 'cowboy' firms: about 10 per cent of vehicles in Greece are uninsured, and their number is thought to be on the increase.[43] This is obviously a problem of poor supervision on the part of the police, or even of not severe enough penalties, but the end result is the same as far as responsible and sound insurance companies are concerned.

Not charging appropriately high car insurance premia is not the only thing characterising 'cowboy' firms. Another is shady investment practices. Now, this is a problem of poor supervision on the part of the Ministry of Trade. Unfortunately, its mentioned weaknesses, despite the efforts of conscientious individuals working in the relevant department, imply slowness in identifying 'problem' cases in the industry. Thinking (sometimes with good reason) that political pressure might pay off, certain companies which have been found guilty on various counts, have chosen to be publicly provocative towards the Ministry. There was this German insurer, for instance, who in 1996 expressed surprise at being fined for not investing its technical reserves properly,

Table 6.5
Greek insurance industry: Basic data

Year	Life branch, 1988 prices: Annual rate of increase in direct premium income (%)	Non–life branch, 1988 prices: Annual rate of increase in direct premium income (%)	Life branch, current prices Annual rate of increase in direct premium income (%)	Non–life branch, current prices: Annual rate of increase in direct premium income (%)	Life branch: Direct premium income as % of GDP at factor cost (%)	Non–life branch: Direct premium income as % of GDP at factor cost	Life income: Share of Greek insurance companies* (%)	Non–life income: Share of Greek companies* (%)	Number of insurance companies (Greek and non-Greek)
1987					0.4	0.9	76.9	81.4	
1988	34.2	6.3	53.0	21.2	0.5	0.9	79.6	85.7	
1989	19.2	0.3	36.8	15.1	0.6	0.9	79.2	84.2	
1990	14.5	6.7	40.6	31.1	0.7	1.0	78.3	82.4	
1991	22.8	–0.5	45.0	17.4	0.9	1.0	75.8	83.5	
1992	15.8	11.3	32.5	27.4	1.0	1.1	77.0	86.0	161
1993	9.8	10.1	23.4	23.4	1.1	1.2	76.5	88.0	156
1994	5.2	4.7	16.7	16.1	1.2	1.3	75.8	89.2	149

	Life branch: Direct premium income per capita in 1991 ($US)	Non–life: Direct premium income per capita in 1991 ($US)	Life branch: Top firms by direct premium income in 1994	Direct premium income in m. drs	Car branch: Top firms by direct premium income in 1994	Direct premium income in m. drs
UK	1 317.7	681.2	Interamerican	46 730.3	Ethniké	16 559.2
France	773.2	639.0	Nation.–Nederl.	27 661.2	AGF–Kosmos	6 605.6
Ireland	726.0	536.6	Ethniké	27 344.6	Interamerican	5 889.9
Germany	505.3	794.6	Alico	17 780.6	Agrotike	5 120.7
Italy	161.1	443.9	Aspis–Pronia	8 747.0	Aster	4 556.3
Spain	159.8	365.8	AGF–Kosmos	5 513.4	Phoenix	4 421.7
Portugal	66.4	183.8	MetroLife	5 266.5	Int'l Union	3 129.0
Greece	53.3	59.5	Aster	5 248.6	European Union	2 691.0

* Some 'Greek' companies are actually affiliates of foreign insurance firms registered in Greece, like Allianz, Nordstern Colonia, ScoPLife (affiliate of Scottish Provident), Generali, Commercial Union, Cigna, or Universal Life. In other cases there is significant foreign participation, as in AGF–Kosmos, or there is significant Greek participation, as in Generali Life (40 per cent of which is owned by the Alpha Credit Bank).

Sources: Union of Insurance Companies of Greece: Annual Statistical Report for 1992, 1993, 1994; NSSG National Accounts.

and asked the Ministry to tell it how to invest them – as if there are no Greek laws (mainly Law 2170/93) which are very specific about this, and which the German company should know and apply.[44]

Life business is another worrying area. After fast growth in 1988–91, the rate of increase in premium income has been coming down fast, in current as well as real price terms (Table 6.5). This may pose a problem for those companies which have overexposed themselves counting on continuous growth in life income. Of more immediate concern, however, is overexposure due to too generous terms contained in health plans, which make up about 25 per cent of the life business. Among the plans, the ones potentially most devastating have been those guaranteeing unlimited hospital cover if the policy holder has avoided hospitalisation for four years after buying the policy. In addition, many private hospitals have been taking advantage of the terms in many of the existing health contracts, and charging insured patients exorbitant prices for treatment – which insurers have had to pay. Already a number of companies, even big and reputable ones, are in the process of rationalising their health plans, and of offering incentives to existing policy holders in order for them to move to new health plans, not likely to break the company selling them. Two other ideas that are currently circulating among insurers are, first, to negotiate contracts with hospitals and clinics not as individual insurance companies but as a group, and, second, to found, perhaps, their own health-care facilities. So the Greek life market is doing some serious soul-searching at the moment, which will probably lead to its transformation over the next few years.

Another source of change is provided by the deregulation and opening up of the domestic insurance market, which has been taking place at an increasing pace for some time now. This, of course, is a process going on throughout the EU, involving directives 357/88, 618/90, 619/90, 49/92, and 96/92. From the point of view of the Greek consumer a welcome result of this process will be the right to better information than is available to him presently, as well as the right not to be sold plans that do not correspond to his actual needs: the scope and application of both rights in the Greek market leaves a lot to be desired at the moment, although there has been improvement.

Increased competition among insurers will be an added benefit of European integration to the Greek consumer, something also that will probably speed up the reduction in the number of insurance companies active in Greece by getting rid of the 'cowboys'. In turn, this necessitates a better-equipped, better-staffed, and tougher supervising authority. But contrary to what some think or hope, neither in Greece nor in other EU members will the consumer find it very easy, for example, to buy insurance from non-resident firms. The reason is that freedom to do insurance business anywhere in the EU is one thing; to go ahead and do it, is another, as before an insurer sells a policy to somebody from a different country, it will need, among others, to have information allowing it to assess the risk represented by the policy buyer. Such information is often not readily available to companies which have not taken the time and effort to investigate the particular national market.

6.6 THE ATHENS STOCK EXCHANGE AND UNIT TRUSTS

Greek companies, most of them family-owned, have traditionally relied either on own funds or on bank loans for their financing – with generous state subsidies occasionally thrown in too. Up to very recently raising capital on the Athens Stock Exchange, or through bond issues, had never been high on their agenda, even though the ASE, which is government-controlled,[45] has been around since 1876. The main, perhaps, reason had been the distrust shown by the general public to financial instruments in general (other, that is, than bank deposits and, to a lesser extent, bonds), and to private financial instruments in particular.

That has begun to change. Already the importance of the ASE as a corporate finance vehicle is much greater than in the past. For example, in 1994 the total capital raised through the ASE was 266 bn drs (167 bn drs by listed companies, 93 bn drs by newly listed ones, and about 6 bn drs raised in the parallel market[46]). The figure contrasts with an increase of 662.5 bn drs in bank advances to the private sector in 1994, barring agriculture and housing, or of 106.5 bn drs in long-term bank advances alone, again barring agriculture and housing.

The ASE came out of the closet in 1987, when the ASE Index more than doubled in value in relation to 1986 (Table 6.6). It doubled again in 1990/89 (probably reflecting positive market expectations after PASOK lost the 1989 elections), elevating the ASE to a more respectable position than it had ever known. Since that year there have been no dramatic changes in the value of the Index from one year to the next, but as of 1992 the turnover of the ASE has been rising, doubling in 1993/92 and again in 1994/93. There are now about 240 companies listed in the ASE main market, and about 20 in the parallel market (begun in 1989).

Table 6.6
Athens Stock Exchange and unit trusts

	Athens Stock Exchange Index	Total turnover (bn drs)	Capital raised in the main market by newly listed (bn drs)	Total capital raised as % of share capital of respective companies	Unit trusts in Greece: Number	Asset net value (bn drs)	Various bourses	market capitalisation ($US bn, Nov. 1993)
1980	100.0		2.10	100			Athens	11.1
1981	86.59						Germany	441.7
1982	93.42						Lisbon	12.0
1983	58.26						Madrid	151.0
1984	59.18						Milan	136.2
1985	70.95						Paris	456.0
1986	103.86							
1987	272.47		1.39	87			Argentina	31.8
1988	279.65		4.74	106			Brazil	95.5
1989	459.43						Chile	39.3
1990	932.00	620.08	31.30	180			China	42.8
1991	809.71	438.55	16.40	268	19	171	India	89.9
1992	672.31	305.25	6.00	157	40	224	Korea	129.9
1993	958.66	624.68	16.40	126	71	886	Mexico	168.7
1994	868.91	1 226.26	93.00	NA	98	1 357	Taiwan	132.2
1995	914.15	1 257.69			119	2 464	Turkey	34.2

Sources: (a) On the Index and on capital raised: Athens Stock Exchange. (b) On turnover: *E Cathemerine*, 13.1.1996. (c) On unit trusts: Bank of Greece Annual Reports. (d) On market capitalisation: Athens Stock Exchange and *Financial Times*, 1994, p. 8.

More fundamental factors causing ASE growth have involved good stock performance on the part of some listed companies, quick capital gains in the case of many new listings, a stream of bond issues subsequently listed on the ASE, the absence of dividend tax, and the presence of tax advantages in investing in unit trusts or portfolio investment holding companies.

As a result the number of unit trusts in Greece has multiplied from 19 in 1991 to 119 in 1995 (Table 6.6). The trusts are owned by other financial institutions. For example, the 98 unit trusts active in 1993 belonged to 25 unit trust management companies (ΑΕΔΑΚ), of which 17 belonged to banks and the rest to insurance companies. Another reason behind unit trust growth is the gradual lifting of exchange controls that has taken place in Greece in the 1990s, and was completed in June 1994. A third, the liberalisation of the money and capital markets over the same period. Finally, treasury bills have been increasingly popular in Greece since the late 1980s, as they are widely considered a low-risk, high-return investment. (Their ascendancy, in turn, is a direct offshoot of governmental needs to service the public debt, a particularly acute problem for the Greek economy in the 1990s.) The four reasons are reflected in the different types of unit trusts available: of the 119 unit trusts active in 1995, 27 were fixed-income funds (investing, among others, in Greek treasury bills), 20 were money market funds, 37 were growth funds, and 35 were international funds.[47]

Despite these developments, the size of the ASE is still minute by international standards. In 1993, for instance, its market capitalisation was smaller than Portugal's (Table 6.6). More than anything else this is due to the Greek economy's deteriorating performance since the early 1980s. There has been, for example, a drop in the ratio of gross fixed capital formation to GDP in 1990–3 (18.4 per cent) in relation to previous years (21.2 per cent in 1960–93).[48] It is quite likely that if Greece had managed to preserve her investment/GDP ratio at past levels, the recent upsurge of interest in the ASE would have resulted in a larger increase in the amount of capital raised through it, and a larger turnover, than has actually been the case. An added difficulty is that much recent investment has been undertaken by transnationals, whose affiliates are typically not listed in the ASE. Yet another is the attraction to many firms of FX financing: as a result of Greek real interest rates in the 1990s being high enough to sustain an overvalued drachma, borrowing from abroad is probably cheaper, or more convenient, than raising capital through the ASE – let alone borrowing in drachmas.

These may be objective constraints on the further growth of the ASE, but there are others. The Greek legal framework governing investment business is still not up to, say, UK standards, despite recent efforts to improve it in the lines of EU directives. There have been, for example, cases of fraud.[49] (Having said that, the Barings affair in 1995 showed the world that no legal framework, and no internal administrative procedure, completely safeguards a financial organisation from fraud or negligence.) Also, the ASE is too inward-looking, too much subject to government red tape. Only in September 1995 did it manage to found a Stock Exchange Centre in Thessalonica, capital of Macedonia,[50] whilst efforts to introduce derivative trading were still in the bill stage.[51] Only in October 1995 were commissions charged by Stock Exchange trading companies deregulated.[52] Its computer hardware needs upgrading,[53] its staff have a public-sector mentality,[54] and its statistical and reporting department is chaotic. Neither is its secure growth helped by government threats to tax unit trusts, like it happened in 1994.[55]

Still, the important thing is that the Athens Stock Exchange has taken off, and that both its past and current Chaiman, although government-appointed, have been competent men, who are aware of the problems. They have been responsible for a series of reports, bills, and laws aimed at streamlining and improving the operation of the ASE and related activities, and have not hesitated to clamp down on shady practices. If such men have their way, the ASE will, with a bit of luck, play an increasingly important role in corporate finance not only in Greece, but in the Balkans too.

Notes

1. In the near future banking in any country is likely to involve a smaller number of traditional-type, bigger branches, and a larger number of modern-type, smaller branches. Assessing, therefore, the comparative significance of number of inhabitants per branch will depend on the definition of branch used. In the meantime, ATMs and EFT-POS are rapidly changing the face of banking everywhere.
2. The mention of Spain may be more surprising to some than that of Britain and Luxembourg. Still, Spanish banks 'have never really succeeded in enforcing [a cartel], such is the rivalry between them. [] Most European countries have between one and five banks that tower over the others. In Spain the power is relatively spread out.' (White, 1987). Moreover, of the eight biggest Spanish banks, seven were private in 1987, while the state-controlled one, Banco Exterior, came last in terms of deposits, and fourth in terms of assets. The biggest bank, Banco Central, had just 17.8 per cent of the deposits of all eight, and Banco Exterior 6.3 per cent.

3. Andronicakis & Gounaridis, 1986; Petoussis, 1986.
4. Andronicakis & Gounaridis, 1986; Catsambas, 1986.
5. Real estate banks were exempted from this obligation.
6. Cf. 'What changes in the banking system', *E Cathemerine*, 19.5.1991, p. 78; Zavvos, 1992b; Tragakis, 1993; Coccolios, 1993; Gortsos, 1993; Nanopoulos, 1993.
7. Bank of Greece Governor's Act.
8. One notable exception still in force at the end of 1995 was that residents in Greece could not open FX accounts in Greece unless they proved that any amount deposited had been earned overseas (and not originally exported from Greece and reimported). See *E Cathemerine*, 12.11.1995.
9. *E Cathemerine*, 25.2.1996, p. 43.
10. Cf. Nicolopoulos, 1996. A different view is expressed in Papandropoulos, 1996. He argues, somewhat caustically, that surplus liquidity would be controlled more effectively if the state cut down its own wasteful expenditure than if the Bank of Greece attempted to curtail consumer spending. Although correct as regards the first part, Papandropoulos is wrong in suggesting, basically, that there is no role for a central bank in a deregulated economy.
11. 'Bank queues that cost a lot', *Ta Nea*, 2.3.1992, p. 18.
12. Archontakis et al., 1994, p. 50.
13. Khaicalis, 1990; Lymperopoulos, 1996.
14. One form opposition has taken is through labour Law 1876/90, which imposes the results of industry-level collective bargaining on all firms in the industry, even where an employers' union does not exist, and irrespective of whether a firm has taken part in the negotiations, or chosen to be represented in them, or not. Foreign banks in Greece have challenged the Law as unconstitutional. Cf. 'Cardinal blow', *Ta Nea*, 8.12.1995, p. 41.
15. 'Ministry of the National Economy priorities as regards state banks', *E Cathemerine*, 14.6.1996, p. 17.
16. It is possible that Hanwha have regretted this. Nearly three years after buying the Bank of Athens from the National Bank of Greece they apparently discovered 1.2 billion drs (£3.2 m.) of bad debts held by the Bank of Athens from before the sale. In 8 June 1995 Mr Kim, President of Hanwha, spent 13 hours at the National Bank's Deputy Governor's anteroom, determined to see him about the problem. Mr Calafatis, however, avoided him equally resolutely. See *E Cathemerine*, 9.6.1995 & 26.10.1995.
17. Bank of Greece Annual Report for 1989 (Athens, 1990), pp. 106–7.
18. *Agricultural Bank of Greece Annual Report for 1994*, p. 10.
19. 'ETBA: "Gordian knot" of a bank', *E Cathemerine*, 8.2.1995, p. 23.
20. 'Bill for cleaning up ETBA through a 492 b. bond issue', *Nautemporica*, 31.8.1995, p. 7–8.
21. 'The state will pay the debts', *Ta Nea*, 31.10.1995, p. 52.
22. *E Cathemerine*, 14.6.1995, p. 1. It's not clear whether all overdue loans of the National Bank were included in this sum.
23. A benefit annihilated in real terms by the capital cost of the 102 bn drs, which the National Bank bought the government bonds with.
24. Mirkos, 1996, p. 25. George Mirkos was Governor of the National Bank of Greece from November 1993 to April 1996.

25. *Bank of Greece Annual Report for 1981* (Athens, 1982), p. 66.
26. *Bank of Greece Annual Report for 1983* (Athens, 1984), p. 70.
27. *Bank of Greece Annual Report for 1984* (Athens, 1985), p. 72.
28. Ibid., p. 73.
29. 'Overindebted firms' fraud against banks', *Kerdos*, 2.7.1995, pp. 1 & 4.
30. A precedent had already been set by the Mortgage Bank, whose Governor resigned in 1993, in protest against the government wanting to continue burdening the bank with the cost of its social housing policy (basically, allowing non-repayment of loans). See 'Mr Georgiadis' accusations, 20 years overdue', *Economicos Tachydromos*, 5.8.1993, p. 27.
31. 'They refuse to lend', *Ta Nea*, 19.6.1995, p. 19.
32. Cf. 'Banks and politics', *E Cathemerine*, 21.6.1995.
33. Cf. Pirounakis, 1994.
34. Ursacki & Vertinsky, 1991.
35. Cf. KPMG, 1992.
36. 'Banks which the public prefers', *Kephalaio*, March 1995, p. 82, reporting on a market research survey by *Focus*.
37. Pirounakis, 1996c.
38. Ibid.
39. Lysimakhou, 1995, p. 20.
40. Pirounakis, 1993b.
41. Indemnity of this type can be claimed from the Assistance Fund only for thirty days after an insurer has gone bankrupt or lost its license.
42. Contonica, 1996.
43. Ibid.
44. Pirounakis, 1996c.
45. Athens Stock Exchange, 1995.
46. Ibid., pp. 46–7.
47. *Bank of Greece Annual Report for 1995*, p. 145.
48. OECD, 1995, p. 73.
49. 'Investment advisers under surveillance', *E Cathemerine*, 5.8.1994
50. 'The Thessalonica Stock Exchange Centre has been founded', *E Cathemerine*, 7.9.1995.
51. 'New products in Sophocleous', *E Cathemerine*, 23.9.1995. Sophocleous St, in Athens, is where the ASE is.
52. 'Capital market's new landscape', *E Cathemerine*, 15.10.1995, p. 52.
53. 'Report on reshaping the ASE', *E Cathemerine*, 29.9.1995.
54. Ibid.
55. 'The institution of unit trusts under threat', *Ependytes*, 16–17.4.1994, p. 63.

7 Social Security – or the Lack of it

'The social insurance peculiarity of Greece, in common with Latin American countries, is that she managed to bring the system to the verge of bankruptcy before her demographics got worse.'
Platon Tenios, Greek social security expert.[1]

With an ageing population and a weak economy, Greece is set to face a most difficult situation in the near future as the time bomb of her social security plight keeps ticking.[2] But Greece's alarming demographics are only partly to blame for what is happening: atrocious state policies pursued over many years made it impossible for social insurance organisations to manage their finances effectively or even prudently. In addition, not keeping welfare policies clearly apart from the running of business enterprises or of the civil service resulted in gross inefficiencies and waste in both the welfare and the production fields. Solutions are now hard to find, and much harder to apply.

7.1 WELFARE IN GREECE

Although the Greek state directly or indirectly accounts for roughly half of Greece's true GDP,[3] in terms of broadly defined welfare (social protection as well as state-provided health care, education, and housing) it appears to lag behind most Western European countries (Tables 7.1 and 7.2). For example, Greece's social security transfers were 10.2 per cent of her GDP in 1960–93, and 15.5 per cent in 1990–3 (Table 7.2), less than the corresponding EU-15 averages (14.6 and 18.1 per cent, respectively). Still, the Greek percentage has increased over time (to some extent an inevitable development, rather than an improvement per se, as the Greek population has been ageing and since the early 1980s the unemployment rate has been rising). Public housing provision, on the other hand, has never amounted to much in Greece, in contrast to Eastern European countries while they were still under communist rule – but also in contrast to Western European ones, even

Table 7.1
Aspects of welfare in the European Union, c. 1990

	Health expenditure as % of GDP, 1981	Health expenditure as % of GDP, 1991	Public expenditure on health as % of total health expenditure, 1989–91	Health bills paid by public insurance, 1991 (%)	Public spending on education as % of GDP, 1991	Total public expenditure on social protection as % of GDP, 1980	Total public expenditure on social protection as % of GDP, 1989	Unemployment benefits in the European Union, 1994: 1st period: Duration in months	Percentage of wage	Thereafter: Duration in months	Percentage of wage
	a	b	c	d	e	f	g	h	i	j	k
Belgium	7.2	8.1	88.9	86.0	5.4	28.0	26.7	12	79	No limit	55
Denmark	6.8	7.0	81.5	85.0	6.1	28.7	29.8	30	73	No limit §	63
France	7.9	9.1	73.9	75.0	5.4	25.4	27.6	12	80	No limit	33–67
Germany	8.7	9.1	71.8	92.0	4.0	28.7	27.5	12	63	No limit	56
Greece	4.5	4.8	77.0	85.0	3.0	12.2	20.7	12	28	0	0
Holland	8.2	8.7	73.1	71.0	5.6	30.8	31.0	24	74	No limit	46
Ireland	8.8	8.0	75.8	90.0	5.5	21.6	20.2	12	41	No limit	32–35
Italy	6.7	8.3	77.5	75.0	4.1	19.4	23.1	6	30	0	0
Luxembourg	7.1	6.6	91.4	91.0	5.8	26.5	25.2	12	85	No limit	46
Portugal	6.4	6.2	61.7		5.5	14.7	16.6	21	81	21	44
Spain	5.8	6.5	82.2	90.0	4.5	18.1	20.1	6	80	18	70
UK	6.1	6.6	83.3	93.0	5.3	21.5	21.9	12	23	No limit	23
EU-12 *	7.0	7.4	78.2	84.8	5.0	24.4	25.2				
USA		13.3	43.9	61.0	5.5		14.6 #				
Japan		6.8	72.0	87.0	3.7						

* EU-12 averages in columns a to e are unweighted.
\# In 1990 (UN Human Development Report 1995, p. 202).

§ It was recently set at seven years, in turn broken down into a 4-yr and a 3-yr period.

Sources: Column a: *Contonica* (1994), on the basis of OECD data.
Column b to d: *UN Human Development Report* 1995, p. 199.
Column e: *UN Human Development Report* 1995, p. 200.
Columns f, g: 'Social Europe', *E Cathemerine*, 9.4.1994, on the basis of EuroStat data.
Columns h to k: *E Cathemerine*, 1.10.1995, p. 20, on the basis of data from the Labour Institute of the Greek Workers' Confederation and the 5th Directorate of the European Commission.

Table 7.2

Social insurance in the European Union, c. 1990

	Pensions as % of expenditure on social protection, 1980	Pensions as % of expenditure on social protection, 1992	Social security contributions as % of GDP, 1991	Social security contributions as % of statutory charges on labour,** 1991	Non-wage labour costs# as % of total hourly labour costs in manufacturing, 1991	Dependency ratios: § 1990 (%)	Dependency ratios: § 2040 (%)	Liabilities of social insurance organisations as % of GDP, 1990	Social security transfers as % of GDP, 1960–93	Social security transfers as % of GDP, 1990–93
	a	b	c	d	e	f	g	h	i	j
Belgium	41.5	44.7	16.0	54.2	46.5	21.9	41.5	128	19.5	23.8
Denmark	35.7	35.1	1.0	3.7	18.4	22.2	43.4	67	13.7	19.4
France	43.9	44.1	19.0	74.8	46.9	21.9	39.2	47	18.3	22.3
Germany	42.7	40.6	16.0	61.8	46.5	23.7	47.1	44	14.8	15.1
Greece	61.9	69.0	12.0	72.7	38.9	20.5	41.7	96	10.2	15.5
Holland	32.9	36.9	18.0	60.6	45.2	17.0	48.5	79	23.8	26.3
Ireland	29.7	27.2	6.0	33.7	30.2	18.4	27.2	102	11.2	
Italy	55.1	62.8	13.0	55.1	51.3	20.4	48.4	98	14.7	18.8
Luxembourg	47.5	48.4	14.0	56.0		20.4	41.2	70	17.4	
Portugal	39.4	38.8	10.0	62.5	42.1	16.4	38.9	68	7.4	
Spain	40.8	41.3	12.0	58.8	38.2	17.0	41.7	45	11.3	17.2
UK	42.8	39.4	7.0	41.9	29.7	23.5	39.1	40	10.3	13.3
EU-12 *	43.4	44.8	14.0	59.6		21.4	42.8	60	14.6	18.1
USA			9.0	46.4					9.1	12.4
Japan			9.0	51.1					7.9	11.5

* The European averages in columns h and i refer to EU-15.
** Sum of social security contributions and taxes on physical persons.
# Non-wage labour costs include employers' contributions to social security and private insurance schemes plus pay for time not worked.
§ Persons 65+ as % of persons aged 15–64.

Sources: Columns a, b: 'Europe in Figures', *E Cathemerine*, 1.9.1994, on the basis of European Commission data.
Columns c, d: 'Growth, competitiveness, employment', White Paper of the European Commission, Dec. 1993.
Column e: OECD Economic Surveys: Italy 1992/93, p. 20.
Columns f to h: 'The Pensions Time Bomb in Europe', a Federal Trust publication, UK, 1995.
Columns i, j: OECD, Historical Statistics, 1960-93, 1995 edition, p. 71.

though the latter were typically associated with far lower levels of public housing provision than the former (a notable exception being the UK in 1946–57). The Greek paradox – a big public sector and a relatively poor welfare record – has happened for a number of reasons:

(a) The family in Greece, in common with other Mediterranean countries,[4] is very close-knit. There is very strong inter-generational support, forward as well as backward, which limits the scope for dependence on the state for welfare. This is a key difference between Greece and Northern European countries in particular. It is common practice, for example, for Greek parents to pay for their children's education and/or upkeep until they are well into their twenties and even beyond – or for children to take care of infirm or senile parents at home until the last possible minute rather than send them off to nursing homes.[5]
(b) Economic activity at a small-scale, family, grassroot level has survived and prospered in Greece,[6] together with private property rights defined in a strongly individualistic manner. Both have been manifested in, and simultaneously allowed, a significant measure of household autonomy especially in the housing field (see Chapter 9), an area often associated with public provision in North-Western Europe. Such individualism was not the typical case in Eastern European countries before 1989 at least, neither has it been typical of North-Western European countries at any time so far.
(c) The unemployment support-net aspect of welfare has always been of little consequence in Greece – overtly, that is (Table 7.1).[7] But this is misleading, since the solution the Greek state found – one palatable to the Greek people – was not one based on handing out unemployment benefits, but on hiring many of the actually or potentially unemployed in the broad public sector – or on keeping 'problem' companies alive at practically any cost to the tax-payer. In effect this has been a much more expensive – and wasteful – way of supporting the unemployed than the Western European systems, as it propagates inefficiencies in the production sphere.
(d) Turning, finally, to pensions and health care, one finds that they are the most prominent aspect of those Greek state policies which involve welfare. For instance, a larger percentage of Greece's expenditure on social protection (62 per cent in 1980 and 69 per cent in 1992) is accounted for by pensions than in any other EU-12 country (Table 7.2). Admittedly, in 1991 Greece spent a smaller proportion of its GDP (4.8 per cent) on health care than any other

Western European, or North American, country; less also than Australia, New Zealand, Japan, Hungary, Czechia, or Poland (but more than Israel – just – Russia, Ukraine, Romania, or Albania).[8] Greece also had fewer hospital beds per 100 000 people (500) than France (1250), Hungary, Italy, the UK, or Holland.[9] On the other hand, the Greek proportion of health bills paid by public insurance was 85 per cent (Table 7.1), higher than the average (77 per cent) for countries ranking high in the UN human development scale.[10] The corresponding UK figure was 93 per cent, and that for the USA 61 per cent, lowest in the bunch.[11]

7.2 THE GREEK SOCIAL SECURITY SYSTEM

This is a compartmentalised pay-as-you-go system, its different parts designed to cater to different professional or occupational groups.[12] In other words, there is not a single social security organisation covering all Greeks, neither is there a minimum national pension. Nevertheless, in 1991 the share of Greece's GDP accounted for by social security contributions was near the EU-12 average: 12 against 14 per cent (Table 7.2). This reflects the compulsory nature of participation in a pension fund[13] in Greece. On the other hand, Greece's share of non-wage labour costs in total hourly labour costs in, say, manufacturing was the fourth lowest in the EU-12 in 1991: 39 per cent, against 18 per cent for Denmark (the lowest) and 51 per cent for Italy (the highest) (Table 7.2). On the strength of this observation one might argue that Greece can improve the finances of her social security system by raising employers' contributions. But this would be wrong, since Greece's productivity is the lowest in the EU-12, and, moreover, in 1991 her share of social security contributions in statutory charges on labour (that is, the sum of social security contributions and personal income taxes) was the second highest in EU-12: 73 per cent, against 75 per cent for France (Table 7.2). Greece, therefore, may respond more effectively to her social security problem by increasing tax revenue from physical persons rather than by raising her labour costs. She does not even need higher tax rates in order to do that: curbing tax, and, incidentally, contribution, evasion should be enough.

The three biggest pension funds, by far, are IKA (Social Insurance Foundation),[14] ΟΓΑ (Peasants' Assurance Organisation), and TEBE (Professionals', Craftsmen's, Traders' Fund). Between them they accounted for 78 per cent of all pension fund members in 1994. Others are the Veteran Seamen's Fund (NAT), the Lawyers' Fund, various bank and public enterprise employees' funds, the Priests' Fund, the Professional Motor Vehicle Drivers' Fund, and so on. A total of 316 organisations,[15] all under state control, make up Greece's social security system (Table 7.3).[16] Some of them have nothing to do with pensions, but play other important social roles. Examples are OAEΔ (which hands out unemployment benefits), OEK (which helps worker households become owner-occupiers), and Workers' Hearth (Ergatiké Estia, which caters for workers' overall welfare, including entertainment). To assist the survival of many of these organisations, the Greek state has imposed what is called 'contributions on behalf of third parties' on a variety of economic activities. In essence, these are taxes imposed on anybody who is involved in those activities, whether they are members of the organisations in question or not. They are also a demonstration of the corporatist nature of the Greek state and society: some groups of people tax the rest if they are powerful enough. One of the champions, in this respect, is the Lawyers' Fund: in 1994 about half of its revenue came from 'contributions on behalf of third parties', whilst its own members' contributions amounted to 13 per cent of its revenue. IKA itself, the main social security organisation of Greece, got 15 per cent of its revenue in the form of 'contributions on behalf of third parties', and only 31 per cent from members' contributions. For TEBE the corresponding figures were 18 and 87 per cent, so TEBE does not tax non-members too much. The overall third-party taxation champion, however, must be OΓA: a full 90 per cent of its revenue came from 'contributions on behalf of third parties', and only 6 per cent from its members.[17]

There is an interesting similarity between the way the Greek state has treated the country's pension funds, all of which it controls, and the way it has treated many of the banks it controls (see Chapter 6). In both cases the state expediently and repeatedly forced the institutions concerned into financially unsound practices and positions, only to foot the bill via tax-payers' money (or by raising debt, which comes down to the same thing) at a later stage, after the institutions concerned had found themselves near bankruptcy. In so doing, however, the state would put itself forward as the country's piggy-bank of last resort, and assert or even expand its own power and influence in the process.

Thus from 1951 to 1990 pension funds were obliged to deposit all of their available monies with the Bank of Greece, ostensibly for prudential purposes, but at interest rates lower than they could get on

Table 7.3
Social insurance in Greece: Basic data

Year	Population of Greece (m.) a	Excess of births over deaths b	Pensioners as % of population c	Ratio of pensioners to selected pension fund members: § All funds d	IKA e	ΟΓΑ f	TEBE g	Government employees h	Lawyers' Fund i
				(4514 th.)	(1830 th.)	(1160 th.)	(519.5 th.)	(273.2 th.)	(42 th.)
1971	8.8	67,307	9.4						
1981*	9.7	54,692	13.9	1:2.78	1:4.02	1:2.38	1:2.77	1:0.89	1:2.53
1991*	10.3 #	6,872	18.9	1:2.18	1:2.80	1:1.65	1:3.96	1:0.82	1:2.93
1994	10.4 #	3,100	20.8	1:2.09	1:2.45	1:1.55	1:3.91	1:0.92	1:2.80

Year	Pension fund assets (bn drs) j	Investment income (bn drs) k	Rate of return on assets % l	Inflation rate % m	Break-down of pension fund revenue by source: Contributions of members % n	Contributions of employers % o	State assistance % p	Investment income % r	Misc. % s
1979					38.6	38.4	17.6	4.9	0.5
1985					37.7	35.7	21.3	4.1	1.2
1992	1 119.4	146.3	13.0	12.1	31.4	29.4	30.2	8.0	1.0
1993	1 464.5	189.5	12.9	10.9	33.1	32.8	24.9	7.5	1.7
1994	1 878.0	210.4	11.2	8.1	32.4	31.5	26.1	8.3	1.6

* The ratios of pensioners to pension fund members pertain to 1980 and 1990 rather than 1981 and 1991.
# Without taking into account most of illegal immigrants (anything between 400 and 600 th.), the great majority of whom arrived from Balkan and Eastern European countries since 1989 and especially since 1991.
§ In parentheses, number of pension fund members in 1994.

Sources: Columns a to i: *E Cathemerine*, 28.12.1995, and Vamvoucas (1995a, 1995b).
Columns j, k and n to s: *E Cathemerine*, 31.12.1994 & 28.12.1995, and Vamvoucas (1995c).

Period	Rate on pension fund compulsory deposits with the Bank of Greece (%)	Rate on 6 m., 1–yr time deposits with commercial banks (%)
1.1.1951–1.4.1951	5	10
1.4.1951–1.8.1954	5	10
1.8.1954–15.2.1974	4	7
15.2.1974–1.1.1977	5	10.25
1.1.1977–1.9.1979	6	10
1.9.1979–1.7.1980	10	14
1.7.1980–15.6.1984	11.5	16
15.6.1984–11.7.1988	15	16.4
11.7.1988–17.10.1990	14.5	19.3
17.10.90–	18	21

comparable time, or even savings, deposits with commercial banks. The various rates involved over that period are listed above.[18]

The data suggest that for at least 40 years Greek pension funds deposited their monies with the Bank of Greece at about four basis points less than what they could get elsewhere. This alone amounts to a huge cumulative loss for them.[19] In contrast, whenever pension funds had to borrow from banks in order to cover their deficits,[20] they would do so at market rates, which inevitably compounded their financial problems. As a result, by 1992 more than 30 per cent of pension fund revenue had to come from the Greek state (Table 7.3), as opposed to less than 18 per cent 13 years before, whilst additional borrowing to cover expenditure has also been required (Table 7.4), along with extensive loan rearrangement under government guarantee. For example, IKA liabilities towards the Post Office Savings Bank and the National Bank (themselves 'problem' financial institutions – see Chapter 6), involving 135 and 31.5 billion drs, respectively, were rearranged in 1991.[21] After all, a series of Greek governments have always preferred shifting various kinds of debt around, in a game of musical chairs, rather than take politically costly decisions.

But what exactly has caused the sizable deficits of Greek social insurance organisations? Is the reason simply a negative rate spread? Actually, it's more than that. Identified factors are listed below.[22]

To these factors one should add the highly prevalent confusion between social security and welfare, and also the very compartmentalisation of the Greek social security system.[23] The first, in particular, tends to burden social security organisations, or the pension arms of such, with payments for disability and for health care, including hospitalisation.

Table 7.4

Seven biggest Greek social security organisations*: Financial trends, 1985–95, in current prices

Year	Total revenue (m. drs)	Of which: revenue from employees' and employers' contributions (%)	In addition: Grants from ordinary gov. budget to total revenue (%)	Total expenditure (m. drs)	Of which: non-capital outlays (%)	Total revenue to total expenditure (%)	Hence: borrowing requirement as % of expenditure	Total revenue minus gov. grants as % of total expenditure	Contributions to non-capital outlays (%)
1985	419 091	87.6	9.2	487 021	92.7	86.1	13.9	78.1	81.3
1986	480 258	85.9	11.3	611 215	89.7	78.6	21.4	69.7	75.2
1987	612 983	75.3	22.9	742 893	89.1	82.5	17.5	63.7	69.7
1988	784 556	66.4	31.1	947 305	84.3	82.8	17.2	57.1	65.3
1989	944 410	65.1	33.1	1 179 627	83.2	80.1	19.9	53.6	62.7
1990	1 177 222	66.3	33.1	1 447 617	87.1	81.3	18.7	56.0	62.0
1991	1 314 593	68.9	26.2	1 730 301	85.4	76.0	24.0	56.1	61.3
1992	1 491 825	70.4	26.0	1 847 713	88.8	80.7	19.3	59.7	64.1
1993	1 887 114	68.1	27.8	2 114 966	88.0	89.2	10.8	64.5	69.1
1994	2 252 880	66.5	28.1	2 450 943	88.3	91.9	8.1	66.1	69.2
1995	2 595 325	69.5	25.0	2 761 373	90.9	94.0	6.0	70.5	71.9

* Up to 1989 the following six social security organisations were included: Social Insurance Foundation (IKA), Peasants' Assurance Organisation (OΓA), Manpower Employment Agency (OAEΔ), Workers' Housing Organisation (OEK), National Welfare Organisation (EOΠ), Workers' Hearth (Ergatike Estia).

In 1990 the Veteran Seamen's Fund (NAT) was added to these.

True pension funds are IKA, OΓA, and NAT. In 1994 IKA alone accounted for 50 per cent of the revenue, and 55 per cent of the expenditure, of the seven, whilst IKA and OΓA together accounted for 66 per cent of all fund members.

Source: Bank of Greece Annual Reports.

Factor	Percentage of responsibility for deficit
Policy regarding investment of available funds	35.0
Contribution avoidance on the part of employers	2.5
Unemployment & recession	12.5
Contribution evasion	12.5
Policies adopted in disregard of actuarial considerations, and other instances of mismanagement	5.0
General social security policy decisions	5.0
Ageing of population	20.0
Third party claims	7.5

To meet these, the organisations concerned often have to resort to utilising pension contributions, a practice which seriously reduces their ability to pay pensions, or at least the level of pensions that their contributing members have a right to expect. Second, compartmentalisation of the system is not a simple matter of individuals freely deciding to contribute to a fund of their choice. That would involve a funding system, which is not the Greek case ('pay-as-you-go'). In Greece compartmentalisation of the social security system, evidenced in a multiplicity of occupation- or industry-specific funds, goes hand-in-hand with a 'pay-as-you-go' system, compulsory fund membership, and lack of an institutionally enshrined minimum income or pension.[24] This set-up is wrong for a a number of reasons:

(a) It causes 'an inflation of promises',[25] which cannot possibly be honoured in cases of funds catering for occupations or industries in decline.
(b) That situation, in turn, creates political incentives for 'passing on' pensioners from 'problem' to relatively healthy funds, or to a 'scoop' fund (which in Greece usually means IKA), to the detriment of the latter. From one day to the next IKA or NAT, for example, have often found themselves burdened with numbers of additional pensioners from whom they had never collected contributions. As a result their own problems have multiplied.[26]
(c) At the same time it makes members of relatively healthy funds resist joining any 'scoop' fund, or taking in 'problem' funds. Such resistance reproduces inequalities and inefficiencies in the social security system, which become especially visible in the long run, whilst it delays any needed clean-up and overhaul of the system.

(d) Politically strong funds can and do divert resources to themselves, or otherwise hinder the necessary restructuring of the social security system, at the expense of weaker ones. Typical examples are bank and public-sector enterprise employee funds,[27] and the Lawyers' Fund.

By 1989 the Greek social security system was close to bankruptcy, even though the liabilities of Greece's social insurance organisations were not the highest in the EU-12 as a percentage of GDP: Belgium, Ireland, and Italy were more heavily burdened (Table 7.2). In regard to the seven biggest social security organisations of Greece, revenue from contributions had dropped to 65 per cent of total revenue, whilst government grants had had to make up 33 per cent of it (Table 7.4). Then the ND government took emergency steps. In 1990 it passed Law 1902/90, against fierce opposition from bank and public-sector enterprise employees, and Law 2084/92 two years later. Law 1902/90, in particular, established higher contribution rates for employers and employees, raised the number of working days required for receipt of pension, increased an insured person's share in the cost of medicine, restricted the granting of disability pensions, accelerated administrative procedures to curb contribution evasion, and adjusted pensions on the basis of pay rises to civil servants rather than to unskilled workers.[28]

These two social security reform laws were by no means the breakthrough the system needs, but at least gave it some respite. For example, by 1995 contributions provided nearly 70 per cent of the total revenue of the seven social security organisations of Table 7.4, the government share in fund revenue had dropped to 25 per cent, total revenue minus government grants had gone up to more than 70 per cent of total expenditure (from 54 per cent in 1989), and, importantly, the borrowing requirement of the seven had gone down to 6 per cent (from 20 per cent in 1989 and 24 per cent in 1991).

The situation has also improved in terms of the funds' freedom to invest their monies more profitably (Laws 1902/90, 2076/92, 2042/92). Since 1990 pension funds have been allowed to invest in treasury bills, bank bonds and shares,[29] and, pending specific ministerial decrees which have yet to be issued, to set up their own unit trusts. Also, their deposits with the Bank of Greece have begun to earn treasury bill rates. Two years later Law 2042/92 allowed funds to invest up to 20 per cent of their deposits with the Bank of Greece in real estate (up to 40 per cent of the said 20 per cent) and/or securities (up to 60 per cent of that).[30] More recently, Law 2217/94 has created a limited opportunity for social insurance organisations to attempt better management of their immobile property.[31] Their new-found freedom has allowed funds to double, almost, the contribution of investment income to their total revenue as of 1992, in comparison to earlier years, and achieve rates of return higher than inflation (Table 7.3).

It may be, however, that it is a case of too little, too late.[32] The compartmentalisation, in particular, of social security among a variety of funds has yet to be tackled, whereas 'the root-cause of the [funds'] financial crisis lies in the unequal distribution of all kinds of revenue [] among different funds and the consequent unequal distribution of the pension "pie", [] against a background of rapidly deteriorating demographics'.[33]

Also, the incidence of contribution evasion seems to spread, particularly regarding contributions to IKA, Greece's biggest employee social security organisation. Some employers go so far as to withhold their employees' IKA contributions in addition to their own liability. The following figures, for example, represent sums owed IKA by employers in the private and public sector (in parentheses, the sums in 1988 prices):[34]

In 1982, 14.8 bn drs (40.7 bn drs);
In 1989, 95 bn drs (82.8 bn drs);
In 1991, 160 bn drs (96.2 bn drs);
In 1995, 234 bn drs (91.5 bn drs), of which 28.3 per cent was owed IKA by public sector entities.

In absolute terms, the 1995 sum represents 76 per cent of IKA's negative financial result (contributions and investment income − outlays) for the year, before, that is, any government grants.[35] The slight decrease in the real amount owed IKA as of 1995, in comparison to 1991, reflects an attempt by the government in 1991 to collect some of the money owed by granting discounts to employers rather than force collection of the entire sum owed in each debtor's case.[36] In the meantime the problem of contribution evasion has been worsening on account also of the many foreigners from the Balkans and the ex-USSR, who have come to Greece since 1991 (maybe up to 600 000), and who almost always work with no security whatsoever. Employers, on their part, are only too happy to take them in, first because they pay them less than what they would have to pay their Greek counterparts, second because they do not pay social security contributions on their behalf, although under Greek law they should. IKA has responded to these challenges by asking the government to pass a law declaring that firing a worker, of whatever nationality or legal status, is illegal if all

Diagram 7.1
Ageing populations and economic performance: OECD (except Turkey and Mexico)

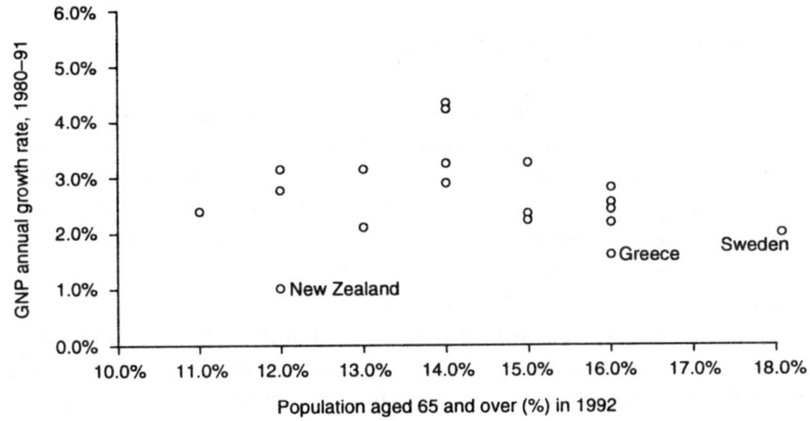

Source: UN Development Report 1995.

the required social security contributions (employee's and employer's) arising from his period of employment have not been paid. To make it easy to identify a worker's period of employment IKA has also proposed that the number of workers employed at an establishment should be registered in the till machine. This should take care of instances of contribution evasion by, among others, eateries, night-clubs, and shops. So far, however, the government has neglected, if not refused, taking these measures, to IKA's great chagrin.[37]

One problem of the Greek social security system is that adverse demographics (Tables 7.2 and 7.3),[38] contribution evasion, and bad fund management policies have coincided with poor overall economic performance. Diagram 7.1 relates GNP annual growth rates in 1980–91 for OECD countries (except Turkey and Mexico) to percentages of population aged 65 and above in 1992. Greece appears to be one of the worst cases: she suffers from a high proportion of aged people (16 per cent) together with low economic growth (1.6 per cent). The other two worst cases are also interesting: New Zealand has experienced a lower growth rate than Greece (1 per cent), but in 1992 had a lower proportion of aged people (12 per cent); whilst Sweden had a higher proportion of aged people (18 per cent), but a higher growth rate (2 per cent). On given trends she may, therefore, be better placed to take care of her ageing population than Greece, something which New Zealand may also achieve simply because she is burdened with a smaller percentage of aged people.

7.3 WHAT NEEDS TO BE DONE

There is no easy solution.[39] Even if the immediate problems of contribution evasion or bad investment policies were to be tackled effectively, the Greek social security system is caught between the Scylla of worsening demographics and the Charybdis of economic stagnation.

Two highly compatible solutions which have been proposed with increasing frequency of late are (a) unifying the various funds into a small number of super funds,[40] probably four,[41] and (b) replacing Greece's 'pay-as-you-go' system with a funding system.[42] Both solutions would face formidable implementation problems, not least of which would be stiff resistance from employees who are currently members of relatively well-off funds (for example, in the banking sector). As, however, even these funds are beset by worsening demographics,[43] their members' resistance to social security restructuring may be curbed if the government and the banks explain to them that when (rather than 'if') in the future the fund deficits grow to unmanageable proportions they will not bail the funds out.

Fund unification may also be helped by a fortunate circumstance which Greece presently faces, if she only decides to take advantage of it. This is the nearly 600 000 economic refugees already mentioned, most of them of working age and quite a few very young, from Balkan and Eastern European countries who are now in Greece. The majority of them have no work permit, even though IKA does not require one in order to collect contributions from them and their employers. Still, because the Greek state does not get round to giving them work permits, they and their employers see fit not to be burdened with social security contributions. Were this problem to be solved (see previous section), and these people be given full rights, their contributions, in conjunction with strict collection policies, would go a very long way towards alleviating the problems of Greece's social security system over the critical period to 2020. At least the hope is that their incorporation would give the system breathing space until the Greek economy itself got out of its present dire straits.

In general, any solution to the problems of Greece's social security system needs to conform to the following five principles:

(a) The system must not hinder economic performance in the production sphere. This primarily means that hiring people in the public sector, simply because otherwise they would be unemployed, has to stop. So must the preservation of 'problem' enterprises, if it is only justified on 'social' grounds. One implication is that modern Greece, for the first time in her history, will have to put in place and streamline a comprehensive and transparent policy regarding the unemployed, involving a combination of unemployment benefit, retraining, assistance in job search,[44] and workfare. Employers' contributions will probably have to be reduced too at the same time that collection of such should be enforced very strictly.

(b) The system must achieve efficiency. This means cutting down operational costs (which would be easier to do if the number of funds were reduced), allowing funds even greater freedom of investment than they have been given recently, making investment and overall management more professional, speeding up computerisation, establishing a better balance between doctors and nurses as well as a better spatial distribution of doctors,[45] and facilitating collection of contributions, especially if deliberately withheld.

(c) The system must aim for equity. To achieve this a number of injustices have to go. One example is young people, some in their forties, or phoney invalids, or phoney war veterans, receiving pensions on account of obscure or suspect laws. Another is the infamous 'contributions on behalf of third parties', mentioned above. A third is contribution evasion. Exactly because employers' contributions will have to drop, the Greek state cannot afford to be soft on employers who basically steal money from employees and pensioners. There is obviously an important moral justification to a change of attitude here, in addition to financial expediency.

(d) Above all, the system must ensure a reasonable minimum pension for all. This requires doing away with the confusion between social security and welfare as well as with the compartmentalisation of the system, and ultimately establishing one social security organisation for all who work or reside in Greece. At least as an emergency, interim measure, it probably also involves partially severing pension rights from social security contributions, with something like the top decile of the population, in terms of wealth, getting nothing, and the rest getting progressively more. This is not equivalent to setting up a national minimum pension funded by tax-payers' money as contributions to the scheme will be independently managed and the government will not be able to spend elsewhere. The idea is to make the social security system a safety net for all in need rather than a promises-generating machine or a personal investment device. There are surely better investment vehicles for individuals than participation in creating and sustaining a social safety net. A minimum pension for all along the above lines could be combined with a funding system, which will grant pensioners additional amounts on the basis of their past contributions and investment returns on them, whilst recourse to private insurance will top up the system.[46] In this way a stronger relationship between contributions and returns is retained than otherwise, whilst greater transparency is achieved than under a 'pay-as-you-go' system.[47] Also, the safety net character which social security should have is retained and/or established comprehensively for the first time in Greece.

(e) Finally, the system must allow individual flexibility and choice. Groups of individuals wishing to set up their own pension schemes must be able to do so (just as when a person decides to buy term life insurance), but only in addition to the main social security scheme, which will be compulsory. These schemes must be voluntary, possible to extend to voluntary agreements between employees and employers, and must enjoy investing freedom within legally prescribed prudential limits.[48] The state will not contribute taxpayers' money to those schemes, not will it ever take up any of their liabilities, but will need to supervise them the same way it needs to supervise insurance companies. This is probably a more appropriate role for the state than forcing people to contribute to schemes offering ridiculously low returns or to subsidise others regardless of need.

The one thing that overshadows the preceding discussion on 'principles' is Greece's worsening demographic trends. On the one hand they dictate measures that may be just possible to enforce simply because there will be no alternative. In the process Greece may come out with a better social security system than she has ever had – or else her present system will simply collapse. On the other hand, these trends call for vitally urgent measures to improve Greece's birth rate (presently below what is required for population replacement). The idea of Greece may be an amalgam of glorious history, philosophy and culture, but unless modern Greeks begin producing more Greeks the nation will vanish in a few decades. More than economic stagnation, corruption and the Turkish threat, the greatest danger to the survival of the Greeks is their unwillingness to have more children.[49] Because of that, the recent infusion of so many foreigners in Greece, most of them Christian Orthodox too, may, with a bit of clever decision-making and planning on the State's part, prove definitely a blessing: what is required is brave measures to incorporate them into Greek society. However, even a recent attempt to streamline the provision of longer-term (6 months to 3 years) work permits to foreigners[50] seems to fall short of the comprehensive measures that are really needed.

Notes

1. Tenios, 1995a.
2. Tzannakis, 1991, Vamvoucas, 1992b, 1995a, 1995b, Tenios, 1992, Venetakis, 1995, Papadopoulos & Demetrellis, 1995a.
3. That is, including the output of the informal economy.
4. Turkey is another example. *The Economist*, 1996b, pp. 12–3.
5. This mentality, very similar to the Japanese, may also be a result of the religiousness of the Greeks. According to European Commission research, more than 75 per cent of Greeks feel that the idea of God is very important to them, followed by 66 per cent of the Portuguese and 46 per cent of the Spanish. *E Cathemerine*, 28.7.1995.
6. Again in common with other Mediterranean countries, like Turkey or Italy.
7. Unemployment benefit in Greece is extended only to people who have been made redundant; high school or university graduates are not entitled to it automatically.
8. *Human Development Report 1995*, p. 199.
9. Ridding, 1995.
10. *UN Human Development Report*, 1995, p. 199.
11. Ibid.
12. See Yfantopoulos, 1990; Leandros, 1996.
13. This is really a misnomer, as the Greek social security organisations which collect contributions from their members and grant pensions have, or at least until very recently had, nothing like the investing freedom and independence that pension funds in the UK or the USA have traditionally enjoyed. See Zavvos, 1992a.
14. The idea of all private-sector employees joining a compulsory social insurance scheme was originally worked out in 1928–32, under Venizelos' government, whilst IKA itself was established by the dictator Metaxas in the late 1930s (Mavroleon, 1986).
15. Pselos, 1995b.
16. According to Yfantopoulos, 1990, p. 219, there were 327 social security organisations in Greece in 1988. Of these 222 were under the Ministry of Health and Welfare, 86 under the Ministry of Labour, 10 under the Ministry of Defence, 5 under the Ministry of Shipping, one under the Ministry

of Finance, and one each belonged to the Greek Parliament, the Public Power Corporation, and the Piraeus Port Organisation.
17. *E Cathemerine*, 1.10.1995, p. 53. See also Karacoussis, 1995.
18. Source: Self-insurance Fund of Bank of Greece and Mortgage Bank Staff, Dec. 1994, mimeo.
19. Although exact figures are very hard to find, the mathematics of annuities suggests a revealing analogy: that one drachma paid in annually over 40 years at 4 per cent yields 95, or 2.4 times the sum invested.
20. The practice was begun by the government of PASOK in the 1980s, in the context of its so-called social policy (Marinos, 1990a, p. 6).
21. *Ta Nea*, 14.5.1991, p. 25.
22. *Ta Nea*, 30.7.1991, pp. 20–1, on the basis of research by Professor J. Kyriopoulos, of Athens Health-care School, Dept of Health Economics. See also Marinos, 1990a; Sterghiou, 1991, 1992; Vamvoucas, 1991a; Tsaoussis, 1992; and Karamouzis, 1995.
23. Karalis, 1994; Tenios, 1995a; A. Karalis is ex-governor of IKA.
24. Pensions in particular have been losing value in real terms on account of inflation. Yfantopoulos, 1990, p. 247.
25. Tenios, 1995a.
26. See Couphalis, 1991 on NAT, and Marinos, 1990a on IKA.
27. Marinos, 1990b; Karalis, 1995; Copsine, 1996c.
28. *Bank of Greece Annual Report for 1990*, Athens, 1991, p. 133.
29. Regarding investment in shares prior approval of the Ministry of Welfare & Social Insurance and of the Bank of Greece is still required.
30. Pselos, 1995a.
31. Ibid.
32. Karalis, 1994; Tenios, 1995a, 1995b.
33. Karalis, 1995.
34. *Ta Nea*, 14.5.1991, p. 25; 21.11.1995, p. 50.
35. IKA's result for 1995 is an estimation included in the government's *Budget Report for 1996*.
36. *Ta Nea*, 14.5.1991, p. 25.
37. Sentiment expressed to the writer of this book by Mr G. Solomos, IKA's Governor, in June 1996.
38. Greece is not alone in this. Apparently two out of three over 65s who had ever lived were alive in 1994. At the same time the average European woman of child-bearing age produced 1.7 children, whilst around 2.1 children are required to replace the population (Willman, 1994).
39. Cf. Tenios, 1995a; Vamvoucas, 1991a; Marinos, 1990b, 1992; Copsine, 1996b.
40. Khaicalis, 1983; Papanicolaou, 1987; Karalis, 1994, 1995; *E Cathemerine*, 24.3.1994, p. 8, *To Vema*, 10.4.1994, p. A50.
41. Karalis, 1994.
42. Tenios, 1995b; Leandros, 1996.
43. Foura, 1995.
44. Greece still does not allow operation of private job-find firms.
45. Karalis, 1994.
46. Leandros, 1996; Copsine, 1996a.
47. Tenios, 1995b.

48. The European Commission proposed a relevant directive in 1991 (*E Cathemerine*, 17.12.1991), whilst Law 1902/90 had already opened the way for pension funds to start their own unit trusts. The first Greek pension fund to try was that of Civil Engineers and Public Works Contractors (ΤΣΜΕΔΕ), in March 1993 (*E Cathemerine*, 6.3.1993): a rather academic decision on their part, as by 1995 the relevant ministerial decrees, setting forth the specifics of the scheme, had not been issued (Pselos, 1995a).
49. Ghiocas, 1994; Polyzos, 1996.
50. *E Cathemerine*, 21.2. 1997.

8 Aspects of the 'Real' Economy

> 'There is no substitute for talent. Industry and all the virtues are of no avail.'
>
> Aldous Huxley. *Point Counter Point.*

A broad definition of the 'real' economy involves the production, transportation, and selling of goods and services – as opposed to the exchange of paper assets, which is the concern of the 'paper' economy of the world of finance. A narrower definition would focus on material goods only; sectors like industry, commerce, agriculture, shipping, supermarkets, construction. Either way, the 'real' economy, directly or indirectly, is, and always will be, the foundation of the economy as a whole. In Greece the survival, and, here and there, good performance of the 'real' economy, despite the weak infrastructure of the country and atrocious state policies, is almost a mystery – until, that is, one realises that, when all is said and done, people need the 'real' economy in order to make a living.

8.1 GREEK INDUSTRY: FROM RETREAT TO PATCHY RECOVERY

The relatively large, by EU standards, percentage of the economically active population of Greece employed in agriculture and related activities (17.3 per cent in 1991) tends to support the layman's notion of Greece as a mainly agricultural country. The notion was probably true until the late 1960s – certainly not now. Still, a tourist enjoying local produce on a picturesquely rustic Aegean island will be surprised to know that from 1973 to 1994 half of total Greek exports have been accounted for by manufactures – even if wines, yoghurt, or preserved fruit and vegetables are not included.[1] Foodstuffs and beverages have made up 24 per cent of total exports, on average.[2]

So there is a Greek manufacturing industry to speak of. Admittedly, its contribution to GDP (at factor prices) is not very high – only

15.7 per cent in 1991 (excluding mining, energy, and water supply). It is also less than it used to be. The contribution of manufacturing to GDP was 14.8 per cent in 1951, 16.2 per cent in 1961, and 19.3 per cent in 1971. It stabilised there for a time (it was 19.4 per cent in 1981), and by 1991 it had gone down almost to its 1951 value. From a highest point of 323 thousand workers with limited and public limited companies in 1981, Greek industry had lost 23 per cent of its workforce by 1994 (Table 8.1). But Greece is not the only country who has been through a process of deindustrialisation recently.[3] From 1970 to 1993 manufacturing employment decreased in all big industrial capitalist countries except Japan.[4] Between 1970 and 1990 the contribution of manufacturing to GDP also went down in those countries, with Japan, once again, showing the most resistance.[5] In the end Greece is not too far below the UK, another deindustrialiser, whose manufacturing sector contributed 23.4 per cent to GDP in 1991.

The 1980s and 1990s have, in addition, seen the Greek industry split into two distinct segments: A relatively profitable, 'dynamic' segment, made up of modernising private firms,[6] and a loss-making, 'problem' segment, made up of an assortment of public-sector and private firms, all heavily into debt, and quite a few into receivership under state control.

A fuller picture emerges from Table 8.1. Even though the number of industrial plcs and limited companies increased by 31 per cent from 1977 to 1994, the number of industrial workers fell by 19 per cent, resulting in 70 employees per firm from a highest point of 114 in 1977. It is also easy to spot the manifestation of deindustrialisation in Greece: It happened in the period 1982–5, when industry as a whole registered losses, year after year.

Most of the new firms appear to have fewer capital assets, in 1986 prices, than the older ones: 380 m. drachmas worth of fixed assets per firm in 1994, as opposed to 564 m. in 1977. Certainly this does not bode well for the average industrial firm in Greece. On the other hand, these fixed assets are combined with even fewer workers than in the past, leading to a higher capital-to-worker ratio in recent years: In 1977–81 each employee worked with an average of 4.6 m. worth of fixed assets; by 1990–94, the figure had gone up to 5.2 m. This suggests productivity gains, as indeed has been the case (see Diagram 8.1), and is one reason behind the recent increase in industry net income: From an annual average of 12.2 m. drachmas per firm in 1977– 81, to 14.7 m. drs per firm in 1990–4 (in real terms). In other words, not only does (a leaner) Greek industry appear to have recovered from the

Table 8.1
Basic data on Greek industrial companies, 1977–94 (million of drs at 1986 prices)

Year	No. of firms*	No. of employees	Employees per firm	Fixed assets per firm	Fixed assets per employee	Total assets	Of which: Fixed assets (%)	Net income	Debt to total assets (%)	Net income to total assets (%)	Net income to net worth (%)	Gross income (standing for value added) per drachma of expenses**
1977	2680	306 689	114	564	4.9	2 332 002	65	37 302	69	2	5	1.10
1978	2944	317 186	108	524	4.9	2 413 392	64	12 782	71	1	2	1.03
1979	3002	322 395	107	487	4.5	2 354 453	62	56 088	74	2	9	1.14
1980	3082	319 254	104	445	4.3	2 336 125	59	50 546	77	2	9	1.13
1981	3210	322 849	101	433	4.3	2 336 104	60	24 752	78	1	5	1.06
1982	2624	291 087	111	615	5.5	2 330 639	69	−19 741	74	−1	−3	0.95
1983	2834	299 934	106	545	5.1	2 334 978	66	−13 508	77	−1	−3	0.97
1984	2959	299 519	101	515	5.1	2 171 508	70	−27 489	81	−1	−7	0.94
1985	2997	288 761	96	453	4.7	2 006 524	68	−33 979	85	−2	−11	0.93
1986	3210	279 600	87	393	4.5	1 954 913	65	14 123	81	1	4	1.03
1987	3453	287 260	83	404	4.9	1 945 627	72	30 423	73	2	6	1.07
1988	3605	293 824	82	431	5.3	2 039 636	76	28 962	69	1	5	1.07
1989	3904	296 158	76	388	5.1	2 077 167	73	35 801	71	2	6	1.08
1990	4112	285 569	69	336	4.8	1 984 895	70	38 541	71	2	7	1.08
1991	3981	269 619	68	332	4.9	1 941 786	68	15 912	74	1	3	1.03
1992	3860	269 385	70	384	5.5	2 018 124	73	69 434	70	3	11	1.15
1993	3476	255 014	73	401	5.5	1 913 421	73	68 490	66	4	11	1.15
1994	3524	247 435	70	380	5.4	1 904 765	70	78 459	65	4	12	1.18

* Firms' refers to limited and public limited companies only.
** Expenses = Gross income − net income.

Data source: 'Greece in Figures', an ICAP publication; volumes 1983 through to 1994 (ICAP: Athens). For 1993, 1994, 'Express', 19.11.1995, based on ICAP data.

Diagram 8.1
Greek manufacturing industry, 1974–95

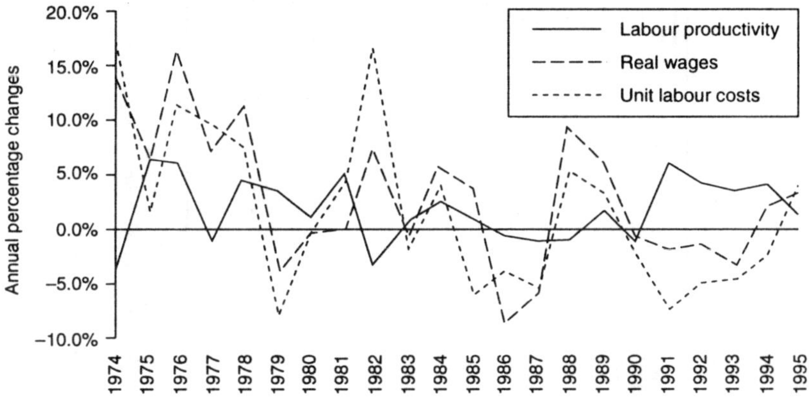

Source: Table 8.5

losses and weak profitability of the middle eighties, but has surpassed its pre-1982 performance.

A number of factors have worked in industry's favour after 1990. The first is higher productivity, already noted. The second is its oligopolistic structure, enhanced by inroads made by transnational firms into Greece (more on this, later). This has allowed market-leading firms in a number of sectors to raise their prices faster than their costs – even if by less than the inflation rate. The third factor involves the reduction of industry's ratio of debt to total assets from 75 per cent in 1977–89 to an average of 69 per cent in 1990–94 (Table 8.1). The fourth has to do with smaller annual percentage changes in industry's real wages since 1990 than previously (see Diagram 8.1). The fifth results from satisfactory domestic sales performance among the profit-making firms (Table 8.2). The sixth and last factor reflects positive annual percentage changes in the real effective parity of the drachma vis-a-vis a basket of appropriate currencies – Greece's main trading partners (Diagram 5.8). This has allowed many firms to buy capital goods and raw materials from overseas more cheaply than otherwise, and to borrow from abroad at lower than domestic rates, thus reducing their interest expenses (since it is the comparatively high Greek interest rates, which have kept the drachma from finding its true value). In effect, those firms, many of which are affiliates of transnationals, have

Table 8.2
Profit- and loss-makers in Greek industry, 1988–94

	Sales by profit-making firms (m. drs)	Percentage change in sales	Number of firms	Sales per firm (m. drs)	Net margin on sales (%)	Return on net worth (%)	Inflation rate
1988	2 029 206		2 626	773	6.9	20.6	14.0%
1989	2 521 006	24.2	2 907	867	7.0	22.6	14.8%
1990	3 205 870	27.2	3 091	1 037	7.0	21.1	22.8%
1991	3 573 765	11.5	3 080	1 160	7.4	22.8	18.0%
1992	4 044 070	13.2	2 940	1 376	8.5	23.0	14.4%
1993	4 528 988	12.0	2 727	1 661	7.4	20.3	12.1%
1994	5 143 859	13.6	2 702	1 904	7.7	19.4	10.9%
	Sales by loss-making firms (m. drs)	Percentage change in sales	Number of firms	Sales per firm (m. drs)	Net return on sales (%)	Return on net worth (%)	Exports of manufactures (all firms, m. $US)
1988	547 397		979	559	−18.6	−68.4	3 113
1989	707 704	29.3	997	710	−17.4	−102.4	3 344
1990	635 747	−10.2	1 021	623	−23.9	−3104.0	3 441
1991	862 501	35.7	1 045	825	−26.4	−944.0	3 321
1992	877 685	1.8	920	954	−19.1	−382.0	3 108
1993	894 519	1.9	749	1 194	−15.9	−84.0	2 429
1994	801 648	−10.4	822	975	−18.8	−272.0	2 426

Data source: For 1988 to 1993, 'Greece in Figures', an ICAP publication, vol. 1990 through to 1995. For 1994, *Express*, 19.11.1995, on the basis of figures released by ICAP. For inflation rates (at year-end) and export figures, Bank of Greece Annual Reports. 'Firms' refers to limited and public limited companies only.

Note: The total number of firms for 1991 does not add up to the figure in Table 8.1 because ICAP revised its records in 1994.

Diagram 8.2
Evolution of Greek trade in industrial goods, 1973–95

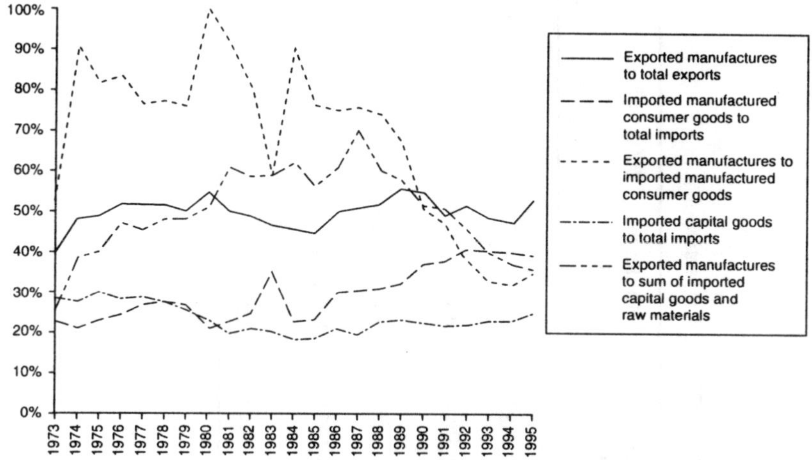

Data source: Bank of Greece Annual Reports.

been able to concentrate profitably on the domestic market, managing, as we said, to raise their prices faster than their costs. These developments have allowed Greek industry to add more output value per drachma of expenses (= gross income − net income). This is a crucial ratio to look for: according to Table 8.1, in 1990–4 it went up to 1.12 from 1.04 in 1977–89 – certainly, a welcome trend.

Not all news is good, though. The export performance, in particular, of Greek industry (excluding food and beverages) is worsening (see Table 8.3 and Diagram 8.2). Despite a rising ratio of imported capital goods to (expanding) total imports since 1984, which implies rising investment in fixed capital, we find that larger imports of capital goods (and raw materials) do not mean necessarily larger exports of manufactures. The ratio of the latter to the former has been declining since 1987, whilst the ratio of exported manufactures to total exports has remained more or less the same over 1986–95, with an average value equal to 51.2 per cent, and a standard deviation of 2.9 per cent. Maybe the high point in Greek industry's export performance was reached in 1980, when the ratio of exported manufactures to imported manufactured consumer goods had achieved unity: Greece had exported and imported manufactured products of equal dollar value. Finally, the ratio

Table 8.3
Greek external trade in industrial goods,* 1973–95; Key ratios

	Average (%)	Standard Deviation (%)	Maximum value	Minimum value	1995 value (%)	Trend since nearest extreme value
Exported manufactures to total exports	50	4	56% in 1989	40% in 1973	53	Declining
Imported manufactured consumer goods to total imports	30	7	40% in 1992	20% in 1974	39	Flat
Exported manufactures to imported manufactured consumer goods	68	20	100%in 1980	32% in 1994	35	Rising
Imported capital goods to total imports	23	4	30% in 1975	18% in 1984	25	Rising
Exported manufacures to sum of imported capital goods and raw materials	50	11	70% in 1987	26% in 1973	36	Declining

* Excluding foodstuffs, beverages, and tobacco products.

Data source: Bank of Greece Annual Reports.

of imported manufactured consumer products to total imports has been rising from 20 per cent in 1974 to 40 per cent in 1992–4. It all means that, although Greek industry, or a segment of it, has been doing some cleaning up of late, it has not been able to contribute to a drastic improvement in Greece's external trade performance, by meeting rising imports of manufactures with rising exports of its own.

The general reason is low international competitiveness.[7] In turn, this has been attributed to a variety of factors[8], such as obsolete equipment and incompetent management in Greek firms, worsening differential productivity between Greece and most industrial countries, an overvalued drachma, high real labour costs, insufficiently skilled workers, poor infrastructure, and very low R&D expenditures. Yet another factor may relate to the increasingly important role of transnational firms in Greece. Since a transnational will usually divide up a regional market among its national affiliates, the latter often tend to focus more on the domestic market each faces than on winning export markets. Let us analyse some of these points in greater detail.

8.2 CAUSES OF UNCOMPETITIVENESS

The main 'background' reason must be the failure of Greece to put in place and streamline a modern, performance-oriented, meritocratic education system, from primary to higher education level (see Section 3.3 in Chapter 3). Certainly the trend, even within manufacturing industry, is for less manual, and more clerical, labour than in the past (see Table 8.4). If Greece had done well in this field, which represents her most important potential resource as she has little of anything else, her economy would be in far better shape, she would be more respected internationally, her various policies (including foreign) would be smarter, and she would have moved much faster and more decisively when the Balkan and ex-USSR markets opened up after the collapse of communism than she has. She would also be doing far more R&D work than has been the case (see below).

The issue of incompetent management is very difficult to quantify for two reasons. First, it presupposes the exercise of value judgement. For instance, one may accuse Greek businessmen of short-termism, inability to anticipate developments, parochialism, vulgarity, neglect of marketing and customer care, and dogged resistance to co-operation with others – all true. But in the context of an opportunistic, alienated, corporatist, and state-pampered society, it could be argued that Greek

Table 8.4
Greek industry: Changes in the labour force, 1961–92

Year	White-collar workers	Blue-collar workers	All workers	Percentage of white-collar to total
1961	25 151	162 812	187 963	13
1963	30 762	170 805	201 567	15
1965	37 508	181 430	218 938	17
1967	43 703	180 552	224 255	19
1969	48 182	175 924	224 106	21
1971	57 869	207 351	265 220	22
1973	69 500	231 907	301 407	23
1975	79 382	256 377	335 759	24
1977	89 023	274 202	363 225	25
1979	97 562	271 715	369 277	26
1981	104 989	269 301	374 290	28
1983	108 724	242 034	350 758	31
1985	113 050	234 619	347 669	33
1987	124 033	225 838	349 871	35
1989	130 690	219 723	350 413	37
1991	127 215	198 111	325 326	39
1992	123 736	192 012	315 748	39

Source: *E Cathemerine*, 25.2.1996, based on a study by professor J. Khalikias, done on behalf of the Panhellenic Union of Exporters. His data are not comparable to ICAP data, as the latter refer to limited and public limited companies only.

businessmen have shown a great deal of competence at skinning consumer, the state, and taxpayer alike. Second, managerial competence can be measured either ex-post, on the basis of success or failure rates of business enterprises (but then how does one separate individual cases from trends affecting the economy as a whole?); or else, on the basis of some objective criterion, like level of educational attainment. The latter course assumes that educational qualifications and business competence are highly correlated, when in fact they are not. Very often ruthlessness is a stronger guarantee of success in business. It is only when an economy opens up, and is exposed to world trade, competition and influences, that the ability to appreciate and utilise novel information (as opposed to familiar types of information) becomes critical. With this in mind, we can look into a study by the Athens Chamber of Craft Industries, conducted in 1994 among a 4000-strong sample of member-firms. The study found (Table 3.1) that 25 per cent of all persons acting as directors of those firms had only finished primary school; 7 per cent had finished a college or polytechnic, 11 per cent had received higher (that is, university) education, and only 1 per cent held post-graduate degrees.[9] Table 3.1 shows that the percentage of managers with university or college education in the sample was slightly higher than in the corresponding population age-group, which was a good thing. But the one in four managers who has not gone beyond primary school, is obviously inadequately equipped to compete against foreign firms, whether in Greece or abroad, or in an information-dependent environment in general, on the way to a unified European market.

Greece's atrocious higher education system accounts, among others, for a very poor R&D record. True, there have been flashes of inspiration. An example is internationally renowned *Heliflex*, a flexible plastic pipe invented by industrialist A. Petzetakis. Another appears to be *LaserLock*, a method for copy-protecting CDs.[10] A third is *Eurodrip*, a hosing system developed by D. Paraskevopoulos. Greek software houses produce good accounting packages,[11] whilst food manufacturers show increasing ingenuity in coming up with innovative, high-quality products, nearly all up to NW European standards, and quite a few even better.[12] Also, Greek wine-makers are gradually managing to produce labels that can stand their ground internationally,[13] and some are simply excellent. But these examples are pitifully few compared to the fantastic stream of inventions and innovations flowing from more advanced countries. Sadly, the broad R&D picture in Greece is dismal,[14] with only 2.7 persons per 1000 employed in R&D in 1991. The figure was on a par with that for Portugal, but was lower than for Spain (4.7), Italy (5.8), Ireland (6.1), and, of course, Germany (12.9) and Japan (14.0).[15] In expenditure terms the picture is even bleaker. In 1991 Greece spent 0.46 per cent of its GDP on R&D, lower than any other EU country.[16] (The figures for the top performers, Germany, France, and the UK, were 2.53, 2.36, and 2.12 per cent, respectively.) In the same year the Greek government spent 0.57 per cent of its budget on R&D, again lower than any other EU country.[17] In absolute terms, total national expenditure on R&D was 267 m. ECUs, once more lower than any other EU country.[18]

The structure of those funds, or their destination, were indicative of who did R&D in Greece, or of the priorities assigned. If anything, the state did more R&D than the private sector. In 1991, only 25.5 per cent of R&D expenditures were undertaken by firms (some, no doubt, public-sector ones): the rest, by the government and universities (which are owned by the state).[19] But whereas, according to 1992 EuroStat

Table 8.5
Greek manufacturing industry, 1974–95
Annual percentage changes in

	Labour productivity (%)	Real weekly wages (blue-collar workers) (%)	Real unit labour costs (%)
1974	–3.8	14.3	17.5
1975	6.3	6.2	1.8
1976	6.0	16.3	11.3
1977	–1.2	6.9	9.6
1978	4.5	11.3	7.4
1979	3.5	–4.4	–8.2
1980	1.0	–0.2	–0.3
1981	5.0	–0.1	4.1
1982	–3.0	7.8	16.6
1983	0.8	–0.8	–2.1
1984	2.8	5.7	4.4
1985	1.0	3.1	–6.3
1986	–0.5	–8.5	–3.6
1987	–0.8	–5.7	–5.2
1988	–0.8	9.3	5.3
1989	2.0	6.2	3.4
1990	–1.1	–0.9	–1.9
1991	5.6	–2.3	–7.5
1992	4.0	–1.8	–5.0
1993	3.0	–3.4	–4.8
1994	4.1	2.1	–2.3
1995	1.4	3.6	4.0

Source: Bank of Greece Annual Reports.

data, the EU as a whole spent 12.1 per cent of its R&D funds on industrial production and technology, Greece spent only 7.6 per cent on same, happily choosing to spend 4 per cent on research into 'social structures and relations'. The corresponding EU average was 1.8 per cent.[20] It is doubtful, however, whether more spending on R&D per se can help industrial Greece modernise, as 'the firms which progress through innovation are in no position to pull the industrial train to higher gear, on account of the rest of industry [] having stuck to counter-productive and inefficient patterns and practices'.[21]

Turning to the issue of labour costs, we find that unit labour costs increased in real terms by 1.6 per cent per annum between 1974 and 1994 (Table 8.5). This is due to a corresponding increase in manufacturing real wages by 3 per cent, which was only partially absorbed by a concomitant rise in labour productivity by 1.9 per cent. In other words, during that period there were excessive real wage increases, in relation to the productivity of labour. The fact that the latter rose by the low rate of 1.9 per cent per annum was caused by a series of factors, many of which were beyond the direct control of the workers themselves. On the other hand, given the low productivity of Greek industry, high real wage increases certainly did not make things easier for industry – or for the workers. The contrast with the period 1990–4, when the productivity, as well as profitability (see Table 8.1), of Greek industry registered positive increases is illuminating. At that time labour productivity went up by 3.3 per cent per annum (almost double the 1974–94 figure), but because real wages dropped by 1 per cent per annum, unit labour costs (a crucial determinant of profitability) fell by 4.4 per cent per annum. Conversely, during the period 1974–89 the productivity of labour rose only by 1.4 per cent per annum: together with an annual average real wage increase of 4.3 per cent, this caused unit labour costs to rise by 3.5 per cent per annum. In short, Table 8.5 and Diagram 8.1 clearly show the effect of excessively high real wage rises on unit labour costs, in conjunction with weak productivity increases in the 1974–94 period. This result is also borne by a statistical regression of unit labour cost changes on, first, real wage changes, and then on productivity changes as well (data from Table 8.5). It showed that real wage changes accounted on their own for 75 per cent of the variations in unit labour costs, whilst together with productivity changes they accounted for 87 per cent of the variations in unit labour costs.

Diagram 8.1 is interesting in other respects too. For example, it reveals those crucial, post-1974 years in the history of Greek manufacturing, during which, given the existence of a low productivity problem, excessive real wage rises, usually achieved through strike action or its threat (Diagram 8.3), made things worse. First such year was 1974 itself; it can perhaps be explained as a backlash against the industrial discipline previously imposed by a military junta (1967–74). The second group of years was 1976–8. The third group, the one that was perhaps decisive for Greece's industrial crisis, was 1982–4; it can be linked to the populist policies of PASOK, Greece's paternalistic version of a socialist party. During 1982, for instance, there was a big rise in real wages (7.8 per cent) which, in combination with productivity's drop in the same year, caused a dramatic jump in unit labour costs (16.6 per cent). It shouldn't be surprising that during 1982–4 Greek industry registered losses, whilst this period marks the formal onset of

Diagram 8.3
Work-hours lost due to strikes throughout the Greek economy in 1976–93, as percentage of period average (= 8.2 m. hrs)

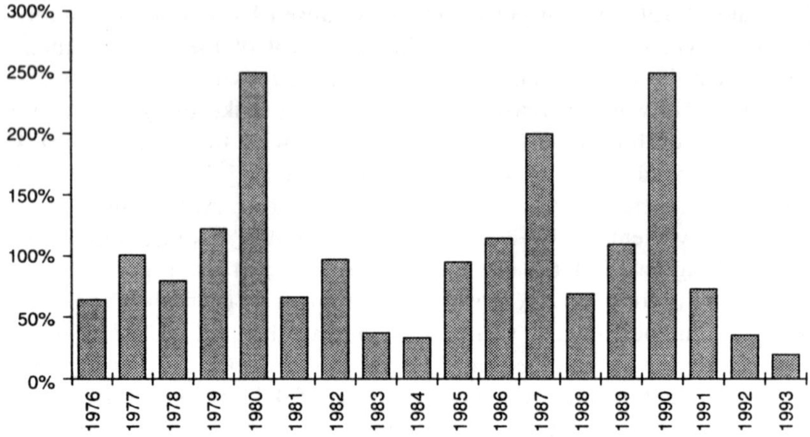

Source: Katsanevas (1995), Lampsias (1990).

deindustrialisation in Greece. Finally, the fourth year group was 1988–9.

The above findings justify neither those who say that deindustrialisation is the industrialists' fault, nor those who fault the workers' and trade-unionists' excessive demands. Quite apart from the fact that there is a global trend towards more services and less manufacturing, as percentages of GDP, both capital and labour bear responsibility for the specific problems of Greek industry – and so do most politicians, who tolerated or encouraged unconstructive attitudes and practices on both sides. On the one hand productivity is primarily the responsibility of governments, who are supposed to provide the right framework, and of businesses, who are supposed to think long-term and take risks; only indirectly and up to a point is productivity the workers' responsibility, as in avoiding absenteeism. On the other hand, if the Greek working class had shown restraint, especially in those times when industry was facing particular difficulties (like the aftermaths of the two oil-shocks, in 1973 and 1979), it would have helped to avoid the worst of the crisis that subsequently developed – assuming, of course, that governments and businesses alike had pursued the right policies. Unfortunately, with rare exceptions neither group in Greece has been known to plan beyond the immediate and the obvious, even if that. In the given context Greece lost more working days per 1000 employees in industry and services in 1985–9 and also in 1990–4 than any other OECD country: 3976 and 3500, respectively, when the corresponding figures for the second biggest loser, Spain, were 647 and 492, and the OECD averages were 145 and 100.[22]

As a result of the incompetence of her governments and of a sizable part of her entrepreneurial class, Greece, according to a European Commission report (December 1994), registered the smallest productivity change from 1985 to 1996 (forecast) in the EU: 11.6 per cent, against 39.5 per cent for Portugal, 46.5 per cent for Ireland, 19.9 per cent for Spain, 23.8 per cent for Britain, and 23.3 per cent for the EU-12.[23]

Lower comparative productivity may have led to larger imports and smaller exports, but were not these two effects enhanced by the supposed 'hard' drachma policy of successive Greek governments since 1986? The answer to this is a bit circuitous. As Diagram 5.8 demonstrated, the annual percentage changes of the nominal weighted exchange parity of the drachma from 1979 to 1994 have all been negative – implying a constantly depreciating drachma, rather than a 'hard' one. Bringing inflation differentials into the picture, however, results in positive APC – at least since 1987. This simply means that, although, year after year, it cost more drachmas to buy, say, a pound sterling (that is, the drachma depreciated vis-a-vis the pound), the latter would buy a smaller quantity of a representative basket of commodities in Greece, due to local inflation. But then the real problem for Greek exporters has not been a 'hard' drachma, but high domestic inflation. Unless, that is, as some have advised, the drachma is devalued by a truly wide margin,[24] or is allowed to depreciate rapidly – in which case, the likeliest effect will be even more inflation in Greece! In the meantime, as said, the relatively 'hard' drachma has allowed Greek firms to raise money and procure capital goods and raw materials more cheaply from abroad than locally.

The poor infrastructure of Greece has been another reason for her low productivity gains over the 1980s. Table 8.6 presents a comparison of indices of productive infrastructures endowment in 1985. At that time Greece managed to surpass Ireland (not in education, though) and Portugal from among the EU-12. Although there are no more recent data, it is doubtful, considering comparative growth rates between the three countries, whether Greece has stuck to her slight lead.

Ultimately, Greece's declining international competitiveness is a result of worsening comparative productivity, excessive real wage changes,

Table 8.6
European Union: Infrastructure data

	Europe: Indices of productive infrastructure endowments in 1985 (EU average = 100)					European Union: Electricity and telephony, 1992			
	Transport	Communication	Energy	Education	Total	Electric power production (kwh per person), 1992	Telephone mainlines per 1000 persons, 1992	Faults per 100 telephone mainlines per year, 1992	Faults per mainlines per 1000 persons, 1992
Belgium	203.6	125.3	265.0	103.4	162.6	7 215	425	8	34
Luxembourg	268.1	184.9	161.5	78.8	158.5				
Holland	244.7	123.9	132.5	70.9	129.9	5 089	487	4	19
France	119.0	123.1	180.8	94.9	126.3	8 089	525	8	42
Germany	163.1	124.4	92.6	134.3	126.0	6 693	457	14	64
UK	152.0	103.1	109.2	81.2	108.6	5 660	473	16	76
Denmark	80.5	142.9	53.8	104.4	89.7	5 983	581		
Italy	105.1	70.2	80.4	104.8	88.8	3 963	410	17	70
Spain	71.1	67.3	50.1	111.9	71.7	4 022	353	6	21
Greece	38.0	90.6	30.8	52.1	48.5	3 624	487	80	390
Ireland	31.8	65.0	32.5	73.1	47.1	4 545	314	38	119
Portugal	47.1	33.4	20.0	37.0	32.8	3 055	306	52	159

Source: Masera (1995).

Source: World Bank, World Development Report 1995, p. 215.

and high inflation. Factors like a poor national infrastructure,[25] an inadequately skilled labour force,[26] insufficient R&D, a starkly incompetent educational system (manifested in functional illiteracy in many, and in depreciating university degrees), substandard management, and obsolete equipment are important precisely because they affect productivity. It all points to the need for more and better investment – in people far more than in machines – and that is not forthcoming to the required extent.

8.3 TRANSNATIONALS LEAD

The bifurcation of Greek industry into a 'dynamic' and a 'problem' segment has already been mentioned. Roughly, sectors such as

- processed food and beverages (first and foremost)
- petroleum products
- pharmaceuticals, cosmetics and detergents (PCD)
- electric-electronic materials and
- rubber and plastics

made up the 'dynamic' segment around 1994. The 'problem' segment comprised

- transportation equipment (the sector includes ship-building, aircraft repairing and truck assembling)
- textiles
- basic metallurgy and metal products
- non-metallic minerals and
- paper products.

Within the 'problem' segment successful firms can, of course, be found here and there, like Thrace PaperMill plc, a paper products factory in Western Thrace. Sometimes, however, success is more apparent than real. This is the case when it has come about by means of state subsidies in various shapes and forms, like debt write-offs, at a tremendous cost to the economy and the tax-payer. Examples are Thessalian Paper Industry plc, Khalkis Cement plc, Eleusis Shipyards plc, and others. Conversely, the absence of loss-maker Pirelli Hellas plc from the rubber and plastics sector as of 1992[27] helped the sector appear even more profitable and dynamic than otherwise, whilst the decision of profit-maker Goodyear Hellas plc in July 1996 to move its operations elsewhere (Turkey or Poland) was expected to have the opposite effect.

The 'dynamic' segment of Greek industry is usually, though not always, associated with the strong presence of foreign capital. Transnationals are certainly among the most dynamic of firms in Greek industry. For example,[28] in 1992 140 firms, or 15.8 per cent of all industrial firms with sales of more than one billion drs (about £2.7 m.), were formally controlled by non-Greek interests, and accounted for 25 per cent of the total sales of firms in this category. Of the 140 foreign-controlled firms, 108 registered profits for the year, which were equal to 26.5 per cent of the sum of the profits of industry's profit-making firms. The return on net worth for all 140 firms was 17.7 per cent, against 11 per cent for the entire large- to medium-size industry, even after taking out special cases (like big-loss firms into receivership). Their net margin on sales was 5.8 per cent, as opposed to 3 per cent for the entire large- and medium-size industry.

Altogether 33 out of the top 100 industrial firms in Greece (in terms of sales), and 61 out of the top 200, were foreign-controlled in 1992. Of the top 100 foreign-controlled firms (again, in terms of sales), 21 were in the PCD sector, 19 in food products, 11 in electric-electronic materials, 11 in chemicals, 5 in beverages. Some of those 100 foreign-controlled firms were found in typically loss-making sectors: four in non-metallic minerals, two in textiles, one in basic metallurgy.

Table 8.7 presents another view of the presence of foreign firms in Greece. It gives the proportion of profitable foreign firms in all profitable firms, with profits of 100 m. drs or more, in all sectors of Greek industry in 1992. It also relates profit per foreign firm to profit per Greek firm in each sector. The evidence in Table 8.7 answers tentatively the question of whether the 'dynamic' segment of Greek industry is associated, or led by, foreign-controlled firms. It appears that in 1992 foreign-controlled profitable firms registered more profits per firm than Greek profitable firms in four out of the five aforementioned 'dynamic' sectors. The sole exception was electric-electronic materials, where the dominant firms are Intracom (Greek) and Siemens (German) – but then Intracom has been accused of winning state contracts through rather shady practices.[29] Finally, Table 8.8 presents the biggest 10 firms, in terms of 1994 sales, in selected sectors of the 'real' economy in Greece, also indicating the foreign-controlled ones and the net margin on sales for each. Again, foreign firms, or firms with significant foreign participation, seem to dominate, with construction the only clear

Table 8.7
Greek and foreign industrial firms* by sector, and comparison of profit per firm, 1992

	No. of firms	Of which: Foreign (%)	Profit per foreign firm to profit per Greek firm
Transportation equipment**	9	0	NA
Basic mettalurgy	10	0	NA
Printing, publishing	16	0	NA
Wood & furniture	11	0	NA
Metal products	28	7	11.31
Non-metallic minerals	27	7	6.22
Miscellaneous	11	18	4.87
Beverages	25	16	2.38
Plastics	20	20	2.25
PCD***	32	44	2.19
Food products	78	21	2.10
Chemicals	20	40	1.95
Machinery – Appliances	8	38	1.31
Electric-electronic appliances	7	14	1.17
Clothing & footwear	22	9	1.03
Minerals	9	44	0.77
Textiles	49	8	0.56
Paper products	17	6	0.52
Electric-electronic materials	20	70	0.30
Cigarettes-tobacco	15	7	0.25
Petroleum products	10	30	0.21
TOTAL	444	19	1.70

* Which in 1992 had profits of more than 100 m. drs, each. Foreign firms which registered losses in that year (e.g., Aluminium of Greece in basic metallurgy, AgroInvest in food produts, or Pepsico-Eve in beverages) are excluded.
** Shipbuilding, aircraft repairing, truck assembling.
*** Pharmaceuticals, cosmetics, detergents.

Data source: Papandropoulos (1995a); *Greece in Figures: 1994* (ICAP: Athens).

exception (followed, at a distance, by foodstuffs and drinks, most dynamic sector of Greek manufacturing).

Despite the comparatively good profitability of many transnational firms in Greece, the country's desirability as an investment location on the part of foreign capital is waning fast. The issue is explored further in the next section, but the broad reason seems to be that over the last 15 years or so Greece has lost her comparative advantage of cheap

Table 8.8
Biggest industrial, commercial, and construction firms in Greece, 1994
(F = foreign controlled, or substantial foreign participation, by 1996)

	Sales in 1994 (m. drs)	Net Profit in 1994 (m. drs)	Net Profit to Sales (%)	Sales 1994 in m. £, at 371 drs/£
Biggest Industrial Firms				
Motor Oil Hellenic Refineries plc (F; Aramco)	178 819	1 638	0.9	482
Petrola Hellas plc	128 284	2 605	2.0	346
Hellenic Bottling Co. (F; Coca-Cola)	98 876	16 912	17.1	266
Athenian Brewery plc (F)	82 991	19 889	24.0	224
Hercules Cement plc (F)	74 741	7 420	9.9	201
Hellenic Sugar Industry plc	74 667	10 855	14.5	201
Papastratos Cigarettes plc	68 992	10 216	14.8	186
Aluminium of Greece plc (F)	66 514	4 135	6.2	179
FAGE Dairy Industry plc	65 230	1 116	1.7	176
Delta Dairy Industry plc	61 215	6 125	10.0	165
Intracom Telecommunications plc	58 994	10 039	17.0	159
Titan Cement plc	58 456	7 819	13.4	157
Lever Hellas plc (F; Unilever)	57 946	3 738	6.5	156
Soya Hellas plc (fats & oils)	57 442	399	0.7	155
Steel Processing plc	53 140	−1 195	−2.2	143
Biggest Goods-trading Firms				
EKO Hellenic Fuels plc	212 975	5 502	2.6	574
Shell Hellas plc (F)	198 817	5 188	2.6	536
BP Greece Ltd (F)	195 816	2 938	1.5	527
Mobil Oil Hellas plc (F)	164 946	−237	−0.1	444
Nike plc (supermarkets) (F)	118 128	219	0.2	318
Sklavenitis J.&S. plc (supermarkets)	87 454	2 653	3.0	236
Texaco plc Hellenic Oil Co. (F)	84 202	2 318	2.8	227
Veropoulos Bros plc (supermarkets) (F)	71 531	1 423	2.0	193
AvinOil plc (Motor Oil affiliate)	69 923	247	0.4	188
MamidOil – JetOil plc (petroleum products)	67 809	−180	−0.3	183
Makro Cash & Carry plc (F)	66 196	909	1.4	178
Mamidakis G. & Co. plc (petroleum products)	64 929	75	0.1	175
A-B Vassilopoulos Gastronomia - Delicatessen plc (supermarkets) (F)	61 919	1 529	2.5	167
Toyota Hellas plc (F)	57 999	2 314	4.0	156
Fiat Auto Hellas plc (F)	51 994	1 391	2.7	140
Biggest Food-product Makers				
Hellenic Sugar Industry plc	74 667	10 855	14.5	201
FAGE Diary Industry plc	65 230	1 116	1.7	176
Delta Dairy Industry plc	61 215	6 125	10.0	165
Soya Hellas plc (fats & oils)	57 442	399	0.7	155
Elais Oleaginous Products plc (F; Unilever)	50 518	4 613	9.1	136
Loumidis plc (coffee) (F; Nestle)	45 624	6 643	14.6	123

Union of Agricultural Co-operatives of Larissa-Tyrnavos-Aya (agroproducts)	27 594	1 045	3.8	74
Mevgal Macedonian Dairy plc	25 479	914	3.6	69
Agno Dairy Industry	20 885	6	0.0	56
ION Cocoa & Chocolate Industry	19 368	969	5.0	52
Soya Mills plc (fats & oils)	18 810	55	0.3	51
Dodona Dairy Industry plc	18 443	162	0.9	50
Nestle Hellas plc (F)	17 344	1 016	5.9	47
AgroInvest plc (fats & oils) (F; Thompson)	17 194	–900	–5.2	46
Hellenic Biscuits Co. plc	16 754	1 427	8.5	45
Biggest Supermarkets & Dept Stores				
Nike (F; Marinopoulos Bros Group & Continent)	118 128	219	0.2	318
Sklavenitis J.&S.	87 454	2 653	3.0	236
Veropoulos Bros (F)	71 531	1 423	2.0	193
Makro Cash & Carry (F)	66 196	909	1.4	178
A-B Vassilopoulos Gastronomia - Delicatessen plc (F)	61 919	1 529	2.5	167
Continent Hellas (F)	46 212	1 816	3.9	124
Metro (F)	43 837	735	1.7	118
Atlantic	33 108	330	1.0	89
Tresco (Marinopoulos Bros Group)	29 833	–439	–1.5	80
Trofo	29 154	437	1.5	79
Pente	28 742	1 375	4.8	77
Massoutis D.	26 133	224	0.9	70
Farma Tetras (Atlantic Group)	23 943	237	1.0	64
Athena (Veropoulos Bros)	23 725	168	0.7	64
HyperMarinopoulos (F; Marinopoulos Bros)	15 037	–774	–5.1	41
Biggest Construction Companies				
Mechanica plc	17 050	4 836	28.4	46
Hellenic Technodomikhé plc	16 119	2 449	15.2	43
AEGEK plc	11 895	3 894	32.7	32
BIOKAT plc	11 659	122	1.0	31
Ergas plc	7 793	1 722	22.1	21
Intracom Construction plc	6 339	652	10.3	17
Eucleides plc	6 217	1 161	18.7	17
Technodomé plc	5 946	1 516	25.5	16
General Construction Co. plc	5 360	1 946	36.3	14
DIEKAT plc	5 246	1 039	19.8	14
GENER plc	4 425	1 338	30.2	12
Technical Co. of Volos plc	4 386	1 610	36.7	12
Hedrasis – M. Psallidas plc	4 276	1 201	28.1	12
ATTI-KAT plc	4 213	1 100	26.1	11
Sarantopoulos K.J. plc	3 984	2 614	65.6	11

Data sources: For industrial and commercial firms, *E Cathemerine,* 13.8.1995, p. 39, on the basis of data supplied by Industrial News & Research and National Communication Statbank, respectively. For food-product firms, National Communication Statbank. For supermarkets and construction firms, ICAP, on the basis of computer print-outs graciously supplied. Makro was included with supermarkets at the author's discretion.

labour to Eastern European countries (which moreover have skilled labour forces) or to Turkey without offering adequate compensation through good infrastructure, trade-union co-operativeness, minimal red tape or a stable regulatory and tax environment. Examples of transnationals which left Greece in the 1990s have been Pirelli and Goodyear, Ucar, Sandoz, Monyal and Nissan.[30] By 1996 more were contemplating leaving or at least had reduced their productive involvement in Greece, such as Warner Lambert, Siemens, Legrand and Procter & Gamble.[31] Even the Greek firm Intracom was thinking about moving its productive arm to Romania. If the movement gathers momentum, talking about the bifurcation of Greek industry into a 'dynamic' and a 'problem' segment will fail to describe the current state of Greek industry: with the possible exception of the food and drink sector, there will be severe deindustrialisation pure and simple.

8.4 FOREIGN CAPITAL AND ATTITUDES TO INVESTMENT

Has Greece, then, been successful in attracting direct foreign investment (DFI)? The short answer is that, especially after 1980, it has not been able to attract much of any kind of 'real' investment, foreign or otherwise. At the same time a small but increasing number of Greece-based companies have been expanding into other countries: Titan Cement (the USA, Spain, France), Ergon (Germany, Japan), Athens Medical Centre (Moscow), Claoudatos department stores (Bulgaria), Delta Dairy Industry (Bulgaria, France, Switzerland, Romania, Ukraine), Hellenic Bottling Co., or 3E (Bulgaria, Ireland), and others. In their case, however, the decision to expand overseas was not really a reflection on their chances at home; it came, rather, in the context of an increasingly global search for greater profitability and/or in order to consolidate their overall position in their particular sectors.

Unfortunately there are no aggregate data on Greece-originated DFI abroad. Related data are to be found in the Monthly Statistical Bulletin (MSB) of the Bank of Greece, and fall under two headings: 'private long-term entrepreneurial capital imported under Law 2687/53', Greece's premier law governing DFI, and 'other private long-term entrepreneurial capital'. Since 1990, however, the last category includes increasing borrowing by Greek firms from overseas – and, of course, repayments on those loans on the debit side. This means that one cannot know the extent to which capital exported from Greece under that heading is for investment or for repayment purposes. By the same token, one cannot know the extent to which imported funds represent DFI or loans to Greece-based firms. In addition, the relevant entries on imported capital (even under Law 2687/53) lump DFI together with working capital.

The importation of capital into Greece for the purpose of DFI is, like we said, governed mainly by Law 2687, which was passed in 1953. Greece was – and ostensibly still is – so desperate for DFI that the law was sanctioned in the Greek Constitution then, and again in the amended Constitution of 1975 (Article 107). Other related laws have been 89/67 (on off-shore companies), Presidential Decree 207/1987 and Decision 825/86 by the Governor of the Bank of Greece (on the exportation of capital by EEC- and non-EEC-residents, respectively), as well as various so-called Development Laws (1262/82, 1892/90, and 2234/94).

Since the liberalisation of capital movements in Greece, which took place in 1993 (for long-term capital) and 1994 (for short-term capital), the aforementioned laws have lost their significance. It is, instead, the European Union Law which has become, or is becoming, the reference framework, as concerns, for example, the taxation of connected companies (Directive 90/435 and Convention 90/436), mergers and acquisitions, or the freedom of establishment.

Looking back on 36 years of attempts to encourage DFI into Greece,[32] one cannot fail to notice two things: First, judging from the trend in capital imports under Law 2687/53, relevant laws and regulations do not appear to have helped much (Table 8.9). If anything, in the period 1986-91 Greece appears to have attracted the smallest share of DFI of all EU-12 member states (Table 8.10). Second, and more importantly, there has been a big difference between paying lip-service to the need for direct foreign, as well as domestic, investment, and creating and sustaining welcoming conditions for it in practice. This is perhaps the reason behind the apparent failure of the legal framework to attract and enable investment capital in sufficient quantities for a low-inflation, high-growth pattern of development.

The following examples will demonstrate the unhelpful, even hostile, environment in Greece for 'real' investments, whether of foreign or domestic origin. They will also show the dramatic, almost pivotal, significance of qualitative factors shaping Greece's investment pattern and subsequent growth chances. In some cases, admittedly, the opposition to investment projects has been linked to environmental concerns. Whether all of these have been justified, even legitimate, the author of this book cannot proclaim with certainty. To a large extent

Table 8.9
Private long-term capital imported into Greece, 1960–95 ($US thousands)

a	Private business capital imported under Law 2687/53 b	Of which: From USA Canada, other America (%) c	From Europe (%) d	Other private business capital imported e	Of which: From USA Canada, other America (%) f	From Europe (%) g	Total business capital imported h	Capital imported for purchasing real estate i
1960	698	83.2	16.8	11 941	0.2	93.5	12 639	34 779
1961	1 396	62.6	37.4	34 712	2.9	97.1	36 108	39 321
1962	3 099	80.4	19.6	15 353	63.6	36.4	18 452	43 269
1963	17 179	59.0	41.0	25 874	45.8	53.8	43 053	48 400
1964	5 650	91.6	6.6	34 254	63.7	36.3	39 904	58 400
1965	49 523	71.3	28.7	38 798	45.6	54.3	88 321	64 000
1966	46 448	82.8	17.2	19 682	35.7	64.3	66 130	70 200
1967	31 985	82.7	17.1	18 270	35.6	64.4	50 255	46 395
1968	8 284	93.2	5.3	42 387	47.9	52.1	50 671	56 717
1969	7 009	48.4	50.8	51 609	34.4	65.4	58 618	65 400
1970	11 048	80.1	19.9	145 017	53.6	46.1	156 065	74 200
1971	24 250	69.9	30.1	74 772	46.9	52.8	99 022	105 655
1972	21 464	63.2	36.8	68 504	50.0	49.3	89 968	172 000
1973	45 262	82.3	15.2	119 362	50.9	48.3	164 624	268 900
1974	42 680	92.4	7.6	144 569	70.1	29.8	187 249	232 900
1975	17 708	68.7	31.3	177 637	70.2	28.9	195 345	299 400
1976	6 579	58.4	41.5	214 559	71.3	28.5	221 138	294 300
1977	8 813	57.7	42.3	264 609	73.0	25.8	273 422	362 800
1978	14 315	38.0	62.0	310 958	66.3	32.6	325 273	409 600

1979	16 305	88.4	11.5	344 309	67.6	32.1	360 614	592 100
1980	40 325	42.4	51.7	428 411	72.7	27.1	468 736	599 000
1981	31 643	70.4	29.4	378 225	64.7	34.6	409 868	487 800
1982	37 145	57.4	42.2	267 205	63.8	34.5	304 350	389 900
1983	16 355	48.7	50.9	297 722	80.6	18.8	314 077	422 900
1984	10 555	23.2	76.7	235 633	68.6	30.1	246 188	473 800
1985	16 187	80.7	18.8	273 528	65.3	32.1	289 715	430 900
1986	7 741	46.0	53.2	292 845	67.0	31.4	300 586	462 700
1987	8 593	68.0	30.6	382 868	65.9	33.9	391 461	674 900
1988	11 154	67.8	31.1	588 016	61.5	38.2	599 170	895 700
1989	12 293	48.5	51.0	627 724	58.4	40.0	640 017	739 500
1990	14 209	45.6	53.7	886 345	71.2	26.3	900 554	990 900
1991	53 043	74.2	24.4	1 296 679	53.4	46.1	1 349 722	1 082 300
1992	61 741	75.9	22.9	1 976 504	36.9	60.6	2 038 245	1 082 400
1993	31 374	58.9	40.6	1 949 864	33.5	63.6	1 981 238	946 000
1994	25 046	57.0	41.5	2 731 479	24.8	63.8	2 756 525	956 400
1995							5 398 800	1 016 000

Source: Bank of Greece Balance of Payments Dept.

Note: Business capital imported does not distinguish between DFI and working capital. Furthermore, since 1990, when Greek firms were first allowed to borrow in FX, 'other' business capital includes that borrowing.

Table 8.10
Direct Foreign Investment (DFI) in EU-12 member-states, 1986–91
(Current prices and exchange parities to the ECU)

	Percentage of total DFI	Percentage of DFI from other member-states
Britain	45.00	19.60
France	12.70	15.90
Holland	9.30	9.30
Spain	8.80	18.90
Italy	7.60	6.60
Belgium/Lux.	6.00	14.10
Germany	3.20	5.00
Ireland	3.00	5.50
Denmark	2.20	0.80
Portugal	1.60	3.40
Greece	0.60	0.80
EU-12	100	100

Data source: *E Cathemerine*, 18.1.1995, on the basis of Eurostat reporting of the findings of a research project sponsored by the European Commission, and involving a sample of 87 firms, including 17 transnationals.

such worries involve value-judgements (which the author happens to sympathise strongly with). But even then, the pertinent issue in the context of the present discussion is about poor co-ordination between government departments, lack of a proper legal framework, and, above all, inability and/or unwillingness to apply the law, such as it is.

(1) In 1986–7 a foreign firm wanted to undertake direct foreign investment (DFI) in Greece, utilising the subsidy scheme that the Greek state had in place. The firm planned to import part of its capital directly, in the form of machinery. The Ministry of the National Economy turned down this request. It asked the company to go through the circuitous route of first importing all the capital in the form of FX, and then re-exporting it in order to pay for the machinery to be imported. Was it because the Ministry wanted to ensure that the foreign firm would not overprice the machinery – which would result in the Greek state subsidising the foreign company to a larger extent than what was legal? No, the reason was more like one a pedantic Shylock might have given: 'If we approve the direct import, the Bank of Greece will lose its commission for

turning FX into drachmas, and also its commission for turning subsequently drachmas into FX' – is what the Ministry actually told the foreign firm![33]

(2) In the middle of 1995 the Canadian firm TVX-Gold won in open bidding the right to mine for gold in the ancient Cassandra mines of Khalkidiké. TVX-Gold's move represented the biggest investment in Greece since 1974, amounting to $200 m. Even though the mining and processing methods chosen were considered environmentally safe, and additional protective measures were being streamlined,[34] a number of local communities have been physically resisting the implementation of the project[35] – which the Greek state had sanctioned in the first place. There have also been reports that behind those locals who protest the project (ostensibly on environmental grounds) are two groups of lawyers with extensive landholdings in the area, which they want to develop for tourist purposes.[36] As a result, by mid-1996 TVX-Gold had suffered financial damage, with knock-on effects on Greece's credibility, it was threatening to quit the project altogether and sue the Greek State, and Greece was foregoing the chance to join the club of gold-producing countries, as well as enjoy a projected 16 billion drs (£43 m.) per year in FX for 15 to 20 years after completion of the works (4–5 years); in addition, 600 people were about to lose their jobs.

(3) For some time now Greater Athens has been under threat of power black-outs. An important reason (other, that is, than strikes by Public Power Corporation staff) is that a third power transfer line, from northern to southern Greece, has not become operational, even though it was essentially completed in 1992. 'Essentially' is the operative word, as the Public Power Corporation (PPC) has not been able to install five required pylons outside Athens, due to local resistance. Unlike the TVX-Gold case, resistance this time is not superficially on environmental grounds. Local land-owners take advantage of the fact that the Ministry of Planning, incorrectly, has categorised the particular area as residential rather than green belt. On their part, PPC does not want to re-site the pylons, fearing this would set a precedent.[37] By 1996 court proceedings on the case were still going on.

(4) Crete is also in increasing danger of finding herself power-less. The PPC has for 15 years been unable to build new power generation plants on the island, as in apparently every site tentatively chosen it has come across arms-bearing Cretans determined to oppose

the project, ostensibly for environmental reasons.[38] This, however, has not stopped the locals from sacrificing the beauty and character of many a place in Crete for the sake of big hotels, neon lights, cafeterias, and bars. The example, and the one involving the Cassandra project, show the extent to which the Greek State is unwilling to enforce the laws of the land because of all governments' fear of an ill-defined 'political cost'.[39]

(5) In 1995 German investors sought permission to build a marina for 500 yachts in Parekia, main port of the island of Paros. After failing to overcome local objections to the project, which were set forth on (probably justified) environmental grounds, the investors secured another area on the island, which they leased from the Greek Church under contract for 50 years. But the Greek Tourism Organisation (EOT) has told the investors that a marina cannot be built on leased land, even though the Ministry of the National Economy had assured the investors that a marina can certainly be built on leased land, provided the contract is for more than 10 years![40]

(6) In September 1995 a shop within a hotel complex in Thessalonica was contracted out to a new entrepreneur. Because of the change in management the authorities requested no fewer than 25 different certificates and forms (weighing 2.6 kilos!) from the management of the hotel in order to grant the relevant permit, although a permit was already in force, only in the name of the previous contractor who had operated the shop.[41]

(7) In 1989 a young man decided to start his own business. Having no own capital, he approached a bank for a loan in order to buy a piece of machinery. The bank asked to see the young man's certificate of registration with the local Chamber of Small-scale Manufacturing Firms. The latter, in turn, wanted to see the purchase invoice, fully paid, before allowing the young man to register. Eventually he got the loan, after signing a promise that he would register with the Chamber within three months, only the bank forced him to buy a life insurance policy from them also. Now, according to Greek law, to get the piece of machinery through customs without paying VAT, he needed to give customs a certificate from Inland Revenue attesting to his small manufacturer's status. Like the bank previously, the Inland Revenue wanted a certificate of registration with the local Chamber of Small-scale Manufacturing Firms – which the young man could not produce yet. When he showed the Inland Revenue official that in similar situations other

IR officials had given the applicants the certificates they required, the official announced that he would never give him one because he considered him 'suspect'. Despite his pleadings, our young man ended up paying the VAT anyway.[42] In this case a tax law which was supposed to help entrepreneurs was nullified by a combination of red tape and narrow-mindedness on the part of an insignificant state official.

(8) The last example concerns the ethics of Greek business. In the words of Mr Ezure, MD of Sony Hellas plc,

> I have worked in Scandinavia, Germany, and elsewhere. Business practices there, are not much different from those in Japan, but Greece is different. [] Let us say that we deliver goods, and the [Greek] businessman asks to pay six months later. Naturally we do not accept this [laughs]. In the end we agree to payment after two months. Payment day arrives, and the businessman is at the hospital feeling unwell, and we have to wait one more week. One week later he has opened a new shop, he needs cash, we have to wait another fortnight, then he is ill again, and we cannot find him. This is local business practice, or tradition, which we have to go along with since we operate locally. [] If this were to happen in Japan, that customer would not have survived following his first such dealing.[43]

One could proceed with dozens of such examples.[44] They are about the discouraging effect on investment in Greece of red tape,[45] frequent tax and business law changes, pervasive unreliability, political opposition to privatisation, governmental tolerance, and at times initiation, of illegal acts, misinformed – hence unjustified – opposition to industry on ostensibly environmental grounds, and an untrustworthy State. If one adds to these factors[46] others already mentioned, like frequent strikes, poor telecommunications, or persistent inflation, the bottom position of Greece in EU as an investment location is easily explained. Worse, these factors have also been discouraging domestic investment by the Greeks themselves.

8.5 OLIGOPOLIES AND COMPETITION

In addition to the dualism between a 'dynamic' and a 'problem' segment, another kind of dualism characterises Greek industry – but also the retail, construction, and other sectors. This comes about as a result of the dominant presence of small numbers of big firms (by Greek standards, anyway), and relatively large numbers of very small firms, with little in-between.[47]

Table 8.11 clearly shows the prevalence of small business units in Greece, as in 1992 the country appeared last among EU-15 member-states in terms of number of employees per business unit: 1.9 against a European average of 6.4. The same table puts Greece last in 1990 in terms of retail outlets per retail firm, just below Denmark, Italy, and Ireland, and first but one (Portugal) in terms of number of retail outlets per 1000 of population. These are all indicators of a country apparently resisting the tendencies to capital accumulation and concentration, which are among the hallmarks of capitalism.

Against that we have phenomena which are more in line with what happens in the rest of the developed world. For example, in 1992 the 50 biggest industrial companies in Greece (in terms of total assets), or 1.3 per cent of the total, accounted for nearly 20 per cent of industrial employment, and 44 per cent of fixed assets.[48] In the same year, the 30 000 largest business units in EU-15 (with more than 250 staff each), or 0.2 per cent of all business units, employed 34 per cent of the corresponding staff total, and accounted for 35 per cent of sales.[49] According to Table 8.12, in 1994 less than five per cent of firms in the Greek supermarket and department store sector accounted for 56 per cent of total sales (among limited and public limited companies in the sector); less than one per cent of construction firms accounted for 25 per cent of sales; and so on. The number of food (grocery) stores has been decreasing annually, which implies increasing concentration of grocery retailing among a smaller number of firms. In particular, food (grocery) stores in Greece were 31 273 in 1978, 28 650 in 1984, and 19 530 in 1994.[50] Additional research by the Greek Ministry of Trade has concluded that in 1994 just 17 large companies supplied 30 per cent of total supplies in the retail sector.[51]

Interestingly, though, these trends do not necessarily imply a lessening of competition in Greek sector-markets. Often the actual extent and significance of competition depend on the inner workings of each particular sector, rather than on concentration ratios. If we compare Tables 8.8 and 8.12, we find that the smallest net margin on sales (= net income to sales) is registered in one of the more heavily concentrated sectors in the Greek economy – supermarkets and department stores. Just ten companies accounted for 56 per cent of sales, and registered a 1.6 per cent average net margin on sales. By contrast, in the

Table 8.11

Business units in Europe, 1992, and retail outlets per 1000 of population, 1990

	No. of business units ('000)	Persons employed (m.)	Persons employed per business unit	Retail trade firms ('000)	Retail trade outlets ('000)	Retail outlets per retail firm	Retail outlets per 1000 of population
Austria	188	2.16	11.5	39.9	52.5	1.32	6.8
Holland	395	4.27	10.8	95.0	119.4	1.26	8.0
Luxembourg	15	0.16	10.7	3.5	4.4	1.26	11.5
Germany	2 420	24.13	10.0	493.0	533.7	1.22	8.4
Denmark	163	1.41	8.7	48.1	51.5	1.07	10.0
Belgium	396	2.95	7.4	127.8	140.0	1.10	14.0
Britain	2 549	18.85	7.4	348.2	466.6	1.34	8.1
France	1 956	14.40	7.4	461.8	546.1	1.18	9.7
Ireland	81	0.54	6.7	29.3	31.7	1.08	9.0
Sweden	341	2.24	6.6	64.9	72.2	1.11	8.4
Finland	199	1.15	5.8	29.5	39.7	1.35	8.0
Spain	2 166	10.37	4.8	454.9	523.2	1.15	13.4
Portugal	626	2.95	4.7	173.3	190.0	1.10	19.3
Italy	3 243	13.49	4.2	929.7	983.0	1.06	17.0
Greece	1 038	1.95	1.9	175.0	184.9	1.06	18.2
EU-15	15 776	101.02	6.4	3 419.9	3 938.9	1.15	11.3

Source on business units: *E Cathemerine*, 26.1.1996, on the basis of data released by EuroStat. The EuroStat study does not include farmers, fishermen, or public-sector employees, but does include self-employed professionals, or sole traders.

Source on retail trade: *E Cathemerine*, 18.7.1995, on the basis of data released by EuroStat. The data on Greece, as well as on retail outlets in Belgium, Britain, and Portugal, are EuroStat estimations. Population data were taken from the 1993 OECD Economic Survey of Greece.

Table 8.12
Greece: Market shares in selected sectors, 1993–4

		Share of sector turnover by top firm (%)	4-firm concentration ratio (%)	10-firm concentration ratio (%)	No. of firms	Percentage of top 4 firms in no. of firms	Percentage of top 10 firms in no. of firms
Supermarkets & dept stores	1992	12.1	30.1	50.5	166	2.41	6.02
	1993	12.7	33.4	57.3	189	2.12	5.29
	1994	11.2	32.6	55.8	212	1.89	4.72
Manufacturers of food products	1993	5.7	17.9	30.4			
	1994	5.2	17.9	30.2	768	0.52	1.30
Fish Farming	1993	4.2	19.8	38.0			
	1994	5.7	18.9	35.0	251	1.59	3.98
Construction	1993	3.3	12.4	18.9			
	1994	4.5	15.1	24.9	1 228	0.33	0.81

Source: ICAP computer print-outs graciously supplied. The total sales of the S-M & dept store sector have been augmented by the inclusion of Makro, at the author's discretion. ICAP has data on limited and public limited companies only.

food-product sector, ten companies had 30 per cent of sales, and a 7.3 per cent average net margin on sales. And in construction, ten companies were responsible for 25 per cent of sector sales, whilst they enjoyed a 20.7 per cent average net margin on sales.

These figures suggest far more competition among supermarkets than among, say, construction companies – which is indeed the case. It's not surprising either, if one considers the workings of the construction sector in Greece and its links to the Greek state.[52] Traditionally, big construction firms bidding for public works (their main source of revenue) would collude with one another in order to share the 'pie' between them. Once agreement had been reached as to who would get what (something which did not always happen), the firms would come up with ridiculously low bids for a project. Normally, the Greek state would grant the project to the lowest bidder. Subsequently, the construction firm would announce various unforeseen 'difficulties' which raised the cost of the project far beyond any initially submitted estimates. In the end the Greek state would feel that it had no choice but to go along with the demands (or blackmail) of the construction firm, since it had already committed funds to the project, and wanted it completed anyway. Eventually the tax-payer would foot the bill.

After 1993, however, the struggle between the big construction companies intensified – to no discernible benefit to anyone. The reason behind their new antagonism had to do with the so-called Second Delors Financial Assistance Package (1994–9), which Greece was awarded from the European Commission in 1992. This represented very substantial potential rewards ('spoils' might be a better word) for the firms involved in the construction projects, which the Package was meant to fund. The situation became more strenuous as a result of the European Commission forcing Greece to make project price reviews on the part of construction companies very difficult, if not impossible (Law 2338/95). A subsequent decree by the Ministry of Planning and Public Works, which effected the same for projects awarded before 10.10.1995, caused additional consternation among construction companies. The profitability of the latter was also bound to be affected by another crucial development: the very low rate at which Greece had been absorbing and utilising the Package funds.[53]

The delays happened because of the new legal framework regarding price reviews, but also because of time-honoured bureaucratic incompetence on the part of government departments, and government efforts to use the funds in ways that would maximise its own political capital. Thus, during the first two years of the programme (1994–5),

Greece managed to absorb just 53 per cent of the ear-marked funds.[54] As a result, the infrastructure projects (not all of them in construction), on which Greece had rested so many hopes for her development, were still crawling in 1996.

In the case of supermarkets and department stores, competition has obviously been good for the Greek consumer. In the case of construction, competition is either seriously distorted (since on the one hand we have instances of collusion among a relatively small number of firms, and on the other a virtual monopsonist – the Greek state); or else brings no social spill-over benefits (since the firm which will win a project, competitively or otherwise, becomes an effective monopolist for the duration, with both the power and enough opportunities to demand and justify price reviews).

With or without competition, though, an oligopolistic market structure, as evidenced by high concentration ratios, may well have interesting side benefits for the economy. Work done by the Centre of Planning and Economic Research in Athens has concluded that high-concentration sectors in Greece are associated with low indicators of import penetration (Table 8.13). This suggests that part of the answer to Greece's development problem may involve fostering conditions that will encourage and bring about more competition together with more concentration. So far, however, a series of Greek governments have done the opposite – on both counts. They have been making it difficult for firms either to amalgamate, or become bigger, or utilise any advantages that large size usually brings.[55] And they have been hindering competition by happily yielding to various groups' demands for more protection.[56] One usual form of protection involves setting the hours of business for retail shops by government decree, under the pretext that workers' hours and shop hours should be one and the same. Another assigns to bakeries exclusive rights to sell fresh bread in their vicinity. A third limits the number of taxi licenses the Ministry of Transport will issue, which is then called upon to control taxi fares. A fourth disallows financial leasing (as opposed to ordinary letting) of residential properties, hoping to discourage the growth of vertical conglomerates (banks together with construction companies) in the housing sphere.[57] And so on.

Such policies are clearly intended to cater to the interests of the masses of various kinds of smallholders in Greece, to the exclusion of other possible, even though sensible, goals – like consumer welfare, lower inflation, a healthier trade balance. Once again, the nature of Greek society and of its political system enforce their own logic on

Table 8.13
Market shares and import penetration in selected sectors of the Greek economy, 1992

Sector	Market share of top firm (%)	Market share of top four firms (%)	Import penetration in sector (%)
Aluminium products	60	91	NA
Beer-brewing	79	90	8
Soaps, detergents	50	86	24
Cigarettes, cigars	46	85	24
Cables	28	79	13
Non-alcoholic drinks	57	77	4
Chocolate, confectionery	36	75	21
Wine-making	18	46	4
Threads, laces	24	44	28
Ceramics and porcelain	18	43	26
Alcoholic drinks		24	45
Yarns, woollens		11	42

Source: 'How oligopolies are made', *To Vema*, 18.6.1995, p. D10, from a Centre of Planning & Economic Research study.

the workings of the economy. It's all the more remarkable since capital concentration and competition are not, as we have shown, necessarily incompatible with one another. True, in most of the cases of Table 8.13 the top firms are either outright foreign or foreign-controlled, not Greek. But in an era of open markets, stunning internationalisation of all economic activities, and Greek firms expanding abroad, as well as others coming to Greece, the question of ethnicity of asset ownership is not pivotal. Performance is.

Notes

1. On the basis of data from various Bank of Greece Annual Reports.
2. Ibid.
3. See Yannitsis, 1994; Tringa, 1994b; Zervas, 1995; Dracatos, 1996, and the excellent survey of deindustrialisation in Greece in *E Cathemerine*, 27.3 to 3.4.1994.
4. *The Economist*, 19.3.1994, pp. 81–2.
5. *Financial Times*, 25.2.1994, p. 11.
6. See Linardos-Rylmon, 1994; Papandropoulos, 1995b.
7. See Sterghiou, 1986; Kephalas, 1994c.

8. 'The six "diseases" of our industry', *Eleutherotypia*, 18.11.1990, pp. 72-3. The article is based on the results of a pan-EU study on the effects of the single market on the industry of the twelve. The Greek report was prepared by D. Mardas and N. Varsakelis, of the University of Thessalonica. See also *Kerdos*, 28.1.1996, reporting on a speech by J. Stratos, President of the Confederation of Greek Industries, at the Institute of Economic and Industrial Research (IOBE).
9. 'Country where primary school graduates shine!', *Eleutherotypia*, 7.12.1995, p. 73.
10. 'Greek lock for CDs', *Eleutherotypia*, 31.3.1996, info p. 5.
11. And Greece has one of the highest rates of employment in computer programming as a proportion of total employment, in the world. Cf. *The Economist*, 1996a, p. 18.
12. 'Greek food and drink: FT Survey', *Financial Times*, 16.5.1995.
13. Ibid., p. iv.
14. Professor N. Christodoulakis, Secretary of the Greek Ministry for R&D, holds a more hopeful view. See his interview to *Economicos Tachydromos*, 29.2.1996, pp. 31–4.
15. *E Cathemerine*, 9.8.1995.
16. Chrysolouris, 1995.
17. Ibid.
18. Ibid.
19. *E Cathemerine*, 5.5.1995.
20. *E Cathemerine*, 11.5.1995.
21. Sarantidis, 1996.
22. *E Cathemerine*, 19.4.1996, p. 17, on the basis of OECD data.
23. Calloniatis, 1995.
24. Anything between 18 and 35 per cent (Aperghis & Carfakis, 1995).
25. By consent of most foreign as well as Greek executives, the worst areas, relevant for business performance, are telecommunications and transport. Pirounakis, 1994.
26. There are notable exceptions. Mr Dombek, MD of Siemens in Greece, has found that, despite cultural differences, Greek workers are not necessarily less productive than, say, German ones. Pirounakis, 1994.
27. There is a sad story here, but very indicative of the way Greeks tend to shoot their own foot. Pirelli began to suffer losses in 1989, which kept increasing thereafter because of persistent strikes by its staff, whom opposition parties encouraged to insist upon maximalist demands. Eventually the company left Greece, and relocated in Turkey.
28. Industrial News & Research, 1994.
29. See 'The Great Looting', *Capital,* 70, July 1995, pp. 44–9.
30. Cacoulidou, 1996.
31. Ibid.
32. See Sterghiou, 1976; 'Current investment incentives', *Economicos Tachydromos*, 14.4.1988; Dryllerakis, 1994; 'Invest in Greece: 1995–96', Hellenic Industrial Development Bank.
33. 'Above all, do not undertake DFI in Greece. . .', *Economicos Tachydromos*, 24.3.1988, p. 11.
34. Arvanitidis, 1995; Papanicolaou, 1995.

35. 'We are driving investors away!', *Eleutherotypia*, 31.3.1996, pp. 88–9.
36. 'Are the Canadians abandoning Cassandra?', *Economicos Tachydromos*, 4.7.1996, p. 17.
37. 'We are driving investors away!', *Eleutherotypia*, 313.1996, pp. 88–9.
38. Ibid.
39. Ms Vasso Papandreou, Minister of Development, is reported to have said in relation to the Cassandra problem: 'What do you want me to do? Send in the Order Restoration Units [MAT]?' *Economicos Tachydromos*, 4.7.1996, p. 17.
40. Ibid.
41. *Economicos Tachydromos*, 19.10.1995, p. 66.
42. *Economicos Tachydromos*, 17.8.1989, p. 71.
43. From an interview to *Eleutherotypia*, 4.2.1996, p. 13 of information section.
44. See also 'How a blossoming small industrial firm was led to bankruptcy by the ruthless State', *Economicos Tachydromos*, 14.4.1988, pp. 71–2; 'Greek Customs views Greek consuls abroad as crooks', *Economicos Tachydromos*, 14.2.1991, p. 62.
45. See Magheiros, 1993.
46. Papandreou, 1994.
47. Papandropoulos, 1995a.
48. Greece in Figures: 1994 (ICAP: Athens).
49. Source: Same as in Table 8.9.
50. 'Greece: Nielsen Census' (Nielsen: Athens), June 1994; For 1994, *Ta Nea*, 10.8.1995, p. 47, on the basis of data released by Nielsen.
51. *E Cathemerine*, 9.6.1995.
52. Cf. Tarpangos, 1996.
53. See Anomeritis, 1996. George Anomeritis was Deputy Minister of Finance, after having served as Deputy Minister of the National Economy.
54. '"Osmosis" of the Community Support Framework, depressingly slow', *E Cathemerine*, 25.2.1996. See also 'We failed to absorb 750 billion drs', *E Cathemerine*, 6.7.1996, p. 28.
55. Cf. Kephalas (1995) on how Greek governments raise obstacles to the enlargement, or amalgamation, of business firms in Greece.
56. See Leventacos (1996).
57. Cf. *Technica*, Feb. 1996, p. 27.

9 Housing Miracle – Planning Blight

'Woe unto them that join house to house, that lay field to field, till there be no place, that they may be placed alone in the midst of the earth.'

Isaiah. *The Book of the Prophet. 5, 8.*

Early in the evening of 22 July 1995 thick smoke blackened the skyline to the north of Greater Athens. Parts of Mount Penteli and the countryside nearby were burning. The fire would rage for three days and two nights, turning 50 000 stremmas[1] (= 50 sq km) of woodland and dozens of homes (mostly villas and cottages) into ashes. Once again, it would also prove the inefficiency of the state apparatus – not so much in fire control terms[2] as in its inability to remove the incentive to commit this type of arson.[3]

Unlawful burning of woodland is something quite common in Greece during the summer months. From 1980 to 1994 more than 21 000 fires destroyed more than 7.6 m. stremmas (= 7600 sq km) of woodland in Greece. Of those fires, 24.3 per cent were due to arson, 21.4 per cent to negligence, and 45.2 per cent to unknown causes (which again means arson in the majority of cases).[4] Why so much cruelty and stupidity? Simply because there are profits to be had from subsequent unauthorised building in the deforested areas – and the buyers or settlers no less than the profiteers can get away with it. Inevitably so, one might say, in the context of the Greek housing system.

9.1 A NATION OF HOUSE-OWNERS – NOT JUST OWNER-OCCUPIERS

In line with a tradition of owner-occupation and smallholding in the countryside, urban Greece, which more or less reached her present order of magnitude in the 1960s and 1970s, has exhibited very high rates of owner-occupation (Table 9.1), correspondingly low rates of renting, and marginal reliance on bank credit for housing. There is no public rented housing in Greece. The role of the state in housing per se is

Table 9.1
Basic data on the Greek housing system.

Year	Total population ('000)	Percentage of population in Athens-Piraeus	Owner-occupying households as % of total*	No. of dwellings ('000)	Dwellings per 1000 of households	Owner-occupied dwellings as % of total**	Secondary dwellings as % of total	Vacant and/or ruined dwellings as % of total
1951	7 633	18.1	76.5	1 864	1 048			
1961	8 389	22.1	80.0	2 318	1 082			
1971	8 768	29.0		2 998	1 203			
1981	9 740	31.1	73.3	3 987	1 340	53.4	17.5	9.7
1991	10 260	30.0	79.6	4 658	1 454	54.3	20.5	11.4

* Including households occupying gratis, that is, rent-free.
** Including dwellings occupied gratis, that is, rent-free.

Source: Pirounakis, 1996b.

limited in a little housebuilding for the purpose of owner-occupation, carried out by the Workers' Housing Organisation (OEK), in granting housing benefit to low-income renting households (again through OEK),[5] in allowing deductibility of 30 per cent of the rent from a tenant's taxable income (with some qualifications), and in subsidising housing loans. The subsidies are of two main forms: interest-rate subvention in the case of loans to buy or build one's primary residence, and deductibility of the interest element from a mortgagor's taxable income, again only in regard to one's first home.

The traditionally small importance of housing credit in Greece may come as a surprise to a Briton. After all, in 1984 60.9 per cent of UK households were owner-occupiers, but 59.3 per cent of those (or 36.1 per cent of all households) were in the process of repaying a mortgage. In Greece, on the other hand, 69.5 per cent of households were owner-occupiers in 1981 (in addition to those, usually relatives, who enjoyed the free use of a dwelling), but only 9 per cent of those were repaying a mortgage.[6] By this book's writer's estimate, that percentage must have gone up to 20 per cent by 1995 (or 15 per cent of all households), equivalent to 480 000 households.[7]

So how have Greeks financed their housing, and their owner-occupation in particular, if not through mortgage loans? By means of four devices mainly, which worked best because their widespread adoption coincided with an era of rapid economic development as well as urbanisation:

(a) Selling rural assets in order to get a foothold in the city. People were able to do this precisely because most of them were owners of land plots in the countryside to begin with. The significance of Greece's non-feudal past, with its myriads of smallholders in the countryside, which was pointed out in Chapter 1, comes to the fore here.
(b) The mechanism of the 'exchange arrangement' ('antiparokhé'). This worked, and still does, like this: an owner of an urban land plot, whether built or not, agrees with a developer/builder ('project taker', or 'ergolavos', is the literal Greek term) to have a high-rise apartment block built on the land. The plot owner contributes the land, and expects to own one or (usually) more of the apartments, whilst the project taker carries the building costs in exchange for the remainder of the apartments. In this way the original plot owner acquires a number of income-earning real assets in addition to a new home for himself, without having had to pay anything for them.

In effect the plot owner could afford to rent those apartments out at prices that were not constrained by the need to recover the capital cost of monetary outlays. This facilitated the entry of newcomers into the city as well as their ability to save in order to become owner-occupiers themselves later. On his part, the project taker could afford to sell his share of the apartments at prices that did not have to reflect any land costs. In the 1960s and 1970s there was no shortage of buyers either, which meant that the project taker did not have to rely on banks in order to finance inventories. Often the apartments were sold before they were built. The buyers would finance their purchases through disposal of countryside assets or through rapidly accumulating savings; retiring state or bank employees would do so through the lump sums they received on retirement day from their employers.

(c) The third device has been unauthorised building. This one is still going strong; the other two have lost impetus, as by the mid-1980s urbanisation, and population and economic growth, came to a virtual standstill. There are many forms of unauthorised building,[8] involving breaches in anything from planning regulations (as when building on public woodland or on a beach) to building regulations, but its usefulness as a device to cut down owner-occupation costs has been mainly based on the following factors:
- It allows building without payment of fees for planning and building permits. This is perhaps the least important factor.
- When done on a plot bought in the process of illegally claiming and subdividing public land (something quite easy to do, as there is no national land and property register in Greece[9]), it avoids substantial land costs. The same happens in the far less frequent case of actually squatting on public land.
- To the extent that it is carried out on land outside formal city plans, and therefore undeveloped, it implies that the owner has acquired the land at less than its potential, or full development, value, as no provision has as yet been made for this land in terms of roads, open spaces, communal amenities, or utility networks. Which means that the total housing cost to the owner is much less than otherwise.

(d) The fourth device for housing oneself and family without reliance on bank credit has worked in the context of authorised as well as illicit building. It is legally possible in Greece to postpone building the second and other floors of a structure at the owner's discretion. Each city area in Greece has its own limit as regards the

> maximum permissible number of floors for buildings, and the maximum height. But that means that in many cases, particularly at the outskirts of cities or in smaller towns and villages, it has been possible to time the building of a second or third floor to the accumulation of family savings and to children coming to marriageable age.[10] And, of course, if the building is unauthorised anyway, raising a second floor will not even require a permit!

The downside of the 'exchange arrangement', together with the licentiousness implicit in unauthorised building, may have already become apparent to the reader: the Greek housing system has provided strong incentives to demolish single or two-storey houses, and build high-rise instead. Whole beautiful neighbourhoods in Athens and other cities, and even traditional towns (like the capital of the island of Chios), have been destroyed in this way. The system has also encouraged proliferation of unauthorised settlements, in addition to individual monstrosities marring a countryside, a beach, or a street.

The appearance of any Greek settlement above the level of a village or small town nowadays is the result of these two trends (high-rise and unauthorised building). Modern Greek cities have evolved without adherence to a plan or to building regulations,[11] or only token such, and without the benefit of environmentally friendly or farsighted regulations.[12] Inevitably they have been plagued by traffic jams, noise and pollution to a greater extent than what would have been the case under a planning system that would be enforced as a matter of course (see Table 9.2). Athens or Piraeus are admittedly nothing like Cairo, Rio, or Bombay (or Vienna, for that matter!), but only because urbanisation and population growth came to a standstill early enough (cf. Table 9.1) – not because of any safeguards in Greece's housing system, its related legal framework, or the ability and willingness of the state to apply it, such as it is.

In the meantime the Greeks have been investing furiously into housing – an average of 28.6 per cent of all investment from 1949 to 1994. By 1991 1000 households came to correspond to 1453 dwellings, and of the total dwelling stock more than 20 per cent were secondary homes, with a further 11 per cent made up of vacant and/or ruined dwellings (which in many cases may well mean secondary homes anyway). In fact the distribution of dwelling wealth in Greece is extremely widespread, as Tables 9.3 and 9.4 demonstrate. For example, between 1981 and 1991 the proportion of owner-occupying households who had no property interests in other dwellings was reduced from 27 per cent of

Table 9.2
Environmental pollution in Athens and the rest of Greece
(late 1970s–early 1990s)

A Free space (sq m per inhabitant) in 1983:

Athens	2.7
Paris	8.4
Rome	9
London	9
Vienna	15

OECD (1983): *Environmental Policies in Greece: A review by the OECD and its Environmental Committee undertaken in 1982/1983 at the request of the Government of Greece* (OECD: Paris), p. 3

B Suspended particles in 1978 (annual mean value in μg/cu m):

Athens	254.7
Los Angeles	173.5
Tokyo	146.0
Houston	98.4
Sydney	95.1
Chicago	87.1
New York	68.5
Helsinki	66.6
Montreal	64.3
Copenhagen	41.2

Source: Ibid., p. 38. The EEC limit was 80 μg/cu m (median value), 40–60 μg/cu m being the target.

C Free space and transportation space: per cent of total land use in 1993:

	Free space	Transportation space
Athens	3,6%	27,8%
Madrid	14,0%	16,0%
London	12,4%	15,3%

Source: 'A city strangled by development', *E Cathemerine*, 27.3.1994, reporting on a study by Th. Aravantinos and J. Cosmaki, of the Athens Engineering University.

D Athens is not the only place in Greece that suffers from pollution:

In a recent report on the environment, the Ministry of Environment and Planning has included a number of Greek counties, in addition to Athens and Thessaloncia, in a list of regions facing environmental pollution problems. These are: Boeotia, the Dodecanese, Euboea, Thesprotia, Carditsa, Corinthia, the Cyclades, Larissa, Magnesia, Rodopi, Tricala, Florina, Phthiotis, and Khalkidiki, with particular mention of the towns of Ptolemais and Megalopolis (where there are Public Power Corporation works)

Source: '17 counties at the mercy of pollutants', *E Cathermerine*, 31.10.1993, p. 14.

Table 9.3
Housing ownership structure in Greece in 1981
Households living in regular dwellings (other than in collective households) or owning such

	No. of households	Per cent %	No. of households	Per cent %	Owner-occupied dwellings	Rented dwellings	Dwellings occupied gratis	Secondary dwellings	Vacant and/or ruined dwellings	DWELLING TOTALS	Per cent %
A. OWNER-OCCUPYING HOUSEHOLDS			2 039 010	69.50							
1. Without ownership interests in other dwellings											
a. Sharing their dwelling	2 945	0.10			2 945					2 945	0.07
b. Non-sharing	785 452	26.77			785 452					785 452	19.75
2. With ownership interests in other dwellings											
a. Letting out to regular (that is, non-tourist) tenants	431 159	14.70			431 159	759 442	37 902	116 413	142 282	1 487 198	37.40
b. Owning dwellings given gratis to others	52 820	1.80			49 897		49 875	15 001	6 127	120 878	3.04
c. With secondary or vacant dwellings only	766 634	26.13			766 634			435 448	177 859	1 379 941	34.71
B. RENTING HOUSEHOLDS			783 630	26.71							
1. Without ownership interests in dwellings											
a. Non-sharing	506 856	17.28									
b. Sharing between them	27 129	0.92									
2. With ownership interests in dwellings	249 645	8.51				9 986		129 815	59 915	199 716	5.02
C. HOUSEHOLDS OCCUPYING GRATIS			111 160	3.79							
a. Non-sharing	64 394	2.19									
b. Sharing with owner-occupiers	2 945	0.10									
c. Sharing between them	43 821	1.49									
TOTALS	2 933 800	100.00	2 933 800	100.00	2 036 065	769 428	87 777	696 677	386 183	3 976 130	100.00
Per cent					51.21	19.35	2.21	17.52	9.71	100.00	

Table 9.4
Housing ownership structure in Greece in 1991
Households living in regular dwellings (other than in collective households) or owning such

	No. of households	Per cent %	No. of households	Per cent %	Owner-occupied dwellings	Rented dwellings	Dwellings occupied gratis	Secondary dwellings	Vacant and/or ruined dwellings	DWELLING TOTALS	Per cent %
A. OWNER-OCCUPYING HOUSEHOLDS			2 405 595	75.35							
1. Without ownership interests in other dwellings											
a. Sharing their dwelling	8 324	0.26			8 324					8 324	0.18
b. Non-sharing	550 472	17.24			550 472					550 472	11.85
2. With ownership interests in other dwellings											
a. Letting out to regular (that is, non-tourist) tenants	619 396	19.40			619 396	632 181	57 937	167 237	204 401	1 681 152	36.21
b. Owning dwellings given gratis to others	74 419	2.33			66 095		66 095	21 136	8 633	161 969	3.49
c. With secondary or vacant dwellings only	1 152 984	36.11			1 152 984			654 895	267 492	2 075 371	44.70
B. RENTING HOUSEHOLDS			651 443	20.40							
1. Without ownership interests in dwellings											
a. Non-sharing	416 290	13.04									
b. Sharing between them	27 527	0.86									
2. With ownership interests in dwellings	207 626	6.50				8 305		107 966	49 830	166 101	3.58
C. HOUSEHOLDS OCCUPYING GRATIS			135 618	4.25							
a. Non-sharing	112 446	3.52									
b. Sharing with owner-occupiers	8 324	0.26									
c. Sharing between them	14 848	0.47									
TOTALS	3 192 656	100.00	3 192 656	100.00	2 397 271	640 486	124 032	951 234	530 356	4 643 379	100.00
Per cent					51.63	13.79	2.67	20.49	11.42	100.00	

all households to 17.5 per cent. Even a number of renting households had property interests in dwellings elsewhere, while over the decade their proportion decreased from 26.7 to 20.4 per cent of the total number of households. In absolute terms, 132 thousand renting households left the sector to become owner-occupiers. Moreover, whereas in 1981 one 'landlord' household corresponded to 1.82 renting households, by 1991 the ratio had gone down to 1:1.05. By 1991 the proportion of all households with no property interests in any dwellings whatsoever had gone down to just short of 14 per cent. It may well be that Greece tops Europe as regards the distribution of dwelling wealth, or the number of second homes.

Nor is the quality of Greek housing bad.[13] In 1991 the proportion of households in dwellings with a number of rooms exceeding, or at least equal to, the number of household members was 62 and 86 per cent, respectively. In the same year virtually 100 per cent of households lived in regular[14] dwellings, and of those only 1.8 per cent shared a dwelling – down from 2.6 per cent in 1981. In addition

- more than 99 per cent of households had a kitchen, electricity, and a bathtub or shower; and 87.5 per cent had a WC with flush inside the dwelling;
- more than 95 per cent were connected to a running water supply;
- 45 per cent had central heating;
- 73 per cent had a telephone;
- 20 per cent had a solar waterheater.

Modern Greek housing is obviously a success story – which, unfortunately, needs to be severely qualified on account of the way the post-war development of Greek housing has damaged the look of traditional settlements, made life difficult for millions of urban Greeks, and spoiled the environment. The fire on Mt Penteli, and others before and, surely, after it, must be seen in this light: an attempt to make more land available for housebuilding in the context of illegal processes of land occupation and development. Official declarations to the opposite notwithstanding, very few of those lands have been reforested successfully afterwards. In most cases they gradually fill up with villas and cottages. The state, far from clamping down on the practice, ends up encouraging it, albeit indirectly. Not six months after the Penteli fire, the Ministry of Agriculture would exempt from reforestation thousands of stremmas of woodland, on the grounds that they had been earmarked for residential development. The Ministry explained that the exemptions would have to apply irrespective of whether the earmarking had been done in breach of woodland protection statutes![15] In a more comprehensive move and in apparent breach of the spirit of the Greek Constitution, the Minister of Agriculture prepared in June 1996 two bills declaring previous decisions to reforest burnt woodland null and void, as long as the fires had occurred before 1975. The bills also contained provisions to the effect that any existing disputes between the State and plot owners in those areas, many of whom have built properties there in the years since the fires, will be declared resolved and settled if the plot owners pay a fine to the State, equal to 25 per cent of the market value of 'their' properties.[16]

It was mentioned in Chapter 1 that one of the characteristics of the Greek political system is that it has allowed reproduction in an urban setting of the smallholder stereotypical feature of rural Greece. Woodland fires are a case in point: since the 1960s many of them may have been started in order to make room for unauthorised building but in 1896 they were an equally illegal means of obtaining grazing land for goats and sheep around Athens. Just like to-day, however, of those fires it was

> impossible to find and punish the universally known perpetrators on account of the fact that trees have no votes whereas goatherds do. These heinous crimes cause a temporary uproar in the press, only to be forgotten soon after [].[17]

Unlike most of the so-called Third World, unauthorised building in Greece typically is not linked to poverty, except during the 1950s and 1960s: it is, rather, linked to cost-cutting, convenience, and expediency. Certainly since the mid-1980s, this kind of building is undertaken by people from virtually all social classes with an eye on a second (weekend or holiday) home. It is ironic, then, that in order to have such a home, which is presumably to function as a haven from polluted, urban Athens or other cities, extensive areas of woodland have to be deforested in this manner. Again, like so much else in Greece, the state allows this to happen for political reasons. Unauthorised building has gone on continuously since the 1950s,[18] involving a corrupt network of house-owners, 'project takers', MPs, political parties, local government representatives, civil engineers, police and planning officers, and public notaries.[19] In response the state will announce now and then that those owners of unauthorised buildings who will pay a fee or fine will save them from demolition. Nonsense.[20] They save them from demolition anyway. When one in five new dwellings built every year in Greece is unauthorised,[21] to demolish a score of those every year (at most) is not only a drop in the ocean, as far as deterrence goes, but positively unfair to their owners.[22]

9.2 INVESTMENT IN HOUSING

As Diagram 9.1 demonstrates, the contribution of investment in housing to the total of gross fixed capital formation for 1949–94 in Greece exhibits a declining trend. For example, the average proportion of housing investment to the total was 23.1 per cent in 1985–94, whilst it had been 29 per cent in 1975–84. Diagram 9.2, on the other hand, shows that, in absolute figures and 1978 prices, the trend in housing investment has been slightly upward from 1950 to 1994. Even so, after 1980 there has been a marked drop in comparison to the excitement of 1968–80. That excitement was only interrupted in 1974 for political reasons (Turkish invasion of Cyprus, general mobilisation in Greece).

A recurring as well as controversial question among Greek economists and civil engineers has been whether housing and industrial investment move together or antagonise one another.[23] Diagram 9.3a correlates the two types of investment for the period 1949–94. At first look the emerging picture is not clear, as the correlation points form a U. Things become clearer if we break down the time series into two distinct periods (Diagrams 9.3b and 9.3c). It appears that in 1949–66 the two kinds of investment were complementary to one another, whilst in 1967–94 they developed an antagonistic relationship. It would be hasty, however, to suppose that housing investment after 1966 has been crowding out industrial investment, since the savings pool of an economy is finite only in the short run. Two things may have happened instead. First, the period of rapid economic development after 1950 gave Greeks the wherewithal to start improving their housing conditions, which they have kept doing down to the present (albeit at a decreasing rate, as their basic housing needs have been satisfied, whilst urbanisation has lost impetus). Second, industry has encountered problems of its own (see Chapter 8), none of which however has been lack of loanable funds. It is these problems which have cost industry the loss of its 1960s dynamism, and not housing investment per se. Taken together, the two trends explain the apparent, though not real, antagonism between housing and industrial investment after 1966. If anything, Diagram 9.4 shows that from 1975 to 1994 a much higher percentage of

Diagram 9.1
Comparative contribution of housing and industry to total gross fixed capital formation (GFCF) in the Greek economy, 1949–94

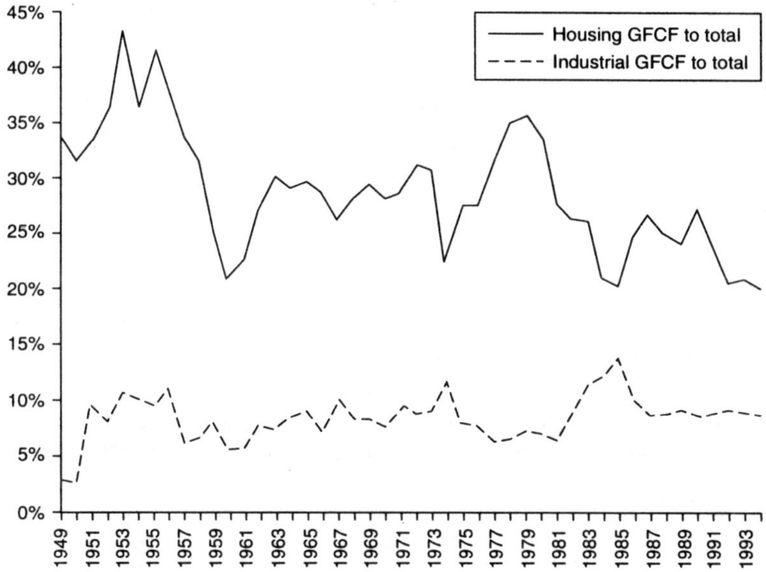

Source: NSSG, National Accounts.

Diagram 9.2
Time series of housing investment in Greece at 1978 prices, 1950–94

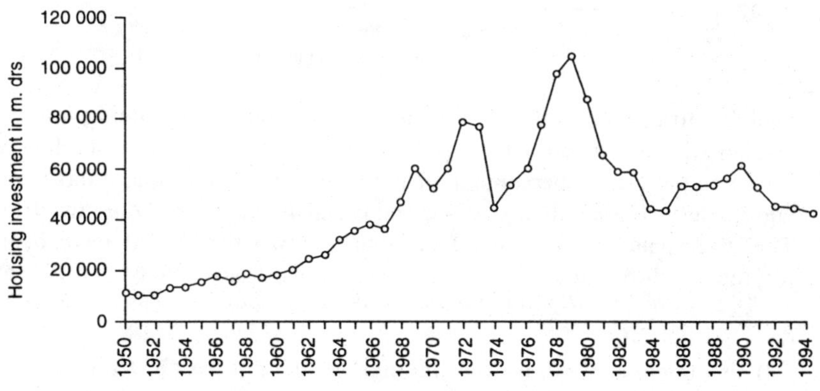

Data source: NSSG, National Accounts.

Diagram 9.3a
Correlation between housing and industrial investment in Greece, 1949–94: Have they moved together or antagonised one another?

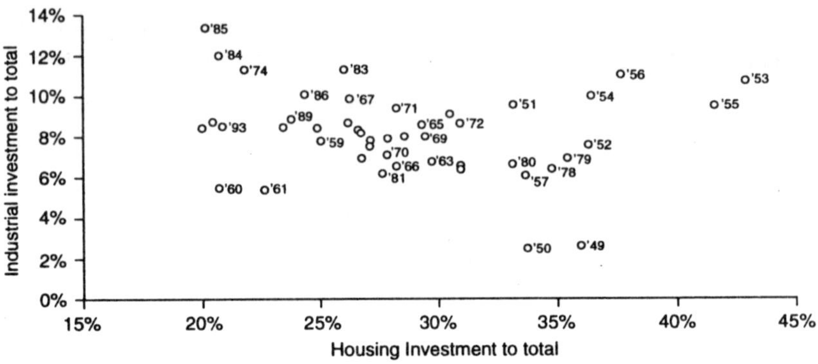

Diagram 9.3b
Correlation of housing and industrial investment in Greece: In 1949–66 (that is, before the 1967 dictatorship) they seem to have moved together.

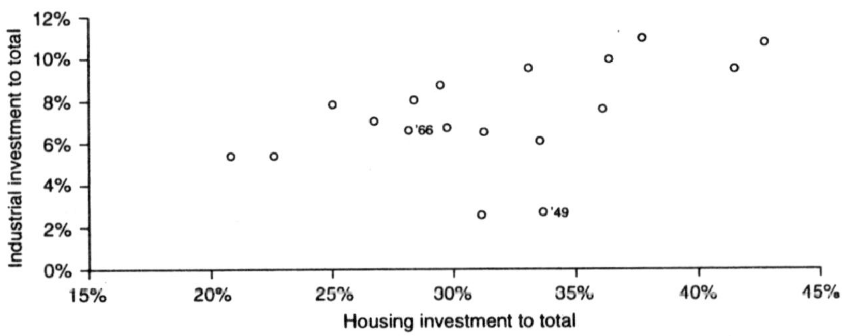

bank credit to the private sector has gone to industry (including mining and small-scale manufacturing) than to housing. By contrast, during the same period the percentage of housing to total investment has been significantly higher than that for industrial investment (Diagram 9.1). The discrepancy reflects the facts that the two sectors (a) have been relying on different financing channels, (b) are governed by different considerations: household choices on the one hand, and entrepreneurial ones on the other.

This conclusion echoes the findings of other research, from Greece and the UK. For instance, in their seminal work on British economic growth, Matthews et al. (1982) concluded that

Diagram 9.3c
Correlation of housing and industrial investment in Greece: In 1967–94 (that is, during and after the dictatorship) they seem to have antagonised one another.

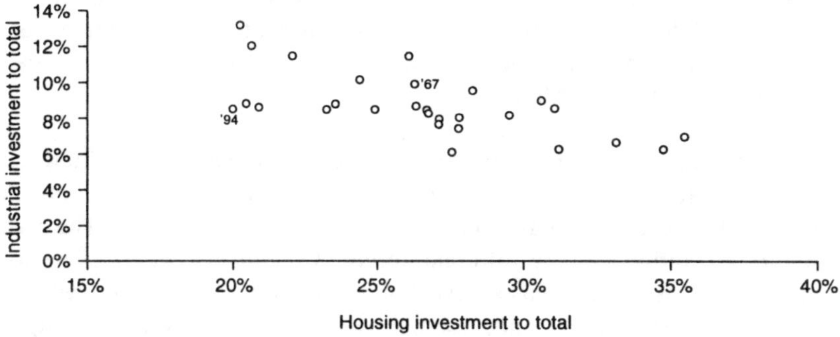

Diagram 9.4
Comparison of outstanding bank loan advances to housing in Greece, to same for industry and tourism, 1975–94.

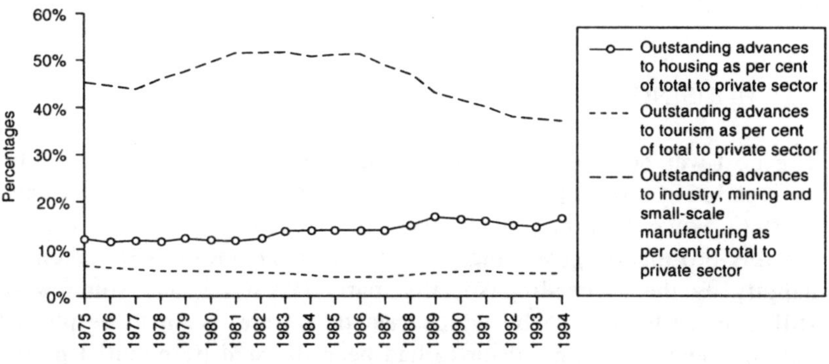

Data source: Bank of Greece Annual Reports.

Much turns on whether a lower level of investment in infrastructure or dwellings would in fact have caused investment in manufacturing to be significantly higher. This must be considered doubtful, since there were in each period good reasons on the [Marginal Efficiency of Investment] side why manufacturing investment was no higher than it was. On this reckoning, lower investment in infrastructure and dwellings would not have helped to speed up economic growth.

And on the Greek side, Emmanuel (1979) was firm that

> the solution to the problem of limited industrial investment must be sought in the domain of *industry* and of related policies, and not in housing policy. The reasons are simple: The 'capital structure' of industrial firms, and the post-war evolution of their capital needs, compared to the available volume of deposits, precluded the emergence of funding problems.

It is therefore quite probable that neither a decrease nor an increase in housing investment will lead necessarily to an absolute increase in industrial investment, which many Greek economists desire. The two sectors are influenced by different forces. Conversely, though, a substantial increase in industrial investment would create incomes which, given the Greeks' preference for possessing dwelling wealth,[24] might revitalise the housebuilding industry. If things were to happen in this manner, then the industrial sector would probably be in a position to benefit from increased investment in housing, and the incomes thus generated. If not, then the discontinuity between the two sectors is likely to persist.

9.3 HOUSING CREDIT

The post-war housing mechanism depended critically on households' savings being directed to housing, and on continued demand for flats. In 1980, however, rent controls were introduced in Greece by the ostensibly pro-market governing party (New Democracy), were taken up happily by the succeeding socialist party (PASOK), and some were still in place by 1996 – by which year they were meant to be phased out completely. The initial move had been dictated by populist political considerations, but was otherwise surprising since by that time urbanisation in Greece, along with population growth, had come to a standstill, whilst only 27 per cent of households were renting in 1981. The 1980s, moreover, saw Greek economic growth peter out, and Greece descend into a crisis which has been getting worse ever since. Under such conditions the sensible move would have been to encourage the housebuilding sector rather than pour cold water on it. In effect, the rent control regime may have caused the number of housebuilding permits issued annually to drop by about 35 000.[25]

These developments ushered in a period of increased reliance on mortgage credit for financing housebuilding or apartment purchase. Until 1985 the Greek housing finance system involved just five specialised credit institutions which had exclusive rights to this kind of business. Two of those (the Post Office Savings Bank and the Loans and Consignments Fund) have been granting mortgage loans exclusively to civil servants, and one (the Agricultural Bank of Greece) to farmers. The other two (the Mortgage Bank and the Housing Bank) have always been open to the general public. Their main source of funds has been savings deposits, which, up to 1985, were topped up substantially by loans from the Bank of Greece. In addition, each has been operating a Housing Savings Department, a form of contractual arrangement between a saver and the bank, which involves him getting the right to a housing loan after saving for a prescribed amount of time.

In 1985 commercial banks were allowed to grant housing loans, but only up to 2 per cent of their deposits. This restriction was lifted in 1991. One year later the first private housing bank came into being (Aspis Bank). The end of 1995 found commercial banks accounting for 13.4 per cent of outstanding mortgage loans. That percentage is forecast to rise much further.[26] In late 1995 Alpha Credit Bank, Greece's biggest private commercial bank, led the industry in rate-cutting, whilst the small Egnatia Bank pioneered the introduction of the endowment mortgage into Greece (in collaboration with ScoPLife, Greek affiliate of Scottish Provident).

Nevertheless the role of mortgage finance in Greece is still much less important than it is, say, in the UK. A statistical regression of housebuilding permits on housing loans outstanding per household at the end of each year from 1960 to 1992, at 1978 prices, has shown that only 36.7 per cent[27] of annual variations in permits could be attributed to variations in mortgage credit.[28] On the other hand a regression of apartment transfers[29] on the same independent variable has thrown up an equivalent figure of 75 per cent.[30] Fuller regression models have indicated the statistical importance of other factors in addition to mortgage credit, as determinants of the demand for permits or of apartment transfers.[31] In the case of permits, one of the additional factors has been the previous year's savings deposits per household (at 1978 prices), whilst in the case of apartment transfers it has been the previous year's time deposits and bond holdings per household (again, at 1978 prices). The same models have confirmed that real mortgage interest rates were one of the least important factors. This result is consistent with the traditionally low reliance on mortgage finance, characteristic of the Greek housing system, but as the role of housing credit in Greece is bound to increase in the future, so will the importance of mortgage rates.

Perhaps unsurprisingly, housing credit itself correlates quite closely with savings deposits (73.9 per cent, adjusted r^2).[32] To explain this one needs to bear in mind three things: (a) savings, rather than sight or time, deposits, are the dominant form of bank deposits in Greece; (b) the state, rather than the private sector, is most Greeks' ultimate source of incomes; (c) until the late 1980s the Bank of Greece determined credit expansion limits for all sectors, including housing, by fiat. It seems, then, that the main reason savings deposits correlate so highly with housing credit is not that they make it happen. Historically, the public's savings have moved along with the contractions and expansions (usually the latter) of governments' overall fiscal and monetary policy, of which housing credit has been, on various occasions since the late 1960s, an important component.

By contrast the statistically significant role of time deposits and bond holdings (including government paper), rather than savings deposits, in apartment transfers can be attributed to the following two factors:

- Housebuilding requires a continuous flow of cash. As a result Greek households planning to build need a lot of liquidity – hence the high correlation between savings deposits and the demand for housebuilding permits. On the other hand, buying a flat requires a substantial upfront payment. Even if the buyer takes out a bank loan, he will still need to find half the purchase price out of his own savings. He therefore needs to have accumulated enough personal capital for the purpose, something usually done by means of investing over a number of years in less liquid financial assets. If he has borrowed in order to buy the flat, he needs in addition an appropriately high income and/or a healthy savings account in order to repay the loan.
- An apartment transfer that is really a parent's gift to a child almost always presupposes a family with more than one dwelling. In such cases the 'surplus' dwellings are more like a personal or family investment than in cases of a family owning only one dwelling. (The latter is then more of a consumption item than an investment.) At the same time a family owning more than one dwelling is in all likelihood better-off than the rest. Hence, a flat transfer by way of a parent's gift is more likely to take place where the sum-total of that family's financial wealth, including time deposits and bond holdings, has reached a certain convenience-allowing level than where

the family actually needs the income from renting the extra flat out. If the latter is the case, the parent will postpone transferring the extra flat to the son or daughter, who may then have to postpone getting married until they are able to afford owner-occupation themselves.

Housing credit nowadays in Greece involves something like 36 000 loans a year (including rehabilitation and house repair loans). Against that the annual number of housebuilding permits issued is about 93 000, that of apartment transfers about 60 000 and that of new unauthorised dwellings[33] about 19 000. The sector has potential for growth though, now that the traditional housing mechanism is running out of steam. That potential can be enhanced if the state removes from the specialised banks their exclusive privilege to advance subsidised housing loans to designated categories of borrowers, and extends this right to all banks (as long as the borrowers meet prescribed criteria). The way things are at the time of writing, two of the so-called specialised institutions, the Housing Bank and the Mortgage Bank, are already on a par with commercial banks in almost all banking areas. The Mortgage Bank, in particular, is the biggest player in the field,[34] and, since 1995, has been moving aggressively into high-risk commercial banking business like derivatives. There is therefore no clear reason to preserve the real estate banks' unfair advantage over commercial banks in the mortgage field.[35]

9.4 THE FUTURE OF GREEK HOUSING

Despite the impressive performance of the Greek housing system from 1951 to 1991, in quantitative as well as qualitative terms, its future looks uncertain. Economic growth is between one and two per cent per year, the productive potential of the country has been severely eroded, and the younger generations are sure not to have the chances for capital accumulation that their parents and grandparents had. On the other hand they are also likely to inherit the substantial dwelling wealth of an ageing population. This is not as much of a gift as it seems. The tax treatment of inherited real property in Greece is excruciating,[36] involving a 5 per cent rate for property values from 4.5 to 15 m. drs (£12 000 to £40 000), 15 per cent from 15 to 60 m. drs, and 25 per cent thereafter – and that's for first degree relatives alone. A son or daughter inheriting, say, three apartments worth £30 000 each – a far from improbable occurrence in Greece – will have in effect to give the state nearly a third of one of these in order to pay the tax. Even if he or she dies immediately after, his or her spouse will again pay the tax – so there goes 60 per cent of a flat in value terms – and when the spouse dies, their child will have to pay the tax also. Considering the demographics of Greece, together with the poor prospects for economic growth, soon there is likely to be a lot of people trying to sell dwellings at the same time in order to pay inheritance taxes. This is certain to depress house prices. Since, however, the Greek Inland Revenue assess property values on the basis of a so-called objective valuation system, rather than as true market prices, the financial burden on an increasing number of inheritors is likely to be fearsome. Unless there is radical tax reform, the Greeks' increasing housing wealth, far from giving them one-upmanship over their fellow Europeans, may become a millstone round their necks.

Increased reliance on mortgage credit in the future may stop another difference between the Greek and the housing systems of more advanced capitalist countries from becoming bigger. That difference is the discontinuity that exists in Greece between the housing and the labour market. In the 1960s rapid urbanisation meant that about half the number of households in, say, Athens and Piraeus had had to rent by the end of the decade. Twenty years later, only 32 per cent did. Between then and now, progressively higher rates of outright owner-occupation in Greece, the fact of widely spreading house-ownership (not just owner-occupation), the very realistic possibility of housing oneself through parental gifts, bequests, or unauthorised building (all three sources reducing, in effect, the need to borrow for housing), and, finally, the high proportion of employers, self-employed, and peasants in the economically active population, have led to little interaction (that is, a discontinuity) between the housing and the labour market. An additional helping factor has worked on the supply side: houses or flats in Greece have been considered traditionally family assets rather than vital devices to support one's income, or investments in a narrow sense, especially since most of them do not represent running mortgage costs. The upshot is that an owner of two or three dwellings could, and to a large extent still can, afford to take his time before renting one out or even selling. Eventually, though, more people taking out housing loans will probably make house prices more sensitive to variations in incomes, and wages in particular, than they have been hitherto. This will re-establish perhaps the links between the housing and the labour market which the diminution of the rented sector had seemed to weaken.

Yet another related as well as worrying development has been taking place recently. Since the collapse of communism in Eastern Europe, about 400 000 economic refugees,[37] equivalent to 9 per cent of the 1995 economically active population of Greeks and non-Greeks together, or maybe even 600 000,[38] have come into Greece, the vast majority of them illegally. Consequently it is highly likely that in the 2001 population census the number and proportion of households sharing their dwellings will have gone up, and so will have the proportion of renting households. Housing conditions will show marked deterioration. The presence of so many economic refugees is a challenge to the Greek State and society, which need to answer the question of whether they are going to try and incorporate these people or throw them out. In time-honoured fashion though, the Greek State will probably do nothing, or very little too late. If the State decides for incorporation, it will also need to review very carefully its housing policy in close coordination with its social welfare policy. Both will be painful exercises for Greek society, but perhaps not as painful as what may happen if it tries to pretend that an immigration problem does not exist.

The pressure of so many refugees housing themselves in the rented sector is bound to raise effective prices in the low-income, low-quality segment of it. It may, eventually, do the same in the upper segments of the sector through the chain effect, but more probably it will give rise to pockets and areas of very bad housing in the main cities of Greece. This country has never had slums before – she may well acquire some now. The better-off from among the Greeks who are still in the rented sector will leave it as soon as they can, so nearly the entire sector will become associated with squalor and foreigners.

In the meantime the Greeks, although building and buying dwellings at reduced rates in comparison to the past, are turning increasingly to the acquisition of second homes. Secondary as well as vacant and/or ruined dwellings were 8 per cent of all regular dwellings in 1951; 15 per cent in 1961; 27 per cent in 1981, and 32 per cent in 1991.[39] It has been estimated that in 1991–2001, 26 per cent of the demand for private dwellings will be accounted for by secondary homes, second largest source of demand next to new household formation; in 2001–10 the figure will go up to 28 per cent, even though total demand will drop further.[40] Not bad for a country in the grip of sluggish economic growth.

Notes

1. *E Cathemerine*, 26.7.1995, p. 6
2. It was quite windy that day and the next; as the fire services of southern France, California, and Australia have also found out, it can be very difficult to tackle the problem effectively under such conditions.
3. The main title of *E Cathemerine* of 23.7.1995 reflects this: 'The state is the arsonist!'
4. Portosalte, 1995. See also *E Cathemerine*, 22.8.1996, p. 1.
5. For example, in 1996 OEK spent 12.5 bn drs (£33.3m.) on this type of subsidy. The terms were as follows: 20 000 drs per month (against 18 000 in 1995) plus 3 000 drs for each child under age, whilst the rent the recipient of the benefit paid should not exceed 61 000 drs (£163) per month plus 9 000 drs for each dependant in the household. (*E Cathemerine*, 17.4.1996.) The number of beneficiaries who received the subsidy in 1996 must have been about 45 thousand.
6. Pirounakis, 1987.
7. Pirounakis, 1996b.
8. See *E Cathemerine*, 14.11.1993, p. 16.
9. 'Since the creation of the modern Greek State [1830] there have been 4000 decrees, laws, decisions, and circulars on the National Land Register, without the latter ever materialising. Greece is the only country in the European Union that does not have a National Land Register. Now, however, it is being streamlined on the basis of two distinct phases: Phase A (1994–99) and Phase B (2000–09).' Laliotis, 1996, p. 25. (C. Laliotis was Minister of Planning in Greece in 1996.) Of course the absence of a National Land Register in turn reflects the unwillingness, rather than the inability (although there is that, too) of the Greek State to clash with the hundreds of thousands, maybe millions, of people who have claimed public land as their own since 1830. (Cf. Rokos, 1982.) Even to-day its absence allows governments on the one hand to avoid really drastic measures against people who squat on, claim, buy or sell public land, a lot of it woodland (burnt or otherwise), and on the other to engage in politically advantageous, piecemeal deals with groups of them on grounds of sensitivity to the 'social problem' aspect of such people's activities, even if the latter are mostly about attempts to secure holiday homes.
10. This practice is quite common in the Eastern Mediterranean, for instance, Turkey, Palestine, and so on.
11. Which is not to say that city plans or building regulations have not existed in post-war Greece.
12. For example, it is only since 1979 (Law 960/79) that any new high-rise apartment blocks have to be built with adequate provisions for car-parking space. Understandably such a law, if it had been introduced in, say, 1955 would have limited the financial gains implicit in the 'exchange arrangement'. Mention of 1955 is not accidental: in that year C. Karamanlis, then Minister of Public Works and subsequent Prime Minister, authored a building law that allowed high building densities. (See Government Gazette 249A, 30.8.1955, and also Government Gazette 86/Δ, 4.6.1960.) Today's ugly, densely built Athens is, to some extent, his doing.
13. See Pirounakis, 1996b.

14. According to the NSSG, a regular dwelling is any permanent and autonomous structure comprising at least one room and meant to house a household.
15. Galati, 1996a.
16. *E Cathemerine*, 15.6.1996, pp. 1 & 19.
17. Roidis, 1996, p. 41.
18. Unauthorised building has not been about dwellings only; the practice has often involved enterprises of various kinds too. See 'The Isthmus [area around the Corinth Isthmus] full of unauthorised buildings: Attorney General to investigate the operation of seven firms', *E Cathemerine*, 10.1.1996.
19. See Galati, 1994, 1996b; 'How Mycenaean tombs became . . . a high-rise block', *E Cathemerine*, 10.5.1992, p. 12; 'He wants to apply the law – Remove him!', *Eleutherotypia*, 15.1.1991, p. 20. The last reference is a report on how a conscientious police officer, George Thanoglou, head of the New Callicrateia Police Dept in Khalkidiké, was removed from his post after nearly all the locals got infuriated at him for stopping them from building illicitly. See, in this connection, Euthymiou (1991).
20. All governments' breast-beating about unauthorised building in Greece is really an exercise in hypocrisy, a sham. The fact is that most owners of unauthorised buildings have always managed to have them connected to water, electricity, and telephony networks, while laws, themselves quite recent, stopping utility companies from doing so are rarely applied. See, for example, 'Circuit for supplying electricity to tens of unauthorised buildings: To the Interrogation Commissioner project takers, electricians and Public Power Corporation employees', *E Cathemerine*, 31.3.1993, p. 4. In June 1996 the State was officially preparing to speed up the connection of 100 to 120 th. unauthorised buildings throughout the country to utility networks, provided the structures concerned were in areas inside a formal city plan. See 'Light to unauthorised buildings', *Ta Nea*, 4.6.1996, p. 19. Such plans are often little more than sketches on a map.
21. Pirounakis, 1992b.
22. Unsurprisingly, little fish are worse off than big fish when it comes to this. It seems that whenever the Ministry of Planning decides to make an example of how tough it can get with unauthorised buildings (an example which invariably stops there), it has its crews demolish small dwellings rather than large ones. '"If you make it bigger, you'll save it": In Ministry of Planning operations "virtue", they don't demolish villas because of the high cost', *E Cathemerine*, 28.7.1995.
23. Emmanuel, 1981. See also the very interesting Petras, 1984 – Skouras, 1984 debate on the relationship between rentierist capital and Greek economic growth.
24. That may be changing, though. Since 1990 a combination of tax reforms and issues of government paper at lucrative rates for the purpose of financing Greece's public debt have made many investors turn away from real estate – but, again, at no benefit to industry or other productive investments.
25. Pirounakis, 1992b, 1996b. The annual average number of permits actually issued in 1980–92 was 105 000.

26. Pirounakis, 1996b. In 1996 the percentage shot up to 19.3.
27. Co-efficient of determination, adjusted.
28. Pirounakis, 1996b.
29. These include legacies and dowries in addition to sales.
30. Pirounakis, 1996b.
31. Ibid.
32. Ibid.
33. Unauthorised buildings cannot be mortgaged.
34. It is also burdened with bad debts, from all three of its lines of business: hotel, housing, and construction. In order to help the ailing bank recover, in 1993–94 the state assumed a substantial part of its bad housing debts (representing unrepaid housing loans advanced to wage earners through the Workers' Housing Organisation, or OEK), in exchange for government bonds.
35. Specialised housing banks have yet another advantage: They are exempted from the obligation to redeposit with the Bank of Greece a percentage of their own deposits from the public, by way of meeting reserve requirements.
36. So is the tax treatment of real estate property in general. For instance, the tax rates on the purchase of dwellings (as it is the buyer who has to pay the tax) are among the world's highest: 11 per cent for the first 4 m. drs and 13 per cent thereafter, in towns and cities where there is a fire service, otherwise they are 9 and 11 per cent, respectively. The tax law does offer considerable relief to first-time buyers though.
37. 'They work for half rates', *Ta Nea*, 8.12.1995, p. 19.
38. 'Attica: Refugees, 10 per cent of the population', *E Cathemerine*, 15.2.1996, p. 6.
39. Pirounakis, 1996b.
40. Ibid.

10 Tourism and Environmental Concerns

'The isles of Greece, the isles of Greece!

....

Eternal summer gilds them yet,
But all, except their sun, is set.'

George Gordon Byron. *The isles of Greece.*

Tourism is one of Greece's five major industries (the other four being agriculture, food and drink processing, construction and shipping). A sixth – entertainment in all its forms – should also be given pride of place, only to a large extent it overlaps with tourism. So does transport, for that matter, and construction, on account of the hotels and rooms-to-let continuously built in Greece in order to accommodate the crowds of tourists. On the face of it, tourism is a success story: in 1995 10.7 m. tourists arrived at Greece, about the same number as the local population. It is also the only industry that is truly universal, open to anybody anywhere, involving entrepreneurs of any financial means, umpteen kinds of businesses, premises of any size, urban as well as rural Greece. But development of the industry has happened haphazardly, often stupidly, with no clear overall direction, and to the detriment of picturesqueness and the environment. One could say that in her opportunistic and frantic attitude to tourism Greece has been killing the goose laying the golden eggs.

10.1 MYRINA, LEMNOS: A CASE STUDY

Until 1973 one of the most beautiful town squares in Greece was in Myrina (or Castro), capital of the Northern Aegean island of Lemnos. In that year, with Greece still under military rule, the mayor of Myrina and a local civil engineer decided to 'modernise' the Perivola square. They had the forty plane trees lining the square cut down and a very broad traffic island built in its middle. They also planted eight palm trees on the island and lots of rose and geranium bushes. Of course, had they thought of building a narrower island, the forty plane trees would have been saved – and modernisation and picturesqueness would have complemented one another. Too often, however, 'modernisers' in Greece, a country only recently urbanised, consider big trees a nuisance rather than a blessing.

The years passed, and Lemnos geared up to tourism. Not explosively, like Rhodes or Myconos or Corfu, but then it was the very calm of the place which in the early 1960s had made Swiss investors choose a small bay near Myrina as a site for one of the most expensive resorts in the Med. Imagine a village of stone-built, red-tiled bungalows covered by climbing plant – only it's not a village, but the Acte Myrina Hotel. The Swiss architect who designed it had actually spent a year in Lemnos, prior to making the plans, in order to study the local traditional architecture and create something which would match it rather than be an affront to it.

By the late 1980s a substantial part of the quiet, picturesque town that used to be Myrina had changed. A number of multi-apartment residential buildings had been added to the exclusively one- and two-storey houses of the not-so-distant past – so much so that in places Myrina now reminds one of certain residential areas of Athens. But the attitude to trees has not changed. The current mayor told the writer of this book that he has no intention of restoring the Perivola square to its former glory because 'the locals don't like plane trees . . . they are too big and produce fluffy bits which are carried away by the wind, causing allergies'. I pointed out that plane trees do not do this – only poplars. 'They are too big, still . . .,' he muttered.

Nowadays there are also many B&B places in Lemnos, and taxis, and more hotels, and jewellery and souvenir shops. But none of the hotels is like Acte Myrina. A couple have tried to imitate it and raised a number of bungalows around one or two main buildings, but there the similarity ends. The main buildings are too massive, concrete has been used everywhere rather than stone and the colour is wrong. For instance, whereas ochre is the typical colour of Lemnos, without thought many of the new constructions are painted sparkling white instead – probably because white is the traditional colour in Santorini, Paros and Myconos, down in the Cyclades . . . The result is an eye-sore. It's not a matter of cutting costs, either (which is what could be argued nowadays in regard to choice of building materials): to a large extent it's a matter of ignorance and bad taste – and of a planning function that doesn't know better and doesn't care.

There are other problems. For example, one of the new big hotel complexes, built in 1994, has been located far away from Myrina, or any other village, at the dug up side of a hill going steeply down to the beach. The beach is very small and is muddy, since cutting up the hill like that has allowed earth to wash down freely. A swimmer who turns to look at the beach is oppressed by the hill looming above. The building of this particular hotel was heavily subsidised by the Greek state: with hindsight, that was very unwise use of taxpayers' money, as the hotel has been doing extremely badly ever since it was built.[1] In 1995 its staff went on strike demanding to be paid several months arrears of wages. It is also said that the owner used illegal immigrants from Albania to build the hotel, whom he reported to the police every six months or so in order to have them deported and avoid paying them. In 1996 the original owner transferred the bankrupt hotel to another entrepreneur and moved away from the spotlight, whilst the future of the hotel looks, if anything, exceedingly uncertain. In another case, while works to build a hotel in Avlon beach, near Myrina, were in progress, excavators unearthed a temple of Artemis. The normal procedure on the authorities' part would have been to stop all development work and declare the site to be of archaeological value. Mysteriously, the hotel was allowed to be completed, whilst in a token gesture towards Greece's heritage the unearthed temple became one of the hotel features. In a third case, a combination of noise and lights from a disco and various kinds of waste washed down or dumped further upstream have decimated the population of sweet water turtles in a stream flowing into the sea at the same beach.[2]

A more general and equally worrying problem is posed by an emerging trend among the bigger hotel complexes in Lemnos (and elsewhere in Greece) to use foreign rather than local staff, particularly illegal immigrants, and in other ways distance themselves from the local economy. In this way they increasingly tend to function as enclaves, actually quite like the mining operations of a number of multinationals in certain Third World countries. It is all the more surprising since it would be relatively easy for the Greek state to require and enforce the cultivation of links between tourist developments and their surrounding local economies – or at least avoid subsidising hotels meant to operate outside such links.

Since the re-introduction of political rule in Greece, a series of Myrina mayors have been busy 'modernising' the town further. Part of a stream in Myrina has been covered with concrete and turned into a parking lot, and a lovely bridge has been destroyed in the process. More trees have been cut. Cobblestone streets have given way to concrete ones. The idea of creating parking lots on municipal land peripherally around

Myrina, so as to conserve the look of the old towncore, apparently has not occurred to the 'modernisers'. Their latest plan involves opening up a short cut in a traditional part of Myrina, through people's courts and gardens (which will be force-purchased for the purpose), in order to save car drivers a couple of minutes ride. Another plan, to raise a bridge for cars over the traditional fishing port of Myrina, has fortunately been turned down by the council, so far at least.

While all this has been going on, B&B and hotel owners have been trying to grab a fast buck. There have been cases of arbitrarily raising prices to existing customers as the season progresses and more people seeking accommodation arrive. A customer who would go to the police complaining about this sort of extortion, would probably have no way of proving it, as the hotelier or landlord could in turn maintain that the higher rate was the one initially agreed upon, and the tourist was trying to defraud him instead. After all, there are no signed agreements or records, especially at B&Bs or the smaller hotels. Taxi drivers, on their part, charge exorbitantly high prices and normally refuse to be hired for short trips.

Unsurprisingly, occupancy rates at Acte Myrina have been falling for some time and dramatically so in 1996. Aside from the adverse effect of two consecutive bad years for tourism, as was the case in 1995 and 1996 all over Greece, there have been other factors behind the fall. One is the changes that have taken place in Myrina and other parts of Lemnos since 1985, including the operation of new hotels; another relates to managerial policies, as the initial owners have walked out and the hotel is now owned by Greeks. For example, long-standing, experienced administrative staff have been fired, on at least one occasion customers – all high-income people – were reprimanded for hiring a local fishing boat (caiqki) for an excursion rather than the hotel's own, and the state of the hotel grounds and of the perimeter fence leaves a lot to be desired; certainly it does not justify the hotel prices, which now look exorbitantly high. Paradoxically, despite falling occupancy rates, in 1996 the new owners, in a move said to herald another attempt at sale of the once exemplary hotel, began expanding the hotel to adjacent land, marring the landscape in the process. The expansion has been financed by bank loans and subsidised, as is often the case, by the Greek state. Needless to say, the new bungalows are made of concrete rather than stone.

10.2 WHERE POLYPHEMUS TREADS

In nearly all other parts of Greece the 'fast buck' ideal also seems to drive the tourist industry. In a convoluted way this stems precisely from the fact that Greece already has in abundance the 'product' to sell – sun, sea, sky, sex. For example, according to a 1995 European Commission report, Greece has the cleanest beaches in Europe,[3] which is all the more remarkable considering the level of pollution in the Mediterranean.[4] Because of those natural gifts, however, a lot of Greeks thought that tourism is an 'easy' industry to join or be in, and that this particular product mix would last forever. As a result Greece's tourist industry lacks organisation, knowledge, direction,[5] and policing. Two aspects of the industry are of particular concern as they undermine its long-term prospects: First, the quality of services and infrastructure offered. Second, the broad environmental impact of the industry. We shall examine these in turn.

A study of quality in Greek hotels, conducted by the Athens Chamber of Commerce and Industry (EBEA) in 1995,[6] found that although 87 per cent of hotels in the sample accepted that securing quality of service is necessary in order to compete in the 1990s, 70 per cent had not installed any quality-measuring and quality-achieving system, 100 per cent had not sought external consultants and had no knowledge of the ISO-9004-2 system, whilst 22 per cent did not want to know. These figures are all the more incongruous considering that all hotels in the sample were 3-star or greater: 32 per cent were 3-star hotels, 42 per cent were 4-star, and 26 per cent 5-star. An explanation, however, may lie in the fact that 63 per cent of those hotels were family-owned (and 16 per cent were 'personal' enterprises, another 16 per cent plcs, and 5 per cent belonged to multinationals). This fact was reflected in the way the hotels were administered: 58 per cent were managed by their owners, only 25 per cent by professional managers, and 17 per cent by their owners and managers both. Unsurprisingly, 56.5 per cent of the hotels did not have an organisational chart, which must mean 'that there is no exact description of duties and tasks, hence there is no staff specialisation either'.[7] Inevitably these characteristics make for resistance to change or improvement on the part of management, who feel they know best and are always right, whilst low-level staff tend to get the blame whenever things go wrong.[8]

The lack of, or perceived small need for, skilled staff was identified in greater detail in another study, conducted in 1993 by the Union of Greek Tourist Enterprises (ΣΕΤΕ), and published in 1995. According to Table 10.1, which reproduces the study results, 35 per cent of staff in hotels of all types was unskilled; by far, however, the largest proportion of unskilled staff was found in the rooms-to-let sector of the industry: 86 per cent. This is also the sector which supplies 67 per cent of the industry beds, so it represents the type of accommodation which most tourists are likeliest to come to contact with. Although many owners of rooms-to-let are by now quite experienced at dealing with tourists, no worse or better than, say, British B&B owners are, it is time that Greece seriously sought to make her tourist industry more professional. Training entrepreneurs and staff, however, is more easily said than done. There is the question of knowing whom to train, part of the much broader question of policing the industry so as to ensure that standards are met and observed: many of those rooms-to-let, and even quite a few hotel rooms,[9] are not registered with the authorities, the main reason being tax evasion. If monitoring who owns what is already a big problem, one can imagine how much more difficult it is to monitor who works where, and what his or her qualifications are.

Then there is the question of who will bear the cost of training, when the whole thrust of the Greek tourist industry up to now has been about attracting as many tourists as possible, at prices that are either too low to justify investment in high standards of service or infrastructure, or too high in relation to the low standards frequently offered. To-day's mass, or packaged, tourism inevitably and increasingly comes at the expense of quality, especially in countries which are not developed enough, or rich enough, to supply, or force the supply of, high standards of service and infrastructure – but if they did, then quite a few of those tourists who have had reason to complain would not have been able to afford their holidays in the first place.

This is not to say that many of those complaints are not genuine and well-justified. There is plenty in the Greek – and other Mediterranean countries' – tourist industry to provide cause enough for such. Apart from complaints about 'ordinary' matters, cases of defrauding, deceiving, or mistreating tourists, both Greek and foreign, are also frequent enough to matter,[10] even if far from typical or normal. But while a number of unacceptable situations can be rectified within the present structure and philosophy of the tourist industry, perhaps with better policing, correcting the majority of such cases, which would ultimately necessitate raising standards substantially, and then enforcing them, would require and presuppose a different tourist industry altogether, involving long-term planning, strict criteria, truly comprehensive policing, and so on. In turn this can only result from a political decision to

Table 10.1
Greek tourist industry, 1993: Number of beds, skilled and unskilled staff

Sub-sector	Beds	% of beds in sub-sector	Skilled staff	Unskilled staff	All staff	Unskilled staff as % of total
Hotels, all categories and types	499 600	30.2	77 700	41 300	119 000	35
Rooms-to-let, declared & undeclared	1 100 000	66.6	13 000	80 000	93 000	86
Camping sites (places)	7 500	0.5	2 200	1 800	4 000	45
Cruising boats	12 200	0.7	4 500	3 000	7 500	40
Yaghts	32 300	2.0	6 000	500	6 500	8
Other (travel agents, rent-a-car, etc.)	NA		20 700	2 300	23 000	10
Total	1 651 600	100.0	124 100	128 900	253 000	51

Source: Daphne, 1995, quoting results of 1993 study by Union of Greek Tourist Enterprises.

clash with the umpteen big and small interests (the small in particular: from taxi drivers to cafe owners), to whom to-day's industry represents an easy and affordable way of living; for some, in addition, it means the only opportunity for employment, especially employment as their own bosses.

Another type of 'complaint' though, the 'trumped up' type, is the result of more sinister and recent trends in the international tourist industry. It involves 'yellow' or 'black' propaganda[11] campaigns against competitor countries, with Greece a prime target. An example is an article in *Sunday Times*,[12] whose author refused to name the English couple who had supposedly had a bad time holidaying in Greece. In this way the Greek Tourism Organisation (EOT) could not make amends, even though the particular 'complaints' betrayed squeamishness and a 'colonial' attitude more than anything else. Neither did *Sunday Times* agree to publish EOT's reply to unsubstantiated accusations,[13] which therefore could easily have been fictitious and made to order. Nevertheless, a lot of people in Greece, some of them people in authority who should know better, have not taken it on board that the damage done to Greece by the thieving taxi-driver, the landlord or small hotelier selling substandard accommodation ('substandard', that is, in relation to what is advertised, implied or expected), or seaports and airports which, mildly put, are chaotic in summer months is too real and too 'sticky' to ignore for the sake of political expediency. Rectifying such practices and situations should be priority one, irrespective of any inevitable howls of protest on the part of the 'fast-buck' crowd. Unfortunately, EOT still thinks that top priority should be given to better advertising abroad of holidays in Greece.[14] That is necessary too, but dealing with the basis for tourists' complaints should have precedence. In turn this requires both political courage and a clear strategy as to what kind of tourism Greece needs. Both are seriously lacking. For example, from April 1950 to June 1996, there have been 31 different heads of EOT, which amounts to 18 months in office for each: not much to allow consistency in strategy, or even the formulation of one. In fact, but for N. Phocas, who headed EOT for 12 consecutive years (from February 1952 to March 1964), the average length of time in office for the rest has been smaller, little more than a year.[15] Leaving the tourist industry practically on its own, has inevitably led to a vicious circle in which low standards command low prices (or, worse, higher than value-for-money prices), they in turn attract low-income tourists,[16] and then investing in high standards appears unprofitable, in the short term at least. This is Gresham's law applied to tourism: the 'bad' (that is, low-income) tourist driving away the 'good' (that is, high-income) one.[17] Despite many hotels and rooms-to-let in Greece offering up-to-standard services, and quite a few more than matching what is expected in their respective categories, it is now difficult, though far from impossible, to re-orientate the industry as a whole towards high quality. Politics apart, one important reason, as both Greeks and foreigners have repeatedly found out, is that hotels and rooms-to-let are not the only aspect of Greece tourists come in contact with: taxis, ports, restaurants, noise levels, and littered beaches form part of the picture too, and they often leave a lot to be desired.

Having geared up to cheap tourism, or giving some tourists less than they expect in terms of personal services and infrastructure, is one of the two main problems of tourism in Greece. Equally worrying is the tolerance, if not encouragement, which the state often shows to environmentally damaging tourist facilities and activities. The phenomenon is not, of course, confined to Greece:

> Build too many hotels and the lovely coast that drew the visitors may become like that of Benidorm; send too many safaris round your nature reserves and one day you will not have much nature to show them.[18]

In addition to that, most Mediterranean countries, precisely because they are relatively undeveloped and at the same time one of the most favoured tourist destinations in the world, seem to have special problems of environmental pollution attributable to tourism, problems of an objective nature:

> Tourists come mainly in a couple of peak summer months, which is when water is most scarce. Village sewage plants, which manage for nine months of the year with a few hundred people, suddenly have to cope with several thousand at the season when nature gives them least assistance.[19]

But instances of environmental degradation in Greece are also the result of a far broader attitude of neglect and yield to expediency.[20] They overlap too with the long-standing practice of unauthorised building – for residential as well as business purposes – which has been typical of post-war Greece (see Chapter 9). It would have been very surprising indeed had the tourist sector escaped the pattern.

One could write volumes of examples. Some were mentioned in relation to Myrina, Lemnos. Five more will suffice.[21] Just before the 1989 elections a new Presidential Decree allowed the construction in the Cyclades of buildings of twice the volume of what was the norm previously. The Union of Greek Architects was furious. They had good reason to be: apart from the general degradation of the traditional Cycladic architectural environment which the new Decree was foreseen to bring about, the Decree did not even exempt from its stipulations such a traditional settlement as the capital of Ios, despite the existence of a state-sanctioned planning study, which had proposed limitations to the right to build in this particular town. Upon official protests from local sources, the Ministry of Planning in Athens admitted that they had made a mistake, which they would correct in due course. In the meantime, a number of enterprising individuals had applied for and received permits to build in Ios according to the new, more lax rules. By the time the Ministry was to issue an official clarification and new guidelines, those permits had given rise to developments which altered the traditional character of the Ios capital. Under the circumstances, the person(s) or department(s) responsible for the mess could not be identified – they never can, in Greece – and the enterprising individuals who had moved quickly can be expected to rest on, and profit from, their new large properties.[22]

The second example is even more suggestive of profiteering interests behind state actions, or inactions. It concerns attempts to build an eyesore of a three-storey hotel in the traditional settlement of Great Papingo in the region of Epirus. Local environmentalists protested to the European Parliament that the volume of the building was three times that of the biggest traditional property in the settlement, and covered an area of 982 square metres. As a result of local resistance to the development, between 1986 and 1991 at least, the hotel plans and the associated permit made the round of various government departments with mixed results. Apparently the Hellenic Tourism Organisation (EOT) did not condone the development, whilst the Ministry of Planning was against it – for it – against it – for it, depending on the committee and the administrative level the plans and protests were referred to.[23]

The third example again implies the presence of profiteering interests, only this time those who press for 'development' are local communities rather than particular individuals. It is a more forceful version of the Lemnos case, but also shows how the State tends to yield to such pressures on the basis of short-term, 'political cost,' considerations. It concerns a place of worship and exceptional natural beauty, the Meteora rocks in the region of Thessaly, atop which are perched a number of Orthodox monasteries. It is supposed to be a place of holy significance to the Greek nation, forming a link to Greece's Byzantine past and to Orthodox spirituality. In September 1995 the Ministry of Planning brought a Bill to the Greek Parliament, recognising the sacred character of the Meteora rocks, thus attempting to safeguard them from the development plans of the nearby communities. At issue, among other things, was the monasteries' traditional and exclusive right to taking and selling pictures of the place. The response of the councils and the communities involved was swift: resignation threats, blocking of national highways through popular mobilisation, seeking and securing the support of locally elected MPs from all parties. Within three days, the Minister had taken the Bill back, for 'further study and consultations.'[24]

In a similar vein, a constellation of local interests has managed to thwart efforts by the Ministry of Planning to delineate land use and building in the island of Patmos (where St John wrote the *Apocalypse*):

> Four years ago the Ministry of Planning commissioned a special planning study of the island, which emphasised the need for a stricter regime governing building activity on it. The idea was to put the brakes on 'convenient', short-termist practices of tourist development there. Official approval of the study is still pending, however. The cause has been resistance on the part of the island authorities (municipal and church), which claim that the proposed building terms are too harsh []. In typical Greek fashion the Ministry's attempt has been forgotten and the situation is now out of control. [] Roads are being built and concrete houses sprout everywhere with no respect for the island's characteristic architecture [].[25]

The last example is perhaps the most horrific. It concerns unauthorised building by inhabitants of the Ionian island of Zante (Zakynthos) on and near beaches which constitute the last remaining breeding grounds in the Med for the big caretta-caretta sea-turtle.[26] They have managed to do that precisely because of corruption and laxity on the part of the authorities, and have even been organising 'turtle-watching nights' for tourists, further disrupting the peace and quiet which these creatures need. Despite being illegally there, the building-owners have been loudly demanding compensation in the unlikely case the Ministry of Planning goes ahead and demolishes their unauthorised constructions, have threatened taking up arms against any demolition crews, and in October 1995 actually exploded a bomb in the premises of the Zante Ecological Movement in order to intimidate its members who have only been asking for existing planning and environmental laws to be observed.

The preceding sentence throws up an important aspect of the problem: in theory, egoistical and opportunistic development interests in Greece do not have an absolutely free reign. There are laws and regulations which are supposed to protect the traditional natural and architectural environment. The Archaeological Service, in particular, is responsible for proclaiming sites and places in Greece to be of archaeological or historic value, and therefore to merit exemption from normal building and planning regulations. But more often than not, it is a losing battle for the environmentalists, as the relevant laws and regulations, even when they do exist, are not applied, or are circumvented, or interpreted in a lax manner by the authorities. A related problem is touristy developments which appear to conform to legality, albeit superficially only. Calocardou (1995) has identified the following reasons for breaches of the legal framework: lack of planning, or only token application of planning rules, by the state; the multiplicity of laws and regulations, which opens the way to vague or multiple interpretations; weaknesses in the system that issues planning permits; and emphasis on short-term profit on the part of entrepreneurs.

More serious, but no less frequent, are cases where planning officials, local councillors, and the police are bribed by businessmen or property owners. The situation is not helped by the fragmentation of conservationist authority among a variety of departments and agencies. For instance, in 1990 the Ministry of Culture, on the strength of advice from the Central Council of Modern Monuments, proclaimed the village of Campos in the island of Chios to be of historic value. But that was not enough: for protection to be enacted, the Ministry of Planning would have to come in, and define the particular building regulations that would apply in the village following the Ministry of Culture decision – a very bureaucratic affair.[27] In the same vein, in order to sanction the building and operation of a pizzeria in, say, Myrina, the following authorities have to be involved:[28]

- The Directorate of Byzantine and Post-Byzantine Monuments, in order to issue a permit allowing works to be carried out 'above ground level'. Incidentally, the Directorate is located in the island of Chios, not in Lemnos.
- The Archaeological Service (located in the island of Lesbos), in order to issue a permit allowing works to be carried out 'below ground level'.
- The local planning office, in order to approve the building plan.
- The Chief of the local Police, the local Health Officer, and the local Council, in order to authorise the operation of the pizzeria.

It may look as if it is really difficult to start a pizzeria in Lemnos (or any other island), and possibly spoil a picturesque environment. It is not so. If anything, the fragmentation of authority among so many departments stops any one of them from having the broader environmental picture in mind that is required for effective conservation. It also makes it very difficult for environmentalists as well as others to challenge the particular development on grounds of incompatibility with the traditional natural or architectural environment. Unchallenged, the businessman involved will secure the permits he seeks as a matter of course. It will be run-of-the-mill procedure, even including the odd bribe. An environmentalist challenging him will have to spend considerable time and money contacting the various departments, even travelling to other islands for the purpose, hiring a solicitor, stating and supporting his case, and otherwise pursuing the matter. Basically, he – not the State – will have to prove that the development in question is in some sense illegal, let alone an eyesore. Even then, his case may be turned down on the grounds that he has no legitimate interests of his own to protect whilst he is challenging the development. That is, an environmental argument based on general principles, even if sanctioned in law, often does not hold water where Greek lower courts are concerned.[29]

A sorely-to-be-missed victim of the above attitudes and practices is Greece's picturesque, traditional settlements. The threat to them was identified and discussed in a 1993 Unesco-supported conference, organised by the Greek Ministry of Planning and the Greek Tourism Organisation (EOT).[30] Cos, Nauplion, Tenos, Naxos, Myconos, and Chios were cited as prime examples. Rhodes is another.[31] In regard to Myconos in particular, it has been argued[32] that her 'tourist system' is in a highly critical and dangerous phase of its development cycle, and is characterised by the following problems: a deteriorating ratio of locals to tourists, extensive change of land uses in and near the traditional town, urbanisation, abandonment of agriculture, environmental degradation, drop in real incomes, land value appreciation, unauthorised building, and, of course, mounting feelings of dislike and discomfort, especially among tourists who are not new to Myconos. Others have extended the analysis to national level:

> The critical situation of the environment and settlements in Greece, as a result of touristy activities, is at last strikingly visible. The crisis has not appeared out of the blue; rather, it has been brought about as a result of a long process . . . related to policy actions and

inactions, as well as long-term structural weaknesses of the social formation.[33]

Is there then an element of inevitability to the present face of tourism in Greece? One is inclined to agree, since a country's political system and her other social characteristics (in Greece's case, large number of smallholders, fragmented land ownership, poverty, and so on) to a large extent determine her future course. On this reckoning, it is probably romantic to expect a different kind of tourism in Greece – one that is oriented towards quality and high-income tourists, and at the same time conserves and sustains the environment – but only if reform measures are confined to the tourist sector narrowly defined. If, on the other hand, reform is much broader in scope, extending to the planning and policing functions of the State, the legal system and framework (particularly as regards environmental protection), the country's infrastructure, local economic development initiatives, and the way the civil service works, then there is reason for optimism. After all, instances of successfully basing a place's touristic development on conservation of the traditional environment have been observed but, sadly, are still very few. Two tentative examples are perhaps Mytilene in Lesbos[34] and St Nicholas (Aghios Nicolaos) in Crete.[35]

In the meantime the way Greek tourism is going, its costs increasingly outweigh its rewards. To this let us now turn.

10.3 PROSPECTS OF GREEK TOURISM

In the 1950s and 1960s Greek tourism was living its innocent, halcyon days. Greece was far more picturesque than she is to-day, and most of her people, even though poor, hard-working, and tormented by memories of the Occupation and the civil war, were charmingly naive. Like to-day, there were many lovely, clean beaches, and thousands of monuments and places of historical interest. The drama festivals enacted every summer in the ancient theatres of Epidaurus and Herodeion were events attracting the interest of European socialites and intellectuals, while Melina Merkouri and Anthony Quinn were capturing the hearts of Western audiences with *Never on Sunday* and *Zorba the Greek*, respectively. The tourist visiting at the time was more akin to the literary traveller of the 1920s and 1930s than to the 'charter flighter' of the present.

The transition from the former to the latter type of tourist began to take place in the late 1960s, and by the middle 1980s it was completed.

Places like Athens, Rhodes, Santorini, Corfu, Paros, Cos, Myconos, Ios, and Khalkidiké are teeming with water sports facilities, and hotels, B&Bs, pubs, restaurants, and souvenir shops with foreign names. Others are mushrooming all the time. The consequences have been two-fold. On the one hand, the number of tourists visiting Greece has expanded dramatically since the 1960s. It passed the one-million mark in 1966, the two-million mark in 1971, the four-million mark in 1976, and it exceeded the population of the country in 1994, when more than 11 million tourists visited Greece – more than 24 times the 1961 figure.[36] In addition, the sector accounts for at least 10 per cent of the country's GDP, and 11 to 18 per cent of total employment,[37] while in 1993–95 it contributed 20 per cent of invisible receipts.[38]

On the other hand, Greece has come to depend almost totally on the international tour operators who manage the flows of mass tourism, rather than basing her tourist development on the higher-income, more discerning type of tourist. This has brought her to a situation where:

(a) The spectacular increase in the number of tourists has been accompanied by sluggish growth in total monetary receipts in real terms (Table 10.2). The discrepancy is even more pronounced when we look into receipts per tourist in real vs current prices, with the real trend actually falling over time: whereas receipts per tourist were about 14 000 drs in 1980, they were about 8500 drs in 1995 at 1980 prices (Table 10.2). At the same time the pressure of the masses of tourists on the available infrastructure and the environment has been increasing. For example, from 1989 to 1994 the number of beds in hotels of all categories (but excluding 'rooms-to-let') went up from 424 thousand to 508 thousand[39] – a 20 per cent rise. Over the same period, the number of foreign tourists, as measured by arrivals rather than nights booked, rose by 32 per cent, and that's not counting Greek tourists. There are, of course, the rooms-to-let to consider too. But as many of these are not formally registered enterprises (partly because they do not meet official standards, partly for tax-evasion purposes), their very proliferation indicates the kind of tourist development that is done haphazardly, often in neglect of planning or environmental considerations, or is of substandard quality. The upshot is that the average tourist who visits Greece pays less every year, in real terms, for consuming her tourist resources, whilst he exacts a heavy toll on Greece's poor infrastructure. These resources and the infrastructure that enables their enjoyment are not, of course, unlimited: increasingly

Table 10.2
Greece 1980–95: Arrivals of tourists and receipts in FX and in drs

Year	Arrivals	Total receipts in $US million	Receipts per tourist in $US	Dr/$ exchange rate	Receipts per tourist in drs	Greek inflation rate (%)	Greek price level (100=1980)	Receipts per tourist in constant 1980 drs	Total receipts in constant 1980 m. drs
1980	5 271 115	1 733.5	329	43.062	14 162	26.2	100.00	14 162	74 648
1981	5 557 109	1 881.1	339	55.427	18 762	22.5	122.50	15 316	85 113
1982	5 463 860	1 527.2	280	66.780	18 666	21.0	148.23	12 593	68 805
1983	5 258 372	1 175.5	224	87.889	19 651	20.5	178.61	11 002	57 853
1984	6 027 266	1 312.8	218	112.681	24 543	18.5	211.65	11 596	69 891
1985	7 039 428	1 428.0	203	138.197	28 034	25.0	264.57	10 596	74 592
1986	7 339 015	1 833.0	250	139.954	34 955	16.9	309.28	11 302	82 946
1987	8 053 052	2 268.0	282	135.429	38 141	15.7	357.84	10 659	85 836
1988	8 351 182	2 396.0	287	141.861	40 701	14.0	407.93	9 977	83 322
1989	8 540 962	1 977.2	231	162.420	37 600	14.8	468.31	8 029	68 574
1990	9 310 492	2 586.8	278	158.515	44 041	22.8	575.08	7 658	71 302
1991	8 271 258	2 567.4	310	182.265	56 575	18.0	678.60	8 337	68 958
1992	9 756 012	3 271.8	335	190.707	63 956	14.4	776.31	8 238	80 374
1993	9 913 267	3 335.1	336	229.250	77 126	12.1	870.25	8 863	87 857
1994	11 301 722	3 904.9	346	242.603	83 823	10.8	964.24	8 693	98 248
1995	10 712 145	4 106.2	383	231.700	88 816	8.1	1 042.34	8 521	91 276

Source: Greek Tourism Organisation (EOT).

they are being depleted as when a pristine beach is overcrowded with tourists, or when a hotel, a taverna, or rooms-to-let are built on an unspoilt beach without heeding the need to use designs and materials that agree with the landscape.

(b) The industry has been geared towards a section of the international tourist market which, above all else, is very sensitive to changes in the price of accommodation in Greece vis-a-vis price changes in competitor countries. This is also the section that is very sensitive to changes in their own incomes. Thus, even though 'cheap' in comparison to, say, Britain or France, Greece can easily be found 'dearer' than, say, Turkey or Spain, especially considering the not obviously superior quality of service she offers. For example, the slight drop in the number of tourists, which Greece experienced in 1995, and she was forecast to experience again in 1996, has been attributed mainly to price changes in Greek hotels vis-a-vis those of other destinations. In particular, the increases in contract prices, agreed between Greek hotels and tour operators in 1994 (effective in 1995), were larger than those for Spain, Portugal, or Cyprus, and certainly larger than those for Turkey, which actually lowered her prices. The increases happened partly because the Greek hoteliers tried to compensate for their low prices in 1993 (effective in 1994; an especially good year for tourism in terms of arrivals), and partly because both Greek hoteliers and tour operators overestimated the extent of the depreciation of the drachma in 1995. Price dependence of this type tends to press the Greek tourist industry deeper into the vicious circle of an increasingly cheaper tourist 'product' which in turn attracts lower-income tourists, driving higher-income ones away.

(c) Tourism's contribution to Greece's balance of payments has also begun to be the object of concern: although its net contribution must still be positive, it is probably far smaller than it is thought, as the industry sucks in imports for the tourists' benefit.

The thing is, most Greek entrepreneurs in the tourist industry used to think, and still do, that the four Ss (sea – sun – sky – sex) would be enough to compensate for other shortcomings, and that, moreover, they would be in high demand always. It is not so. First came AIDS. Then the hole in the ozone layer, which is making long exposure to the sun increasingly dangerous. Pollution of the Mediterranean in the foreseeable future will be getting worse, not better. Finally, according to the English Tourist Board,

> many tourists have become more interested in attractions that have retained some of their traditional character and are beginning to shun the featureless concrete cities that occupy large parts of the Mediterranean.[40]

One might, of course, say that there is an element of wishful thinking in the ETB's observations, as it is in the interests of North-Western European countries to keep their tourists at home. They have, after all, better managed to conserve and gift-wrap many of their traditional, mostly medieval, towns and villages than Mediterranean countries. But concrete cities and constructions are ugly compared to traditional settlements and houses, so the latter were, or are, bound to start featuring high in tourists' preferences sooner or later.[41] Fortunately Greece by and large does not entertain her tourists in concrete cities, Benidorm-style. But the increasing destruction of her traditional picturesqueness, evidenced in many towns, villages, islands and beaches, is taking away from her the one thing that may give her the competitive edge in tomorrow's international tourist market: with careful planning, her combination of sunny skies, clean seas, picturesqueness, quality of service and multi-varied tourism (agro-tourism, ecological tourism, conference tourism, and so on) would have been hard to beat.

It is sad that although all five aspects of this combination are either already at Greece's disposal or within her capability to achieve, she has adopted a completely short-termist and opportunistic model of tourist development. True, more people nowadays are beginning to realise that this model has failed, including, among others, the current head of the Greek Tourism Organisation[42] and Vasso Papandreou, Greece's Minister of Development.[43] But a recent attempt to move to a different model, by means of establishing so-called Areas of Integrated Tourist Development (AITD), has been rather unfortunate: these Areas are to be the result of ad hoc, special regulations and arrangements rather than part of a more general and comprehensive land-use and town-planning policy. More specifically, the law governing AITD (2160/93)

> betrays complete ignorance of (a) the spatial processes of tourist development [ ] and (b) the particularities of the tourist sector. Tourism is not an assembly-line industry, nor can it be modelled, in planning terms, after Industrial Areas. [What is needed, is] (a) maximising forward and backward linkages between tourism and other sectors, principally at county or regional level; (b) harmonising tourist infrastructure, existing and new, with the social, cultural, and environmental

resources and parameters, which are, after all, the main poles of attraction to tourists.[44]

On the basis of the preceding discussion, we can, perhaps, see why the government has opted for the AITD model as a token gesture to the increasingly perceived need to go for quality tourism, rather than, for example, introduce and/or apply environmental protection and planning laws comprehensively, or police taxi-drivers more strictly. The reason is that otherwise it would have to clash with the multiplicity of interests that have been profiteering at the expense of the environment and of quality, and which have been consistently undermining in this way the industry's long-term growth prospects as well as, ultimately, Greece's image abroad. From this point of view, the Areas of Integrated Tourist Development are not, nor can they be, a genuine alternative to the present, bankrupt model.

In short, what Greece needs is to turn the traditional model on its head: instead of relying on the backfiring combination of low standards and (usually) low prices, Greece can and must, whatever the reactions of various entrenched interests, aim primarily for high-quality tourism. She can achieve this in three mutually complementary ways. First, by putting in place and then enforcing a planning and environmental framework specifically meant to conserve or (re)establish the natural and architectural picturesqueness of Greece. Second, by defining and enforcing across the board higher standards of service than today's, not only as regards hotels, restaurants and taxis, but also the country's ports. Third, by using tax revenue from model hotel developments which attract high-income tourists by capitalising on picturesqueness (the way the Acte Myrina hotel, mentioned above, did in the past) in order to subsidise, say, restaurants or cafes in near-by towns and villages, so that small businesses spend more on environmental aesthetics in turn. This circuit would also be in the interest of the more expensive and more heavily taxed hotel complexes as it would help preserve or accentuate the overall character of an area. Rather than causing Greece to price herself out of the international tourist market, the whole process would simply result in Greece becoming more popular with higher-income tourists, even if less so with lower-income ones. Inevitably, restructuring and reorienting the industry along those lines would cut into the profits and raise the costs of a great many haphazard or 'cowboy' entrepreneurs currently in the sector – which is why they would oppose the effort. They would also have assistance from people from outside the industry, and even help from local communities. Let us not forget that the tourist industry in not an island unto itself: an environmental or planning law applied universally would not hurt just the hotel- or room-to-let-owner who has built in breach of planning regulations, but dwelling-owners who have done, or are thinking of doing, the same too. After all, 'osmosis' between the many smallholder interests in Greece is perhaps the main reason why particular measures or attempts at rationalisation fail so often.

It is a worthwhile bet that if some visionary government found the courage to enforce the rule of law and at the same time remodel the tourist industry as indicated, Greece would find that, far from sacrificing the environment and picturesqueness to her present kind of tourism, she would have reason to conserve and cultivate both as her top assets; such protection, moreover, would pay for itself in the long run. But Greece needs to move fast, or there will be precious little left to protect in the end.

Notes

1. The owner of that hotel has not been the first (probably not the last either) to try and take advantage of state subsidies and development laws by building a hotel without any forward planning or careful thought, and eventually, perhaps inevitably, finding himself in financial trouble. Apparently the crisis concerns more than 1000 hotels all over Greece. See Stereopoulos, 1994; Sophoulis, 1995.
2. Sadly, the Ministry of Planning & the Environment in Athens has failed to respond to this writer's pleas for measures to protect the turtles.
3. *E Cathemerine*, 15.5.1996, p. 28; *Ta Nea*, 29.4.1996, pp. 20–1.
4. *The Economist*, 1992.
5. Comilis, 1995, p. 78.
6. Papadopoulos, 1995.
7. Ibid., p. 55.
8. Ibid., pp. 58 & 61.
9. 'Informal economy worth 30 bn drs in hotel sector: Checks found 30 000 rooms added without permit', *Kerdos*, 6.6.1995; 'Plethora of illegal rooms', *E Cathemerine*, 13.7.1995.
10. The following incident was certainly over the top, although no less true for that. In July 1995 a cafe in the Constitution (Syntagma) Square in Athens charged three Japanese customers 1 000 000 drs (£2667) for three bottles of lager (*E Cathemerine*, 23.7.95, p. 43). They did, of course go to the police, and the culprits were arrested, but the episode is indicative of a widely spread pattern of attempts to defraud tourists.
11. 'Yellow' propaganda does not disclose its source; 'black' propaganda discloses other than its true source.
12. Clark, 1995.

13. EOT, 1995a.
14. Coussounis, 1996.
15. Ibid.
16. 'Greece has allowed herself to be rated as a cheap tourist package', *Kerdos*, 10.6.1995, p. 7.
17. Courmoussis, 1991.
18. *The Economist*, 1989, p. 22.
19. *The Economist*, 1992, p. 21.
20. See Chapter 9; also 'The Greeks kill their environment', *E Cathemerine*, 5.6.1996, p. 6.
21. See also Dorovinis, 1992a, 1992b; 'Tourism threatens Pefkias', *E Cathemerine*, 10.1.1996.
22. 'Let Ios be covered in concrete,' *Eleutherotypia*, 31.12.1989, p. 58.
23. 'Threat to the landscape in Papingo,' *E Cathemerine*, 26.5.1991.
24. *E Cathemerine*, 5, 6, 7 Sept. 1995. See also Calokairinos, 1995; Papathanasopoulos, 1995.
25. 'Loss of character danger to Patmos', *E Cathemerine*, 22.8.1996, p. 7.
26. Papademetriou, 1995; 'Blast in the careta-careta "house"', *E Cathemerine*, 3.10.1995.
27. 'Chios: Campos breathes again,' *Eleutherotypia*, 18.11.1990.
28. Pirounakis, 1992a.
29. The only definitely pro-environmental court in Greece is the Supreme Administrative Court [Συμβούλιον Επικρατείας] (up to now at least). In a series of decisions it has annoyed the Ministry of Planning no less than crowds of property owners for whom environmental concerns are of low and of no priority at all, respectively. Recently the Court surpassed even its past record by declaring, among others, that building on plots smaller than 15 stremmas (1/10 of a hectare) in the islands, building hotels outside Ekistic Development Zones, or building roads along beaches and less than 100 metres from the sea, are wrong and to be made illegal. See *Express*, 1996.
30. Bouzali, 1993.
31. Zachariadis, 1995.
32. Parpairis, 1995.
33. Hadjidakis, 1995, p. 91.
34. Magheiros, 1995.
35. Papandropoulos, 1995c.
36. Greek Tourism Organisation (EOT) data.
37. Catokhianou, 1995. In Britain the corresponding figure was 10 per cent in 1991 (Skapinker, 1991).
38. Bank of Greece Annual Report for 1995.
39. EOT data.
40. Skapinker, 1991.
41. See Barley, 1990, writing about 'the West's relentless quest for novelty and authenticity as we move up the holiday market'.
42. 'The competitiveness of Greek tourism has been based up to now exclusively on price . . . a new strategy is needed, focusing on quality', *Kerdos*, 16.6.1996, p. 5.
43. 'Greece is too beautiful to sell cheaply'. Papandreou, V., 1996.
44. Comilis, 1995, pp. 79–80.

11 Lessons and Insights

'The words of Immortality were placed in your hands. But, o fool . . . how have you invested them?'
Themis A. Vassiliadis, Lemnian mystic. *The Steps of the Passage.*

11.1 HOW IS GREECE DIFFERENT?

One can start with the trivially obvious: that different countries differ from one another. One of the main points of this book, however, is that Greece for a variety of reasons has been backsliding for some time now. Does this make her somehow unique?

The short answer is sadly no. Growth rates in the advanced capitalist world have been lower since the oil-price shocks of 1973 and 1979 than they were before. Recessions are endemic. Although inflation has become less severe than it was in the 1970s, unemployment is on the increase, with many millions apparently out of work permanently. Job prospects for the majority of young people look particularly gloomy. Criminality and drug use rates are rising fast. Educational standards have been suffering throughout the advanced capitalist countries, not just in Greece (even if the deterioration is more comprehensive and pronounced in her case). Social inequalities are worsening and poverty is once again becoming highly visible, with homelessness and malnutrition the foremost signs. Specific groups, like the old, the unemployed, economic refugees or single-parent families, are exceptionally vulnerable to cuts in the welfare state, which appear all the more 'logical' or 'inevitable' as the opening up of the world economy upsets established social orders and economic patterns and whips up competition between continents, countries, regions and cities. The disruption and its social consequences are more prevalent in the ex-communist European countries, but America and North-Western Europe are inexorably and increasingly its victims too. Corruption, tax evasion and informal economy growth seem to spread throughout the Western world – once a model of benevolent rationality, welfare, the rule of law and ethical conduct, at least outwith the realm of foreign affairs. Western foreign policy (or policies?), in turn, seems to become rapidly more disjointed, unethical and outright imperialist than the carefully constructed facade of care for human rights had led some to expect of it whilst the Cold War was going on.[1]

If these are the trends of the times anyway, isn't the backsliding of Greece merely a localised, national case of a broader phenomenon? After all, what could one expect of less rich or powerful countries when advanced ones are in trouble?

Although there is a strong element of truth implied in the above rhetorical questions, they can also be misleading. For too long has Greece, her people and her politicians, accused foreigners of all of the country's ills, real or imagined. This line of thinking needs to be severely qualified even if it is partly justified. There is no doubt, for example, that the intervention of Britain and America in Greece during the 1940s served to link the country decisively to Western interests henceforth. Together with many of Greece's socio-institutional characteristics, like the very wide distribution of land and dwelling property, those events broadly defined the development path Greece was to follow. Did this subsequently make each and every government decision, law and regulation virtually inevitable? It is hard to accept that, for even quite rigid social structures or political frameworks never quite manage to determine fully the scope of human choice and individual or group action. In Greece's case this can be seen over two different periods, one covering the years from the end of the civil war to the fall of the 1967–74 military dictatorship and another covering the years thereafter. As regards the 1950–74 period the regime was powerful enough to carry out policies which, far from threatening its survival, would have taken care of many of to-day's problems. That it did not do so may have been more a matter of convenience, ignorance and political expediency than of iron-clad inevitability – or of foreigners imposing their will on Greece. Examples of different policies which could have been adopted but were not are:

(a) A model of urban development based on zoning and on expropriation of peripheral urban land rather than on high rise and unauthorised building.
(b) A funded and comprehensive social security system rather than a corporatist version of a pay-as-you-go one. If nothing else, the regime could have allowed pension funds greater investment freedom, could have separated the pension and health arms of social insurance organisations and could have allowed their obligatory deposits with the Bank of Greece to earn 'market' rates of interest rather than deliberately lower ones.

(c) A model of economic development involving export-led growth, competitive banking and less protectionism in all walks of economic life than was actually the case.
(d) A better educational system; probably one that would have included acquisition of technical and vocational skills, along with languages and history, at high-school level, and research at university level.

The same argument goes essentially as regards the post-1974 period, with one important difference: the civil war years, with their hatreds and exigencies, had by now receded into the past, the Greek people had achieved an unprecedented measure of prosperity and the essentially pro-Western regime was in no way under threat domestically. Yet as this book has demonstrated it is during this period of relaxed parliamentary rule and the legal and safe operation of all political parties that Greek governments and a multiplicity of vested interests at grass-roots level carried out the most determined and far-reaching assaults against all the factors that are normally expected to contribute to good economic performance. This happened particularly in the 1980s. If anything, Greek democracy helped bring this outcome about as an unintended consequence of its populist, clientelist character.

If Western imperialism is not the main or at least persistent factor behind the malaise of the Greek economy, world economic developments or Greece's relative resource scarcity bear perhaps even less of the blame. In vindication of this conclusion, Chapter 2 showed that Greece's economic performance over the 1966–90 period was worse than expected in comparison to any other OECD country – not just the ones making up, say, the Group of Seven. Thus, it is into Greece's *domestic* socio-political patterns and forces that one must seek most of the explanation for her current economic problems and backsliding. Put another way, Greece's socio-institutional features, precisely because and to the extent that they have *deviated* from those normally associated with the kind of development typified by advanced capitalist countries, must be the main reason behind her relatively poor economic performance. This cannot be said in the same way in regard to those countries. Their socio-institutional characteristics make them far more similar to one another than Greece is to any one of them. It can also be reasonably argued that their characteristics are highly compatible with and probably necessary conditions for successful capitalist economic development – almost by definition since it is mainly these countries which determine or at least generate the dynamics of global capitalism.

Greece's pattern of capitalist development, by contrast, has taken very strenuous routes, mostly around her continuously reproduced multitudes of smallholders and proprietors and her all-pervasive public sector. Herein lies Greece's fundamental difference from advanced capitalist countries. From this point of view Greece's relatively poor physical infrastructure or low GDP per capita are in a certain sense trivial. They are not as important 'differentiators', analytically speaking, as Greece's inherent socio-institutional characteristics themselves – those that have given rise to her statist smallholder form of capitalism (see Chapters 1, 3 and 9 in particular).

Greece is also different from the so-called Third World, even if her backsliding may eventually place her there in GDP per capita or quality of life terms. For instance, Greece does not have an abundance of cheap labour or of one or more primary products for export (whether minerals or cash crops) like many Third World countries do. She is, as mentioned in the Introduction, in-between, like Argentina, Portugal or some of to-day's ex-communist countries of Europe.

Consequent upon the depiction of Greece as a statist smallholder form of capitalism, there is a variety of related phenomena, ranging from Greece's clientelist, populist politics to her big, inefficient public sector, the ineptitude of her educational system, the lack of meritocracy in nearly all walks of life, endemic tax evasion, neglect of citizen or consumer rights, investment short-termism, corporatism, the non-rule of law and unauthorised building. Together they shape the pattern of Greek underdevelopment rather than being caused by it, in some sense. Indeed, this may be the proper way to define and view the process rather than the state of 'underdevelopment': Greece shows that particularly in the case of 'medium-level' countries, when absolute scarcity of resources relative to population size is not the critical issue, the main obstacles to economic growth (barring the possibly adverse state of the world economy) may have to be sought in the socio-institutional superstructure of those countries.

While Greece has been struggling with herself, global capitalism, nowadays manifested primarily in the opening up of national economies to the forces of international competition and free trade, has been creating problems for all countries, including advanced ones: it is, in other words, responsible for many of the social ills and instances of economic malaise mentioned above. Some people, of course, might not describe such phenomena as 'backsliding', preferring to explain them away as the pangs of a new growth phase and of an allegedly necessary economic restructuring. This is not our view. Be that as it may, the specific causes of Greece's current condition were identified as stemming primarily from within Greece rather than from outside, even if, inevitably, the Greek economy is also influenced by trends in global capitalism. In 'normal' circumstances, therefore, one might say that since it was mostly Greece's 'fault' that she is faced with her current predicament, it should also be possible to pull herself out of it. Certainly there is no other way but to try, as no one else will do for Greece what she needs to do for herself. The topic will be revisited in the last chapter of this book. The point, however, is that from now on Greece's efforts at (capitalist) economic and social restructuring, even if she ever gets serious about undertaking them, can only take place in the context of an open economy; therefore of an international economy which is already exerting tremendous pressures on participating national economies, some much richer and more developed than Greece's. This means that the latter, having let her problems and structural weaknesses fester for too long, needs to embark on a course of recovery in an unusually difficult, unsafe, ruthless world (by the standards, that is, of the developed world during 1950–1990), whilst being inherently ill-equiped to deal with the challenges global capitalism throws upon her.

It is worth summing up at this point some of the conclusions of this book.

(1) Since 1974 Greece has been 'backsliding' in economic and social terms; on the other hand she has been 'enjoying' an unprecedented level of formal democratic freedoms. Certainly she is far more democratic than any of her neighbours.
(2) The causes of her economic and social malaise are by and large related to her socio-institutional features and the way these have interacted with exogenous factors, like the two oil-price shocks, periods of world recession and the on-going globalisation of economic activities.
(3) These features – encapsulated in the cliché 'statist smallholder society' – and their related phenomena have affected the Greek economy adversely mostly because, while Greece is part of the world capitalist system, they tend to be antagonistic to the growth of capitalist relations, to capitalist rationalisation and restructuring and to capitalist economic performance, the way the latter is defined at the level of the advanced capitalist countries themselves.
(4) Of the various socio-institutional features that meet this description or play this role, the single most important one involves the role of the state in Greece. Strong capitalism requires a strong

state, one that upholds the rule of law, does not hesitate to use force where necessary and works reasonably efficiently and on the basis of merit. This is not a reflection of any innate ethical tendencies of capitalism itself as much as of the need for the capitalist state to mediate between conflicting private interests. To-day's Greek state, however, is weak, inefficient, corrupt and favouritist. It is also indulgent and domineering and, since it systematically fails to observe or enforce the rule of law, is in truth quite undemocratic. Oddly this is the result of, in a sense, too much 'democracy' rather than of too little; the latter was the case, for example, during the junta rule or in present-day Turkey.

(5) Inevitably the economic policies of all Greek governments since the civil war and approximately up to 1991 have revolved around the poles of protectionism and demand management. To have done anything else – like attempting restructuring on the supply side – would have necessitated a kind of intervention that Greek society did not – and does not – find acceptable; one, moreover, that only a strong, hegemonic state could have carried out. Even the term 'demand management' is a misnomer: whilst fiscal profligacy was the rule in the 1980s, the debt-ridden 1990s have seen Greek governments exercise a measure of fiscal restraint, but only because they had no choice. In other words fiscal contractions and expansions have typically happened irrespective of the economic cycle. This dichotomy, explained as regards the 1980s by the excessive 'politicisation' of fiscal policy, has certainly meant that the latter has been a far cry from Keynesian economics proper in Greece.

(6) The monetary consequences of the fiscal profligacy of the 1980s caused inflation – originally sparked by exogenous factors – to become endemic in Greece. Indeed the analysis in Chapter 5 showed that deviations from the long-run trend in the money supply were one of the two most important determinants of inflation, the other being faltering real economic growth. This result is consistent with a monetarist view of inflation and, by extension, with a classical view of the importance of the supply side. From this point of view, 'excessive' rises in wages and in labour costs during the 1980s (see Chapter 8) were not seen to have caused inflation directly; rather they have done so indirectly, by first affecting adversely real output.

The above conclusions involve a harsh indictment on PASOK, Greece's self-styled socialist party which governed the country in 1981–9 (and again from October 1993 to the present), and on its economic policies. On the redeeming side, PASOK's victory in October 1981 contributed to a breach with the repressive and discriminatory practices of the post-civil war authoritarian state. Significantly, though, the breach began with the CPG's legalisation in 1974, effected by C. Karamanlis, a right-wing politician, after the fall of the junta, and was completed in symbolic fashion in the summer of 1989, when the CPG and the right-wing ND party formed a government. The latter was a good thing for an added reason: the event allowed the Greek Parliament to pursue charges against A. Papandreou, the 'socialist' ex-PM, and other PASOK ministers implicated in various scandals, notably the Koskotas affair.[2] If this had not happened then, and another election been held, it would not have been legally possible to press those charges later.[3]

One important topic which the discussion in this section has not explored sufficiently is the precise nature of Greek capitalist development. Greece may well be a 'statist smallholder society', but to what extent is it also capitalist? Is Greece developing capitalistically and how fast? To these issues let us now turn.

11.2 DEVELOPMENT AND UNDERDEVELOPMENT

In the 1970s a certain controversy among Greek intellectuals (economists mostly) and political parties from the broad Left about the nature of Greek society and the way it had been developing (or not) reached its peak. On the one hand there were those in the Communist Party of Greece (CPG) and in PASOK (the 'socialists')[4] plus a few individual authors outside mainstream parties whose views, despite various differences in emphasis and sometimes in substance, amounted to considering Greece as the victim of Western imperialism; Greek capitalism as distorted, backward, parasitic and underdeveloped; the Greek economy as dependent on foreign capital, with Greece's bourgeoisie or capitalist class subservient to foreigners, in typical comprador fashion; the immediate task ahead, therefore, was national liberation rather than the overthrow of capitalism, with the vast majority of Greek people (including, in some analyses, a so-called endogenous or national bourgeoisie) having common interests against those of a pitiful minority of exploiters and oppressors sold out to foreign capital and acting as lackeys of Western, mainly American, imperialism.[5] Within the 'people – or the nation – vs the oligarchy' camp but outside the CPG or PASOK, a small number of authors argued that by the mid-1970s Greek capitalism, at least in economic terms, was not, after all, distorted and underdeveloped but perhaps sufficiently well developed to merit placing Greece in the capitalist metropolis rather than the periphery; politically, however, Greece was still a 'dependent' country, little more than a USA colony.[6]

A few radical intellectuals, chiefly centred around the Athenian bimonthly *Theses*, begged to differ however.[7] In their view, Greece not only was and is a developed capitalist country, but by the 1970s any dependency of Greek capitalism was already largely a myth, unlike the case of, say, Latin American or African countries; Greece was, indeed, part of the capitalist metropolis, although she belonged to its third layer, along with Denmark, Ireland, Spain and Portugal, whilst the USA comprised its hegemonic core and, in Europe, Germany, France, Italy, Britain and Sweden made up the second, also hegemonic, layer;[8] foreign capital in Greece, far from acting 'colonially' (that is, in ways that do not contribute to capital accumulation within a country), has actually fostered the development of Greek capitalism and on that basis is to be considered equivalent to Greek national capital;[9] the growth of the tertiary sector in Greece, again far from implying a parasitic, distorted or backward capitalism, has in truth proven the high level of the development of capitalism in Greece;[10] the main antithesis permeating Greek society in the 1970s or later has not, therefore, been one between the people or the nation on the one hand and foreigners and their Greek lackeys on the other but between workers (whether in the primary, secondary or tertiary sector) and capitalists, whatever the national origin of the latter. The *Theses* approach to the issue of Greek post-war development was later taken to extremes: in Melios and Joachimoglou (1987) the crisis in the Greek economy was downplayed as merely a national instance of the general crisis of Western capitalism rather than stemming from any Greek peculiarities; and in Catsoridas (1995) the subsequent worsening of the Greek economic crisis was brushed aside as 'restructuring' in the context of a fundamentally sound and well-developed capitalist economy.

There are strong and weak points in both camps' arguments. The analysis of the Greek economy pursued in this book allows us to evaluate them critically and proceed to a new synthesis. Thus:

(1) Capitalism has indeed matured and spread throughout Greek society since the war. In capital accumulation terms Greece is not as developed as advanced capitalist countries (witness the relatively small size of Greek firms – see Section 8.5); hence she merits being conveniently described as semi-developed, part of the growing

group of, sometimes quite disparate, countries between typical Third World and advanced capitalist. The only problem with this label is that, perhaps inadvertently, it implies a unique development path for all countries, an inevitable movement forward, an expectation that full development will one day come. This is not necessarily so – as the Greek experience, among others, demonstrates. Nevertheless there is no doubt that over the last forty years Greece has been transformed from a predominantly agrarian to an urban, commercialised, money-using society. The vast bulk of the Greek production of goods and services is now in commodity form. Many industries, moreover, are dominated by a few large (by Greek standards) firms, like banking, insurance, petroleum products, ship-building (or what remains of it), most other branches of manufacturing, retailing of groceries and white goods, public works construction and, inevitably, minerals. Even in the eateries sector fast-food chains are now making inroads into what once was exclusively the domain of small, family-owned restaurants and tavernas. About half of the Greek labour force are employees (see Section 1.3), while the rest (farmers, self-employed professionals, traders and capitalists), although fiercely resisting their being turned to employees, are open to the vicissitudes and vagaries of the domestic and world market.

Still, the development of Greek capitalism has taken a parasitic and distorted form, in comparison to the archetypical capitalism (or capitalisms) of, say, the Group of Seven. Greece's development path has been conditioned by her peculiarity as a statist smallholder society and its attendant phenomena, described throughout the book. In other words, Greece demonstrates that parasitic or distorted capitalism can also be well-developed capitalism from the point of view of urbanism, commodification, exposure to the market, capital concentration and money-use – though not necessarily in terms of growth of dependent labour (particularly in the private sector), of capital accumulation, or of a sufficiently distinct separation between the economic and political spheres (on account of the size and dominance of the Greek public sector). There is no logical inconsistency or historical impossibility here. There is, however, a *real* contradiction or antagonism between the uncapitalist, or capitalism-resisting, features of Greek society and the economic pressures to perform better applied on Greece by global capitalism. The contradiction, whose tangible expression is the deepening crisis of the modern Greek economy, can only be resolved through removing all obstacles to further capitalist restructuring of the Greek economy and society (or through a socialist revolution; but that is not on the agenda). If it is not resolved, Greece will inexorably experience long-term decline (already begun) and may even disappear as a distinct nation-state. The obstacles or distortions may have an objective basis in, say, the large numbers of smallholders and of public-sector employees in Greece, or in the extent of economic activity accounted for by the public sector, but exert their discouraging influence primarily through political practice and behaviour: they involve the nature of the Greek state (inefficient, clientelist, weak and so on); the pitiful state of the rule of law in Greece, manifested in systematic tolerance of law-breaking as well as in instances of arbitrariness on the part of the executive authority; and the ability of groups and individuals to resist both the processes of capital accumulation and the rationalisation of socio-economic activities to the direction of improving economic performance in the short- and the longer-term. Examples from the former area of resistance were cited in Chapter 8: they involved instances of hostility against industrial investment; systematic protection granted to categories of professionals; and regulatory difficulties put in the way of achieving economies of scale. Examples from the latter area of resistance are to be found in town planning (Chapter 9), tourism (Chapter 10), consumer protection (quite poor by, say, UK standards), tax collection (Chapters 3 and 4), privatisation (Chapter 4), education (Chapter 3), social security (Chapter 7) or in the substantial diminution of the managerial prerogative, chiefly in the public sector. Together these phenomena fully justify labelling Greek capitalism as distorted, backward and rough.

(2) In the two preceding paragraphs the *Theses* evaluation of Greek capitalism as well-developed was qualified by 'marrying' it to the 'distorted capitalism' view of the traditional Left. No such 'marriage' between the two 'camps' is possible in regard to the issue of Greek dependence though: for in truth Greece has always been dependent on the West, first and foremost politically and militarily[11], but also economically. Certainly after the civil war 'the government's dependence for its political and military survival on external patronage effectively made Greece a client state of the United States'.[12] On this, the traditional Left is more correct than on other areas – or than *Theses*. One important implication of accepting the dependence view is that relatively well-developed

capitalism and dependence are not necessarily incompatible with one another. Well-known examples besides Greece are Taiwan and South Korea.

Thus the first phase of the post-Second World War dependence of Greece on the West began during the civil war – for obvious reasons – and lasted until 1974. It involved Western political support for the regimes that governed Greece during those years as well as money (in the form of USA aid) and weapons. The second phase began after 1974: it again involved weapons, whose importance in fact has been increasing in proportion to rising levels of Turkish aggression in Cyprus and the Aegean. The Turkish threat has also led to renewed political reliance on the West, particularly, it seems, on the USA, in the hope that in this way Greece will gain some measure of protection from her obstreperous neighbour. Significantly, economic dependence has also been on the rise, after a relative lull during the 1960s and 1970s: Since 1981 Greece has been relying on EC transfers to make up for dropping invisible earnings from other sources; and since 1989, when her debt problem reached frightful dimensions, she has been desperately relying on those same transfers as well as world capital markets in order to make ends meet.

(3) The *Theses* argument regarding the tertiary sector is two-pronged: its large size in Greece, they say, suggests a well-developed capitalist society since the sector is also very big and expanding in the advanced capitalist countries; moreover, the sector in Greece, again in line with those countries, is not the exclusive province of small proprietors and self-employed professionals but exhibits strong capitalist tendencies, manifested in the presence of many capitalist firms and the spread of wage labour in it.

Even if borne by the facts (which is not precisely the case), the assertions regarding the size and other characteristics of the tertiary sector in Greece do not necessarily describe a society as highly developed as those of the advanced capitalist countries. Let's look at the factual part first: although the services sector did supply about 57 per cent of Greek GDP in 1991 (see Table 1.1), in 1990 it was also shown to contain the largest percentage of self-employed in the EEC (34.4 per cent – see Section 1.3). Looking at total employment, which will bring, among others, peasants into the picture (something appropriate since the discussion is about the degree of Greek overall capitalist development), discloses a more startling figure: in 1993 the proportion of non-employees in Greek total employment (47 per cent) was way above that of any other EU country – but, significantly, lower than Turkey's, which was 60 per cent (see Section 1.3). It is of course true that particular industries within the Greek tertiary sector are strongly capitalist in their organisation – like banking and insurance – but many others – like tourism, food and drink serving, grocery retailing, solicitors' and architects' services – are associated with large numbers of small proprietors and self-employed professionals. Also, most public sector employees, although formally subjected to the wage relationship, fail to serve as 'suppressors' of the level of wages in the private sector on account of their enjoying permanent tenure.[13] In their case, a sizable part of the working class does not and cannot function as a 'reserve army' of the potentially unemployed; this kind of situation helps retard the process of capital accumulation in Greece. The same, incidentally, can be said about Greek peasants (who are not, of course, in the tertiary sector), virtually all of them self-employed smallholders: despite Vergopoulos' (1975) view that the Greek state has been helping them remain so because capitalism somehow requires smallholder agriculture, it is more appropriate to explain their perseverance as a social class in terms of their political weight (a force to be reckoned with throughout the EEC too). Keeping them on the farm, however, again helps limit the number of urban workers seeking jobs, and indirectly discourages capital accumulation.

Turning to the interpretation of the existence of a large tertiary sector from the point of view of capitalist development, we should first note that typically Third World countries can have sizeable such sectors, no less, in percentage terms, than advanced ones: poverty can give rise to services (provided by street hawkers, pedlars, prostitutes and others) at least as much as post-industrialism can[14] – but for different reasons. The Greek figure, therefore, is not very enlightening on its own.

Conversely, the strong presence of self-employed people in the Greek tertiary sector and elsewhere in the economy need not always imply underdeveloped capitalism. Indeed, the present trend in advanced capitalist countries towards flexible forms of work may[15] bring about a rise in the proportion of self-employed workers in the labour force:[16] they will still be workers though, subject to capitalist domination rather than masters of their own destiny, whereas in Greece, so far at least, the norm was for the self-employed and the small- to medium-sized traders to enjoy a high degree of autonomy and self-reliance (be their own bosses, as the phrase goes). This was achieved by means of various protective measures enshrined in law and aimed at curtailing competition, by governmental tolerance of tax evasion, by the corporatist organisation of Greek society and by political activism. In the same way public-sector employees have found it possible to perpetuate their advantageous position which, by offering them security of tenure, enables them to press for wage rises and other perks more successfully than private-sector workers. Since, as a result, both the self-employed and public-sector employees tend to make a living at the expense of the rest of society and of each other,[17] the state of the tertiary sector in Greece justifies describing Greek capitalism as 'parasitic'.

It is thus more appropriate to consider the large size of the Greek tertiary sector in conjunction with other characteristics: the strong presence of the self-employed, the smug public-sector employees and the relatively low degree of capital accumulation in Greece. Looked at in this way, the sector is not a safe indicator of capitalist development: rather, its specific characteristics render it as one of the distortions of Greek capitalism.

(4) In regard to the role of foreign capital in Greece the *Theses* view is more correct than that of the traditional Left. With the partial exception of Pechiney (Aluminium of Hellas) and the more appropriate exception of offshore companies, no foreign firm in Greece has acted as an enclave in relation to the Greek economy. Moreover the extent of repatriation of profits has been far less than what was allowed under Law 2687/53 (see Section 8.4), Greece's main law governing DFI: apparently from 1954 to 1975 foreign investors under Law 2687/53 could have repatriated \$470 m., yet they repatriated only \$220 m.[18] Also, the net inflow of capital into Greece was positive throughout the 1954–75 period, with the exception of 1961, 1969 and 1972,[19] although the sign of the capital account is not a safe indicator of whether foreign capital, in the form of DFI, contributed to capital accumulation in Greece or not. The reason for the unreliability of the sign as an indicator has to do with the relatively small proportion of inward DFI in relation to total capital inflow (which includes foreign borrowing, importation of capital for investment in real estate and so on). Since 1975 too the capital account of the balance of payments has been positive, but, again, non-DFI items, on both sides of the account, have been by far the most important. Accurately identifying and separating

DFI from non-DFI items, particularly outwith Law 2687/53, is, in addition, virtually impossible (see Section 8.4). Many foreign (and Greek) firms have of course been exporting or saving FX through overpricing their imports and underpricing their exports, respectively:[20] but this is a different consideration from profit repatriation as such. At any rate the dramatic development of Greek capitalism in the 1960s and 1970s can hardly be attributed to investment or re-investment of domestic (Greek) capital alone. It can be safely concluded that foreign capital into Greece has broadly helped the process of capital accumulation in the country, whilst most foreign manufacturing firms have been known to sell mostly to the domestic market (Section 8.1). From this point of view foreign capital has functioned precisely like national capital: hence, any distinction between Greek and foreign capital on the basis of ethnicity of ownership (even assuming that the latter can be identified at all), a distinction the traditional Left has for some reason been particularly fond of, is unwarranted. In fact nowadays it is the departure, rather than the arrival or operation, of an increasing number of transnationals from Greece (Section 8.3), along with the country's general failure to attract or welcome foreign investment (Section 8.4), which have been causing consternation and anxiety among those Greeks who care. Finally the position of the traditional Left on the subservient role of Greek vis-a-vis foreign capital is weak also. At least two kinds of Greek capital – shipping and construction – are anything but subservient and 'play' even on the international arena.[21] Lately a number of Greek industrial and commercial firms from other sectors have been expanding overseas (see Section 8.1), particularly the Balkans and the ex-USSR,[22] while Greek banks and insurance companies have been spearheading the movement to those destinations.

To sum up: Greek capitalism is relatively well-developed, to the point where a number of Greek firms from outside the traditionally global Greek shipping sector have been becoming international. It is nevertheless distorted and parasitic, a result of Greece being a statist smallholder society. The particular features of the Greek tertiary sector make it, despite its large size, compatible with and an instance of Greece's form of capitalism. On account of the distorted and parasitic characteristics of the latter, the country is currently in deep, long-term crisis. The crisis unfolds while Greece is politically, militarily and economically dependent on the West. Foreign capital in the form of

DFI, however, far from contributing to Greece's dependence, has instead helped capital accumulation in post-war Greece and thus assisted the development of Greek capitalism.

No matter how interesting a discussion of the nature of Greek capitalism can be, the main thing to-day is to recognise that the Greek economy and society are in a mess and to decide what to do from now on in order to remedy the situation. There are two aspects to this problem, the internal, or domestic, aspect and the external, or foreign relations, one. Both affect one another; together they determine Greece's chances of survival. The domestic aspect of the problem is dealt with below, along with suggestions for a way out drawn from the preceding discussion of the Greek economy and society. The crucial issue of Greece's position in to-day's unstable, even threatening, international environment is taken up in the final chapter of the book.

11.3 'KEYS' OF ECONOMIC AND SOCIAL RECOVERY

One of the most important questions posed in the Introduction to this book was, 'how can a besieged, alienated country with a broken economy hope to move forward? What is required?' Throughout what followed the problems, indeed the crisis, of the modern Greek economy were highlighted. It is time we discussed the way forward.

It is convenient to start with the obvious: Greece needs to reduce her public sector debt and lower her inflation rate (and do so independently of the fact that success in these fields would enable Greece to join Emu). Achieving both targets presupposes smaller budget deficits and certainly larger, actually far larger, primary budget surpluses than has been the case in the 1990s. Less inflation, in turn, will not just help foster conditions of economic stability; it will also make servicing Greece's public debt that much easier, on account of the lower real interest rates it will make possible. Finally, easier servicing of the public debt will allow smaller budget deficits. This is the scenario all Greek governments have been pursuing since 1990. They hope that, with a bit of luck, a delicate mix of fiscal and monetary policies and 'creative' debt management will prove enough by itself to enable Greece to meet her targets for economic convergence on the road to Emu (see Section 2.3).

If anything, however, the preceding discussion of the Greek economy has shown that Greece's economic malaise is primarily the result of structural and institutional factors. PASOK's policies precipitated the descent into economic stagnation during the 1980s (in marked contrast to the rapid growth of the 1960s) but the underlying structural and institutional factors were already there – since the 19th century in fact (see Section 1.2). Some authors (for example, Alogoskoufis, 1995a, 1995b – see Section 2.1) have directed attention to the institutional breach with the first three post-Second World War decades which 1974 has come to represent: in that year, it will be recalled, the military dictatorship, which had governed Greece since 1967 but was also an inevitable offshoot of the post-civil war police state and the anti-Left hysteria of the regime, crumbled, on the wake of the Cyprus tragedy which the dictatorship itself had triggered. Following 1974, post-war Greece reverted to political normality and became perhaps more democratic than ever before. In that sense Greece's institutional framework has been different since 1974 than it was from 1945 to 1974. But in a more fundamental sense it has also been more in line with the long tradition of the type of parliamentarism (clientelist and populist) which has been characteristic of the modern Greek state almost since its inception; as a result it has allowed free expression and play to the smallholder and statist interests making up the bedrock of Greek society. Thus the institutional features of the 1945–74 period cannot be looked upon as a recipe guaranteeing future economic performance, for two reasons: first, Greek economic growth at the time was helped by Greece's very low starting point, by rapid urbanisation and by a favourable international economic environment – rather than by police repression on its own; second, no government of that period, not even the military junta, attempted to embark on fast-track capitalist development, involving the introduction of competition and meritocracy, export-led growth, cracking down on tax evasion, or expanding the wage relationship. To the extent they made no such attempt and bowed, instead, to the myriad smallholder and statist interests which even then were taking shape and form, they have been responsible for Greece's distorted capitalism (see previous section). It can therefore be argued that economic growth from the 1950s to the 1970s was incidental and circumstantial rather than deliberate, only a little helped by the institutional framework or government policies of the time and probably less than what could have been, had, say, a Japanese model of development been adopted.

This means that Greece still needs to take her smallholder-cum-statist interests head-on if she is to tackle her economic and social 'backsliding'. The momentous task is in truth nothing short of a revolution – one that has yet to happen in Greece. The revolution should be about enabling

Greece to meet, first, the performance criteria of to-day's open, competitive, globalised economy and, second, the threat from Turkey. The two goals are highly complementary. An economically strong Greece can finance her defence effort far more easily than a weak one; she can also afford to shrug off some of the more unpalatable political pressures from her friends in the West in regard to Greece's own regional interests.

In the meantime the 1990s policy of trying to deal with Greece's deepening economic crisis through fiscal and monetary means (and poorly at that, as, for example, both the ND and PASOK governments have shown singular unwillingness – or inability – to privatise state assets or proceed to deep cuts in the budget expenditure) is reaching its limits. The policy should have bought governments time in which to start effecting the structural changes which the Greek economy requires. For political reasons, however, no government has attempted such, nor one is likely to under the present political system. Unsurprisingly to those with knowledge of modern Greece, political and administrative inertia has even stopped or delayed other much needed changes, which do not directly threaten the sensitive balances on which Greek society is based (but which do threaten localised interests), like speeding up pubic works, modernising the country's telecommunications and transportation facilities, or putting in place an efficient defence industry.

Inevitably the 'hard' drachma effect of the necessarily high real interest rates that accompany the 1990s economic policy has begun to affect adversely and dramatically Greece's trade balance (see Chapter 1). On current trends devaluation or a market-led run on the drachma will have to occur at some point in the future. That point will probably not be later than 1999, when the current inflow of funds from the EU, in the context of the so-called Second Delors Package, stops. Already EU funds and receipts from tourism are the main invisible items that allow Greece to cover, roughly, her trade deficit – and tourism has run into problems of its own (see Chapter 10), whilst a combination of inefficiency and politicking is not allowing Greece to absorb the EU funds timely or effectively.[23] Quite probably, too, devaluation-induced inflation will make it harder to service Greece's (mostly short-term) public debt, but the real hope is that the ensuing acute crisis will give, perhaps, a coalition of parties (or a new type of leadership) the excuse to embark on a programme of structural reform.

It is useful to categorise the main components, or 'keys', of such a revolutionary programme under different labels: the economy, the society and polity, and foreign relations. Below we sum up the first two, leaving the last one for the next chapter.

(A) Keys of economic reform

Key 1: A strict separation of the welfare, or social protection, aspects of state policy from the running of private and public-sector enterprises and organisations and the civil service. Henceforth the unemployed, for example, must be taken care of by means of unemployment benefits, retraining programmes and workfare – not by the state employing redundant staff and a government's political friends. Unsuccessful private or public-sector firms must close down rather than burden the state budget and ultimately the taxpayer, whilst financing of such enterprises by state-controlled banks must stop. The allotment of state subsidies should be accompanied by stringent controls and carry severe penalties in case of misuse of public funds. The Greek state should stop act as a scoop fund, shouldering the financial consequences of mismanagement, embezzlement or miscalculation.

Importantly, the above policy should be part of a two-pronged strategy, involving on the one hand an emphasis on economic performance and on the other a strengthening and upgrading of the welfare state. The latter, although necessary for securing social equality and cohesion in the long run, should be more appropriately targeted to those in actual need rather than the labour aristocracy, it seems, of the public sector. In this connection, guaranteeing a minimum income might be better than enforcing a minimum wage.

Key 2: A complete overhaul of the public sector. Main and tangible aspects of such an overhaul should be a comprehensive privatisation programme, starting with private 'lame duck' firms under state control, abolition of permanent tenure and other perks for public-sector staff, and aiming to offer value for money to the taxpayer.

Even if, on the basis of defence or market failure considerations, some ΔΕΚΟ stay with the public sector, they must henceforth operate on a combination of financial performance and service-to-the-public criteria. Since, in fact, the Greek Constitution forbids making civil servants redundant, until that changes one idea is to hire new ones on private-law contracts only and reshuffle old staff on the basis of departmental or regional needs.

Selling off state enterprises and making public-sector staff non-permanent is not simply about the Greek state collecting more non-tax revenue or helping competition and the consumer. Because of the pivotal role of the state in Greece, such an 'incision' into its size and mode of operation would constitute a dramatic shock to the entire Greek society – a message that the long-standing 'contract' between the state and the people (see Chapter 3) is about to change. But to avoid a relapse to the pre-1920 model, whereby the state was about as inefficient as it is to-day, with the added horror of firing existing civil servants and hiring new ones on every government change, a number of measures should be institutionalised. No more than, say, three per cent of civil service staff could be fired following a change of government; any staff fired would be compensated and/or put on welfare, just like private sector staff made redundant; firing more staff could only result from cuts in the government budget (so that new staff could not be hired to replace the old), or from overhauling particular departments (in which case these could not continue in operation); and so on.

Key 3: Introducing zero-based central government, ministry and ΔΕΚΟ budgeting. This, too, would help control favouritist appointments in the public sector. It would, in addition, avoid the accumulation and growth of unnecessary expenditure items and keep the entire public sector on its toes, as every item would have to be justified and accounted for separately. Another idea, as far as the central government budget is concerned, might be to prepare it in consultation with the opposition in Parliament; certainly more transparency in its preparation and openness to control are in order.

Key 4: Cracking down on tax evasion (for specific ways to do it, see Section 4.2). Tax law should be simplified, codified, treat all investments equally and change rarely. Bringing the informal economy under the taxman would go a long way towards tackling the pervasive disregard for the rule of law, and towards reducing the influence of smallholder interests in Greek society. One needs to be careful, though: the smallholder interests meant here are of the traditional type, involving protected, corporately organised professional and property owner groups (for example, owners of unauthorised holiday homes or rooms-to-let). Presently, however, another type of 'smallholder' in the developed capitalist world is emerging: he or she works on a contract or fee basis, may telework, uses computers, faxes and modems, may work at home, works flexibly. The difference is that this type, although outside the discipline of the shopfloor, is a more advanced form of proletarian[24] – one who uses brain rather than brawn and who, moreover, may own his or her house. The traditional type of smallholder, by contrast, has been inimical to the spread of capitalist relationships as such, functioning as an enclave in the capitalist economy and securing institutionalised forms of protection for his special, usually advantageous, position. Historically he descends from the medieval guilds and from steam engine capitalism, whilst the new 'smallholder' is child of post-industrialism. Thus the need for Greece to diminish the influence of her smallholder interests makes sense only to the extent that these interests are of the traditional type (as by and large is the case) – and therefore exercise a distorting influence on Greece's capitalism or the pace of its development. (In this connection it might be interesting to know which type of 'smallholder' Britain's Labour party under Tony Blair has in mind when it advertises its 'smallholder capitalism' thesis: Greece's type has been shown to affect the country's economic performance in ways that leave a lot to be desired; the post-industrial type is probably the future. A modern political party should deal with the smallholders' issue bearing this in mind, perhaps devising appropriate social security schemes and suchlike.)

Key 5: On the supply side Greece needs to enhance competition, facilitate mergers and, in general, the achievement of economies of scale, increase consumer protection, force strict quality criteria on producers of goods and services, enable her embassies and consulates abroad to assist Greek exporters, and take all measures necessary to make Greece a more desirable investment location (as implied, for example, in Sections 8.2 and 8.4). Greece should also try hard to put in place and streamline her own defence industry.

Key 6: Greece's geographical position is ideal for allowing her to act as a link and a transport route between Eastern Europe's low-wage industries and 'Third World' and Middle East markets for cheap, even if second-best, consumer products. Moreover, Greece can capitalise on her regional lead in certain sectors (chiefly financial, consultancy, information and medical services, retailing, food and drink, shipping, tourism and petroleum products) for the purpose of economic expansion to the Balkans and the ex-USSR.[25]

Key 7: In the same vein, Greece should opt for an active policy of encouragement and assimilation of immigrants from Eastern European countries (more on this, in Chapter 12).

(B) Keys of social and political reform:

Key 1: Establishing the rule of law. It cannot be stressed enough how important this is for Greece – probably the country's greatest institutional weakness (see Chapters 3, 4, 6, 7, 9 and 10). The conspicuous absence of the rule of law from Greece – a result, it will be recalled, of the combination of a perverted sense of democratic sensitivity or tolerance, the supremacy of smallholder interests, statism and a clientelist political system, accounts for most of the country's present ills. Unfortunately, the way things now stand in Greece, establishing the rule of law is a Herculean task: it would require both an attack on Greece's structure of socio-economic interests and, perhaps more importantly, a different political system (see below) from to-day's bankrupt and corrupt one as well as a different leadership (on how that might come about, see Chapter 12.): one, for example, that would be willing to uphold the rule of law impartially and by force whenever necessary.

Key 2: Educational reform. Its urgency stems from two facts: the collapse of the existing educational system and the needs of the times. The first (see Section 3.3) is manifested in poor linguistic and mathematical skills and deficient general knowledge among Greece's younger generations; in the absence of a viable, respectable, properly supervised layer of college (technical, vocational) education between high school and university; in widespread functional illiteracy; in the devalorisation of university degrees; and in the lack of meritocratic ethos at all educational levels. Against this background, Greece needs to strengthen her national heritage and identity (for reasons of morale but also in order to assimilate immigrants from abroad – see Chapter 12); hence the need to reintroduce formal modern Greek on formal occasions, the teaching of ancient and formal modern Greek at school, and proper spelling everywhere – and to cultivate language skills, whilst emphasising Greek and European history and culture.

Greece also needs to be able to compete in today's knowledge-based global economy. One of her problems in this respect is that her labour force is high-wage, low-skilled. To enable her to compete on this front requires meritocratic, efficient and flexible schools and universities – particularly the latter; hence the need to make university entrance examinations stricter, give work permits to professionals only on condition they pass state exams (thus ensuring equality of treatment between Greek and foreign, and between public- and private-sector, university graduates), allow university students only one or two resits per subject, permit and then supervise private-sector universities and colleges, forge research links between universities and enterprises, protect university grounds from vandalism and remove student influence from the management of universities.

Key 3: Reform of the political system. Since Greece suffers from strongly clientelist and populist politics, she needs to change that. Three measures seem especially apposite: (a) Increase the number of years between elections to, say, five. This should go some way towards countering the effect of the political business cycle, from which Greece has been suffering since the early 1980s (see Diagram 4.1). (b) Give real powers to the Presidency – like the power to call elections or plebiscites, send a bill back to Parliament with recommendations, or demand a more substantiated justification for a proposed law before signing it. Ideally the Presidency should balance the socialist concerns of the Left with the economic performance ones of the Right. Both concerns are legitimate; they have their time and their place, but either type can defeat its own purpose if taken too far. (c) Truly separate the Bank of Greece from the country's government (perhaps by having an all-party committee appoint the Bank's governor, who will then keep his or her job for at least twice a government's term of office). At the same time, give the Bank of Greece a statutory duty to fight inflation, regardless of other considerations. This should make it very difficult for any government to exercise fiscal profligacy again.

The above 'keys' or components of Greece's much needed revolution are sure to be met with stiff, perhaps even hysterical and violent, opposition from a multitude of interests. This is why they cannot be pushed through unless in the context of a precipitous national and/or economic crisis – and by a new leadership too. So far Greek society has shown that it prefers the slow, perhaps, but no less inexorable, backsliding of the country to suffering the pangs of reform. It refuses to see or believe that 'there is greater hope in managing the modernisation process than in rejecting it'.[26] It chooses, instead, to 'vegetate in the teeth of time', waiting for a miracle which will save the smallholder and statist interests that make it up, so that things can go on as before. But even if an economic crisis – like a drachma devaluation and/or a dramatic rise in inflation – won't happen, or, if it does, won't jolt Greek society to action, a foreign crisis will. The latter is bound to have grave economic consequences, anyway. Is a foreign crisis likely or imminent though? The answer is, sadly, very much so. Our discussion of this prospect, in the next chapter, will help us appreciate both the foreign policy pressures applied on the Greek economy, at a time when it is already struggling with its inherent problems, and Greece's likely future.

Notes

1. Examples are Western manipulation of and support for the break up of Yugoslavia, Western prejudice against and persecution of the Serbian nation, Western tolerance of the slaughter of Kurds or torture of prisoners in Turkey – not to mention that country's aggression towards Greece or her proprietary attitude as regards her use of the waters of Euphrates.

Other examples involve USA sanctions, or threats of sanctions, on European companies dealing with Cuba, Libya or Iran; American bullying of Japan to buy USA products irrespective of the preferences of Japanese firms or consumers; European Commission over-reacting to research findings as regards BSE in Britain (a country 'unfortunate' enough to have better monitoring procedures in place than most), ostensibly in order to protect European consumers but also, one suspects, in order to stifle British objections to a German- and French-dominated process of European integration.

2. Clogg, 1992, p. 198.
3. Clogg, 1992, p. 200.
4. At that time PASOK deliberately appeared far more radical than it actually showed to be or became later; it was probably the only way for Andreas Papandreou, its founder, to steer large masses of voters thirsty for 'Change' away from the CPG and towards his party.
5. For a critical evaluation of these views see Mastrantonis & Melios, 1983; Mavris & Tsekouras, 1983; Melios, 1984.
6. Examples are Marios Nicolinacos, Nicos Poulantzas, Nicos Psyroukis. See Mastrantonis & Melios, 1983.
7. See Mastrantonis & Melios, 1983; Mavris & Tsekouras, 1983; Melios, 1984; Mavris, 1984; Melios & Joachimoglou, 1987; Catsoridas, 1995.
8. Mavris & Tsekouras, 1983, p. 69.
9. Mavris & Tsekouras, 1983; Melios, 1984.
10. Mavris, 1984. Cf. Moschonas, 1986.
11. Political-cum-military dependence is manifested, among others, in the way Greece has deployed her forces, 'chosen' her weapons systems and used her geographic morphology in view of the Turkish threat. Without getting into sensitive details, suffice it to say that as a result of this kind of dependence the myriad Greek islands in the Aegean have become a liability whilst they could have been Greece's greatest asset in a possible confrontation with Turkey. Broadly, this has happened because the USA do not want Greece to be able to ensure victory in case of a Turkish attack. An additional problem affecting Greek choices of weapons systems is corruption among politicians and officers responsible for procurement decisions – which is, after all, another instance of dependence.
12. Clogg, 1992, p. 146.
13. Tsoucalas, 1983, 1986.
14. Connolly, 1985.
15. See European Commission, 1994 (the White Paper).
16. See 'Workers – "free-lance professionals": German employers press employees to declare themselves free-lancers', *E Cathemerine*, 27.9.1996, p. 22.
17. Cf Marinos, 1988, 1994a.
18. Mavris & Tsekouras, 1983, p. 52, quoting Roumeliotis, 1978, p. 109.
19. Mavris & Tsekouras, 1983, p. 52, quoting Roumeliotis, 1978, p. 106.
20. Roumeliotis, 1978.
21. Mavris & Tsekouras, 1983; Tarpangos, 1996.
22. Of particular significance – on account of its scope and size – is the 1995 deal between MotorOil, owned by Vardinoyannis brothers, and the Ukrainian government.

23. See Section 8.5; 'Lost chance', *E Cathemerine*, 15.8.1996, p. 3; Khaicalis & Collias, 1996.
24. Cf. note 16, above.
25. See Dragassakis, 1995; Hassid, 1995a, 1995b.
26. Kephalas, 1996a.

12 What Future for Greece?

> 'Blessed be he who expecteth the worst, for verily he shall ne'er be disappointed'
>
> L. Sprague de Camp, *The Unbeheaded King*

In some ways this is perhaps the most important chapter of this book. Even though Greece's on-going economic and social crisis (analysed in the previous chapters) is serious enough, it is her problems with Turkey which may precipitate the overall crisis which will force Greece, finally, to confront her 'backsliding' in a creative and resolute manner. Those problems are exacerbated by current Western foreign policy thinking that Turkey is very important strategically to the West.[1] They also determine the context in which Greece must attempt her economic recovery as well as the dire urgency of the task. In a broader but no less compelling sense the post-Cold War international environment is an interesting set of opportunities and threats: on the one hand the Balkans and the ex-USSR are opening up to world trade and private investment; on the other Greece's foreign policy options currently appear to be circumscribed by Russia's weakness and the West's supremacy, while the twin processes of Emu in Europe and of global economic deregulation put her already weak economy under severe pressure to perform better or else.

12.1 RUDE AWAKENING

There is no doubt that, following the collapse of the Warsaw Pact, the international framework in which Greece currently finds herself is, from her point of view, quite adverse. Of particular concern to Greece are three elements of this framework:

- The Turkish threat;
- Western tolerance of Turkish aggression, inside and outside of Turkey;
- The demise of communist regimes in Eastern Europe, the break-up of Yugoslavia and a currently weak Russia.

Let us briefly discuss the situation Greece faces.

The antagonism between Turks and Greeks (or should one say between Turks and Europe?) goes back to the 11th century, when the Seljuk Turks, coming from Central Asia, first made inroads into Asia Minor. They were succeeded by the Ottoman Turks, who over four centuries (14th–17th) managed to conquer nearly all lands surrounding the Aegean, traditional cradle of Greek civilisation, including the islands,[2] Cyprus and, of course, the city of Byzantium (Constantinople) itself (in 1453). The latter was capital of the Byzantine empire: what had started as the Eastern half of the Roman empire but since the 7th century had become the political entity housing and expressing predominantly Greek-speaking populations sharing the Christian Orthodox faith in this part of the world. The reason why the 7th century marks the 'Hellenisation' of Byzantium is that during it Greek became the official language of the State, in addition to being spoken by most of the empire's subjects, many of whom were of Greek origin anyway.

On the issue of ethnic origin Greek official ideology proclaims the direct descent of modern from ancient Greeks. This is only partly correct: due to the many foreign invasions and population migrations into Greek lands since Roman times (Vandals, Goths, Avars, Slavs, Arabs, Franks, Turks), modern Greeks are certainly not terribly related in blood terms to ancient ones; but then, on average, they are more directly and closely related to them (and to Byzantine Greeks) than any other nation on the earth is. Be that as it may, the bloodline argument is not really necessary to justify modern Greeks' pride in their linguistic and cultural lineage, and their sense of being part of the same nation. Quite like the Jews, actually,[3] most of whom, moreover, came to speak Hebrew again as their main tongue only in very recent times (on account of religious and ethnic persecution during the Diaspora). The Greeks, on the other hand, although they have kept using Greek as their main language throughout the ages, adopted Christianity at some point (without, perhaps, ever completely forgetting the Olympian religion), while the Jews chose to stick by Moses' teachings.[4]

There are thus solid reasons why modern Greeks, irrespective of any blood purity nonsense, view both sides of the Aegean, along with Constantinople and Cyprus, as their historic heartland, wrested away from them and from large parts of which they were eventually expelled by the Turks. These, Greek folk tradition has always seen as nothing more than ruthless invaders from the East whose conquest of Byzantium led to the subjugation of most Greeks for more than half a millennium. After all, that a modern Greek nation-state exists at all is the result of a Greek revolution against Ottoman rule begun in 1821 (and brought to fruition a few years later through the decisive help of Britain, France and Russia) as well as of subsequent successful campaigns to liberate more of Greece. Greece, however, because of internal political strife and because the tide of international politics had turned against her this time, lost her most recent war with Turkey in 1919–22, as a result of which most Asia Minor Greeks were thrown out of their homelands (see FactFile and Chapter 1), to be followed a few decades later by Constantinople Greeks and, on the wake of the Turkish invasion of Cyprus in 1974, by northern Cyprus Greeks.

Despite Greek nostalgia about lost homelands, most Greeks after 1922 were content to accept the verdict of history and prepared to live in peace with their long-standing antagonists. There is no doubt, indeed, that friendly relations between the two countries are going to be extremely advantageous economically to both if they are ever realised, not least because of a much lessened defence burden but also because this will give them a chance to become politically and militarily more independent of the West than they are presently (this goes mostly for Greece). A Greek-Turkish rapprochement would also mean Turkey's only opportunity to become more democratic and calmly receptive of European culture and political practice, with beneficial results for all her different peoples.[5]

After the 1940s civil war the Greeks let down their guard in another sense too. They felt safe during the Cold War, basking in the sun and enjoying their unprecedented economic growth. Avid bon-viveurs, they would reap the fruits of economic protectionism and statism at home, crossing the Aegean every summer in order to have their beloved holidays. It never occurred to them that on those sea trips they would now and then travel through formally international, rather than exclusively Greek, waters; taking the international status quo for granted, they knew that no one was likely to direct territorial claims at them. The balance of terror between NATO and the Warsaw Pact ensured that NATO could be relied upon to help Greece counter any moves by, say, the Yugoslav republic of Skopje ('Macedonia') or Albania against her and to suppress possible Turkish designs on Greek territory before they could even be voiced. Turkey of course knew that. It was, overall, a good world for the Greeks.

What came later was a hard awakening for them. The first shock happened in 1955, when the Turks organised purges against the Constantinople Greeks in breach of the 1923 Lausanne Treaty. Greece did not counter the Turkish move by throwing out of Western Thrace a Turkish minority remaining there.[6] One important reason was that the USA told the Greek government not to: that was the first sign that even then Western peace-keeping in the region was tilted in favour of Turkey. The purges were therefore brushed aside. The second shock occurred in 1974, when the Turks invaded Cyprus after the fascist military government of Greece had been duped by the CIA into organising a coup in Cyprus in an attempt to oust Archbishop Makarios. Soon after, however, Greek governments conveniently chose to live with the Turkish occupation of northern Cyprus too. (With hindsight, if the Cyprus struggle for independence from British rule in the 1950s had taken a more evolutionist route, Turkey would not have been called in to act as one of the three guarantor powers – along with Greece and the UK – over Cyprus, the West would not have been feeling anxious about Makarios and by now Cyprus would probably have been united with Greece – or at least be whole and free.[7] Also, having worked together towards a non-confrontational solution of the Cyprus issue, Greece, Cyprus and Britain would have cultivated closer links between them to the long-term benefit of all three.)

The Greeks had their third and most decisive shock with the collapse of communism in Eastern Europe and the dissolution of the Warsaw Pact that followed it. First, Yugoslavia broke up; to the consternation of Greek public opinion, moreover, in the civil wars that accompanied that event the West, far from acting as impartial umpire, took sides unilaterally and consistently against the Christian Orthodox Serbs. Second, the break-away Republic of Skopje decided to call herself 'Macedonia' and include in her Constitution articles allowing the subsequent formulation of territorial claims on Greece, to whom the largest part of geographical Macedonia belongs. Articles or no, the Greeks felt particular disquiet at a neighbour with avowed intentions on the Greek province of Macedonia adopting the name and the symbols of the same-name ancient Greek kingdom, when Alexander's Macedonia and modern Greek Macedonia largely coincide on the map. (Of course that Yugoslav republic had been calling herself by that name since the 1950s; Greece had swallowed it then, once again because of USA pressures so as not to upset Tito, who was then following a neutral course between the West and the Warsaw Pact.) Yet the West, for no apparent reason this time, sided with Skopje rather than Greece on the matter.

Third, post-communist Albania too made some noises regarding the Greek region of Southern Epirus, whereas Greece would have been far more justified to lay claims on Tirana-controlled Northern Epirus on account, among others, of the large number of Greeks living there – only she didn't; she watched, instead, the USA supporting wholeheartedly the largely undemocratic new Tirana regime. Finally, Turkey, who had been systematically infringing Greek air space in the Aegean since 1974, threatened war should Greece extend her territorial waters to 12 miles (something which Greece is perfectly entitled to do in the context of current international sea law) and in December 1995 actively began to dispute Greek ownership of rocks and islets (though not islands, yet; that was to come later) in the Aegean, despite past treaties. Worse, the West has refused to quell Turkish aggression, thus encouraging it further. The Greeks now gravely fear that, should Turkey attack Greece and even if (a big 'if', this . . .) she ends up occupying any number of Greek islands or Western Thrace, the West will turn a blind eye and may even actively support Turkey; in all likelihood the West will merely supervise the eventual 'peace' talks, to which what will remain of modern Greece will be dragged in order to ratify what in the most optimistic scenario for her will be Turkish control of half the Aegean, if not half the islands also. In effect, Greece, a EU member, will have become Turkey's vassal.

Taking, therefore, all four aspects of Greece's third shock together, it appears that her post-1940s days of relaxation and ostrich politics are well and truly over. For her, the so-called 'peace dividend' which all Western countries seem to have enjoyed since the collapse of communism has been a heavy liability instead, whilst on all regional issues the West has systematically sided with everybody else but Greece. Recognition of this fact is a particularly difficult dish for the mainstream Greek parties to swallow. It requires of them to start formulating and pursuing a dynamic and independent national strategy for Greece rather than subsume any such under the dogma of Greece 'belonging' to the West.

12.2 GREECE IN THE INTERNATIONAL ARENA

International foreign policy developments after 1990 have posed a number of crucial questions for Greece's future. Why have nearly all of Greece's immediate neighbours, except Bulgaria, been laying claims on her? Why is the West being apathetic about it? Should the West help Greece? Why does the West support Turkey in particular so much? What can Greece do about her predicament? Let us examine these.

An important reason for Greece's neighbours' aggressive stance against her, with Turkey at the forefront, is very simple: they have sensed Greece's current weakness. The country's state of the economy, public administration, degree of social cohesion, moral readiness to identify and stand for the broader good, and even defence capability leave a lot to be desired. A second reason is that the claim-makers can get away with it, taking advantage of the West's indulgence – particularly Turkey, towards whom the West has been following a policy of appeasement very reminiscent of the one Britain and France had adopted towards Hitler's Germany, until, of course, it was too late. Thirdly, foreign adventurism has historically been a convenient outlet for regimes facing internal problems. Turkey's military elite, the country's true power behind government, are in a particularly sensitive position as the political structure and ideology put in place by Kemal Ataturk[8] have come under increasing pressure at home due to widespread poverty, conspicuous inequality, overpopulation, high inflation (more than 80 per cent), urbanisation, the rise of a Turkish middle class and the Kurds' struggle for independence. Of course a genuinely democratic Turkey might have gone a long way accomodating the Kurds, quite like the USA have done with their ethnic constituents; Turkey apparently cannot achieve this without dropping the extreme nationalist aspect of her Kemalist tradition and without transforming her power structure. In the meantime the only half-baked alternative to Kemalism, Erbakan's Islam,[9] is in many respects even less capable of tolerating ethnic and religious differentiation than the Kemalists are. Against this background, challenging Greece abroad offers the regime a useful distraction and a rallying point.

But why Greece? Surely, many Europeans seem to think, to-day's chances of mutually advantageous co-operation between the two countries should not be thwarted by historic animosity; even France and Germany reached an understanding after World War II despite past hatreds and wars. True, but in the case of Greece vs Turkey there are a couple of crucial differences. The religious one is the most obvious even if not the most important. The second is continuing Turkish occupation of fundamentally Greek lands – Eastern Thrace, northern Cyprus and the western coast of Asia Minor. The Greek element is so strong there – temples, ruins, churches, place names – that it renders the Turkish presence alien. To legitimise the latter, an authoritarian and nationalist Turkey needs to press for expansion to the west as the very existence of Greece makes, for example, the sight of Turkish guides showing Greek temples and churches to tourists appear highly incongruous. By analogy, it is doubtful whether France and Germany would have been reconciled so spectacularly were Germany still in possession of, say, the whole of eastern France. The upshot is that renewed Turkish aggression several decades after the 1923 arrangements (the Lausanne Treaty) has shattered Greek resignation and complacency and may well put back on the agenda Greek irredentist claims instead.

The brewing conflict is overshadowed by Western foreign policy in the region. It is now understood that this has lacked foresight and depth and/or has had little to do with containing the so-called Islamic threat – or else the West would not have recently helped create the first Islamic state in Europe (Bosnia) since the 19th century. Apparently the West's overriding considerations are the following:

(a) To keep Russia (and Ukraine and other ex-Soviet republics) weak, forever if possible.
(b) To have in place a strong, pro-Western Turkish state which will
   - guard the routes to the oil reserves of the Caspian sea and of the surrounding (predominantly Moslem) republics and offer military back-up 'as needed' to Western oil ventures there;[10]
   - supply a base of operations against the equally sensitive, from the point of view of Western interests, Iran, Iraq and Syria, and for ensuring friendly regimes in the Gulf;
   - act as a permanent counterweight to Russia.

The twin, complementary goals of a weak Russia and a strong Turkey illuminate a number of more specific policies which the West adopted from 1991 to 1996. The encouragement of the break-up of Yugoslavia, the anti-Serb stand, the subsequent creation of a Moslem-dominated Bosnia, and Western support for the Republic of Skopje and for Berisha's regime in Albania have temporarily averted an alliance between a united and potentially strong Yugoslavia and Greece – an alliance which would have easily been extended to include Bulgaria (10 per cent of whose population are of Turkish origin, whom Turkey stirs up), Romania and Albania.[11] This Balkan federation would have been a formidable opponent of Turkey, should the latter still entertain expansionist notions against Greece and Bulgaria or foment unrest among Yugoslavia's or Albania's Moslems. It would also be a vehicle for a broader co-operation between Christian Orthodox peoples in the Balkans as well as in Russia and other ex-Soviet republics. The West's policy in the region has therefore been about precluding the formation of just such an alliance, keeping the Balkan countries disunited and weak (that is, balkanisation revisited), kindling strife and then protecting local Islamic contingents.[12] In short, anything that keeps Turkey strong, saves her face and does not diminish her ability to be useful to the West is to be welcomed and supported. The West's dismissive attitude towards Kurdish demands for independence or towards official Turkish treatment of the press,[13] MPs, political prisoners, or Kurdish civilians is also a manifestation of this policy decision.

In this world Greece's scope for manoeuvre is severely limited. Because she is weak and, more importantly, allows herself to be so, the West no less than Turkey cannot take her seriously; on the face of it, Turkey's geographical position, autarchic, ruthless regime and ostensible military strength[14] make her a more reliable vehicle for seeing to regional Western interests – or so the West presently seems to think.[15] Because Russia is weak,[16] Greece cannot turn to her for protection from Turkish aggression. Because Yugoslavia has been dismembered, Serbia nearly brought to heel, the Bulgarian government relies on a vote of confidence from the Bulgarian-Turkish contingent, and Berisha's regime in Albania is highly mercenary and undemocratic, a Balkan federation to act as deterrent to Turkey's designs in the region and as a platform for resolving local disputes without outside interference is now quite difficult, although not impossible, to build. Finally, because the West has so far kept a united front regarding all serious international issues,[17] Greece's opportunities for exploiting differences between major Western powers in order to play one against the other appear few and far between.

12.3 TWO MODELS OF REGIONAL STABILITY

There is nothing wrong or wicked with Western plans to secure long-term access to Caspia's oil reserves until other sources of energy are found or existing ones become economically viable. What is wrong is a couple of Western assumptions with bearing on the issue. The first erroneous assumption is that Russia is, or will be, a threat to those plans and, more generally, an a priori enemy of the West; the second is that relying on a Turkey which bullies every one of her neighbours and represses political dissidents and ethnic groups at home is a sensible way to ensure regional stability in the medium to long run. These two assumptions probably reflect American influence on current Western foreign policy thinking: because a rapprochement and close links between Russia and the European Union in particular would threaten America's aspired hegemonic role in the post-Cold War world, it is more convenient and natural for her to keep treating Russia as an Other opposed to Us. Also, America has for too long relied on repressive regimes abroad and on regional policemen. Both devices were probably necessary ways to serve USA interests during the Cold War, even though they backfired on a number of memorable occasions, as in Iran and Iraq.[18] For this reason America finds it hard to come to terms with the idea of regional security structures based on co-operating, non-aggressive, tolerant democracies. It may of course be that the idiosyncrasies and choices of American foreign policy are deliberate rather than an unfortunate carry-over to the post-Cold War world of the ingrained reflexes and practices which allowed America to lead the West successfully during the previous period. If so, Western Europeans in particular will need to start challenging USA hegemony. If, however, post-Cold War American foreign policy is merely the result of a certain lack of diplomatic sophistication and adaptability, the sooner America learns to be flexible and wise the easier it will be for her to gain the world's genuine respect and, on that basis, lead it too. (An additional factor that may increasingly and worryingly shape USA foreign policy in the new era is the torrent of information from all sorts of lobbies and largely autonomous organisations flooding the Administration: strangely, at a time when America feels less constrained than ever before in the international arena, the process of decision-making at home is becoming more disjointed and less capable of achieving depth and consistency.)[19]

Of course Russia may indeed turn out to be once again the West's antagonist – even though during the two world wars her interests had made her side with the democracies against German aggression. At this historic juncture, however, such an eventuality is more likely to be the result of lingering Cold War stereotypes precipitating a self-fulfilling prophecy on the West's part than of anything else. After all, in culture and religion Russia is part of the broad European, Graeco-Christian tradition, unlike China, for example, which probably poses a more serious long-term threat to American interests than Russia.

The question of Turkey's role in the region's stability is more concrete than the one about Russia's future status and policy, since Turkey *already* behaves in a destabilising manner.[20] In this connection Western interests would, as already implied, be better served through a regional political model involving a balanced structure of democratic nation-states roughly equal in power to one another, which the West would assist on their road to economic and political development, than through the current model of an undemocratic, expansionist regional superpower acting as neighbourhood bully. The democratic, non-aggressive power structure would extend from the Adriatic to Caspia and from Cyprus to the Black sea, with Russia and Ukraine getting their rightful share of the responsibility of supervision. Whatever the difficulties of achieving this structure, the other model, which the West currently strives for, is clearly unworkable and is likely to keep or make happy only weapons manufacturers for decades to come.

Suppose, for example, that Turkey attacks Greece and the latter loses the war.[21] The West cannot really expect either that the Greeks will swallow that (even if a Greek quisling government is found to sign any documents with the victors) or that Turkey will not next turn her attention, say, to Bulgaria (on the excuse of the presence there of Bulgarians of Turkish origin) or to Bosnia, Albania, Armenia, Syria or even Russia. It is imperative for the current Turkish militarist regime, like the Ottoman regime before it, to be imperialistic,[22] or the hold of the military over Turkey will crumble and the country's multi-ethnic, multi-religious population, having no democratic outlets, will tear her apart. The recent resurgence of Islam in Turkey is of course an additional problem: fed by poverty and originating independently of the military, Islam in Turkey will either become fundamentalist and aggressively anti-Western in Iran's fashion, or else will be used by the mostly Kemalist military in a forced attempt to glue Turkey's society together; either way, democracy will suffer – and, of course, most of Turkey's neighbours, Greece above all. Actually, even a genuinely democratic Turkey might now find it difficult to absorb and contain the centrifugal ethnic and religious pressures which have surrounded her. The military's and/or the Turkish Islamists' agenda is therefore powered by the country's internal dynamic and the need to hold unto power; it does not and cannot coincide with the West's agenda.[23]

Even if Greece suffers a temporary military defeat, in all probability a Greek national leader will emerge who will forge whatever alliances he or she can, galvanise Greek society, force Turkey to wage again war against Greece and drag Turkey either to defeat or to the point, for example, where the West will seriously have to agree to the complete annexation of Greece by Turkey and either the enslavement or massacre of 10 m. Greeks or their seeking asylum in Western Europe. In the meantime the other Balkan countries and Russia will not of course sit idly by. Russia, in particular, seeing the West provide this kind of unconditional support to Turkey will have reason to fear both the growing power of Turkey to her south and that the West itself will next use Turkey in ventures around the Caspian – and Russia, though weak, does have nuclear weapons.

The democratic, non-aggressive power structure is feasible but requires a dramatic policy about-turn on the West's part. Among others, it calls ensuring the transformation of Turkey into a decidedly secular, non-expansionist, multi-ethnic democracy which will jettison the extreme nationalist and autarchic aspects of her Kemalist tradition as well as fundamentalist Islam. Failing a peaceful transformation along those lines, the West would probably have no choice but to consider seriously accepting or even assisting Turkey's dissolution: the south-eastern part would form the independent Republic of Kurdistan; another part, in the north-east, would be returned to the Republic of Armenia; and the remainder might have to be divided between a secular, Europeanised part, made up of Eastern Thrace and the western coast of Asia Minor, and an ethnic and/or Islamic Turkic part in central Asia Minor.

Obviously any Western attempts to realise the above scenario are conditional upon Turkey refusing to change herself in ways that make her democratic and tolerant at home and non-aggressive abroad. They are also predicated upon the West deciding that the regional model it presently supports is not, ultimately, to the West's best interests. On the basis of its current choices, however, the West has no inclination and no reason to side with, say, Greece even though the latter is at the receiving end of Turkish aggression. International politics, unfortunately, has never been founded on considerations of right or wrong. At best the West, without going to extremes, will attempt to stop the antagonism between the two countries escalating to full-scale war – which is not an insignificant contribution, albeit a minimalist one – all the while trying to press Greece into talking with Turkey on all 'issues' between them – including, it seems, Turkey's territorial claims.

12.4 GREECE'S RESPONSES TO FOREIGN CHALLENGES

Since the 1940s civil war Greece has been very much dependent on the West, the USA in particular.[24] Even Andreas Papandreou's 1970s rhetoric about closing down American military bases on Greek soil were forgotten as soon as his party came to power in 1981 – to be remembered triumphantly for reasons of domestic consumption only when the Americans themselves decided to close down their Athens base. Old habits die hard; when the post-Cold War world began to emerge from the ashes of communism, Greek politicians never took the trouble of trying to formulate an independent long-term strategy for their country in the context of the new, unstable world order. As one national crisis or problem piled itself upon another (Skopje, Albania,

Turkey) Greek governments monotonously and predictably would seek the West's help or protection on no other ground than the sadly thin one of justice and rights – or the conveniently forgotten one of Greece's contribution to the cause of democracy and freedom during two world wars.[25] Having no clear goals of their own, no imagination, no taste for power politics and no alliances policy other than the one involving Greece in NATO and the EU, they would be surprised and dismayed when their overtures to the USA or the EU invariably received the cold shoulder. The Greek attitude, moreover, has played into the hands of a large part of the Western press and media for whom running highly biased anti-Greek (and anti-Serb) campaigns since 1991 has been their idea of assisting their governments' current policies in the region.[26]

Above all, no Greek government to this day has found the courage to attempt a dramatic restructuring of the Greek economy and society, without which the country's weaknesses and backsliding will only get worse, never better or reversed. In this way Greece foregoes the chance to earn the respect of other countries and the credibility that goes with good housekeeping. Her singular aversion to formulating and pursuing a pro-active foreign policy does not help either. There is certainly something incongruous, even ludicrous, in Greece's appeals for assistance with her problems – whether economic or foreign – when she herself does precious little about them.

Below we discuss four areas of foreign policy of special import to Greece: the problem with the Republic of Skopje in regard to the name 'Macedonia'; the triangle Turkey–Greece–EU; dealing with Balkan, Eastern European and ex-Soviet economic refugees in Greece; and Emu.

(a) Skopje ('Macedonia')

Partly due to a couple of initial mistakes Greece failed to convince her European partners that they should not recognise the break-away Yugoslav republic as long as the latter, through the device of a carefully chosen name ('Macedonia') or through other devices (articles in her new Constitution; flag symbol) entertained notions on Greek territory. Because of her 'all or nothing' attitude on the issue, by now Greece may have also failed to make her neighbour adopt at least a derivative name, like 'Slavomacedonia' or 'New Macedonia'. Be that as it may, the main point is that Greece should have closed the matter as soon as the West had made it clear that it was not going to show *esprit de corps* with her on the issue; the important thing for Greece was and is that she herself must never recognise the Republic of Skopje under the name 'Macedonia', even if the international community does. Greek border and customs officials would calmly use removable self-adhesive strips of tape to cover the name 'Macedonia' on all passports, bills of lading or number plates bearing it, which their counterparts on the other side would subsequently take off.[27] In the meantime economic relations between the two countries would thrive. Within 10 or 20 years, assuming that the Republic of Skopje ever lasted that long (as it is really a multi-ethnic amalgam of groups, each with their own aspirations), the Republic would to all intents and purposes have been another Greek province. Because of her small size, her sizeable and rapidly growing Albanian contingent, her economic dependence on Greece and the centrifugal pressures she faces, the Republic's leaders would also come to see Greece as an ally rather than a country to have territorial claims on. All that may still happen, but there was no reason for Greek governments to show panic, waste time or organise nationalist rallies, especially in view of the far greater and far more real threat from the east (Turkey). If she had kept her nerve at the outset, Greece might even have avoided applying an 18-month embargo on the Republic in 1994–5 – although, the way the situation had developed, the embargo did result in the Republic removing the Vergina star – symbol of Alexander's dynasty – from her flag and the irredentist hints from her Constitution, in exchange for Greece lifting it. On this, the Greek government (PASOK) was moderately successful and might have been more so had it seized the chance to strike a deal on the Republic's name too.

(b) Turkey–Greece–EU

The way Greece has handled Turkey's relations with the EU, or her own with Turkey, has been rather unfortunate, betraying, once again, Greece's lack of strategic vision. In 1995, for instance, the Greek government (PASOK) chose not to veto the customs union between Turkey and the EU, without getting anything concrete in return other than a vague and probably unworkable promise regarding the future start of talks on Cyprus joining the EU. Having fruitlessly waived its objections then, the Greek government subsequently, perhaps in another genuflexion to the exigencies of Greek domestic politics, went on to stall funding of Turkey by the EU over many months (in the context of the MEDA programme), only to back down eventually in July 1996, again at only a token gesture of EU sympathy with Greece's problems with Turkey. Greece's inconsistency had also shown when the question of the customs union between Turkey and the EU had come to a vote before the European Parliament in 1995, after the Greek government had chosen not to veto the prospect at governmental level: nearly all Greek Euro-MPs, including those elected with PASOK, voted negatively (one abstained) and tried to convince others to do the same. In short, the Greek government behaved as if Greece's interests are or should be primarily the responsibility of individual Euro-MPs rather than its own.[28] A more consistent and responsible policy, on the other hand, might have incorporated the following aspects:

First, Greece should never have foregone her right of veto unless she got back something solid like a blanket solution to the problem posed by the Turkish invasion and occupation of Cyprus, whose 'ghastly results are still with us all'.[29] That might have involved the withdrawal of Turkish troops from the island (in line with UN resolutions), its reunification under one government, and guarantees of respect for all Cypriots' human, civic and property rights, irrespective of religion. At the very least Greece should have pressed for Turkey pledging and undertaking to respect Greek sovereignty in the Aegean, on the basis of past treaties but also of Greece's right to extend her territorial waters to 12 miles; to uphold Europeans', including, therefore, Greeks', property rights in Turkey – like the right to have, obtain or transfer property; to return to Greeks their, or their relatives', property in Turkey, taken away from them since 1955 on the basis of Turkish discriminatory laws (which were enacted in breach of the 1923 Lausanne Treaty); to return the church of St Sophia, in Constantinople, to the jurisdiction of the Greek Patriarchate there, and to allow its subsequent operation as a Greek Orthodox church.

Second, all Greek governments' unwillingness to talk with Turkey on the issues she continually raises is in many ways understandable since Greece's, or any other country's, territorial sovereignty is not negotiable unless in the context of military defeat – and, in time-honoured fashion, Turkish territorial claims have increasingly come to involve Greek soil, in addition to parts of the Aegean sea and airspace. Cyprus apart, modern Turkey's claims on Greek soil were first formally made in January 1996 in relation to a rock in the Dodecanese cluster in the Aegean, then in relation to an inhabited islet to the south (sic) of Crete, in August 1996 were extended to more than a hundred rocks and islets in the Aegean and Cretan seas – even to the inhabited and larger than the rest island of Calymnos, near Rhodes,[30] – and there is no end in sight. One wonders, though, whether Greece too easily confuses non-negotiability with a refusal to talk at all. Suppose, for example, that

Greece went to such talks and Turkey demanded Athens and the Parthenon: Greece could always say a polite no, and prepare for a Turkish attack.

Ultimately, though, the above suggestions are about tactics, whereas Greece's main problem is lack of strategy. It is not clear, for example, what the Greek and Cypriot governments actually want in regard to Cyprus: to come to a deal with Turkey or throw her out of the island?[31] Choosing to do nothing is perhaps the worst thing they could do – and yet this has been the case since 1974. Similarly, no Greek government seems to have appreciated (a) that Turkey has a determined expansionist policy concerning the Aegean and Western Thrace and probably the rest of Greece too; (b) that Turkey has been pursuing this policy on a long-term basis; and (c) that Greece's, or any country's, defence effort cannot rest mainly on appeals to the international community for help or understanding. As a result Greece's Turkish policy is passive, sentimental and shallow: it would have made sense if Greece were playing for time – only she pathetically lets the time thus gained go to waste: no efforts at economic restructuring, no better organisation of defence. Why so? The answer has a by now familiar ring to it: domestic political cost considerations on the one hand; susceptibility of Greece's mainstream political class to 'advice' from the West, particularly the USA. Both aspects are the mark of, to put it mildly, poor leadership and an inefficient political system.

What should be Greece's strategy towards Turkey then? The following five elements would seem the most important:

(1) A strong Greece, in economic, social and defence terms. In the meantime, and rather urgently, Greece, faced with the dilemma 'war or appeasement', needs to put in place a credible deterrence mechanism,[32] whilst pursuing a more actively friendly policy towards Turkey's Kurds and a more determined regional alliances policy.
(2) Turkey has stated that, should Greece expand her territorial waters to a 12-mile zone (even though Greece is entitled to do so), that will be a cause of war (*casus belli*). Greece should decide that the Turkish on-going occupation of nearly half of Cyprus is *already* a cause of war of liberation, which Greece, unless Turkey concurs to a united Cyprus with equal rights for all her citizens, will launch at at time of her own choosing, in co-operation with the Cypriot government.
(3) Greece should make a list of Turkey's breaches of the Lausanne Treaty; add a number of other 'compensatory' claims (like Greek

control of the St Sophia church in Byzantium and the return to Greeks of their properties there); then accept Turkey's request for 'all-encompassing' talks, still aiming for genuine peace.

(4) Above all, Greece should make it plain that she will give no surrender, no recognition of faits accomplis, ever, even if Turkey does manage to occupy Greek soil in the Aegean or Western Thrace. (Certainly a Turkish attack looks quite likely now – all the more reason for Greek politicians and the Greek people to get serious about preparing to meet it.)

(5) Greece, finally, does not need to antagonise her Western partners over their Turkish policy. If she works calmly and quietly in order to put her own house to order and build her strength, all the while pointing to Turkey's destabilising role in the region, she will place herself in a position to benefit from the West's inevitable disillusionment with to-day's Turkey. Greece, in particular, needs to put herself forward as the one country that will guarantee that a resurgent Russian influence in Southeastern Europe will be based on Christian Orthodox, rather than pan-Slavist lines, and thus be benignly disposed to the West; in the long run the latter will probably have to accomodate Russia as an ally against a potentially antagonistic China.

(c) Economic refugees

The number of economic refugees from the Balkans, Eastern Europe and the ex-USSR in Greece is currently estimated to be anything between 400 and 600 thousand.[33] On the other hand the number of Greeks in Greece is about 10.4 m, while the birth rate has been falling to an extent where growing fears of Greeks suffering extinction sometime during the next century seem sadly well-grounded.[34] On the other side of the Aegean, Turkey's population is about 62 m. and rising fast; even if one subtracts the Kurds, that still leaves about 42 m. ethnic Turks and Islamified Greeks of largely Turkish allegiance. The time, therefore, may have come for a brave Greek government to consider killing two birds with one stone: first, to embark on a policy of welcoming and assimilating economic refugees in Greece rather than pretend that their presence is inconsequential, unimportant or, worse, merely troublesome (which it often is, the way things now stand); second, to do something about Greece's worsening demographics. If Greece decided to be clever, she would go out of her way to invite lots of Russians and Ukrainians in particular into Greece, most of whom nurse nice feelings about her but for various reasons (economic depression, Chernobyl) would like to leave their country.[35] Two or three million of them coming into Greece would go a long way towards revitalising Greek society and improving her demographic prospects. But for this to happen, to-day's Greeks must first face and admit the harsh reality of the country's demographic trends, especially in view of the threat from Turkey. Then they must accept the measures that will make assimilation possible – some necessary in their own right, anyway. These are:

- A flexible policy regarding minimum wages and quotas of Greeks vs immigrants. In some sectors – probably industry or construction – wage floors would need to be abolished: put differently, a situation which already exists would have to be recognised and accepted precisely in order to be better controlled in other respects, for example social security. In other sectors – relatively lucrative ones like tourism, banking or supermarkets – wage floors could remain and quotas on the employment not just of Greeks but of locals be established (particularly in small towns and the islands).
- Taking immigrants into Greece's social security system by giving them stakes in it; an incentive, therefore, for them to pay contributions and also to co-operate in forcing their employers to pay such. As an additional bonus the policy would remove the threat of bankruptcy currently hanging over the system.
- Giving immigrants landplots on which to build homes; arranging for gangs of them to work together in establishing their own settlements on public land; allowing them property rights, consequent upon their having full rights to work and stay in Greece, and facilitating their housing efforts by devising appropriate credit schemes.
- Integrating immigrants culturally into Greek society by means of an education system which will emphasise Greek language and history, teach, where appropriate, the immigrants' children their own languages and also cultivate technical skills. In this connection, upgrading Greece's bad educational system is a must both for obvious economic reasons and for salvaging and strengthening the Greek identity.[36] After all, the latter has always been about culture and education, never about race.
- Expecting first generation male immigrants to do some kind of minimal or auxiliary service in the Greek armed forces for three months or so, and their children to do so fully when they come of age, just like Greek young people.

- Expelling from, or not allowing into, Greece those economic refugees or immigrants who will not accept the obligations (like being law-abiding and doing the minimal service mentioned) accompanying the above rights. Careful and decisive use of this 'stick' (along with the 'carrot' of assimilation) would also allow Greece to gain influence vis-a-vis the immigrants' countries of origin. At the moment, for example, Greece finds herself in the awkward and odd situation of being Albania's largest source of income – yet having no, or very little, influence with Berisha's regime which more often than not mistreats the Greeks (and Albanians) of Northern Epirus, shows hostility to Greece and even makes territorial claims on her.

Of course Greece could always throw her economic refugees out rather than try and assimilate them fruitfully. But this would not solve her demographic problem whilst it would be bad for her image among many ordinary people in countries to Greece's north and north-east – people and countries whom Greece can ill afford to alienate and most of whom are Christian Orthodox too.

(d) Emu in the EU

The official Greek position on Emu is that the EU should be single- rather than multi-speed; that deepening European integration should take precedence over, or at least go together with, enlargement; that the opening up of markets and more competition should be accompanied by the building of social Europe – that is, measures to protect the excluded and the unemployed and uphold workers' rights; and that a united Europe should also be prepared to protect her constituent members from the aggressiveness of other countries.

These are not bad ideas, except that they cannot substitute a country's responsibility to herself. Economic and social development proceeds unequally anyway, not only between countries but also between different regions within the same country. This cannot change except, perhaps, at the cost of overall development. The Greek position on social protection and rights may be well-intentioned but loses some of its force to the extent that Greece herself does not take steps to put her own house to order – in fields such as contribution and tax evasion, or in terms of a workable model 'marrying' a better social security system with better economic performance. In other words, the Greek position is suspect and unconvincing because it seems to rely too much on fund transfers from the richer to the poorer members of the EU and too little on structural and institutional changes within a given country.

Moreover, for labour protection to work, it has to be done in ways that do not compromise one country's competitiveness vis-a-vis others'. Relevant measures need therefore to be combined with social security and tax arrangements which will be applied by all countries participating in the Union. The way things now stand, the UK labour market model appears more successful at combating unemployment than the more heavily regulated labour markets of other EU members. Unsurprisingly the British see no reason to change it substantially.[37] And a common defence policy that, dramatically put, looks as if it might require Germans or Frenchmen getting killed along with Greeks in the Aegean is decidedly unpalatable at a time when the West still attaches strategic precedence to Turkey over Greece's rights or Turkey's wrongs.[38] On the other hand there is something incongruous, even ludicrous, in a Union which strives for a common currency but not for borders defended in common. Thus Greece, like the UK already,[39] needs to accept the inevitable reality of the nation-state as the fundamental unit of analysis in Europe and to pursue her interests in the EU and in her proximate geographical region on that basis. To do otherwise, would be substituting dangerous illusions for the responsibility she must show regarding her own future. Europe may indeed help Greece eventually, but only if Greece helps herself first. Unfortunately, Greece so far has not even managed to absorb EU funds rapidly and wisely[40] – let alone revolutionise her economy and society or gear up to the Turkish threat.

12.5 WHO WILL LEAD?

Greece's fundamental institutional problem is how to move from a society organised around possession-protecting interests (like groups of public-sector employees, unauthorised housebuilders, recalcitrant businessmen or public procurement 'rodents') to one organised on the basis of merit and performance (a meritocratic society). At the same time, perhaps unsurprisingly, Greece has no governing elite (see Chapter 1). Its absence strongly reinforces the present social framework (which antagonises the emergence of probably any true – that is, merit-based – elite) and is certainly highly compatible with it.

There exists a difficulty: for Greece's social and political order, through the clientelist and populist policies it fosters, has given Greek people reason to believe that socio-economic advancement is possible – and perhaps only possible – to achieve through free-for-all individual action, use of middlemen, politicking and disregard for the law. This framework encourages osmosis between various interests and groups in Greek society and a melting down – along with the continuous recreation – of class differences. It has certainly allowed Greeks to achieve a remarkable degree of upward social mobility. That the latter is mostly illusionary, or at least ephemeral, as it depends on the tree of the national economy growing further, escapes them. What they do know, through instinct if not through conscious reasoning, is that a meritocratic society implies a hierarchically organised one, or at least one with much fewer chances for those with not enough merit to move upward. Let us expand on this.

Economic crime (stealing, robbing, defrauding) is usually a way for the have-nots to get what they want but lack. It is, in other words, an income and wealth redistributive mechanism. Indeed, the line between social revolution (like when starving peasants seize the lands of latifundistas) and ordinary crime is often very fine. Now, in Greece there is ordinary economic crime, like everywhere else, but there is also very widespread disregard for the letter as well as the spirit of the law, in countless minute respects (operating a noisy bar late into the night; paying or receiving bribes; building illicitly; hiring staff as a political favour). This institutionalised law-breaking has allowed many Greeks to become rich far quicker and more easily than otherwise: say, by benefiting from tourism or by becoming owners of holiday homes or by evading taxes. The noisy bar owner who would have been made to operate quietly might lose customers: he might therefore not earn enough to buy his own or a second house within three years, or a speed boat; he might even be forced to close down and go back to farming or fishing or working for wages. From this point of view, the 'flexible' application of the rule of law in Greece is precisely a way to reduce class differences.

Let us, on the other hand, take a law-abiding citizen who has advanced purely on the basis of merit – say, by being a hard worker or a good professional. That person uses his or her rightfully earned savings in order to buy a house – next to which a noisy bar later opens. If at that point the law regarding noise pollution is not applied, the law-breaker will benefit at the expense of the law-abider – not because of merit but because he is smart or brazen enough to go around the law. Be that as it may, any class differences between the two will be reduced. If the law *is* applied, however, the bar owner may end up losing his business and tending the law-abider's garden instead. Class differences will be more pronounced. Hence the reason why, whilst most Greeks and all political parties pay lip service to the need to introduce reward on the basis of merit (meritocracy, or, in Greek, *axiocratia*) and to uphold the rule of law, they do not really want it.

Yet meritocracy and the rule of law must happen, or Greece will go down the drain: her internal economic problems and the external threats she faces are simply too many and too urgent to ignore any longer.

But who will take on the task of transforming Greek society and making Greece capable of meeting the challenges thrown upon her? Who, in other words, will lead? In addition to the absence of a merit-based governing elite from Greece, there is grave doubt that the present political system can produce the kind of leadership Greece requires. It is simply too dependent on the way Greek society is structured and functions, too accustomed to bowing to foreign interests, and too sensitive to considerations of political cost. No Greek party, for example, espouses an aggressive, pro-active foreign policy along with a radical (that is, capitalist) restructuring of Greece's economy: it's either one or the other (you can have, say, a nationalist and at the same time statist party, or one that supports economic liberalism but is 'accomodating' abroad), or, worse, statism and economic corporatism combined with a meek foreign policy.

In this author's view a new leadership is more likely to come from outside the present system and probably on the wake of an economic catastrophe or war. Let us look into three possible scenarios:

(a) An acute economic crisis destroys the way of life of large groups of Greeks. The structure of economic interests (smallholder, statist) that through continuous transformations has sustained Greek society since the 1950s is broken. The clientelist 'contract' between the Greek people and the state (see Chapter 3) is abandoned. Existing political parties adapt their policies and programmes to the requirements of the times and produce new leaders. Some break up. New parties are also created. Strong possibility of a coalition government with a radical mandate; alternatively, a single party led by a probably charismatic figure manages to win the inevitable election on the basis of a promise of radical reform, along the lines of capitalist modernisation.

(b) There is, again, economic collapse and social turmoil, but more probably a war with Turkey, which Greece loses, perhaps along with a few islands and/or Western Thrace. A military figure – perhaps one who has shown courage or competence during the short war – leads a successful coup and/or forms a party which wins the elections, sweeps away the old political order and ruthlessly pushes through radical reform. Alternatively, the military cleanses the old political order and clears the way for new parties or a new, charismatic, civilian though, statesman to emerge – again with a radical mandate. Either way the pace of reform is faster and more determined than under the previous scenario. There is a severe drawback: for this scenario to materialise, the national catastrophe must have already happened – a potentially bad bargain. Quite like, actually, the 1909 army revolution at Goudi, in Athens, which led to the country's revival but had to come after the 1897 defeat of Greece by Turkey. On that occasion the bargain ultimately turned to Greece's advantage. Or – an ugly twist of events that – like 1974, when 'out of the disaster of Cyprus came the freedom of Greece',[41] which was then under the colonels.

(c) Even if an acute crisis does arrive, there is no guarantee that a new kind of leadership will automatically rise out of the ashes. The ground for a new political order may have to be prepared. Since Greece is kept low by her web of short-termist, opportunistic, selfish interests; since, moreover, she lacks visionary, honest or at least competent leadership, that is, a merit-based governing elite: the way forward may have to be paved by means of a society of dedicated patriots which will act as a focus for Greece's increasing number of disaffected from all walks of life. Such a society, a national-spiritual Order actually, may eventually give rise to a political party or may not. Its task will be to speak for the Greek nation without regard to partial or petty interests; to attach continuity and vision to that voice; and to help Greece recover and remain strong.

There are historical precedents: Greece's own Friendly Society ('Philike Hetairia') organised and launched the, ultimately successful, 1821 Greek revolution against Ottoman rule. Turkey's Young Turks, a century later, managed to modernise and strengthen Turkey in opposition to the backward and corrupt Ottoman regime. And Britain's or America's 'old boys' networks', operating in the context of more cohesive societies and more powerful countries, achieve much the same thing by supplying an inter-temporal dimension to the so-called 'national interest'.

Whichever of the three scenarios comes to pass, there is bound to be social and political turmoil, which the government will have to deal with harshly. Economic collapse, military defeat and/or national humiliation are their own demons. In the long run, however, none of the scenarios is inimical to genuine democracy: the latter, we have shown, is violated in modern Greece not because of police repression, as in Turkey,[42] but because of, on the one hand, widespread, grass-roots disregard for the rule of law and, on the other, a state that at once tolerates illegality and treats Greeks like subjects or children. Restoring the rule of law and introducing genuine citizenship are therefore steps towards democracy, let alone better economic performance.

In the same vein Greeks might have to learn that successful capitalism requires a strong state: one that would not hesitate to confront crowds of owners of unauthorised buildings or vandalisers of property but would also put behind bars or execute 'respectable' and powerful people who embezzle public funds.

Such a state cannot emerge painlessly or in the context of polite discussion. The Greeks' days of complacency and anarchic individualism have to come to an end. Whether some will label the required revolutionary transformation of to-day's Greece 'undemocratic' is ultimately immaterial. At stake is the country's survival.

It is perhaps appropriate to finish our discussion of Greece's future by questioning the oft-made supposition of a likely dramatic event of national import prior to the emergence of a new leadership; also that such an event, should it occur, will usher in a new leadership through the dynamic it will set in motion. Greece, that is, may be unfortunate enough not to know ever the cleansing effect of an acute crisis. She may instead keep on backsliding, gradually and inexorably, basking in self-pity, embracing pettiness and vulgarity and rejecting efficiency, meritocracy and visionary thinking, seemingly for ever. Her future course may well become an example of T. S. Eliot's vision in *The Hollow Men*:

> This is the way the world ends
> Not with a bang but a whimper

All the more reason, then, for Greeks who care to do something about their country before it is perhaps too late.

Notes

1. The term 'West' as used here means something more specific than modern European civilisation broadly defined as an amalgam of democracy, individualism, human rights, the rule of law, gender equality and so on. Of this culture Greece largely is and wants to be a part, despite as well as

because of various aberrations, most of which are the result of the long centuries of Turkish occupation and oppression. The term, rather, refers to the set of foreign policies emanating from and designed to further the international interests of the USA and, in varying degrees, a number of Western European countries.

2. Crete was last to fall, in 1669, after a 25-year struggle with Venice, during which the Cretans sided with the latter.
3. Cf. Lazaridis, 1996d.
4. The fact that both Greeks and Jews have no close relatives among the nations of the earth may explain, among others, the support and protection offered Greek Jews by Christian Greeks during the Nazi occupation of Greece – an attitude not often found in other European countries during the Second World War.
5. The population of Turkey in 1995 was about 62 m. Of these, ethnic Turks were 16 to 19 m. (26 to 31 per cent), Kurds 18 to 20 m. (29 to 32 per cent), descendants of forcibly islamified Greeks about 20 m. (32 per cent). See Macris, 1995.
6. Not to be confused with Pomaks, an ethnic Moslem group also living in Western Thrace.
7. Cf. Iordanidis, 1996.
8. See note 1 in Chapter 3.
9. In July 1996 Mr Necmettin Erbakan, leader of the Islamic Refah party, became Kemalist Turkey's first Islamist Prime Minister, in a coalition with Mrs Tansu Ciller's True Path party.
10. Andrianopoulos, 1996; Hill, 1996.
11. On Greece's scope for regional alliances, see Lazaridis, 1995a, 1995b, 1995c.
12. Germany's support for an independent Croatia in particular had no doubt also something to do with co-operation between Nazi Germany and many Croats during the Second World War as well as with the fact that of all the occupied European peoples outside the USSR the Serbs (along with the Greeks and the Poles) offered the Nazis the most determined large-scale resistance.
13. See 'Turkey: Press ganged', *The Economist*, 3 Aug. 1996, pp. 30–1.
14. But not her economic potential as a market for Western goods. This, despite Western statements to the contrary (see note 9 in Chapter 1 and Mortimer, 1996) has been greatly exaggerated.
15. Cf. *The Economist*, 1996c; Mortimer, 1996.
16. See 'Russia: Soldiers of misfortune', *The Economist*, 3 Aug. 1996, pp. 28–30.
17. This may change. Britain sees the process of European integration, which is spearheaded by France and Germany, differently from those two countries (see John Major's article in the Greek economic weekly *Economicos Tachydromos*, 25 July 1996, pp. 20–1). The friction between the USA and the EU over sanctions against companies investing in Libya and Iran is another example (*Financial Times*, 18 July 1996, p. 1). And Jacques Chirac's France resuming nuclear testing in 1995 made a statement about French military strength which was read, no doubt, by Germany also, France's main European ally for the time being.

18. Lazaridis, 1996b.
19. See Lazaridis, 1996e.
20. Lazaridis, 1996b.
21. Cf. note 11 in Chapter 11.
22. See Loucas, 1996.
23. An example is Turkey's, under Erbakan, deal with Iran, in August 1996, involving construction of facilities for transporting large quantities of natural gas from Iran to Turkey, in disregard of USA efforts (D' Amato law) to stop trade with or investment in Iran. The deal was accompanied by Turkish declarations to the effect that 'Turkey is nobody's vassal and will follow the policy she herself chooses in order to meet her energy requirements'. *E Cathemerine*, 13.8.1996, p. 23.
24. See note 11 in Chapter 11.
25. See note 4 in Introduction.
26. At times the campaign has gone to ridiculous lengths; for example, Kerin Hope, of the *Financial Times*, attempted to belittle the Greek athletes' successes in the 1996 Olympics by suggesting (31.7.1996) that some of them were not 'really' Greeks – as if the dozens of black athletes taking part in, say, the British or French teams are of pure Anglo-Saxon or Frankish descent, respectively. Two notable exceptions to the campaign of Greece-bashing have been Adam Nicolson (*Spectator*, 13.11.1993) and Heinz Burghart (*Deutsches Sonntagsblatt*, 1.3.1996).
27. If, that is, they could be trusted to keep their cool. It seems that Skopjan police are infuriated to the point of physical violence when interrogating Greek travellers from the Greek province of Macedonia who do not speak the Skopjan dialect (the Skopjan police think they should) or insist on calling themselves Greek first and foremost rather than 'Macedonian'. See 'Greek manhandled in Skopje', *E Cathemerine*, 8.8.1996, p. 6.
28. Cf. Lazaridis, 1996a.
29. Levi, 1983, p. 185. The Turkish argument, incidentally, is that they invaded Cyprus in order to protect the Turkish minority there. That was certainly the excuse (even if it holds no water in terms of international law), as Greeks and Turks in Cyprus did live in peace together until Turkey began to foment unrest among them. To their dismay, Turkish Cypriots have now found that they have to share their part of the divided island with Turks brought there as colonists from Turkey.
30. These claims were made in a report prepared by the Turkish War Academies HQ and announced in the Turkish newspaper *Cumhuriyet* on 7 August 1996. See *E Cathemerine*, 8.8.1996, p. 5; *Rizospastis*, 8.8.1996, p. 3.
31. Lazaridis, 1996c.
32. See Lazaridis, 1996c, 1996d.
33. Pirounakis, 1996b.
34. Ghiocas, 1994; Polyzos, 1996.
35. In the experience of this book's writer, who has talked with Ukrainian refugees in Greece, it appears that most ordinary Russians and Ukrainians even now feel that they belong to one nation, really.
36. It is perhaps utopian to expect that Greece's current educational system will be able to play this role when since 1974 it has increasingly failed to teach succeeding generations of Greek students proper Greek language

skills and pride in their history and identity (see Chapter 3). But this touches upon one of this book's tasks: to stress the need for Greece to put her own house to order before, or simultaneously with, attempting to deal with international pressures and challenges – otherwise Greece will not be up to them.

37. Major, 1996.
38. In this writer's estimate, Europe's young people may well have to confront Turkish expansionism at some point in the future anyway, when the time to reap the bitter fruits of appeasement arrives.
39. At least under the Conservatives.
40. See 'Lost chance', *E Cathemerine*, 15.8.1996, p. 3.
41. Levi, 1983, p. 185.
42. This is not an empty or sentimental accusation. Even *The Economist* (1996c, p. 17) recently warned that the main reason 'why Turkey will not get closer to Europe in the near future [] is its lack of democratic values and its violation of human rights. Europe is simply not keen to get closer to a country where torture and imprisonment without trial are still reported with disturbing frequency'.

Bibliography and References

Alogoskoufis, G. & Prodromidis, C. (1995): 'Absorption of EU funds means nothing!', *Express*, 16 Nov., p. 10.

Alogoskoufis, G. (1993): 'How we 'll come out of the crisis', *Economicos Tachydromos*, 25 Feb., pp. 29–32.

Alogoskoufis, G. (1995a): *The crisis of economic policy* (Athens: Critique).

Alogoskoufis, G. (1995b): 'The two visages of Janus: Institutions, Political Regimes, and Economic Performance', *Epiloghe: Annual Economic Review 1995*, pp. 70–82.

Anderson, P. (1978): *Passages from antiquity to feudalism* (London: Verso).

Anderson, P. (1979): *Lineages of the absolutist state* (London: Verso).

Andrianopoulos, A. (1996): 'The new geopolitics of oil and Greek foreign policy options', paper presented at Kennedy School of Government, Harvard University, March.

Andronicakis, S. & Gounaridis, C. (1986): 'How bank interest rates are determined', *Economicos Tachydromos*, 19 June, pp. 65–71.

Andronopoulos, M. (1992): 'The Bank of Greece is modernised', *E Cathemerine*, 15–16 Aug., p. 32.

Andronopoulos, M. (1993): 'From Tricoupis to Manos', *E Cathemerine*, 1 August., p. 44.

Angelopoulos, A. (1994): 'Deficits and the black economy, a nightmare: Interview to V. Mathiopoulos', *Ta Nea*, 28 Feb., pp. 12–3.

Anomeritis, G. (1996): '"Commission-grabbing" interests, guilds, and monopolies undermine utilisation of the Second Delors Package', *Economicos Tachydromos*, 15 Feb., pp. 24–6.

Aperghis, N. & Carfakis, J. (1995): '"Hard" drachma and inflation', *Economicos Tachydromos*, 20 April, pp. 34–5.

Apostolou, N. (1995): 'Dangerous gaps in the Real Estate Register bill', *Economicos Tachydromos*, 6 July, pp. 41–2.

Archontakis, A., Papadias, D. & Tsantilas, P. (1994): *Information technologies in the Greek banking system* (Athens: ΕΠΥ).

Arouch, A. (1994): 'The owl's fare' [the fare for bringing coal to Newcastle], *Kerdos*, 11 Nov.

Arouch, A. (1995a): *Economic parody* (Athens: Anubis).

Arouch, A. (1995b): 'Illiterate economy', *Kerdos*, 29 Sept.

Arvanitidis, N. (1995): 'Tragic misconceptions on the way of a most important productive investment', *Economicos Tachydromos*, 30 Nov., pp. 26–8.

Athens Stock Exchange (1995): *Guide to the Stock Exchange* (Athens).

Bank of Greece (1980): *Long-run statistical series of the Greek economy* (Bank of Greece: Athens).

Bank of Greece: Annual Report (Bank of Greece: Athens).

Bank of Greece: Economic Bulletin (Bank of Greece: Athens).

Bank of Greece: Monthly Statistical Bulletin (Bank of Greece: Athens).

Barber, L. & Marsh, D. (1994): 'Emu fans ready to move the goalposts', *Financial Times*, 12 May, p. 2.

Barber, N. (1988): *Lords of the Golden Horn* (London: Arrow Books).
Barley, N. (1990): 'Tourist herds moving across the world', *The Independent*, 19 May.
Baumol, W.J. & Blinder, A.S. (1991): *Economics: principles and policy* (Harcourt Brace Jovanovich).
Botsari, P. (1994): 'How we became richer', *Agora*, 183, 26 May, pp. 80–90.
Bouzali, L. (1993): 'Traditional settlements: sacrificed to "development"', *E Cathemerine*, 31 Oct., p. 32.
Bowen, S. (1991): 'Peru collects taxes at point of a cannon', *Financial Times*, 10 Dec.
Butler, C. (1994): 'The frontrunners in a race for world trade', *The European*, 9–15 Sept.
Cacoulidou, I. (1996): 'Why multinationals are leaving Greece', *E Cathemerine*, 28 July, p. 41.
Calliri, Ph. (1993): 'Decades come and go, but the Public Administration remains . . . unscathed', *E Cathemerine*, 5 Dec., p. 18.
Calliri, Ph. (1994a): 'Research into public administration, Part IV: Big parties are chiefly to blame', *E Cathemerine*, 3 March, p. 6.
Calliri, Ph. (1994b): 'Public Administration is living in the past', *E Cathemerine*, 2 Nov.
Calliri, Ph. (1995a): 'Public-sector employees populating', *E Cathemerine*, 20 May.
Calliri, Ph. (1995b): 'Public Administration: 100,000 appointments within two years', *E Cathemerine*, 13 Dec.
Calliri, Ph. (1996): 'Wretched conditions in the civil service', *E Cathemerine*, 24 March, p. 23.
Calloniatis, C.G. (1995): 'The competitiveness of the Greek economy once again to the fore', *Express*, 4 June, p. 6
Calocardou, R. (1995): 'Structured environment and tourism: a difficult relationship', *Synchrona Themata*, 55, April–June, pp. 81–7.
Calokairinos, Gr. (1995): 'Meteora: political cost and interests', 17 Sept., p. 12.
Catephores, G. (1983): 'Greece: The empiricist socialism of PASOK', in Sawyer M. & Schott, K., eds, *Socialist Economic Review 1983* (London: The Merlin Press).
Catokhianou, D. (1995): 'Economic and spatial development of tourism in Greece: a first view', *Synchrona Themata*, 55, April–June, pp. 62–71.
Catsambas, Th. (1986): 'The role of the Bank of Greece in shaping economic policy', *Economicos Tachydromos*, 19 June, pp. 27–8.
Catsanevas, Th. (1995): 'Workers' strikes in Greece from 1976 to 1993', *Epiloghe*, Nov., pp. 34–6.
Catsoridas, D. (1995): 'A "backsliding" economy? (Notes on the post-war capitalist development', *Theses*, July–Sept., no. 52, pp. 59–72.
Catsoridas, D. (1996): 'Foreign workers in Greece and their conditions of living', *Theses*, 56, July–Sept., pp. 127–46.
Chrysolora, I. (1991): 'The 700 which are leaving the public sector', *E Cathemerine*, 17 Oct., p. 18.
Chrysolouris, G. (1995): 'Achieving growth by means of R&D', *Economicos Tachydromos,* 8 June, pp. 33–4.

Clark, S. (1995): 'What fun we never had', *Sunday Times*, 30 July.

Claudianos, P. (1990): 'Unacceptable and continuously worsening our tax system, according to OECD', *Economicos Tachydromos*, 22 Feb., pp. 13–5.

Claudianos, P. (1995): 'Restructuring and modernisation at the Finance Ministry', *Economicos Tachydromos*, 23 Feb., pp. 26–8.

Clogg, R. (1992): *A concise history of Greece* (Cambridge University Press).

Coccolios, G. (1993): 'Implications of the new Law 2065/92 for the income tax liability of banks', *Bulletin of Union of Hellenic Banks*, 37–8, pp. 111–15.

Comilis, P. (1995): 'Tourist policy and Areas of Integrated Tourist Development', *Synchrona Themata*, 55, April–June, pp. 77–80.

Connolly, P. (1985): 'The politics of the informal sector: A critique', in Redclift, N. & Mingione, E., eds (1985): *Beyond employment: Household, gender and subsistence* (Oxford: Basil Blackwell).

Contonica, C. (1994): 'Due to excessive overdose . . .', *E Cathemerine*, 9 Oct.

Contonica, C. (1996): 'Assistance Fund – insurance companies: threatened by an 11.4 bn "hole"', *E Cathemerine*, 16 June, p. 53.

Copsine, C. (1996a): 'A single minimum pension for all', *E Cathemerine*, 8 March, p. 19.

Copsine, C. (1996b): 'The social security issue opens for discussion', *E Cathemerine*, 10 March.

Copsine, C. (1996c): 'The "blank cheque" of the Public Power Corporation's social insurance system', *E Cathemerine*, 7 April.

Couphalis, S. (1991): 'How vulgar populism shipwrecked NAT', *Economicos Tachydromos*, 8 Aug., pp. 76–7.

Courmoussis, G. (1991): 'How in Greece bad tourists drive good ones out', *Economicos Tachydromos*, 27 June, pp. 32–4.

Coussounis, S. (1996): 'Advertising, priority one for tourism', *E Cathemerine*, 8 Feb.

Cyprianidis, T. (1983): 'Monetarism and leftist neo-liberalism', *Theses*, Oct.–Dec., no. 5, pp. 9–29.

Dalamangas, B. (1995): 'Stabilisation and/or development?', *Economic & Statistical Bulletin*, National Bank of Greece, 4, July, pp. 4–10.

Dalamangas, B. (1996): 'Investment and interest rates: Myths and reality', *Economic & Statistical Bulletin*, National Bank of Greece, 6, April, pp. 25–33.

Daphne, C. (1995): 'Wanted(?): Skilled staff', *Touristike Agora*, 74, Sept., pp. 62–5.

Delithanassi, M. (1995): 'Olympic Catering stands to lose 12 bn', *E Cathemerine*, 19 March, p. 21.

Demetrellis, S. & Papadopoulos, Th. (1995a): 'The fountains of social security funds are drying out', *Ta Nea*, 20 Nov., pp. 46–7.

Demetrellis, S. & Papadopoulos, Th. (1995b): 'A 500 billion deficit for IKA in 1996!', *Ta Nea*, 21 Nov., pp. 50–1.

Dempsey, J. (1990): 'Rocky road leads to the market', *Financial Times*, 17 Oct.

Diamantopoulos, Th. (1995): 'University graduates by decree, a new shame', *Economicos Tachydromos*, 4 May, p. 44.

Dinopoulos, A. (1994): 'In the constellation of the informal economy!, *E Cathemerine*, 13 Feb., pp. 18–9.

Dorovinis, B. (1991): 'How a waterland reserve is being destroyed by common consent', *Economicos Tachydromos*, 8 August, p. 62.

Dorovinis, B. (1992): 'Destruction of waterland reserve in Roumani, Argolis, going on regardless', *Economicos Tachydromos*, 30 April, pp. 69–70.

Doxiadis, A. (1977): 'Ekistic policy for the reconstruction of Greece and a twenty-year plan', *Ekistics*, 260, July, pp. 9–11.

Dracatos, C. (1996): 'Deindustrialisation or restructuring?', *Epiloge*, 1996 Survey of the Greek Economy, pp. 92–8.

Dragassakis, J. (ed.) (1995): 'Greece and the Black Sea countries: Problems and prospects', *Kerdos*, special publication, May.

Drettakis, M. (1996): 'The dramatic growth of the public debt 1981–96', *Economicos Tachydromos*, 21 March, pp. 117–18.

Drosos, N.G., Kraloglou, G., Louca, L. (1996): 'In the jaws of the state', *Kephalaio*, May, no. 80, pp. 74–96.

Dryllerakis, J. (1994): 'Investment subsidies for development', *Economicos Tachydromos*, 8 Dec., pp. 24–8.

Dukas, P. (1993): 'How the public debt was created', *E Cathemerine*, 26 Sept., p. 64.

E Cathemerine (1994a): 'TAXIS: Electronic taxation', 1 Dec., p. 23.

E Cathemerine (1994b): 'The "objective income" criteria for taxing peasants', 10 Dec.

E Cathemerine (1995): 'The vicious circle of the public debt', 16 April, p. 59 (reprint from *The Economist*).

Economicos Tachydromos (1995): 'Reprint of the Casanegra Report', 16 Feb., pp. 29–32 & 130, and 23 Feb., pp. 28–9.

Eleutheroudakis (1927–31): *Encyclopaedic Dictionary*, 1st ed. (Athens: Eleutheroudakis plc).

Emmanuel, D. (1979): 'Housing investment in a context of balanced social & economic development', paper presented in Greek Chamber of Engineers Conference on 'Construction in Greece', June, Athens, mimeo.

Emmanuel, D. (1981): *The growth of speculative building in Greece: Modes of housing production and socioeconomic change* (London School of Economics, PhD Thesis).

EOT (1995a): Press release, 21 August.

EOT (1995b): Press release, 27 Nov.

Ependytes (1996): 'Tourism: A survey', 25–26 May.

Epiloghe (1984): *The Greek economy in figures 1984* (Athens: Electra Press).

Epiloghe (1993): *Annual Economic Review* (Athens).

Epiloghe (1994): *Annual Economic Review* (Athens).

Epiloghe (1995): *Annual Economic Review* (Athens).

Epiloghe (1996): *Annual Economic Review* (Athens).

European Commission (1994): *Growth, competitiveness, employment: The challenges and ways forward into the 21st century* (Office of Official Publications of the European Communities: Luxembourg).

Eurostat (1988): *1986 Labour Force Survey* (Office of Official Publications of the European Communities: Luxembourg).

Eurostat (1991): *1989 Labour Force Survey* (Office of Official Publications of the European Communities: Luxembourg).

Eurostat (1995a): *1993 Labour Force Survey* (Office of Official Publications of the European Communities: Luxembourg).

Eurostat (1995b): *Basic Statistics*, 32nd ed. (Office of Official Publications of the European Communities: Luxembourg).

Euthymiou, P. (1991): 'The policeman's "scandal"', *To Vema*, 6 Jan., p. A4.
Express (1996): 'At least 15 stremmas for building in the islands!', 2 June, p. 7.
Featherstone, K. & Ifantis, K. (1996): *Greece in a changing Europe: Between European integration and Balkan disintegration* (Manchester University Press).
Feldstein, M. & Horioka, C. (1980): 'Domestic saving and international capital flows', *The Economic Journal*, June, 90, pp. 314–29.
Financial Times (1993): 'Turkish finance and industry: A survey', 3 Nov.
Financial Times (1994): 'Emerging markets: A survey', 7 Feb.
Foura, G. (1995): 'Greece: A bottomless pension fund for veterans', *E Cathemerine*, 11 June.
Frankos, J. (1995): 'State-owned universities at the service of Public-Sector mediocrity', *Kerdos*, 15 June, p. 6.
Freris, A.F. (1986): *The Greek economy in the twentieth century* (New York: St Martin's Press).
Fukuyama, F. (1994): 'Mysteries of "Civil Society"', *To Vema*, 13 Nov., p. B4.
Galati, P. (1994): '"Legal" land squatting by means of illegal contracts', *E Cathemerine*, 27 Feb., p. 15.
Galati, P. (1996a): 'They are using concrete to erase burnt woodland from the map . . .', *E Cathemerine*, 25 Jan.
Galati, P. (1996b): 'Local self-government is going bankrupt', *E Cathemerine*, 7 April, pp. 20–1.
Galati, P. (1996c): 'Woodland: Five ways to appropriate it', *E Cathemerine*, 12 May, p. 20.
Galiatsos, C. (1994): 'The deregulation of capital movements and the banking system', *Economic & Statistical Bulletin*, National Bank of Greece, 1, April, pp. 13–5.
Gaunt, I. (1991): 'Germany sets the pace on privatisation', *Financial Times*, 29 Aug.
Gellner, E. (1994): *Conditions of liberty, civil society and its rivals* (London: Hamish Hamilton).
Georgiou, P. (1986): 'The invention of the informal economy', *Scholiastis*, 42, Sept., p. 14.
Ghiocas, M. (1994): 'In fifty years there will be no Greeks left!', *Economicos Tachydromos*, 12 May, pp. 26–31.
Gortsos, C.V. (1993): 'Financial & credit market integration and monetary union: The two components of the community programme for the banking sector', *Bulletin of Union of Hellenic Banks*, 37–8, pp. 34–51.
Gritzalis, A. (1992): 'How many the State pays', *E Cathemerine*, 21 June.
Hadjidakis, A. (1995): 'Impact of tourism on the structured environment: a framework for analysis', *Synchrona Themata*, 55, April–June, pp. 88–92.
Hassid, J. (1995a): 'If you want to invest in the Balkans', *Economicos Tachydromos*, 8 June, pp. 26–30 & 93–5.
Hassid, J. (1995b): 'If you want to invest in the Balkans', *Economicos Tachydromos*, 15 June, pp. 39–42.
Hassiotis, V. (1995): 'The gist of the problem of the Eleusis shipyards', *Economicos Tachydromos*, 7 Dec., pp. 77–9.
Hill, F. (1996): 'Greece in a Caspian oil maelstrom', *Economicos Tachydromos*, 26 Sept., pp. 24–30.

Hope, K. (1990): 'Greeks develop a more sophisticated taste for wine', *Financial Times*, 2 Jan.

Hope, K. (1994): 'Out of sync with their partners', *Financial Times*, 1 June, p. 15.

Hope, K. (1995): 'Greek food and drink: A survey', *Financial Times*, 16 May, pp. i–iv.

Industrial News & Research (1994): 'Multinational, 25% of Greek industrial turnover', *Success*, Feb., pp. 34–9.

Iordanidis, C. (1996): 'Greece–Cyprus: how the Union did not happen', *E Cathemerine*, 18 Feb., p. 12.

Jones, C. (1985): *Patterns of social policy: An introduction to comparative analysis* (London: Tavistock).

Karacottas, Th. D. (1994): 'That's why taxes are not collected any more', *Economicos Tachydromos*, 24 Feb., pp. 24–6.

Karacottas, Th. D. (1995): '"Objective income" criteria, over the top', *Economicos Tachydromos*, 20 March, pp. 26–9 and 86–8.

Karacoussis, A. (1995): 'A flood of "contributions on behalf of third parties"', *E Cathemerine*, 26 Sept., p. 19.

Karaiskaki, T. (1995): 'The financial suffocation of universities', *E Cathemerine*, 26 Feb., p. 20.

Karalis, A. (1994): 'Cleaning up the social security system, a burning issue', *E Cathemerine*, 15 May, p. 48.

Karalis, A. (1995): 'Creating groups of social insurance funds, an unfortunate proposal', *E Cathemerine*, 18 Nov.

Karamouzis, N. (1995): 'Management of the reserves of social insurance funds', *E Cathemerine*, 7 May, p. 54.

Kelly, J. & Tett, G. (1996): 'A nibble out of the tax base', *Financial Times*, 15 April, p. 17.

Kephalaio (1995): '1944–1994: 50 years of the Greek economy', annual collector's edition, pp. 8–83 and 94–143.

Kephalas, A. (1991): 'Privatisation errors', *Economicos Tachydromos*, 12 Sept., pp. 102–4.

Kephalas, A. (1994a): 'The stunning tale of Olympic Catering', *Economicos Tachydromos*, 17 Feb., pp. 94–6.

Kephalas, A. (1994b): 'The public debt at 140% of GDP', *Economicos Tachydromos*, 3 Nov., pp. 15–6.

Kephalas, A. (1994c): 'The productivity game and why our country's lost it', *Economicos Tachydromos*, 29 Dec., p. 17.

Kephalas, A. (1995): 'Gross disregard for any notion of competition', *Economicos Tachydromos*, 16 Feb., pp. 35–6 and 123.

Kephalas, A. (1996a): 'The true shield-droppers', *Economicos Tachydromos*, 4 April, pp. 13–4.

Kephalas, A. (1996b): 'New measures knocking at the gates', *Economicos Tachydromos*, 13 June, p. 14.

Khaicalis, S. & Collias, F. (1995): 'Will we get, at last, a Real Estate Register?', *Economicos Tachydromos*, 19 Jan., pp. 24–7.

Khaicalis, S. (1983): 'Arguments for and against unifying privileged and non-priveleged health funds', *Economicos Tachydromos*, 29 Sept., pp. 25–30.

Khaicalis, S. (1990): 'Greek (especially state-owned) banks to tread bare-foot on the thorns of "1992"', *Economicos Tachydromos*, 15 Feb., pp. 28–30.

Khaicalis, S. (1994): 'Has generalised impunity become an institution now?', *Economicos Tachydromos*, 3 March, pp. 3–6.
Khaicalis, S. & Collias, F. (1996): 'The Second Delors Package at a crucial crossroads', *Economicos Tachydromos*, 15 August, pp. 22–5.
Kharalampopoulou, I. (1995): 'The changes in education', *E Cathemerine*, 2 July, p. 3.
Kolmer, C. (1995): *The bankruptcy of the Third Hellenic Republic* (Athens: Delos).
Kotzamanis, B. & Maloutas, Th. (1985): 'State intervention in workers' and people's housing', *Review of Social Research*, 56, (Athens: EKKE), pp. 129–54.
KPMG (1992): *Banking to the Year 2000* (London: KPMG Management Consulting).
Kyritsis, N. & Polymeridis, G. (1992): *Topical problems of the Greek economy* (Athens: Synchrone Epoche).
Lacopoulos, G. (1994): '100,000 employees missing!', *To Vema*, 6 March, p. A42.
Lacopoulos, G. (1995): 'The antics of the Public Administration mandarins', *To Vema*, 23 April, pp. A30–1.
Laliotis, C. (1996): 'Interview to Stathis Khaicalis', *Economicos Tachydromos*, 16 May, pp. 24–6.
Lampsias, P. (1990): 'Strike champions', *To Vema*, 7 Oct., pp. D10–1.
Lazaridis, C. (1995a): 'Strategic convergence with Albania', *Economicos Tachydromos*, 6 April, pp. 88–9.
Lazaridis, C. (1995b): 'In search of a substantial foreign policy', *Economicos Tachydromos*, 27 July, pp. 39–42.
Lazaridis, C. (1995c): 'Meaning of a national policy on alliances', *Economicos Tachydromos*, 16 Nov., pp. 18–9.
Lazaridis, C. (1996a): 'The worst "anti-Europeans"', *Economicos Tachydromos*, 25 July, p. 19.
Lazaridis, C. (1996b): 'Turkey: in the constellation of doubt . . .', *Economicos Tachydromos*, 1 August, pp. 33–5.
Lazaridis, C. (1996c): 'Defence and Deterrence – Now!', *Economicos Tachydromos*, 15 August, pp. 11–3.
Lazaridis, C. (1996d): 'Let's be like the Hebrews . . .', *Economicos Tachydromos*, 12 Sept., pp. 33–5.
Lazaridis, C. (1996e): 'The USA's "chaotic" behaviour', mimeo.
Leandros, N. (1996): *The crisis in social security and guidelines for reforming the system* (Athens: IOBE).
Lecatsas, E. (1995): 'Actual GDP more than twice the official', *Economicos Tachydromos*, 12 Oct., pp. 88–9.
Lee, J.J. (1989): *Ireland 1912–1985: Politics and society* (Cambridge University Press).
Leventacos, D. (1996): 'Who asks gets', *E Cathemerine*, 5 April, p. 18.
Levi, P. (1983): *The hill of Kronos: a vividly personal discovery of Greece* (London: Zenith).
Linardos-Rylmon, P. (1994): 'Two-speed modernisation in industry', *Economicos Tachydromos*, 29 Sept., p. 77.

Liveracos, P. & Macrydemetris, A. (1996): 'How many are the public-sector employees?', *Economicos Tachydromos*, 9 May, pp. 24–30 and 77.

Loucas, J. (1996): 'The "imperial model", Turkey and the new international system', *Strategica*, 22, July, pp. 98–103.

Lymperopoulos, C. (1996): 'State-owned banks and syndicalism', *Economicos Tachydromos*, 4 April, pp. 60–1.

Lysimakhou, T. (1995): 'The Greek insurance market in 1995–9', *Economic & Statistical Bulletin*, National Bank of Greece, 5, Nov., pp. 19–21.

Macris, P. (1995): "Pure" Turks, a national minority in Turkey', *E Cathemerine*, 14 May, p. 18.

Magheiros, Ev. (1993): 'Red tape and lost man-hours', *E Cathemerine*, 28 Feb., p. 40.

Magheiros, S. (1995): 'Mytilene: Model of development', *Ta Nea*, 8 Dec., p. 16.

Major, J. (1996): 'What will determine Europe's future', *Economicos Tachydromos*, 25 July, pp. 20–1.

Manessiotis, B. (1993): *The public sector: Implications and prospects arising from EEC membership* (Academy of Athens, Centre for Research into Greek Society, vol. 4).

Manessiotis, B. (1995): 'A tax-collecting mechanism worthy of its name: Interview to Paul Claudianos', *Economicos Tachydromos*, 16 Feb., pp. 26–9.

Marinos, J. (1987): 'Making a habit of breaking the law', *Economicos Tachydromos*, 7 May, pp. 3–6.

Marinos, J. (1988): 'The harmful implications of the guilds' domination of Greek public life', *Economicos Tachydromos*, 4 August, pp. 3–6.

Marinos, J. (1990a): 'Social security: The story of a heinous crime', *Economicos Tachydromos*, 16 Aug., pp. 3–8.

Marinos, J. (1990b): 'Solution of the social security problem, a one-way street', *Economicos Tachydromos*, 23 Aug., pp. 3–5.

Marinos, J. (1991): 'Lawlessness reigns!', *Economicos Tachydromos*, 6 June, pp. 3–7.

Marinos, J. (1992): 'Solving the social security problem whilst leaving various entitlements intact is ultimately impossible', *Economicos Tachydromos*, 28 May, pp. 3–7 and 96.

Marinos, J. (1994a): 'If they really wanted to collect the taxes . . .', *To Vema*, 10 April.

Marinos, J. (1994b): 'The wrecking of Public Administration', *Economicos Tachydromos*, 10 Nov., pp. 3–6.

Marinos, J. (1995): 'How law-breaking has become a "democratic" right', *Economicos Tachydromos*, 20 April, pp. 3–6 and 89.

Masera, R. (1995): 'Motives for the private sector to contribute to collective infrastructure', *Proceedings of European Investment Bank Forum on Infrastructure Provision and the Role of the Private Sector* (Luxembourg: EIB).

Mastrantonis, T. & Melios, J. (1983): 'The Left's theory of the dependence of Greek capitalism: Conditions and implications', *Theses*, Jan.–March, no. 2, pp. 31–43.

Matthews, R.C.O., Feinstein, C.H., Olding-Smee, J.C. (1982): *British Economic Growth* (Oxford: Clarendon Press).

Mavris, J. & Tsekouras, Th. (1983): 'Foreign capital and the development of Greek capitalism', *Theses*, Jan.–March, no. 2, pp. 45–82.
Mavris, J. (1984): 'The problem of petty bourgeoisie in Greece', *Theses*, Oct.–Dec., no. 9, pp. 39–76.
Mavris, J. (1995): 'Syndicalism's social profile', *E Cathemerine*, 12 March, p. 22.
Mavroleon, B. (1986): 'Social non-insurance', *Ethnos*, 14 Aug., p. 35.
Mazower, M. (1991): *Greece and the inter-war economic crisis* (Oxford: Clarendon Press).
Melios, J. (1984): 'The "dependence" theories of the Left, and the dependences of Greek capitalism', *Theses*, Oct.–Dec., no. 9, pp. 5–22.
Melios, J. & Joachimoglou, E. (1987): 'Capital accumulation indices in Greece (1958–1985)', *Theses*, April–June, no. 19, pp. 95–114.
Mikhas, T. (1994): 'The myth of foreign capital', *Eleutherotypia*, 25 August, p. 32.
Mikhas, T. (1995): 'Greece's position has worsened', *Kerdos*, 29 Sept., pp. 18–9.
Mirkos, G. (1996): 'Interview to Demetris Sterghiou', 25 April, *Economicos Tachydromos*, pp. 24–31.
Monthly Review (1972): *Greece: Neocolonialism and revolution*, Dec., vol. 24, New York.
Mortimer, E. (1996): 'A place at the centre', *Financial Times*, 12 June, p. 10.
Moschonas, A. (1986): *Traditional petty bourgeois strata* (Athens: Foundation for Mediterranean Studies).
Mourdoukoutas, P. (1994): *The Experiment* (Acton, Massachusetts: Copley Publishing Group).
Mouzelis, N. (1978a): 'Class and Clientelistic Politics: The Case of Greece', *Sociological Review*, vol. 26, pp. 471–97.
Mouzelis, N. (1978b): *Modern Greece: Facets of underdevelopment* (London: Macmillan).
Mouzelis, N. (1986): *Politics in the Semi-Periphery: Early Parliamentarism and Late Industrialisation in the Balkans and Latin America* (London: Macmillan).
Mouzelis, N. (1988): 'Structure and ideology of Populism', *To Vema*, 3 Jan., pp. 24–6.
Nanopoulos, N. (1993): 'Greek banks in the European competition ground', *E Cathemerine*, 13 June, p. 42.
Nautemporica (1991): 'Returns on fixed capital in the economy', 3 July, pp. 1 and 11.
Nautemporica (1992): 'The convergence plan of the Greek economy 1993–1998', 4 Dec., pp. 6–12.
Nautemporica (1992): *Dealing with the multi-faceted phaenomenon of tax evasion*, special publication, Athens, Jan.
Negreponti-Delivani, M. (1979): *Analysis of the Greek economy* (Athens: Papazessis).
Negreponti-Delivani, M. (1990a): *The economics of the informal economy in Greece* (Athens: Papazessis).
Negreponti-Delivani, M. (1990b): 'Dangers of clamping down on tax evasion', *Economicos Tachydromos*, 15 March, pp. 35–8.

Negreponti-Delivani, M. (1995): 'The peculiar face of Greek unemployment', *Eleutherotypia*, 20 August, p. 28.
Nicolacopoulos, D. (1995): 'Mayors' five "sins"', *To Vema*, 12 Nov., p. A55.
Nicolaou, N. (1990): 'Why the economic crisis is not believed', *Economicos Tachydromos*, 15.3., p. 16.
Nicolaou, N. (1996): 'A government in search of political stamina', *Economicos Tachydromos*, 13.6.1996, pp. 3–4.
Nicolaou, S. (1995): 'The informal economy permeates the entire society', *Economicos Tachydromos*, 24 August, pp. 41–2.
Nicolopoulos, Gr. (1992): 'Greece's unfavourable image among foreign entrepreneurs', *E Cathemerine*, 22 Nov., p. 53.
Nicolopoulos, Gr. (1996): 'Deregulation and interventions', *E Cathemerine*, 16 June, p. 55.
Niskanen, W. (1971): *Bureaucracy and Representative Government* (Aldine-Atherton).
Norman, P. (1996): 'Shadow economy could help Emu fly', *Financial Times*, 10 June, p. 7.
OECD (1983): *Environmental policies in Greece: A review by the OECD and its environmental committee undertaken in 1982/83 at the request of the government of Greece* (OECD: Paris).
OECD (1986): *Living conditions in OECD countries: A compendium of social indicators* (OECD, Social Policy Studies no. 3: Paris).
OECD (1993a): *Economic surveys: Greece 1992–93* (OECD: Paris).
OECD (1993b): *Historical statistics 1960–90* (OECD: Paris).
OECD (1994): *Economic surveys: UK 1993–94* (OECD: Paris).
OECD (1995): *Historical statistics 1960–93* (OECD: Paris).
Ormerod, P. (1994): *The death of economics* (London: Faber and Faber).
Paleologos, J. (1995): 'Stop the overvalued drachma policy', *To Vema*, 1 Jan., p. Δ11.
Panayotarea, A. (1995): 'Public procurements: How the public administration is cheated', *E Cathemerine*, 17.12.1995, p. 23.
Papademetriou, Ev. (1995): 'Illegal builders vs careta-careta', *E Cathemerine*, 18 June, p. 21.
Papadopoulos, J. (1995): 'Quality in Greek hotel units', *Touristike Agora*, 74, Sept., pp. 54–61.
Papageorgiou, Th. (1995): '95 per cent of agricultural co-ops are capable of operating on a healthy basis', interview in Annual Survey of the Agrarian Economy', *Express*, Nov., p. 17.
Papandreou, V. (1994): 'Investment incentives and investment', *E Cathemerine*, 7 Aug., p. 36.
Papandreou, V. (1996): 'Greece is too beautiful to sell cheaply', a survey of tourism in *Ependytes*, 25–26 May, p. 3.
Papandropoulos, Ath., ed. (1985): 'How and why so many companies became problem firms, and their present state', *Economicos Tachydromos*, 9 May, pp. 53–8.
Papandropoulos, Ath. (1995a): Unhealthy deviations in the business sector', *Economicos Tachydromos*, 12 Jan., pp. 84–5.
Papandropoulos, Ath. (1995b): 'The deindustrialisation myth and why it is being promoted', *Economicos Tachydromos*, 16 Nov., pp. 3–6.

Papandropoulos, Ath. (1995c): 'An example of quality tourism', *Economicos Tachydromos*, 7 Sept., pp. 56–7.
Papandropoulos, Ath. (1996): 'Back to the "ledger" age', *Economicos Tachydromos*, 13 June, p. 85.
Papanicolaou, G. (1987): 'The maze of the social security system in figures', *Economicos Tachydromos*, 30 July, pp. 49–52.
Papanicolaou, G. (1995): 'Do we really care to have industrial investment?', *Economicos Tachydromos*, 26 Oct., pp. 128–9.
Papasoteriou, Ch. (1991): 'ΔΕΚΟ [public-sector enterprises & organisations]: the gangrene in Greek society', *Kerdos*, 18 Oct., pp. 7–8.
Papathanasiou, C. (1995): 'The failure to privatise the Scaramanga Shipyards, a new economic crime at the expense of taxpayers', *Economicos Tachydromos*, 15 June, pp. 30–3.
Papathanasiou, J. (1995): 'Privatisation model that failed', *Economicos Tachydromos*, 31 August, p. 24.
Papathanasopoulos, G. (1995): 'Liemongering under the Meteora rocks', *Economicos Tachydromos*, 2 Nov., p. 43.
Papatheodorou, C. (1995): 'The end of the pattern of subsidies and self-deceptions', Annual Survey of the Agrararian Economy, *Express*, Nov., p. 15.
Papayannakis, El. (1983): 'The different phases and the basic characteristics of Greek industrialisation', *Economicos Tachydromos*, 24.3.1983, p. 70.
Parpairis, A. (1995): 'Life cycle of the tourist product: the case of Myconos', *Synchrona Themata*, 55, April–June, pp. 93–103.
Pavlopoulos, P. (1987): *The informal economy in Greece* (Athens: IOBE, Special Reports series, no. 17).
Pavlopoulos, P. (1996): 'On the informal economy and tax evasion', *Epiloghe: Annual Economic Review 1996*, pp. 150–3.
Petoussis, M. (1986): 'Are credit rules the cause of, or an excuse for, the low returns of Greek banks?', *Economicos Tachydromos*, 14 Aug., pp. 27–31.
Petras, J. (1984): 'Rentierist capital: Source of Greece's dynamic development and industrial underdevelopment', *Economicos Tachydromos*, 8 March, pp. 27–30.
Petrochilos, G.A. (1989): *Foreign direct investment and the development process: the case of Greece* (Aldershot, Hampshire: Avebury).
Phillips, A.W. (1958): 'The relation between unemployment and the rate of change of money wages in the United Kingdom, 1861–1957', *Economica*, New Series, vol. 25, Nov.
Pirounakis, N.G. (1987): *A European market in mortgage credit: Comments* (Discussion Paper 15, Centre for Housing Research, University of Glasgow).
Pirounakis, N.G. (1990): *Housing system dynamics: An interdisciplinary comparative approach* (PhD Thesis, Glasgow University).
Pirounakis, N.G. (1992a): 'How we waste our (limited) tourist resources', *Touristike Agora*, 37, April, pp. 79–85.
Pirounakis, N.G. (1992b): *Estimation of the correct number of dwellings built in Greece per year* (Report prepared for the NSSG: Athens).
Pirounakis, N.G. (1993a): 'The ghost of the National Real Estate Register', *Economicos Tachydromos*, 9 Sept., pp. 38–41.
Pirounakis, N.G. (1993b): 'The life and health insurance market in Greece today', a survey in *Economicos Tachydromos*, 14 Oct., pp. 47–70.

Pirounakis, N.G. (1994): 'Transnationals in Greece', a survey in *Economicos Tachydromos*, 24 Nov., pp. 51–82.

Pirounakis, N.G. (1995a): *Basic economics for students, business managers, and politicians* (Athens: Anubis).

Pirounakis, N.G. (1995b): 'Public-sector enterprises in the Greek economy', a survey in *Economicos Tachydromos*, 5 Oct., pp. 49–71.

Pirounakis, N.G. (1995c): 'The kind of Budget Greece needs', *Information*, Dec., pp. 38–45.

Pirounakis, N.G. (1996a): 'A dying country's craven democracy', *Economicos Tachydromos*, 4 Jan., pp. 35–7.

Pirounakis, N.G. (1996b): *Housing credit in Greece* (Athens: IOBE).

Pirounakis, N.G. (1996c): 'The insurance market: trends, problems, products', *Information*, April, pp. 40–54.

Ploritis, M. (1994): 'Pressures and "solutions"', *To Vema*, 13 Nov., p. A20.

Polyzos, N. (1996): 'Our tragic demographic problem', *Economicos Tachydromos*, 11 April, pp. 42–3.

Portosalte, A. (1995): 'How we are going to protect our forests', *E Cathemerine*, 11 June, p. 23.

Powell, D. (1941): *Remember Greece* (London: Hodder and Stoughton).

Pselos, G. (1995a): 'The wealth of social insurance organisations', *E Cathemerine*, 19 July.

Pselos, G. (1995b): 'The profile of social insurance', *E Cathemerine*, 26 July.

Rallis, G. (1996): 'The truth about modern Greek', *E Cathemerine*, 21 April, p. 21.

Ridding, J. (1995): 'Weighed down by burden of care', *Financial Times*, 1 Nov.

Roidis, E. (1996): *Athenian strolls et cetera* (Athens: Castaniotis).

Rokos, D. (1982): 'Property and land policy in Greece: the distribution of national lands', *Epistemonike Skepsis*, Jan.–Feb., pp. 99–104.

Roumeliotis, P. (1978): *Multinational enterprises and overcosting–undercosting in Greece* (Athens: Papazessis).

Ryder, J. & Silver, H. (1970): *Modern English society: History and structure, 1850–1970* (London: Methuen).

Sakellaropoulos, S. (1996): 'Elected self-government at county level in the context of capitalist restructuring', *Theses*, 56, July–Sept., pp. 61–77.

Samaras, J. (1982): *State and capital in Greece* (Athens: Synchrone Epoche).

Sarantidis, S. (1996): 'Stagnation and competitive advantage in Greek industry', *Epiloghe: Annual Economic Review 1996*, pp. 100–4.

Skapinker, M. (1991): 'Tourism industry travels new road', *Financial Times*, 11 Dec.

Skouras, Th. (1984): 'Rentierist capital and development: A reply to J. Petras', *Economicos Tachydromos*, 28 June, pp. 25–8.

Sloman, J. (1991): *Economics* (Harvester Wheatsheaf).

Sophoulis, C. (1995): 'Crisis of overindebtedness in the tourist sector', *Economicos Tachydromos*, 26 Oct., p. 99.

Sophoulis, C. (1996): 'Seven sins of the educational system', *Economicos Tachydromos*, 28 March, p. 40.

Spanou, C. (1994): 'Public-sector appointment policies, a reflection on society', *E Cathemerine*, 2 March, p. 6.

Stereopoulos, N. (1994): 'Umpteen hotels on the verge of closing down', *Economicos Tachydromos*, 3 March, pp. 105.
Sterghiou, D. (1976): 'Thirty laws comprising the network of privileges to industrialists', *To Vema*, 14 March.
Sterghiou, D. (1985): 'Seven years and many billions lost', *Economicos Tachydromos*, 4 July, pp. 3–6.
Sterghiou, D. (1991): 'How IKA reached a dead end', *Economicos Tachydromos*, 21 Nov., pp. 26–30.
Sterghiou, D. (1992): 'How the social security system was toppled', *Economicos Tachydromos*, 28 May, pp. 26–32.
Sterghiou, D. (1994): 'How law-breakers are in truth rewarded!', *Economicos Tachydromos*, 3 March, p. 19.
Sterghiou, D. (1995a): 'The looting of Greece', *Economicos Tachydromos*, 8 June, pp. 4–5.
Sterghiou, D. (1995b): 'The ever-deadly threat of problem companies', *Economicos Tachydromos*, 31 August, pp. 18–20.
Sterghiou, D. (1995c): 'The abolition of Greece', *Economicos Tachydromos*, 19 Oct., pp. 3–6 and 92.
Sterghiou, D., ed. (1986): 'The despairingly low productivity of the Greek economy, a national tragedy', a survey in *Economicos Tachydromos*, 11 Sept., pp. 33– 86.
Sterghiou, D., ed. (1994): 'Development: Will it come to us, or will it leave us behind?', a survey in *Economicos Tachydromos*, 22 Dec., pp. 47–118.
Sterghiou, D., ed. (1995): 'Economic policy and development' a survey in *Economicos Tachydromos*, 21 Dec., pp. 43–170.
Syrigos, A. (1994): '10 questions and answers on the 12 miles', *To Vema*, 20 Nov., p. A22.
Tarpangos, A. (1996): 'Economic developments and social conflicts in the construction sector', *Theses*, 56, July–Sept., pp. 111–26.
Taylor, A. (1991): 'Hungary seeks foreign cash for toll roads', *Financial Times*, 29 Aug.
Tenios, P. (1992): 'Social insurance: Past and Future', a survey in *E Cathemerine*, 20 Sept.
Tenios, P. (1995a): 'A vicious circle that goes on forever', *E Cathemerine*, 12 March, p. 54.
Tenios, P. (1995b): 'How are future pensions going to be paid?', *E Cathemerine*, 15 Oct.
Tett, G. (1996): 'Three EU economies are revised upwards', *Financial Times*, 29 May, p. 14.
The Economist (1989): 'Third-world tourism', 11 March, pp. 21–4.
The Economist (1992): 'Cleaning up the Mediterranean', 21 Dec., pp. 21–4.
The Economist (1996a): 'A world gone soft: A survey of the software industry', 25 May.
The Economist (1996b): 'Economic growth', 25 May, pp. 23–4 and 29.
The Economist (1996c): 'The elusive golden apple: A survey of Turkey', 8 June.
The Economist (1996d): 'Arguments for enlargement', 3 August, pp. 27–8.
Tragakis, G. (1993): 'The institutional framework for exercise of the credit function in Greece', *Bulletin of Union of Hellenic Banks*, 39–40, pp. 29–40.

Tragakis, G. (1994): 'The independent central bank model and the Bank of Greece', *Economicos Tachydromos*, 29 Sept., pp. 24–8.

Triantafyllou, A. (1992): *Industrialisation, foreign capital, and economic development: The case of Greece, 1960–88* (PhD Thesis, University of Manchester).

Tringa, N. (1994a): 'Privatising problem companies', *Economicos Tachydromos*, 19 May, pp. 22–30.

Tringa, N. (1994b): 'Deindustrialisation, and how to counter it', *Economicos Tachydromos*, 2 June, pp. 30–1.

Tsakalotos, E. (1991): *Alternative economic strategies: The case of Greece* (Aldershot, Hampshire: Avebury).

Tsaliki, P. V. (1991): *Greek economy: Sources of growth* (USA: Praeger).

Tsaoussis, C. (1992): 'Social insurance funds: Losses of many billions due to commissions to banks', *To Vema*, 26 April, p. Δ3.

Tsoucalas, C. (1983): *Social development and the state: the structuration of the public domain in Greece* (Athens: Themelio).

Tsoucalas, C. (1986): *State, society, work in post-war Greece* (Athens: Themelio).

Tsuru, Sh. (1993): *Japan's capitalism: Creative defeat and beyond* (Cambridge University Press).

Tzannakis, S. (1991): 'Social insurance: the young people of to-day will have to foot the bill', *Ta Nea*, 22 Oct., p. 25.

Tzouganatos, G.A. (1992): *The development of the Greek economy, 1950–91* (USA: Greenwood Press Inc.).

United Nations (1994): *Economic survey of Europe in 1993–1994* (UN, Economic Commission for Europe: New York and Geneva).

United Nations (1995): *Human development report 1995* (Oxford University Press: New York).

Ursacki, T. & Vertinsky, I. (1991): 'Market positioning and performance of foreign banks in Korea', *International Journal of Bank Marketing*, 9, 5, pp. 14–22.

Vamvoucas, G. (1990a): 'While Greece is at the bottom of the international economic league, her informal economy – fortunately – is thriving', *Economicos Tachydromos*, 15 March, pp. 39–41.

Vamvoucas, G. (1990b): 'The excessive tax burden has reduced real incomes', *Economicos Tachydromos*, 13 Dec., pp. 28–32.

Vamvoucas, G. (1991a): 'Causes of the collapse of our social security system and proposals for its recovery', *Economicos Tachydromos*, 29 Aug., pp. 26–9.

Vamvoucas, G. (1991b): 'Fiscal drag and its meaning', *Economicos Tachydromos*, 12 Dec., pp. 112–5.

Vamvoucas, G. (1992a): 'Half of Greek employees get their pay-packets from the state!', *Economicos Tachydromos*, 26 March, pp. 26–8.

Vamvoucas, G. (1992b): 'The gist of the social insurance problem', *Economicos Tachydromos*, 6 Aug., pp. 28–30.

Vamvoucas, G. (1994a): 'Greece sets the tax-burden record', *Economicos Tachydromos*, 1 Dec., pp. 102.

Vamvoucas, G. (1994b): 'How big is Greece's public debt, anyway?', *Economicos Tachydromos*, 1 Dec., p. 18.

Vamvoucas, G. (1994c): 'The size of the public debt', *Economicos Tachydromos*, 8 Dec., pp. 115–6.

Vamvoucas, G. (1995a): 'Our social security system in jeopardy!', *Economicos achydromos*, 6 July, pp. 72–3.
Vamvoucas, G. (1995b): 'The demographic crisis crushes social insurance', *Economicos Tachydromos*, 13 July, p. 100.
Vamvoucas, G. (1995c): 'The wealth of social insurance funds', *Economicos Tachydromos*, 27 July, pp. 86–7.
Vardas, Th. (1994a): 'Significant benefits of a bravely-done devaluation of the drachma', *Express*, 6 March, p. 7.
Vardas, Th. (1994b): 'Aggressive depreciation of the drachma, the "answer" to the crisis', *Express*, 22 May, p. 6.
Vassiliadis, Th. A. (1985): *The steps of the passage* (Myrina, Lemnos).
Venetakis, B. (1995): 'A dismal future for pensioners', *Economicos Tachydromos*, 12 Oct., pp. 102– 3.
Vergopoulos, C. (1975): *The peasant question in Greece* (Athens: Sextant).
White, D. (1987): 'Modernisation brings changes at the top', *Financial Times* survey: Spanish Banking & Finance, 17 July, p. ii.
Willman, J. (1994): 'With a greyer picture of the future in mind', *Financial Times*, 8 March, p. 10.
World Bank (1988): *World Development Report 1988* (Oxford University Press: New York).
World Bank (1994): *World Development Report 1994* (Oxford University Press: New York).
Yannaras, Christos (1995a): 'Turkish transmogrification of our polity's life', *E Cathemerine*, 12 July, p. 3.
Yannaras, Christos (1995b): 'Functionally illiterate', *E Cathemerine*, 25 Oct.
Yannaras, Christos (1996): 'Rallis' language reform', *E Cathemerine*, 28 April, p. 33.
Yannaris, N. (1996): 'Public debt and higher education in Greece', *Economicos Tachydromos*, 29 Aug., pp. 32–3.
Yannitsis, T. (1994): *Dynamics of specialisation between Greece, Spain, Turkey and Portugal, and foreign investment in Greece in the 1980s* (Athens: Papazessis & EKEM).
Yfantopoulos, J. (1990): 'The welfare state and pension policy in Greece, and in OECD and EEC countries', *Review of Social Research*, (Athens: EKKE), pp. 199–249.
Zachariadis, G. (1995): 'Sacrifice to tourism', *Ta Nea*, 7 Dec., p. 26.
Zarkovic Bookman, M. (1994): *Economic decline and nationalism in the Balkans* (Macmillan).
Zavvos, G. (1992a): 'Pension funds and the Community's new perspective', *To Vema*, 26 Jan., p. Δ19.
Zavvos, G. (1992b): 'The reformation of the Greek financial system in the 1990s', *Bulletin of Union of Hellenic Banks*, 35, pp. 9–12.
Zervas, D. (1995): 'Why we experienced deindustrialisation', *Economicos Tachydromos*, 14 Sept., 29–32.

Index

Acté Myrina Hotel, 230, 232
Administrative Court, Supreme, of Greece, 249n29
Aegean, 4, 10, 124, 260, 275–6, 278, 287–9, 292
Aghios Nicolaos, Crete, 242
Agricultural co-operatives in Greece, 56, 68n46, 133–4
Agriculture, Greek,
and EU subsidies, 55, 68n46
and share in GDP, 16
smallholder characteristic of, 12–13, 261
vs industry, 170
Albania, 276–97, 280–1, 283–4, 291
Albanian contingent in Skopje, 286
see also Berisha's regime; Tirana
Alogoskoufis, G., 34, 36, 46, 47, 265
Aluminium of Greece, 187, 262
Angelopoulos, A., 28
Archaeological Service, Greek, 240
Area(s) of Integrated Tourist Development, 246–7
Armenia, 283–4
Assistance Fund, 141, 150n41
Ataturk, Mustafa Kemal (1880–1938), 66n1, 279
Athens Medical Centre, 190
Athens Stock Exchange, 145–8;
Athens, environmental pollution in, 211

Balkan federation, 280–1
Balkans, 274, 280, 289
Bank
ABN-AmRo, 136, 138
Agricultural, 68n38, 68n46, 121–3, 124, 133, 221
Agrotiké, *see* Agricultural
Alpha Credit, 122, 221
Aspis, 122–3, 221
ATE, *see* Agricultural
Barclays, 136, 138
Bayerische Vereinsbank, 136, 138
Citibank, 136, 138
Commercial, 122, 133
Egnatia, 221
Emporiké, *see* Commercial
ErgoBank, 122
ETBA, 89, 122–3, 133–4
ETEBA, 122–3, 138
Ethniké, *see* National
Euromerchant, 138
Housing, 122–3, 221, 223
Investment, 122–3
Ionian, 54, 122, 131
Ktematiké, *see* Mortgage
Midland, 136, 138
Mortgage, 122–3, 132–3, 150n30, 221, 223; and the Bank of Greece, 132
National, 53–4, 67n30, 121–2, 124, 133–4, 149n16, 149n23, 158
NatWest, 136–8
of Athens, 131, 149n16
of Attica, 122, 131
of Central Greece, 131
of Crete, 131
of Scotland, 136
Piraeus, 131
Post Office Savings, 122–3, 158, 221
Royal, of Scotland, 136, 138
Bank of Greece, 99, 122, 190
and exchange rate policy, 105
and housing credit, 222
and monetary financing of GGBd, 110n2
and monetary policy, 95–6, 111n4
and money supply, 96–7
and pension funds, 158, 161
and regulation of banking system, 126–8, 149n10, 222; to-day, 128

and success at supervision, 7, 97, 121
and the Mortgage Bank, 132
government borrowing from, 73, 96–7
Banking, 121–140
in Spain, 148n2
Practice, Code of, 128
system, deregulation of, 127–8, 131; modernisation of, 128, 130–1; oligopolistic structure of, 124; productivity in, 130; regulation of, 126–8;
Banks
and ATMs, 130–1, 148n1
and confidentiality of bank accounts, 86
and DFI, 137–40
and public-sector enterprises, 127
and reserve requirements, 128
and write-offs of non-performing loans, 133
and ΔΕΚΟ financing, 131–2
commercial, 121–2, 124, 127–8, 135, 223; and 'engage-disengage' system of control, 12; and treasury bills, 127; returns to savers with, 109
financing to various sectors by, 128–30
foreign, in Greece, 136–40; and collective bargaining, 149n14; customer profile of, 140
Greek public-sector, customer profile of, 140
in Greece, asset/employee ratio, 124–5
public sector, development role of, 124
real estate, 122, 223, 228n35
Barings affair, 148
Berisha's regime, 280–1, 291
Blair, Tony, 269
Bosnia, 280, 283
Bourgeoisie, national Greek, 13, 14
Britain
and smallholder capitalism, 269
corruption in, 61
housing investment in, 218–19
labour market of, 292
mortgage finance in, 208, 221
on the EU, 292
owner-occupation in, 208
productivity in, 183
public housing provision in, 154
R&D in, 179
role in Greek civil war, 14, 17
tax evasion in, 86, 92n26
BSE, 272n1
Budget, Greek government, 70–8, 91n1
for 1996, 100; for 1997, 78
in surplus, 75
Budgeting, zero-based, 76, 268
Bulgaria, Bulgarians, 278, 280–1, 283
Byzantine empire, smallholders in, 10; the state in, 10–11
Byzantium, Hellenisation of, 275
Byzantium, the city, 11, 275, 289

Callas, M., 4
Calymnos, 287
Canellopoulos, Ath., 76
CAP, 55, 68n38, 68n46
Capital
flight from Greece, 86, 112n18
foreign in Greece, 190–7, 262–3; *see also* DFI
imported into Greece for purchasing real estate, 192
imported into Greece under L. 2687/53, 192
'other' business imported into Greece, 192
Capitalism, Greek, developed but distorted, 257–9, 263–4
Caretta-caretta sea-turtles, 239
Caspia and the West, 30n9, 280–1, 283
Castro, Lemnos, 229
Cavafy, C., 3
Centre for Planning & Research, 28, 203
China, 289
Chios, 240, 241
Ciller, T., 30n8, 297n9

Cities, Greek, appearrance of, 210
Civil servants in Greece, permanent tenure of, 52, 262
Civil service, Greek, chaos in, 52
  corruption in, 61
Civil society in Greece, 13
Claoudatos dept stdre, 190
Clientelist politics, Greek, 12, 19, 36, 50
Clogg, R., 36, 272n2, 272n3, 272n12
Communist Party of Greece, *see* CPG
Competition in Greek economy, 197–203, 262
Constantine IA' Paleologos (1449–1453), 11
Constantinople, 275, 287
  as Byzantium, 11, 275, 289
  Greeks, 276
  St Sophia church in, 287, 289
Construction industry, Greek, 201–2
  biggest firms in, 189
Contribution evasion, 162
Corruption, in Britain, Germany, Greece, 61
  in the Greek civil service, 61
CPG, 17, 256, 272n4
Crime, economic, 293
Cyprus, 245, 260, 265, 275–7, 279, 282, 286–8, 295, 298n29
  Turkish argument for invasion of, 298n29

Dalamangas, B., 46
Davelis, 91n8
Defence spending, Greek, 74–5
Deficits, Greek government Budget, 8, 70–78;
  and 1967–74 junta, 66n9
  and economic growth, 74–5;
  and foreign debt, 96;
  and tax evasion, 79;
  as percentage of GDP, 72
  monetary financing of, 110n2;
ΔEH, *see* Public Power Corporation
Deindustrialisation in Greece, 171
  whose fault it is, 182
ΔEKO, financing of, 126, 131
Delors package, 22, 201, 266
Delta Dairy Industry, 190
Demographics, Greek, 163, 166
Depreciation of drachma, *see* drachma
Dept service ratio, Greek, 71
Devaluation of drachma, *see* drachma
Development of Greece, 256–64
DFI, 26, 32n47, 137–40, 190–4, 262–3
Direct Foreign Investment in Greece, *see* DFI
Dodecanese, 9, 287
Doxiadis, C. A., 48n3
Drachma
  depreciation of, 104–10; nominal vs real, 112n16
  devaluation, and public debt servicing, 266; expected, 266; of April 1953, 110; of October 1985, 104
  effects of devaluation, depreciation, 108–10
  exchange rate policy re., 183
  hard, anti-inflationary role of, 104–10; as effect of high interest rates, 21, 266; effect on export performance, 183
  parities of, 105, 107, 173

EC transfers to Greece, 26
Economic growth, Greek, 8, 16, 34–5
  and institutional features of 1945–74, 34–7, 265
  in 1958–73, 18
  and budget deficits, 74–5
  and rentierist capital, 227n23
  export-led, 18, 252
Economic performance, Greek comparative, 37–42
Economic policy in Greece, 255
  and Keynesian economics, 255
  counter-cyclical dimension of, 95, 255
  discontinuity between fiscal and monetary, 95–6
  fiscal, 95–6, 100

monetary, 95–6; and Bank of Greece, 97
re. exchange rate of drachma, 21–2, 110, 183
Economic refugees into Greece, 104, 164, 167, 225, 269, 289–91
work permit for, 167
Economy, informal, in Greece, 21, 28–9, 79, 268
in Belgium, 92n27
in Germany, 92n27
in Turkey, 28
Education, Greek, 19, 61–66, 298n36
Greek students abroad, 63, 69n78, 252, 270
illiteracy, functional, in Greece, 65
Eleusis shipyards, 88, 91n6
Elytis, O., 3, 6n5
Emigration from Greece, 55
Employees, in Greece, 15
public-sector, 16–17, 56
Employers and self-employed in Greece, 8, 15
Emu, 291–2
and Greece, 46–7, 76, 94
convergence criteria, 46–7
English Tourist Board, 245
Environmental concerns in Greece, 191, 195–6, 210, 229–48
Environmental pollution in Greece, 210–11, 237
ΕΟΠ, 159
EOT, 196, 236, 238, 241
Epirus, 12, 124
Northern, 277, 291
Southern, 277
Erbakan, N. (1926–), 279, 297n9, 298n23
Ergatiké Estia, 156, 159
Ergon, 190
Ethniké Insurance plc, 56, 143
Euphrates, 271n1
Evert, M., 76
Expats' remittances, 26
Exports, Greek, 170
manufacturing, 175–7
and 'hard' drachma, 183
and inflation, 183
Export-led growth, 18, 252
Ezure, Y., 197

Family, in Greece, 154
assets of, 224
workers, 15
Fiscal drag, 83
Fiscal expansionism, 75
political dynamic of, 78–9
Fiscal policy, *see* economic policy
Fiscal profligacy, and 1981, 70
in the 1980s, 255
Fish-farming, Greek, 7
Food consumption, Greek, 29n1
Food-product makers, biggest firms in Greece, 188
Foreign debt, Greek public sector, 71
Foreign firms in Greece, 186
Franchise in Greece, 12
in Britain, 12
Friendly Society, 295
FX, and Greece's real interest rates, 101
firms borrowing in, 110, 147

GDP, Greek
and trade deficit, 24–5
compared to Portugal's, 34
contribution of insurance industry to, 140; of tourist industry to, 243
growth rates, 1951–95, 35
old and new method of estimation, 32n45
taxes, direct, indirect, proportion of to, 80–1
required growth rate for Emu, 47
sector shares, 1951–91, 16, 27–8
Germany
and Croatia, 297n12
corruption in, 61
Goodyear Hellas plc, 186, 190
Goudi, 1909 army revolt at, 295
Greece,
and a Balkan federation, 280–1
and Albania, 277–8, 291
and customs union between Turkey and EU, 286–7

and Emu, 46–7, 76, 94, 291–2
and EU, 22, 26, 36, 47, 68n46, 292
and her post-1989 shock, 277–8
and her Western partners, 9, 285, 289
and required strategy towards Turkey, 288–9
and Skopje, 277, 285–6, 298n27
and Russian influence in SE Europe, 289
and Turkey, 3–5, 10–11, 14, 30n8, 272n11, 274–84, 286–9, 292, 294– 5; *see also* War
as capitalist society, 257–64
as investment location, 187, 190, 194
as statist, smallholder society, 10–15, 17, 56, 198–9, 206–10, 212–16, 242, 248, 253–5, 258–62, 268–9
corruption in, 61; in Greece's civil service, 61
dependence, political, on the West, 259–60, 272n11, 284
economic importance of geographical position, 269
educational reform, required, 270
in Byzantine times, 10
international competitiveness of, 46
leadership scenarios about, 294–5
ownership of TVs, 24; of passenger cars, 24
political reform, required, 270–1
prevalence of small business units in, 198
Turkish policy of, 288
West's attitude towards, 278–81, 285
Greeks, modern, ethnic origin of, 275

Hanwha Group, 131, 149n16
Hellenic Bottling Co., 190
Hotels, Greek, beds in, 235, 243; quality in, 233; skilled staff in, 233–4
Housing credit in Greece, 220–3
and the labour market, 224
and the Bank of Greece, 222
Housing in Greece, 206–25
and rent controls, 220
'exchange arrangement' and, 208–10
quality of, 214
see also owner occupation; unauthorised building; urbanisation
Housing investment in Greece, 216–220
vs the UK, 218–19
Housing, public provision of, 151, 153

IKA, 53, 155–60, 162–4, 167n14
sums owed to, 162
Illiteracy, functional, in Greece, 65
Import penetration in Greek economy, 203
Industry, Greek
biggest firms in, 188
changes in labour force of, 178
dynamic segment of, 186
export performance of, 175–7
labour productivity in, 173, 180–3
problem segment of, 171
profit- and loss-makers in, 174
real wages in, 173, 180–1
two segments of, 171
unit labour costs in, 173, 180–1
Inflation in Greece, 8, 22, 94–101, 113–15
and fiscal policy, 95
and public debt, 109, 266
and supply side of economy, 101
and the drachma, 104–10
and uncompetitiveness, 183
causes of, 97–9
in 1995, 22, 94
in 1996, 22, 94
Infrastructure in Greece, 183–5
Inland Revenue, Greek, 59, 81, 83, 86, 196–97
Insurance industry, Greek, 140–5
'cowboy' firms in, 141, 144
life business, 144

opening up of domestic market, 144
Interest rates, Greek, 21, 108
effect on drachma, 266
on pension fund deposits, 158
relation to investment, 46
Intracom, 186, 190
Investment
and interest rates, 46
comparison of role of, 42–6
housing, 216–20
Invisible earnings of Greece 25, 26
Ios, 238, 243

Jews, Greek, 297n4
Jews and Greeks, 275
Junta, Greek military (1967–74), 19, 35, 50, 66n9, 67n10, 251, 255–6, 265, 277

Karamanlis, C. (1907–), 1, 226n12, 256
Kazantzakis, N., 3, 6n5
Kemalism, 279
Khalkidiké, 195, 227n19, 243
Koskotas, G., 256
Kouvelakis, G., 68n59
Kurdistan, independent Republic of, 284
Kurds, 271n1, 279, 281, 288

Labour market and mortgage credit in Greece, 224
Latsis family, 30n5
Lausanne Treaty, 276, 280, 287–8
Law
89/67, on off-shore companies, 191
396/68, on write-offs of non-performing loans, 133
960/79, on car-parking space, 226n12
1262/82, on development, 191
1386/83, on privatisation, 90
1599/86, on disclosure in the public sector, 59
1892/90, on development, 90, 135, 191
1902/90, on social security, 161
2000/91, on privatisation, 90
2042/92, on funds' freedom to invest, 161
2076/92, on banking business, 128, 133; on pension funds, 161
2114/93, on banking business, 128
2160/93, on AITD, 246
2170/93, on insurance, 144
2217/94, on funds investing in real property, 161
2218/94, on local authorities of the second degree, 57
2234/94, on development, 191
2240/94, on local authorities of the second degree, 57
2324/95, on banking business, 128
2338/95, on project price reviews, 201
2687/53, on DFI, 137–8, 190–2
2804/92, on social security, 161
Lawyers' Fund, 156, 157, 161
Lecatsas, E., 28
Legrand, 190
Lemnos, 229–32, 241
Life expectancy in Greece, 7
Life-style, Greek, 24, 29n2
Linguistic backsliding in Greece, 65, 69n79
Livanis, A., 68n59
Loans & Consignments Fund, 122–3, 131, 221
Local authorities in Greece, 56–58

Macedonia, 1, 12, 148, 277, 285–6
Managers of BEA firms, educational level of, 64, 178–9
Manos, S., 94
Manufacturing, Greek, contribution to GDP, 170–1
export performance of, 175–7
Marinos, J., 32n39
Markezinis, S., 110
Marxism, 2
MEDA programme, 286
Meritocracy, 294
Merkouri, M., 4, 242

Metaxas, J., 17, 167n14
Meteora, 238–9
Mirkos, G., 149n24
Monetary policy, *see* economic policy
Money supply, 97–100
Monyal, 190
Mortgage finance in Greece, 208, 220–4
 vs the UK, 208, 221
Mouzelis, N., 11
Mt Penteli, fire on, 206, 214
Myconos, 241, 243
Myrina, Lemnos. 229–32, 237, 240
Mytilene, Lesbos, 242

NAT, 156, 159, 160
National Land and Property Register, 86, 209, 226n9
National Welfare Organisation, see ΕΟΠ
ND, 76
 and 1989, 256
 and banks, 131
 and GGBd, 72
 and nationalisation, 75, 91n6
 and privatisation, 90, 266
 and public-sector employment, 30n16
 and rent controls, 220
 and social security, 161
 and spending, 75, 78, 266
 and UBTO, 87
 and university exams 62
Negreponti-Delivani, M., 28, 29
New Callicrateia, 227n19
New Democracy party, *see* ND
Niarchos, S., 30n5
Niskanen, W., 51, 67n14
Nissan, 190
Nuclear testing, French, 297n17

ΟΑΕΔ, 156
ΟΓΑ, 155–7, 159
ΟΕΚ, 132, 156, 159, 208, 226n5, 228n34
Oil-price shocks, 4, 34
Oligopolies in Greece, 197–203
Olympic Airways, 58, 88, 91n6, 93n48
Olympic Catering, 88
Onassis, A., 30n5, 58
Organisation for Restructuring Business Enterprises, 90, 93n45
OTE, 31n35, 61, 91, 93n48
Otto A' (1832–1862), 11
Owner-occupation in Greece, 15, 208, 212, 213
 devices for achieving, 208–10
 outright, 208; vs the UK, 208

Papadopoulos, A., 70
Papandreou, A. (1919–1996), xviii, 1, 68n59, 69n59, 67n29, 91n2, 256, 272n4, 284
 his indictment by the Greek Parliament, 256
Papandreou, G., father of Andreas, 67n29
Papandreou, V., 30n16
Paros, 196, 243
PASOK, 35–6, 87, 134, 255–6, 287
 and banks, 131
 and capital flight, 112n18
 and CPG, 272n4
 and economic decline, 74–5, 264
 and fiscal deterioration, 72
 and fiscal expansionism, 75
 and local authorities, 57
 and Olympic Catering, 88
 and patronage, 36
 and populism, 74, 181
 and privatisation, 90, 131, 266
 and public-sector employment, 30n16, 53
 and rent controls, 220
 and Skopje, 286
 and spending, 75, 78, 266
 and the 1989 election, 75, 145
 and the Left, 91n2, 272n4
 and Turkey-EU customs union, 286
 and UBTO, 31n35, 88
 and university exams, 62
 and victory in 1981, 256
Patmos, 239
Pavlopoulos, P., 28
Pechiney, 262

Pension funds, Greek, rates on deposits of, 158
  reasons for deficits of, 160
Pension, need for minimum, 165–6
Pensions in Greece 154, 160
Petroleum products industry, Greek, 7, 30n5
Phillips curve in Greece, 101–4
Phocas, N., 236
Piraiké-Patraiké, 89
Pirelli Hellas plc, 185, 204n27, 190
Political business cycle in Greece, 72
Political parties, Greek mainstream, dependence on West of, 278, 288
  positions of, on capitalist restructuring, 294
  on foreign policy, 294
Polytechneion, *see* Technical University of Athens
Population of Greece, 16
Privatisation in Greece, 87–91, 131, 267–8
Productivity in Greece, 171, 173, 180–3
  in Greek public sector, 53
Procter & Gamble, 190
Prodromidis, C., 46, 47
Property in Greece, imported capital for purchasing, 192
  tax treatment of, 78, 223–4, 228n36
PSNBR, 70, 73, 96–7
Public debt, Greek, 8, 70–8, 91n12
  and devaluation, 266
  and inflation, 109, 266
  compared to EU, 76
Public Power Corporation, 54, 30n16, 93n48, 195
Public sector, Greek, 49–66
  bonuses in, 93n48
  contribution to GDP, 66n4
  dichotomy of roles in, 53
  educational profile of staff in, 64
  effect on economy, 19, 56
  employment in, 15, 17, 56
  foreign debt, 71
  Net Borrowing Requirement, 70, 73, 96–7
  role in curbing unemployment, 53, 55

R&D in Greece, 177, 179–80, 185
Rallis, G., 69n80
Revolution of 1821, Greek, 11, 275–6
Ritsos, Y., 3, 6n5
Roidis' commentary, 12, 215
Rule of law in Greece, 50, 58–61, 195–6, 240, 255, 269
Russia, 30n9, 280–3, 289

Sandoz, 190
Scaramanga shipyards, 88, 89
ScoPLife, 221
Scottish Provident, 221
Seferis, G., 3, 6n5
Semitis, C., xviii
Serbia, Serbs, 271n1, 277, 281, 285
Shipping, Greek, 7, 30n4, 229
  receipts from, 26
Siemens, 186, 190, 204n26
Skopje, 276–7, 280, 284, 285–6
  Albanian contingent in, 286
Smallholder interests in Greek society, see Greece
Social security, in Greece, 151–67
  funded system of, 160, 164, 166
  pay-as-you-go system of, 155, 160, 164, 166;
  transfers, 151
  see also IKA
Solomos, G., 168n37
Sony Hellas plc, 197
Spanish banking, 148n2
Strikes in Greece, workers', work-hours lost due to, 181–2
St Nicholas, Crete, 242
St Sophia church, 287, 289
Supermarkets in Greece, 198, 201–2
  biggest firms, 189
Supply side, Greek, need to overhaul, 269

Tax burden, personal, 83
Tax data, Greek, for 1995, 92n18
Tax evasion in Greece, 79, 81, 83, 86, 268
  in the UK, 86

Taxation system, Greek
  regressiveness in, 79, 81
Taxes, 78–87
  on property in Greece, 78, 223–4, 228n36
TAXIS, 86
TEBE, 155–7
Technical University of Athens, 60
Tertiary sector, Greek, 260–2
Thanoglou, G., 227n19
Theodorakis, M., 4
Theses magazine, 257, 259–60, 262
Thessalonica, xvii, 1
  Stock Exchange in, 148
Thessaly, Greek land-holdings in, 13
Thrace, 124
  Eastern, 279, 284
  Western, 276, 278, 288–9, 294
Tirana, 277–8
Titan Cement, 190
Tourism, Greek, 229–48
  prospects of, 242–8
  receipts from 26, 244
  required development model for, 247–8
Tourist arrivals in Greece, 243–4
Tourist industry, Greek, 7
  Area(s) of Integrated Tourist Development, 246–7
  contribution to employment, 243; to GDP, 243
  number of beds, 235, 243
  skilled and unskilled staff in, 233–5
  smallholder interests in, 242, 247–8
  tour operator influence in, 245
ΤΠΔ, *see* Loans & Consignments Fund
Trade deficit, Greek, 21, 24, 25, 101, 109–110, 183, 266
Transnationals in Greece, 173, 185–190
  profitability of, 186–7
Tricoupis, Ch. (1832–1896), 9
ΤΣΜΕΔΕ, 131, 169n48
Tsovolas, D., 75
Turkey
  and Cyprus, 287–8, 298n29
  and democracy, 299n42
  and Europe, 286–7, 299n38
  and Greece, 3–5, 10–11, 14, 30n8, 272n11, 274–84, 286–9, 292, 294–5; *see also* War
  regional stability, 282–4
  Greek strategy towards, 288–9
  Islam in, 279, 283
  population of; 297n5; ethnic components of, 297n5
  possible dissolution of, 284
  required transformation of, 284
  territorial claims on Greece, 287–8; war threats to Greece, 30n8, 278
  West's attitude towards, 9, 30n9, 271n1, 274, 279–80; in the future, 283–4
TVX-Gold, 195

Ucar, 190
UK, *see* Britain
Unauthorised building in Greece, 209, 214–16, 224, 228n33, 237–8, 239
Uncompetitiveness of Greek economy, causes of, 177–85
  and inflation, 183
Underdevelopment of Greece, debate on, 256–64
Unemployment in Greece 19, 20, 53, 95
  and inflation, 101–4
  benefit, 152, 154, 167n7, 267
  effect on Exchequer, 20
  public sector as device for containing, 51, 53, 55
Unit labour costs in Greek industry, 173, 180–1
Unit trusts (ΑΕΔΑΚ) in Greece 147, 169n48
Urban Bus Transport Organisation, 87–8
Urban development, ideal model of, 251
Urbanisation in Greece, 13, 15, 16, 207, 210, 224, 265
USA
  bases in Greece, 284

post-cold war foreign policy, 280–2
pressures on Greece, 277, 288
role in Greek civil war, 17
sanctions on European companies, 272n1, 297n17
support for Berisha's regime, 277–8

USSR, 274, 289

Vangelis, 4
Vardinoyannis family, 30n5
VAT, in Greece, 82, 86, 196
in Britain, 86, 92n26
Venizelos, E. (1864–1936), 9, 13, 167n14
Vergopoulos, C., 261
Vranopoulos, M., 87

Wages, real, in Greek industry, 173, 180–1
War
Greek civil, of 1944–9, 3, 14, 17, 23; role of Britain in, 14, 17; of the USA, 17
Greek-Turkish, of 1897, 9; of 1912–13, 3, 9, 12; of 1919–22, 14, 276; in the future, 278, 283
Second World: and Germany's support for Croatia, 297n12; and Greek Jews, 297n4; and loss of Greece's building wealth, 48n3; Greece in, 3, 6n4, 14, 48n3, 297n12; reversal of moral values after in Greece, 17

Warner Lambert, 190
West, definition of, 296n1
WHO, *see* OEK
Workers' Hearth, *see* Ergatiké Estia

X-inefficiency, 102, 112n14

Young Turks, 295
Yugoslavia, 271n1, 274, 277, 280–1

Zante, 239
Zolotas, X., 31n37